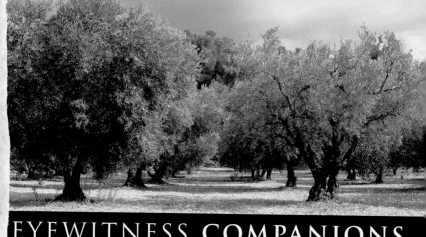

EYEWITNESS COMPANIONS

Olive Oil

CHARLES QUEST-RITSON

"THE OLIVE TREE IS
SURELY THE RICHEST
GIFT OF HEAVEN"

Thomas Jefferson

LONDON, NEW YORK,
MUNICH, MELBOURNE, DELHI

Senior Editor	Simon Tuite
Project Art Editor	Sara Robin
Executive Managing Editor	Adèle Hayward
Managing Art Editor	Karla Jennings
Art Director	Peter Luff
Publisher	Corinne Roberts
DTP Designer	Julian Dams
Production Controller	Mandy Inness

Produced for Dorling Kindersley by
Cooling Brown Ltd

Creative Director	Arthur Brown
Project Editor	Jemima Dunne
Designers	Juliette Norsworthy, Tish Jones, Peter Cooling
Editors	Constance Novis, Mandy Lebentz, Claire Cross
Picture Research	Louise Thomas
Illustration	Tom Coulson – Encompass Graphics
Special Photography	Fritz Curzon

First American Edition, 2006

Published in the United States by DK Publishing, Inc.,
375 Hudson Street, New York, New York 10014
A Penguin Company
06 07 08 09 10   10 9 8 7 6 5 4 3 2 1

Library of Congress Cataloging-in-Publication Data
Quest-Ritson, Charles.
   Olive oil / Charles Quest-Ritson. -- 1st American ed.
     p. cm. -- (Eyewitness companions)
   Includes index.
   ISBN 0-7566-1530-5 (flexi binding with flaps)
   1. Olive oil. 2. Olive oil industry.   I. Title. II. Series.
TP683.Q47 2006
641.3'463--dc22

2005033581

ISBN-13: 9-7807-5661-530-7
ISBN-10: 0-7566-1530-5

DK books are available at special discounts for bulk purchases
for sales promotions, premiums, fund-raising, or educational use.
For details, contact: DK Publishing Special Markets,
375 Hudson Street, New York, NY 10014 or SpecialSales@dk.com

OD015
Color reproduced by Colourscan, Singapore
Printed in China by L Rex

Discover more at
www.dk.com

CONTENTS

OLIVE OIL IS THE PUREST OF PLEASURES. IT IS MORE THAN JUST A COMMODITY YOU CAN BUY AT THE SUPERMARKET. ITS VERSATILITY IS INFINITE. THERE ARE TWICE AS MANY OLIVE VARIETIES AS THERE ARE GRAPES, AND TWICE AS MUCH VARIABILITY IN THE TASTE OF OLIVE OIL. IT IS THE VERY ESSENCE OF MEDITERRANEAN CULTURE

This book is for everyone who wants to know how to recognize high-quality oils and where they come from. *Olive Oil* is the first truly comphensive guide to the subject. It tells you which are the most important oil-producing countries, it shows you how to identify oils, read bottle labels, and understand what is meant by terms such as "extra virgin" and "cold pressed."

FROM ANCIENT STOCK
There are many old olive trees in the Mediterranean, like this one in Patrí, in Greece. Some are hundreds of years old.

Our understanding of olive oil is roughly at the same level now as some people's knowledge of wine 30 years ago. Like wine, olive oil varies greatly according to where it is made and from which varieties, or cultivars, it comes from. Quality and flavor also depend on the maturity of the fruit, the storage of the fruit before processing, the processing itself, and the way the oil is stored. These variables explain the differences between *Koroneïki* oil from Sitia, in Greece and *Frantoio* oil from Tuscany, in Italy. The European Union has a classification system for oil based on the *Appellation Controllées* system begun

in France for wine. This system ensures consistency of quality, determines which olive varieties can be grown where, and what the essential qualities of their oils should be (*see p.36*).

During the course of writing this book, I tasted more than 2,000 different oils. There were three main reasons for deciding which oils to include. First, I felt that the book must contain a description of the national brands, country by country, because they are the names that people are most likely to be familiar with, even though they are not always the best. These oils are generally sold on price, exported in quantity, and found on the shelves of supermarkets all over the world.

Second, I wanted to include oils from high-quality local producers, including provincial brands and cooperatives. Some have a limited

MATURING OLIVES
Unripe olives are green. They turn purple, then black as they mature. Some olives are picked while still green; other are left to ripen.

following; others are more widely available. Third, I wanted to describe and recommend the best single-estate oils (high-quality oils from skilled producers around the world). The leading examples are oils with the European recognition of locality and content and stamp of origin, known as a DOP (Italy, Spain, and Portugal), AOP (France), and PDO/ΠOΠ (Greece), (*see p.39*). These oils have an exceptional reputation for quality and the best are consistent winners of national and international prizes. Some are only available locally, perhaps directly from the producer, but many are widely available in gastronomic retailers worldwide.

This book is a celebration of extra virgin olive oil. I have concentrated especially on those that are intended for sale outside their immediate area of production. I have not featured the bijou or "garage" oils that are often made to an extremely high standard but available only in very small quantities and very locally. Likewise, I have omitted oils made in large quantities that have powerful local followings but are not always of

FRESHLY PICKED OLIVES
This mixture of green, black, and intermediate-colored olives will produce good oil. The leaves are sifted out before pressing.

OIL IS THE DRESSING Extra virgin oil is one of the healthiest and tastiest accompaniments to food. It is delicious on freshly grilled vegetables.

high quality and were never intended to be sold elsewhere. Likewise the book makes no mention of hybrid concoctions with names like "lemon," "garlic," or "herb" oil.

The biggest section of the book looks at oils from the main oil-producing countries, principally Spain and Italy, but also Portugal, France, and Greece. Each of these countries has an introduction and a map showing their main oil-producing regions, followed by articles about each of those regions working from north to south. I have also given detailed accounts of the newer producers, such countries as the United States, Australia, and New Zealand, where a quality-led industry has developed fast in recent years. There is less space allocated to Turkey, the Middle East, and North Africa, where most of the oil produced is of an inferior quality.

I have given a description for each of the oils I have included in the book, and divided the lists for the most part into Leading Producers and Other Producers. It is not possible to give star ratings to individual bottles because, unlike wine, oil deteriorates with age. When looking for oils it is important to seek out the youngest and freshest, from the most recent harvest. All the producers included make oils of above-average quality, and can be recommended as reliable. All of the oils look and taste different every year. My notes describe the oils as they were in the year or years that I tasted them.

Charles Quest-Ritson

CHARLES QUEST-RITSON

THE WORLD
OF OLIVES

THE OLIVE OIL INDUSTRY

Olive oil is a wholesome food, rich in history, and is the indispensable adjunct to good cooking. Its virtues have been praised by poets and writers for more than 3,000 years. Once the most highly prized commodity in the ancient world, olive oil has been a source of trade and revenue for thousands of years; taxation in Imperial Rome depended on it. It has been the maker of empires and nourisher of children throughout the ages.

THE INDUSTRY TODAY

Olives and olive oil are associated above all with the Mediterranean basin. At least 90 percent of world production comes from the two sides of the Mediterranean—of which 75 to 80 percent is produced on its northern shores. The olive's tolerance of poor soils means that for centuries it has been used to extend areas of land under cultivation or to reclaim scrubland.

World production of olive oil is still rising slowly but fairly steadily, even allowing for variations in the size of the annual harvest in different parts of the world. It is difficult to obtain accurate national production figures, first because the olive has a tendency to biennial cropping (*see p. 27*)—which makes for great swings in volume—and secondly, because countries tend to use statistics from an exceptional year to inflate the size of their industry. Olive yields can vary by as much as 100 percent from one year to another.

Olive-oil production in Europe increased significantly in the 1990s as a result of new plantings and major investment in modern production and extraction methods. This is a trend that will continue. The most significant expansion in recent years has been in the Southern Hemisphere, notably in Argentina, which has a large home market, and in Australia, where government tax incentives have led to large new olive plantings.

INSPECTING OLIVES
There are many small producers who still manage their olive groves by hand, often with the help of extended family.

DEMAND IS INCREASING

World consumption of olive oil is also increasing slowly but steadily. Much of this growth is in the nonproducing regions such as northern Europe. The major olive-growing countries (Spain, Italy, and Greece) are also the leading consumers. However, these countries also export large volumes. Italy's exports are for the retail market; Spain and Greece's are overwhelmingly wholesale to the Italian blenders. The main importers of European olive oil are the United States of America, Australia, Japan, Germany, Canada, and Brazil. Olive oil is seen as a gourmet product that also offers health benefits.

It is worth remembering that, although popular, olive oil is by no means the most widely grown or plentiful of vegetable oils. Olive oil actually accounts for no more than 2.2 percent of the world vegetable oil production. Compare this with the figures for soy (27.3 percent), palm oil (20.3 percent), rapeseed oil (14.4 percent), and sunflower oil (12.2 percent).

◀ LECHIN DE SEVILLIA These distinctive olives dominate the province of Seville, in Andalusia.

WELL MAINTAINED OLIVE TREE

Olives Around the World

This map shows the main olive-growing countries of the world. The actual area within each country that is devoted to the cultivation of olives is small. In the United States, for example, it extends only to California, with traces in Arizona and Texas. Nevertheless, the leading oils from these countries are the main subject of this book.

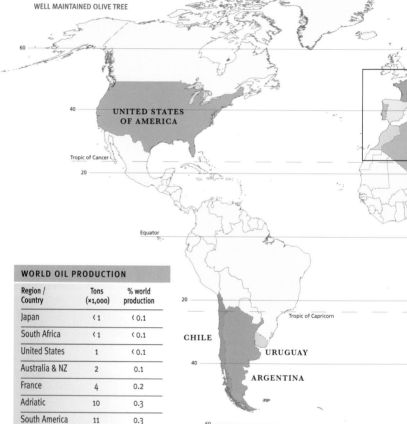

WORLD OIL PRODUCTION

Region / Country	Tons (×1,000)	% world production
Japan	⟨ 1	⟨ 0.1
South Africa	⟨ 1	⟨ 0.1
United States	1	⟨ 0.1
Australia & NZ	2	0.1
France	4	0.2
Adriatic	10	0.3
South America	11	0.3
Portugal	34	1.0
Turkey	121	3.4
Middle East	179	7.0
North Africa	189	7.4
Greece	405	15.8
Italy	633	24.7
Spain	978	38.1
Others	42	1.6

Figures averaged 1998–2004. Source Inernational Olive Oil Council 2004 & others

WHERE OLIVE OIL IS PRODUCED

The table on the left shows the olive production figures for the leading countries we describe in this book. Olive trees tend to be biennial croppers (*see p.27*), so the figures are averages, taken over a number of years. Spain, Italy, and Greece are the largest producers by far, and account for nearly four-fifths of the world crop. These countries are also the main high-quality producers, the largest per capita consumers, and the biggest exporters of olive oil. Middle-ranking

FRANCE
SLOVENIA
CROATIA
MONTENEGRO
ITALY
ALBANIA
SPAIN
40
TURKEY
PORTUGAL
GREECE
TUNISIA
MALTA
CYPRUS
LEBANON
SYRIA
MOROCCO
ISRAEL
PALESTINE
ALGERIA
JORDAN
LIBYA
EGYPT
THE MEDITERRANEAN BASIN

40
JAPAN
Tropic of Cancer
20
Equator
20
Tropic of Capricorn
AUSTRALIA
SOUTH
AFRICA
40
NEW
ZEALAND
60

countries like Turkey, and geographical areas such as North Africa and the Middle East, tend to produce oil largely for their local markets. Quality is variable but their best oil is often shipped to Europe for blending. In addition to the countries shown on the map, oil is produced in small quantities in Brazil, China, Iran, Iraq, Mexico, Pakistan, Peru, Saudi Arabia, and the Ukraine. With a few exceptions the oil is consumed locally and of poor quality.

OLIVE AND PALM TREES TOLERATE SIMILAR CLIMATES

The History of Olives

Olive farming has always been a symbol of a settled society. It requires stable political and economic circumstances, and advanced cultivation skills. Its development coincides with the origins of Mediterranean civilization. From age to age, its history follows the changes in social, economic, and political conditions.

ANCIENT GREEK VASE
This vase depicts three men shaking olives from a tree, while a fourth gathers the harvest into a basket.

ORIGINS OF THE OLIVE

No one is sure exactly where the olive tree originated. Archeologists and paleobotanists have found traces of wild olives over much of the Mediterranean basin that date back for several thousand years B.C.E. The earliest confirmation of olives as a cultivated crop date from the eastern seaboard of the Mediterranean in about 6000 B.C.E. Excavations in Knossos, in Greece, have revealed sophisticated techniques for extraction and storage, from which it is clear that olive oil was an important commodity by 1500 B.C.E. Olive oil found in the Egyptian tomb of Tutenkhamun dates to about 1325 B.C.E. In Ancient Egypt oil was used for cooking, as medicine, for religious purposes (including anointing the dead), and for light—olive oil was the principal source of fuel for lamps. Its spread throughout the Mediterranean basin was often associated with religious practices as well as its usefulness for fuel, food, and embrocation.

Every ancient civilization has its own account of the origins of the olive tree. Gods like Osiris and Athena or heroes such as Aristaeus and Heracles each had their part to play. All were agreed that olive oil was a precious gift to mankind. Olives were sacred to the Ancient Greeks, especially among the Athenians who worshiped an ancient olive tree on the Acropolis that they believed had been planted by Pallas Athene herself. When Aristotle wrote the Constitution of the Athenians, he prescribed the death penalty for anyone who uprooted or felled an olive tree. Olive oil was widely traded all over the eastern Mediterranean. Oil amphoras from Athens have been found not only in Greek overseas colonies but also in Tuscany, Phoenicia, and "barbarian" lands beyond the Straits of Gibraltar.

THE ROMAN EMPIRE

Olive trees, like vines and wheat, were an economic staple of ancient Rome. They were planted throughout the empire wherever conditions were suitable, and much of the imperial taxation took the form of bulk oil tributes sent to the imperial city itself. The oil trade was second only to the grain trade in importance. By the time of the Emperor Constantine in the 4th century, there were more than 2,000 oil dealers in Rome itself. Ancient writers such as Cato, Columella, and Saserna sought to improve

GREEK MANUSCRIPT
Harvesting olives as depicted in an 11th-century Greek manuscript from the Opiano Codex, a treatise on hunting and fishing.

cultivation, pruning, fertilizing, harvesting, processing, and the storage of oil. "*Olea prima omnium arborum est*"— the olive is first among trees—declared Columella in *De Re Rustica* written in the first century C.E. Two thousand years later, the sentiments are still correct.

OLIVE OIL IN RELIGION

The instability that followed the collapse of the Roman Empire greatly reduced the scale of olive growing. Olive oil survived in religious communities, where it was employed for liturgical purposes. Lamps that lit the altars where the Blessed Sacrament was kept had to be fueled by olive oil.

14TH-CENTURY OLIVE-OIL MERCHANT

The Jewish religion also has a long association with olives. In the story of the great flood, the dove returned to Noah's ark with an olive twig. The Hebrew Ark of the Covenant was consecrated with olive oil. The kings of Israel were anointed with it to bestow authority, power, and wisdom, and it is still used for the coronation of European kings and the consecration of bishops.

FROM THE MIDDLE AGES ONWARD

The cultivation of olives picked up toward the end of the Middle Ages. The greatest expansion took place during the Renaissance; it was after the 16th century that the olive became so firmly associated with the landscapes of Tuscany in Italy and Catalonia in Spain. Improvements in transportation led to a thriving trade between northern and southern Europe. Olives were one of the first European exports to the New World. By the 18th century, vast quantities of oil were required to supply the soap manufacturers of Provence.

OLIVE OIL MUSEUMS

There are olive museums in all major olive-growing countries. Especially good are the Museo dell'Olivo in Imperia (*see p.60*) and the Parc Temàtic de l'Oli near Los Borges Blancos in Lérida (*see p.150*). Other good olive museums can be found in Nyons, in France, Sparta in Greece, and in Cisano del Garda and Masseria Sant'Angelo de' Graecis, in Italy.

THE OIL MILL The oil-making processes in this 16th-century engraving by Stradanus are still the same today.

The Olive Tree

*The olive has adapted so well to the Mediterranean basin that it naturalizes in uncultivated land all around its shores. Wild olives (*Olea europaea *var.* sylvatica*) are small, spiny shrubs; it is as a result of cultivation and selection over thousands of years that the olive has developed into a tree. Olive trees grow equally well in fertile and rocky barren soils. Neglected, a tree will go into decline but it never dies. It will start into production again once it is properly cultivated, pruned, and managed.*

CHARACTERISTICS OF THE OLIVE TREE

There are countless different types, or cultivars, of olive. They share many characteristics; all are evergreen, have arching branches, and narrow, gray-backed leaves that grow in pairs at right angles to the branches. Older trees have gnarled trunks. There is a tendency for vertical branches to continue growing upward and to produce new tree growth, while horizontal branches bear flowers and fruit. Olive trees produce tiny, white flowers, on small racemes ("spikes" of flowers arranged along a single elongated stem), in the late spring, which will develop into olives. Only a small fraction of the flowers develop into olives; trees naturally shed their surplus fruit before it develops too far, so that they are not overburdened by more olives than they can support. Olive trees are normally biennial croppers (*see p.27*), which means that a big olive harvest one year is followed by a small one the next, while the tree puts its energy into a bumper crop again in the third year.

Olive fruit

The fruit of the olive is a drupe (which means a fruit with one stone) and consists of a skin (epicarp), flesh (mesocarp), and a stone (endocarp) in the middle. The size of the fruit and the ratio of flesh to stone varies considerably from one cultivar to another. There are olives of many types and qualities, from primitive near-wild olives to the fattest of selected cultivars (*see p.24*). Some are grown for their oil, others for table olives.

PHYSIOLOGICAL VARIATIONS

There are enormous physiological variations between the different olive cultivars. Some are pendulous in growth, while most are upright or spreading. The olives also differ in color, size, shape, and oil yield (*see p.26*). In addition, the same cultivar can perform in different ways in different climates. *Arbequina* olive oil tastes fresher and fruitier if produced from trees in its native Catalonia, than it does when grown in the hotter climate of Andalusia. The leading olive-growing countries recognize the importance of this biodiversity and have built up national collections of all their rare and local cultivars. Meanwhile, work continues on the study of their genetic makeup and usefulness. As an olive tree ages, it becomes less productive and is often replaced by new plantings.

NATURALIZED OLIVES
The ruins of this ancient settlement are strewn with abandoned olive trees, relics of a long lost civilization.

CULTIVATED OLIVES IN LECCE, PUGLIA Ancient trees have gnarled trunks and a spreading habit.

Nevertheless, there is a growing awareness that ancient trees, though seldom of economic value, should be preserved for their historic or environmental importance.

PERFECT GROWING CONDITIONS

Olives need hot, dry summers, mild, wet, temperate winters, and enough wind for pollination—in other words a Mediterranean climate. They require lower temperatures in the winter than in the summer, because cool winter temperatures induce the flowerbuds that turn to olives later in the year. Olive trees are killed by hard and prolonged subzero temperatures. Nevertheless oil from olives grown in cool areas at the limit of their cultivability are noted for their fineness, delicacy, and fluidity.

Olives need well drained soil, and prefer alkaline conditions but can tolerate most acidic soils. They grow especially well in limestone soils that retain water deep down but whose surface decomposes to create a fertile "terra rossa." Olive trees need open, well ventilated positions where fog is rare. Their evergreen leaves are especially susceptible to mold and cannot tolerate prolonged humidity, especially in winter. They do, however, respond well to irrigation during the growing season by producing larger crops of fruit.

EFFECT OF CLIMATE ON OIL YIELD

Olives yield 10–30 percent of their weight in oil, according to the cultivar grown. Climate and weather also have a significant effect on productivity. Following a serious drought in 1995–96 in Spain, for example, the 1996 crop produced no more than 372,600 tons of olive oil, just over one-third of the following year's 1,044,000 tons. Winter frosts are a problem in northern areas such as Provence and Tuscany. French farmers still discuss the great frosts of 1956 and 1985 and whether they were as bad as that of 1709. In exceptional conditions, trees are frozen to ground level and it can take many years for new growth from the roots to grow to fruiting size. But these areas often produce oil of exceptional quality.

At the opposite end are areas that are almost too hot for oils. In southern Tunisia, on the edge of the Sahara desert, olive trees are planted at about one per acre (4/ha) because of the low water supply in the subsoil (40 per acre [100/ha] is normal in Italy, and can be up to 810 per acre [2,000/ha] in modern, irrigated plantations). Olives can tolerate very high temperatures but they do need a cold spell in winter. Hot climates tend to produce thick, smooth, rich, unctuous oils with a mild nutty flavor. Cool-climate oils are more likely to taste fruity and fresh.

Cultivating Olives

There are three types of olive farming: traditional groves of ancient trees, often scattered and lightly managed (with little or no irrigation or fertilizing); old groves that are actively managed, with a measure of irrigation, the use of fertilizers, and regular pruning to increase production; and thirdly, intensive modern plantations, usually irrigated and managed in a highly mechanized manner, from planting to harvesting.

MIXED PLANTING

Olive trees are sometimes planted as an adjunct to other crops—perhaps as an edging to arable crops. But more often they are interplanted with vines and fruit trees. Only in a few areas like Jaén and Bari are they planted to the exclusion of all other economic activity. Catch crops are often planted near olive trees because the canopy of a cultivated olive is open, and does not take more than a small percentage of the light. In the early years after planting vines are often grown between the trees until they are large enough to crop regularly and give a good return. Olives grow slowly whereas vines establish quickly.

MODERN PLANTATIONS

Olives are traditionally associated with dry-land farming, often in poor, marginal land. Much of the great expansion of olive growing in the 19th and 20th centuries was the result of taking marginal land into cultivation.

Now the tendency is to plant dense, intensive lines or selected cultivars that grow to no more than 8ft (2.5m) tall and require active management. These trees give higher yields and crop more evenly.

IRRIGATION

Olives make good use of water and installing irrigation is the most effective way to increase crop size. It also counteracts the olive tree's natural tendency to biennial cropping, and helps ensure regular, steady yeilds. Irrigation is most economically installed using water seepage hoses on the surface of the soil, or trickle irrigation. The installation of irrigation is a major activity in such countries as Spain, where government grants are available to help with the expense. About one-third of

> ### Organic cultivation
>
> There is a growing move to use no artificial chemicals or fertilizers in the cultivation of olives. This is often pioneered by innovative producers who are aware of the commercial benefits because organic oils sell at premium prices. Every country has institutes that certify organic practices and you will often see evidence of their affiliation to these regulators on the producers' labels.
>
> In my experience in the course of writing this book, organic does not equate with improved quality. There is always the danger that organic crops will be vulnerable to attack by the olive fly, which gives the oil a dirty taste. Generally speaking, nonorganic oils taste cleaner and fresher. However, there are some outstanding exceptions at the top end of the market.

Andalusia's olive groves are now irrigated. They benefit from a major big dam-building program throughout Spain.

IMPORTANCE OF PRUNING

Olive trees are often trained to make them easier to spray and pick and to "open" them up so that they are less susceptible to disease. There are various shapes that are sometimes adopted for pruning younger trees, including the "vase," the "monocone," and the "umbrella." The aim of pruning is to structure a tree, with well balanced branches that are equal in size and regular in shape. Pruning also helps fructification by increasing the number of fruit-bearing growths. Trees in modern intensive plantations are often machine-pruned to a slanting, conical shape. Using mechanical pruning cuts labor costs substantially, but there are drawbacks because the machines cannot

OLIA EMPELTRE TREES These trees in La Rioja have been pruned back hard to encourage new growth.

select specific branches to prune. To counter these negatives some owners still prune their trees the traditional way—by hand—every three or four years.

Modern cultivation and pruning methods mean that a greater density of trees is possible. Forty trees per acre (100/ha) is normal in well managed traditional groves, but 500, 650, or 800 per acre (1,200, 1,600 or 2,000/ha) is usual in modern intensive plantations.

PRUNING OLD TREES
Overgrown or badly managed olive trees sometimes need drastic pruning to bring them back into productivity. Modern techniques encourage the continuous production of new fruiting wood and the first stage in the process is to prune the old tree back very severely.

Sometimes trees need to be reshaped so they are easier to manage. The problem that confronts a grower is how to correct a tree's shape without reducing the olive crop while the tree is undergoing regeneration.

FERTILIZING OLIVE TREES
Mature olives trees are traditionally fertilized every three years—ideally every other year—toward the end of winter. Further fertilizers are sometimes added at the end of the spring, when the plant has just flowered, or at the end of the summer when rains in the fall will aid its absorption. This too can help counter the natural tendency of some trees toward biennial cropping (*see p.27*). Intensive cultivation requires much more feeding of the trees.

Pests and diseases

Olive trees are subject to a number of different pests and diseases including bacterial and parasite infections, olive gall, scale insects, moth larvae, and beetles. Birds, especially blackbirds and thrushes, eat the ripening fruit. The olive fly is the most harmful pest because of the effect it has on oil quality.

The olive fly, known as *Bactrocera oleae* is a small iridescent fly that is especially

OLIVE FLY

prevalent in mild, maritime climates. It lays an egg in the developing olive, and the larva feeds on the pulp. Eventually the olive drops off but, if it is picked before it drops, the larvae gives a distinctive, dirty taste to the oil —one of the most common defects among oils from badly managed groves.

Several generations of olive fly occur each year, starting when the fruit is the size of a pea. Most olive growers use chemicals to control infections. There is, however, a movement toward using organic controls based on pheromones that mimic the hormones of the female flies and lure the males to their death before they can mate.

Olive Cultivars

For thousands of years, farmers have selected and propagated plants that are best suited to their particular environment and needs. There are thousands of different olive cultivars grown throughout the Mediterranean and the rest of the world, some with only a very local distribution. Italy alone has morre than 700 olive cultivars and each has a distinct character that gives a unique flavor to the oil it produces.

THE DIFFERENT TYPES OF OLIVE

Olive cultivars differ from each other in innumerable ways, most notably in the size of their olives and in the size and shape of the stones. Primitive olives produce small fruits with little pulp and large stones. Cultivars selected for the production of table olives have large fleshy fruits and small kernels but may not offer such a high oil content as those that are specifically grown for oil. Some cultivars need rich fertile soils, while others—most of them—will thrive on poor soils. Hardiness also varies between cultivars and clones of cultivars. This is measured not only by reference to a plant's resistance to extremely low temperatures, but also to the length of time cold temperatures can be endured, and by the tree's resistance to late frosts. Occasional severe winters, like that of 1929 in Tuscany, have enabled growers to select those that seem to be hardiest. Traditional growers tend to see what does well in their area and remain loyal to the local cultivar. But if a superior cultivar is introduced, they are not slow to replace older trees. That perceived superiority may come from higher yields, hardiness, or resistance to disease.

PLANTING FOR POLLINATION

Some of the best olive cultivars are self-sterile, and must be planted alongside other varieties for cross-pollination. The Tuscan olive, *Leccino*, for example, is self-sterile and usually grown alongside a good pollinator such as *Morchiaio*, *Pendolino*, or *Maremmano*. Some cultivars are partially self-sterile, so they set small crops when self-pollinated, but bear their fruit abundantly when cross-pollinated. Most Spanish cultivars are self-fertile, so do not need to be planted alongside other cultivars; *Gordal* and *Manzanillo* are about the only Spanish self-sterile trees.

VARIANCES IN OILS

The choice of cultivar and the ripeness of the olive affect the oil content, the relation between the pulp and the nut, the resistance to picking, the color of the skin, the consistency of the pulp, and the taste and nutritional content of the oil. Biodiversity means that the same cultivar will perform differently in different conditions: *Arbequina* is widely planted in Andalusia but gives a much fruitier oil in its native Catalonia. Similarly, oils made from *Leccino* olives are richer and more rounded in Puglia than *Leccino* oils from Tuscany. Nevertheless, if all olive oils were made in the same way, with olives grown in identical conditions and picked at exactly the same degree of maturity, then the different taste of each oil would depend upon only one factor—the variety of olives used.

Local popularity of an olive does not however mean excellence or adaptability

outside its area of origin. Most olive cultivars are inferior to the few whose qualities of hardiness, productivity, health, vigor, and adaptability have made them widely dispersed throughout the olive-growing world. *Picholine* (from Spain), *Koroneïki* (from Greece), *Leccino*, and *Frantoio* (both Italian) olives, for example, are now widely grown not just in their countries of origin, and in "new" countries like Australia and Argentina, but also in other major oil-producing areas within Europe. The advance of these "super cultivars" threatens the historical choice and biodiversity that consumers enjoy but also guarantees an increasingly high-quality product. Leading producer countries are now investigating clonal selection to improve yields, hardiness, drought-resistance, ease of picking, and resistance to disease. They seek also to counter the natural tendency toward biennial cropping and look out for types that are adaptable to modern methods of cultivation.

Considerable research and experimentation has led to the selection of superior clones. Good examples are *Koroneïki I-38, Arbosana I-43,* and *Arbequina I-18,* all characterized by early production, high yields, and suitability for intensive cultivation. There is no

> ### Biennial cropping
>
> Olive trees have a natural tendency toward biennial, or alternate-year, cropping, because it fruits on previous year's growth. This is a common feature of other economic crops, including apples, raspberries, and citrus fruit. It means that a year of plenty is followed by a year of paucity. This creates economic problems for the growers in poor years and quality problems in good years because a large crop deteriorates while it waits to be picked and processed. Biennial cropping can be countered to some degree by regular pruning, irrigation, and manuring. It is initiated by climatic factors, like winter cold, which are beyond the grower's control. Only the most intensive olive growing with selected clones cultivated in artificial conditions can even up production.

doubt that these selections will set a worldwide standard for large-scale high-quality production against which all other oils will come to be judged.

ARBEQUINA OLIVES

This cultivar originates in Catalonia (*see p.146*), and is now widely grown in Andalusia as well (*see p.166*). The tree is of low to medium vigor, has a weeping shape, and crown of average size. *Arbequina* olives are popular because they produce reliably high yields, have little or no tendency to biennial cropping, adapt well to dense planting, and are self-fertile. Selected clones (for example, *Arbequina I-18*) are sold worldwide for intensive cultivation at densities of up to 650 plants per acre (1,600/ha). *Arbequina* oil is noted for its intensely fresh and fruity taste, which is particularly pronounced in cold climates.

CORATINA OLIVES

This cultivar takes its name from the town of Corato, near Bari, in Italy. It is the most important olive in the region of Puglia (*see p.101*) and widely found

OLIVE TREES GROWN FROM CUTTINGS
National research stations around the world test, select, and propogate superior olive clones for specific conditions.

throughout southern Italy. Also, there are new plantings in areas like Australia and Argentina. It makes a medium-sized tree, with a dense canopy and a rounded shape. It comes into production early but adapts well to different soils and climates. It is self-sterile, so needs to be planted alongside another cultivar. *Coratina* is not prone to biennial cropping but has a very high, very constant yield (up to 25 percent when irrigated). Its oil is very fruity (some people detect suggestions of apples and leafiness), bitter, and peppery with a hint of sweetness. *Coratina* oil is also high in polyphenols, which makes it very stable and long lived. Unusually for olive oils, the strong flavor of *Coratina* oil improves with age and becomes gentle, aromatic, and almondy.

CORNICABRA OLIVES

This cultivar, sometimes called *Cornezuelo*, is said to originate in central Spain, near Toledo. *Cornicabra* olives make one of the most stable, long lasting of all oils, and so are popular with blenders.

The name *Cornicabra* refers to the long, asymmetric shape of the olive, which is slightly curved like a goat's horn. The trees are moderately vigorous, upright, and thickly leaved. The olives ripen late; picking starts when they turn from green to purple at the end of October and continues until January by which time they are black. Late-picked oils have a ripe balance between light bitterness, pepperiness, and mellow fruitiness, reminiscent of tropical fruits and avocados. Younger oils are more pungent and "greener" in taste, but always aromatic, thick, smooth, and velvety on the palate. Sometimes they have an almondy aftertaste.

MISSION OLIVES

DNA analysis shows this to be a clone of the *Cornicabra* olive (*left*). Spanish missionaries took it to the west coast of America in the 18th century. During the first half of the 20th century, it was widely planted in California to supply the table-olive trade. *Mission* olive trees are strong, upright, and vigorous growers, with a fairly dense canopy. They are very hardy. The olives are medium sized and slightly asymmetrical in shape with a yield of around 21 percent of their weight in oil. The olives ripen rather late in the season. *Mission* oil is fruity, with more pepperiness and (especially) bitterness than *Cornicabra* oils, with which it shares a thick, velvety texture and a suggestion of almondy sweetness in the aftertaste. It is regarded as long lasting, but is perhaps less stable than *Cornicabra*.

Treating and preserving table olives

Green table olives are unripe fruits. They are preserved in one of two ways. Spanish or Sevillian olives are soaked in sodium hydroxide to remove the bitterness and then fermented in brine by yeasts and malolactic bacteria. This method is used for *Manzanillo* and *Gordal* olives in Spain, and *Picholine Marocaine* in Morocco. The American style is to soak the olives first in brine and then in sodium hydroxide, and to change the water frequently until all the bitterness has come out. The olives are then packed into cans

TABLE OLIVES

or bottles, covered with brine and vinegar, and sterilized under heat. This is the way *Manzanillo* olives are preserved in California, and *Picholine* and *Lucques* olives in France.

Black olives (ripe olives) are preserved in brine, which is regularly replenished and stirred so that the bitterness is dispersed, and the salt penetrates the flesh of the olives to preserve them. The olives are then packed in brine and sealed with oil. This process gives the olives a slightly bitter taste. *Kalamáta* olives from Greece are a good example of this type. There are many other processes used to prepare table olives, including drying olives in salt (popular in northern Greece).

HOJIBLANCA TREE Even a well cultivated tree may be bowed down by olives in a bumper year.

FRANTOIO OLIVES

This Italian cultivar, originally from Tuscany (*see p.70*), is now one of the most widely grown olives, appreciated throughout Italy, where it accounts for some 250,000 acres (100,000ha). The *Frantoio* olive is also extensively planted in Argentina and Chile, and it is popular too in California and Australia, as well as New Zealand.

There are many different clones in cultivation, but they all produce high-quality oil. The trees are only of medium height and vigor, with a naturally dense habit of growth. They are very hardy as well as self-fertile, which guarantees a high and constant production. The olives are medium small and ripen quite late in the high, cold region of Tuscany but comparatively early in warmer areas.

Frantoio olives are best picked half-ripe, when they are turning from green to purple. The oil is then very fruity, aromatic, and well balanced by a good measure of pepperiness and bitterness. Late-picked olives yield a soft, gentle, almost sweet, oil that has a mild, almondy taste and very little aftertaste. *Frantoio* oil is not naturally long lived, but the best producers take great care to preserve it under vacuum or covered by inert air so that it keeps its flavor at least until the new season's crop is ready.

GALEGA OLIVES

This cultivar accounts for about four-fifths of all olive trees grown in Portugal. *Galega* gives Portuguese olive oil its distinctive character, and its consistency of taste. The olive's great virtue is its hardiness and adaptability, which make it easy to grow in a wide variety of soils and climates. The trees are naturally short and compact but not always productive. The olives are small and ripen early, but their oil content is low (14–18 percent), and they show a marked tendency to biennial cropping (*see p.27*). The oil has a fruity smell and a soft, smooth taste of green fruit and grass, with sometimes a suggestion of almonds. It is not very stable and tends to deteriorate quickly, especially if it is made from late-harvested olives.

HOJIBLANCA OLIVES

This Spanish cultivar gets its name from the brilliant pale underside of its abundant foliage—*hojiblanca* in Spanish means "white leaf." Its relatively low oil content (17–18 percent) explains why it has not spread significantly beyond its native Andalusia. There are about 544,000 acres (220,000ha) of *Hojiblanca* trees in the region, however, which makes it the world's third most-planted olive. The trees are vigorous, with a characteristic broad and pendulous shape and long, twiggy tips. They are

NOCELLARA DEL BELICE TREES Originating from Sicily, this olive is widely planted elsewhere.

among the most beautiful of all olive trees. *Hojiblanca* olives are medium large and often used for the production of black table olives. They ripen late, but stand up well to cold weather. *Hojiblanca* oil is variable in taste, but is usually sweet and slightly fruity at first, followed by a mild pepperiness, a long, light bitterness, and sometimes a surprising aftertaste of rich fruit and almonds.

KORONEIKI OLIVES

This cultivar originates from Koroni in the Mani Peninsula in the Pelepponese and it now accounts for two-thirds of the olives in Greece.

Koroneïki is an olive tree of medium vigor with a spreading habit and an open canopy. It is usually found in low-lying and coastal areas where the climate is warm. The olives are very small but they ripen early and give high and constant yields. *Koroneïki* oil is fruity, with a slight touch of green apple and somewhat more of a fresh, leafy, grass taste. It has a pleasant pepperiness and light bitterness in its aftertaste, and is very well balanced overall.

KORONEÏKI OLIVES

Koroneïki is one of the longest-lasting olive oils. A clone called *I-38* was selected in Spain for super-intensive cultivation and is widely planted all over the world.

KALAMATA OLIVES

This is the principal table olive in Greece, though it also offers a high yield of good-quality oil. It originated in the region of Kalamata in the Peleponnese, where a 700-year-old specimen claims to be the original tree. It is now widely cultivated in other parts of the Peloponnese (*see p.232*) and around Lamía in the prefecture of Fthiótida. The tree is vigorous and upright, with distinctive, large, soft leaves. The *Kalamata* olives are generally large and have a good flesh-to-stone ratio as well as being "freestone" (the stone is not attached to the flesh of the fruit). The olives turn black when ripe and are renowned for their flavor and firmness.

LECCINO OLIVES

The *Leccino* olive originates in Tuscany, where it is still an important component of oils, but it spread quickly into Umbria and Lazio and is now planted throughout the peninsula. It is probably the most widespread of all Italian olives and is an expanding cultivar that has also been extensively planted outside the Mediterranean region.

The reasons for its popularity are twofold. It is the hardiest of all widely grown cultivars, and it produces good quantities of consistently high-quality oil. It is also very adaptable to different growing conditions. The tree is vigorous and broad, with a dense, slightly pendulous habit. It is self-sterile, so it must be interplanted with other cultivars. The olives ripen early and simultaneously. The optimal time for picking them is when they have turned purple. They are medium-small olives with an oil content of around 18–20 percent that remains constant even when the trees are irrigated to increase yields. The oil is pale, gentle, mellow, and only lightly fruity—"delicate" is the usual word for it—with little in the way of bitterness or pepperiness but sometimes a hint of sweetness. These characteristics are accentuated if it is grown in a hot climate. The oil is reasonably stable and very popular as a blending oil to tone down the strong flavors of oils from such olive cultivars as *Frantoio* and *Coratina*.

LECCINO OLIVES

NOCELLARA DEL BELICE OLIVES
This Sicilian cultivar had a fairly local distribution until recently. The town of Castelvetrano, in Marsala province, is still its epicenter but excellence and the popularity of its oil has led to it being widely planted throughout Sicily and on the mainland of Italy.

The tree is unremarkable—somewhat short and expansive. It needs good soil and does best when irrigated. The olives are regularly produced and large, with crisp, firm flesh and a delicious taste.

PICHOLINE OLIVES
This is France's best (and most widely distributed) olive, both for oil and table olives. *Picholine* is grown all over Languedoc, Corsica, and Provence. It is very adaptable and dependable, so that it is now increasingly planted also in Puglia and the New World.

Picholine trees are narrow and upright at first, but broaden out with age. Annual pruning produces regular crops, and irrigation increases the yield. The olives are medium-large (0.10–0.14oz/ 3.5–4.5g) and uniform in size, with a thin stone that makes it good as a table olive, picked green in November. Oil is made when it is ripe and reddish black (December, January), with a yield of 18–20 percent. *Picholine* oil lacks bitterness, being mild and almost sweet. It is full of fruitiness and sometimes quite peppery but almost always pale, well balanced, rich, and elegant.

PICUDO OLIVES
This Spanish olive gets its name from the prominent point at its tip. *Picudo* are most extensively planted in southern Córdoba, and in the adjoining areas of Jaén, Málaga, and Granada. It makes a very vigorous, hardy tree with an unusually dense canopy. The fruit are large (0.14–0.17oz/4.5–5g) and useful also as table olives.

Picudo oil is fluid and smooth in texture with a strong and distinctive taste—sweet and grassy at first, with a pungent aroma of bitter oranges, followed by a light pepperiness, and a long, light bitterness. The flavor is always well balanced and combines especially well with strong-flavored foods. Low levels of polyphenols in *Picudo* oil cause early oxidization. Good producers are meticulous in their storage of *Picudo* oil to preserve its freshness.

PICUAL OLIVES
This is the world's most prolific olive. It accounts for half of Spain's olive trees and 97 percent of the olives in Jaén. The trees are vigorous, hardy, and adaptable, with an expansive, leafy crown. The olives are medium-sized (0.07–0.14oz/2–4g), with an off-center point at their tip. They are copiously borne and can yield as much as 28 percent of their weight in oil.

Picual oil has a distinct bitter and pungent taste that recalls figs and wet wood, which is highly esteemed by some Spaniards. The *Picual* oils from cooler areas are lighter and fresher. *Picual* oil also has a very high polyphenol content, which gives it a long shelf life.

Extracting Oil

The starting point for making high-quality oil is healthy olives. Once harvested, olives must be conveyed to the mill as soon as possible—ideally the same day. Traditionally, oil is extracted by a series of procedures, which, if the machines are not thoroughly cleaned between pressings, can result in dirty oil. These are being phased out by fast modern systems that produce a more consistent oil and have a greater capacity.

HEALTH AND MATURITY OF THE OLIVES

The most important factor in making high-quality oil is the health of the olives when picked. They must be unblemished and free from pests like olive fly (*see p.25*), which impart an unpleasant flavor to the olives. Any rupture of the skin or cells of the fruit will start off a process of deterioration, leading to infection by bacteria, yeasts, or fungi, and ultimately to defects in the oil, namely mold, fermentation, or mustiness, which taint the oil.

The taste and other qualities of an oil also depend on the maturity of the olives when they are picked and milled. Oil builds up in the flesh and kernels to reach its maximum (up to 30 percent of the pulp, depending on the cultivar, *see p.26*) just as the fruit starts to ripen— young olives are green, and most cultivars turn red, purple, or black as they mature. The first pickings are usually made just as this ripening process begins. By this stage the oil is fully developed and will not benefit from further maturation. If the fruit is left longer the percentage of oil may increase but only because some of the water in the olive evaporates and, with it, some of the oil's fruity flavor.

Small private estates can choose the optimum time to pick their olives to produce their oil. However, in areas like Andalusia where there are large crops of olives, the producers start picking them as soon as they yield a good volume of oil. In good years, there can be four months between harvesting the first olives and picking and processing the last. In mixed plantations, where several cultivars are grown together, growers will pick the early-maturing cultivars first, and the late-maturing olives last. In cool

PICKING OLIVES   Large nets are laid out under the trees during harvesting to catch the olives that fall.

climates like upland Tuscany, where there is a shorter growing season, growers traditionally pick their olives before they are fully ripe (*see p.70*). This has advantages for the longevity of the oil, because young olives are high in polyphenols and low in linoleic acid, which are characteristics that help delay the oxidization, decay, and rancidness that ultimately affect all oil.

PICKING THE OLIVES

This is by far the most expensive part of the production process for traditional growers and mechanized estates alike. There are several methods of harvesting olives. Whatever the method of picking, it is essential that the fruit is kept intact, as undamaged as possible, and transported to the mill for immediate pressing. The process of picking usually damages the olives. Their skin may be broken by falling and they are often bruised in the course of handling. All sorts of undesirable processes may ensue that affect the taste of the oil (*see opposite*). The European DOP rules state that olives should be milled within a specified period, typically 24 hours. Oils processed in modern mills taste cleaner and fresher than oils from traditional mills in non-European parts of the Mediterranean.

Manual harvesting is a time-consuming process that involves running the hand along the branches toward their tips, stripping the fruits on the way, and placing them in baskets, without splitting or bruising the olives. There are hand-held machines that speed up manual picking, though these may injure the quality of the fruit. Nets are often laid out under the trees to catch and collect the falling fruit and ladders are needed to reach the ones in the crowns of the trees. Hand-picking is used mainly in low-density areas, in small plantations where mechanization is not

ANCIENT OLIVE-GRINDING WHEEL

viable, and in hilly terrain where it is not possible (slopes greater than 15° cannot be harvested mechanically).

Mechanical picking is widely used and involves harvesting machines, or shakers, that are linked to a catching frame. Some machines shake the trunk of the tree, others the main branches. There are also machines that work like a vacuum cleaner, but they are more likely to damage the fruit. Modern, intensive plantations with row on row of trees no more than 6ft 6in–10ft (2–3m) tall have machines that drive up and down the lines to harvest the olives. While being transported to the mill, the olives are best kept in flat, shallow, open-sided containers where the air can circulate around them, minimizing the risk of decay before pressing.

TRADITIONAL OIL EXTRACTION

The first part of the extraction process involves crushing the olives so completely that the cell structure is destroyed. The traditional method was to grind the olives, stones included, into a paste between large stone wheels (turned by men, donkeys, or horses).

Once the olives are pulped, the paste was kept turning to help the oil coagulate. In some areas hot water was added to the mash to assist the process. Nowadays this disqualifies an oil from DOP status because it has the effect of vaporizing some of the polyphenols that give taste and character to the finished product. High-quality producers insist that temperatures should never exceed 82°F (28°C) at any stage of the production process, hence the expression "cold-pressed." The next stage in traditional oil extraction is to load the paste into circular mats that are stacked high on a press and squeezed until all the oil and other liquids drip down the outside of the stack into a collector below. The press used to be made with a large wooden screw at the center that

CONVEYING THE OLIVES
Long conveyor belts take the olives, when they
arrive at the mill, for deleafing, grading, and
washing before they enter the extraction plant.

was turned by men or beasts, but
hydraulic machines began to be used
toward the end of the 19th century.

The liquid from the press runs into a
series of tanks where it sits for about a
day. The oil separates out and floats to
the surface because it is lighter than the
vegetable water from the olives. The oil
is then skimmed off, though particles of
olive pulp remain suspended in the oil.
Freshly made oil therefore looks opaque
or cloudy, but the impurities continue to
settle over a period of months until they
appear as a sediment and the oil itself is
clear. Some people believe that the tiny
pieces of olive impart a special fruity
taste to newly made oil. However,
filtered oils last longer and are less likely
to disappoint the consumer.

Olive oil was traditionally kept in
terra-cotta jars or stone or cement
containers, which were difficult to clean
and did not exclude contact with
atmospheric oxygen, which is responsible

for rancidness. Some oil was transported
for sale in animal skins. Wooden barrels
were the preferred form of containers
for transportation to northern Europe.

MODERN OIL EXTRACTION
When the olives first arrive at the mill,
they are washed to remove all traces of
dirt and any leaves that they may have
acquired in the process of picking and

MODERN PRESS Olives are mashed to a fine paste as here, before being pressed to extract the oil.

transportation. If leaves are left in the press, they give a bitter taste to the oil and impart an unnatural green color (oil made from ripe olives is naturally yellow). Toward the end of the harvest, however, when the olives are very ripe, some producers add a few olive leaves to "improve" the color.

Modern, automatic, enclosed systems then pulp the olives with hammers, churn the paste, and separate the pure oil from the vegetable water and pulp by centrifugal force. There are two main systems, called "two-phase" and "three-phase." Two-phase plants, which are preferred in Spain, are thought to give a better product. This is because the three-phase system adds fresh water,

which takes away some of the polyphenols and antioxidants that maximize taste and conserve the oil. The water is also contaminated by the process and needs to be treated before being released. However, the two-phase system leaves lots of rather wet residue, and the pulp needs to be heated to extract the rest of the oil, hence the large volumes of sansa and refined oil in Spain. There is a third system of extracting oil, using a machine known as Sinolea. This works by attracting the oil molecules in the mash to thousands of tiny fibers by surface tension. It produces a high-quality oil but seldom draws out more than two-thirds of the potential oil, so the residue is put through a centrifugal extractor. Sinolea systems are most commonly found in Italy.

MODERN STORAGE

Newly extracted oil is stored under nitrogen or inert gas in sealed stainless steel vats at a temperature of 50–64°F (10–18°C). Temperature and storage regulation is essential: oxidization is catalyzed, or accelerated, by heat and light. Below 50°F (10°C), oil starts to crystallize, and may not reconstitute satisfactorily when temperatures rise again. Modern storage vats also have conical bases, so deposits collect in the bottom and ease the extraction of deposits that form in unfiltered oils.

Dennocciolato oil

This is oil made from fruit that has had the stones removed. The technique for making this oil has recently been reintroduced, especially in Italy. Advocates believe that denocciolato oil has a more intense flavor and lasts longer than conventional oil. Others maintain that pulping the stones releases enzymes in the kernel that aid the development of flavors.

The Quality Factor

Olive oil is a very complex mixture of components, although at least 98 percent is made up of fats and only two percent of polyphenols and other chemicals. The latter include tocopherols and sterols (such as cholesterol) that give the oil flavor and character, and contribute to its stability. Polyphenols are antioxidants while cholesterol is a vital component of every cell in the body (see p.46).

GEOGRAPHICAL ORIGIN & QUALITY IDENTIFICATION FOR OILS

The main olive-producing countries of Europe—Italy, Spain, Portugal, France, and Greece—have developed their own geographical guarantees for many of their olive oils. These are based on the familiar system of *Appellation d'Origine Contrôlée* (AOC) that the French use to denote high-quality wines. More reliable, however, is the system of quality controls that the EU (European Union) has developed to guarantee the standard of olive oil. There are two types of EU guarantee, and you need to distinguish between them. One is a guarantee of quality and the other a guarantee of geographical origin. The EU quality guarantee is based on the Italian national laws of *Denominazione di Origine Protetta* (DOP) and is variously known in other countries (*see p. 39*). The lesser guarantee (of an oil's geographical origin) also has different names in the main producing countries. Some governments continue to make their own national awards, and do not distinguish them from EU guarantees.

CONDITIONS FOR CLASSIFICATION

All potential DOP oils (oils from within the EU-defined areas) have to undergo more than thirty compulsory chemical tests every year before an oil can be

MODERN OLIVE PLANTATION In southern Andalusia especially the land is dominated by huge olive groves.

classified and sold with a DOP certificate. Oils are also tested for smell and taste by a panel of qualified tasters. The tasters will look for such defects as rancidity, mold, and anaerobic fermentation, as well as checking that the oils exhibit the distinctive character set out in the particular DOP's legislation. The rules ensure that every individual olive tree in a given area is registered with the DOP authorities. They also specify such details as the permitted density of the planting of trees, the cultivar type, the season of picking, and the maximum time allowed between picking and processing.

All these tests guarantee the origin and quality of an oil. Nevertheless, some DOP oils remain more dependable than others. In a few cases, the DOP parameters are so widely drawn that the oil may qualify but seem defective to most palates—the AOC for Corsican oils is an example. Some national AOCs have been made for political reasons, or to encourage improvements in quality in a producing area rather than guarantee it. Sometimes, the tasters are not uniformly and universally impartial. But these are exceptions. The vast majority of DOP olive oils are high quality, dependable, and delicious. You may buy any DOP oil from the leading areas like Terra di Siena and Valli Trapanesi in Italy, Siurana in Spain, and Trás-os-Montes in Portugal with absolute confidence that the oil will be worth everything you pay for it, provided it is no more than 12 months old, and has been stored in cool, dark, air-free conditions.

In Italy and Greece, the great majority of oil is extra virgin. In 2000 this accounted for 78 percent of the olive oil in Italy and 85 percent in Greece. Most of the olive oil consumed in the rest of Europe is also extra virgin. In Spain, only 20 percent of

USING DARK BOTTLES
High-quality oils are sealed in dark glass or terra-cotta bottles to help combat oxidation caused by light.

Categories of olive oil

There are four categories of olive oil: virgin olive oil, refined olive oil, olive oil, and sansa oil. Virgin olive oil has the highest quality but all the oils featured in this book are extra virgin.

VIRGIN OLIVE OIL

This is oil that has been obtained from olives using mechanical or physical processes that do not treat or alter the oil in any way. Oil that has been treated with solvents, distillation, or chemicals is expressly excluded. There are three types of virgin olive oil, which are classified by the European Union according to how much free acidity they contain (that is, acid that does not form part of a chemical compound but exists on its own in its natural state). Acidity is a measure of quality and freshness (it increases as oils age) but is not discernible by the human tongue until it reaches about 6%. The three types are:

Extra virgin olive oil—this contains no more than 0.8% oleic acid.
Virgin olive oil—this oil's acidity is within range of 0.8–2%.
Lampante olive oil – the acidity of this oil exceeds 2%. The word lampante indicates that its historic use was not for consumption but for lighting lamps.

REFINED OLIVE OIL

Refined oil should be called rectified oil; there is nothing refined in the positive sense of the word about refined oil. It has been chemically cleaned to eradicate excessive acidity, oxidization, or an unpleasant taste. Refined oil is usually made from lampante, and has an acidity not exceeding 0.3%.

OLIVE OIL

This is a blend of the two previous categories, virgin (excluding lampante) and refined, and has no more than 1% acidity.

SANSA OIL

This is made from the pressed waste from which oil has been extracted and from which a debased type of oil may be obtained. There are several types of sansa oil, none of them worth serious consideration.

the oil sold at retail is extra virgin. The rest is "olive oil," which is a mixture of refined and virgin oils.

QUALITY CONTROL OUTSIDE THE EU

The EU system of quality control is widely followed by producers in other parts of the world. When the EU reduced the maximum permitted acidity for extra virgin oils from 1% to 0.8% in 2003, the new definition was accepted almost universally. However, the laws are not binding outside the EU, so a little skepticism is occasionally desirable when considering the claim of a non-European oil to be extra virgin. Only the Americans exercise effective quality control, through the California Olive Oil Council. There is no equivalent in Australia as yet.

DOP LABEL FROM MONTES DI GRANADA, SPAIN

FILTERED OR UNFILTERED OILS

Unfiltered oil is sometimes thought to be better than filtered, being more natural, and having more elements that help protect the body from such diseases as cancer and heart disease. Factory-produced oils, and many estate oils, are filtered to take out suspended particles,

protect the oil from decay, and give it a longer shelf life. Health fanatics believe that the process also removes the oil's health and nutritional qualities. "Real olive oil is not filtered," they claim. There is no evidence that filtration alters the taste of the oil. In fact the opposite is true. Pure oil is clear, and keeps its fresh taste for longer than unfiltered oils. Cloudy oils contain impurities, such as pieces of olive that act as a catalyst for early deterioration.

THE DETERIORATION OF OLIVE OIL

Oil does not improve with age, but starts to degrade from the moment it is squeezed from the olive. The rate of deterioration is usually slow at first, and depends on many factors, including how well made the oil is and what olive cultivars it is made from. *Arbequina* and *Biancolilla*, for example, lose their freshness quickly, while *Cornicabra* keeps it for several years.

There are two phases in the chemical deterioration of olive oil. First, oxygen attaches to the fats (a reaction known as oxidization) to produce hyperperoxides. These are odorless and tasteless, so they

EU classification for olive oil

COUNTRY	EU QUALITY GUARANTEE	NATIONAL GUARANTEE	EU GEOGRAPHICAL GUARANTEE
France	Appellation d'Origine Protegee (AOP)	Appellation d'Origine Controlee (AOC)	None
Italy	Denominazione d'Origine Protetta (DOP)	None	Indicazione Geografica Protetta (IGP)
Portugal	Denominacao de Origem Protegida (DOP)	Denominacao de Origem (DO)	None
Spain	Denominaciones de Origen Protegida (DOP)	Denominaciones de Origen (DO)	Denominaciones Geograficas Protegidas (DGP)
Greece	Protected Designations of Origin (PDO) / Προστατευόμενη Ονομασόα Προέλευσης (ΠΟΠ)	None	Protected Geographical Indication (PGI) / Προστατευόμενη Γεωγραφική Ένδειξη (ΠΓΕ)

have no effect on the flavor of the oil. Second, the hyperperoxides themselves break down and give rise to rancidity, which has a distinct and disagreeable smell and taste. Peroxides therefore indicate oxidization, which is why EU rules stipulate that the best oils must be tested for peroxides before they can be classified and sold as extra virgin.

Top producers keep their oil under nitrogen, or in a vacuum, to ensure that it is in good condition when it leaves their premises. Their bottling plants leave no space at the top of the bottle. Light

and heat are catalysts that accelerate the oxidization of olive oil, so oil should ideally be stored in the dark at 57–61°F (14–16°C). Far too many oils are already spoiled by the time the consumer buys them because it is difficult to display olive oil in a cool, dark environment. Consumers should, however, try to store it correctly at home (*see p.41*).

SMALL OLIVE PLANTINGS
Olives are grown on a very small scale to maximize land use, as here, as well as on large estates dedicated to olive growing.

Buying and Storing Olive Oil

High-quality oil will generally keep longer, which is why it is important to determine an oil's pedigree by reading the label on the bottle. You should also look for any signs of deterioration before you buy, and store the oil carefully in order to keep it as fresh as possible. The crucial factor is that it should be stored in the optimum conditions, before and after you buy it (see below).

RECOGNIZING A GOOD OIL

Too much oil leaves a producer in good condition, of the quality and taste it purports to be, but is then stored under the wrong conditions and spoiled by the time it reaches the end consumer. Many people who buy olive oil are unaware that they are getting a poor-quality product, but it explains why, at least in Mediterranean countries, people prefer to buy their oil directly from a producer. In certain traditional olive-growing regions, a defect like rancidness is sometimes considered desirable. But there is a growing awareness everywhere that high quality means adherence to the international standards that define extra virgin olive oil (*see p.37*). If you buy an olive oil that is rancid, or fails in some way to come up to the standard promised by its label, you should always make the seller aware of your concerns. Legal liability for the quality of the oil rests with the seller.

In newer markets, many people do not know how to interpret olive oil labels. Nor do they realize that some producing countries may dump their inferior oil on them. Olive oil is often promoted as health giving, yet more than half the oil sold in North America, for example, has been refined, a process that removes the health benefits. But change is afoot. The appearance of high-quality extra virgin oils in countries like the United States provides greater choice, but there is no opportunity to pretaste even a fine oil on the supermarket shelves nor can we know how well it has been stored.

CHARACTERISTICS TO WATCH FOR

The principles of best practice that apply to bulk storage also apply to bottles of olive oil. Humidity, light, air, and heat are enemies of olive oil. Avoid oils in clear glass because oxidization will be accelerated by light. Look for bottles with little or no headspace in the neck of the bottle and reject any that show signs of leakage, because the lost oil will have been replaced by an injection of air.

The color of oil is usually yellow, but may be anything from pale to deep golden yellow, sometimes with a green tinge and occasionally more green than yellow. Oils tend to darken as they age

and oxidize. Look very carefully at any oil that has a sediment at the base of the bottle. Any darkening of that deposit indicates an anaerobic fermentation that will already have begun to have an adverse effect on the taste of the oil. Do not be deceived into thinking that unfiltered oil is in any way tastier or more natural than filtered or that you can judge the flavor of an oil by its color. Professionals taste oil from colored glasses so that they are not influenced by perceived color or hue.

Always check when the oil was made, or its sell-by date. Unfiltered opaque oils do not last as long as filtered oils. You should aim never to use a filtered oil that is more than 12 months old; unfiltered oils spoil even sooner.

STORING OLIVE OIL AT HOME

Olive oil usually deteriorates slowly at first, depending on how well it was made and from which olive cultivars. *Arbequina* and *Biancolilla* oils, for example, lose their freshness quickly, while *Cornicabra* keeps well for years (if unopened). Store your olive oil at a temperature of 57–61°F (14–16°C) away from light, and sealed from the air (ideally in a dark bottle). High-quality oils are sold in bottles made of opaque or very dark glass. Do not decant your oil into a different bottle. Below 57°F (14°C) some of the component flavors crystallize out and may not reconstitute perfectly. Bottles should be finished within one month of being opened.

Understanding labels

Most olive oil bottles have two labels. The front one sells the bottle; the back one tells you what it contains. Look at both.

Look for the date of harvest Do not buy any oil more than 12 months old. This is not the same as the sell-by date, which may give a false impression of freshness. The taste will already have deteriorated by the time you approach the sell-by date.

Buy only extra virgin oil Ignore anything that says "cold-pressed" (all extra virgin oils are). Be wary of "made from selected olives" (it means they bought them in) or "made in Italy" (it probably came from somewhere else first).

Work out where it comes from Look for a DOP sign. It is a guarantee of quality. So are marketing devices like Laudemio in Tuscany. Try to work out if the oil is estate-made and estate-bottled; these usually indicate quality. Avoid anything saying "product of" or "blended"; these are often rather ordinary oils masquerading as upscale products.

Look for how much acidity the oil contains This is a measure of quality. For example, 0.8% is only just extra virgin; 0.5% is better; 0.3% is good; 0.2% is very good.

Think hard about "organic" and "unfiltered" These are not marks of quality, but descriptions of the cultivation and processing.

SELECTING A BOTTLE OF OLIVE OIL
Not all these bottles found their way into this book. Pretty labels are no guide to quality. Choose oil sold dark bottles that protect it from light. Avoid oils with cork stoppers because they can let in air.

Olive Oil Tasting

There are broadly three categories of taster—professional, expert, and consumer. Professional and expert tasters must make objective judgements on either quality or consistency for the institution, producer, or blender they work for. An amateur consumer, however, is in the happy position of being always right. He or she can make a personal and subjective assessment and then declare "I like it" or "I do not like it" and does not even have to give any reasons.

WHICH OIL IS THE BEST

Almost every producer, farmer, village, company, region, and country believes its own oil to be the best in the world, without being able to say why. Few can taste another oil and explain why it is inferior to his own except by saying that "it is different" and "I simply do not like it as much." Choice is a matter of personal preference. There are many different styles of olive oil but none is more correct or more desirable than the rest. The traditional taste—made from fully mature olives—is soft, gentle, and almondy. The modern style, championed in Tuscany and Umbria, is for strongly fruity, peppery, and bitter oils. There is a place for each of them and many more besides. Look for an attractive appearance, a pure smell, a pleasing taste, a degree of complexity and balance, and a long aftertaste.

Remember that the taste of an oil will begin to change after you open the bottle. Most will deteriorate, but a few will start to lose their harder edges and become more accessible. And remember, too, that oils from the same cultivar have much in common with each other, especially if the olives are pressed at the same degree of maturity.

NOBIL DRUPA

FOODS FOR OLIVE OIL

Every oil is said to be delicious when accompanying salads or poured over fish and white meats. There are no forbidden combinations like the convention that prevents sweet white wine being drunk with beef stew. In fact, there are no rules at all for olive oil. You should feel able to experiment and discover for yourself what oils go best with what food, at least for you. Be wary

My Ten Top Oils

FOR QUALITY		
Name	Country	Page
Nobil Drupa Terra di Brisighella	Italy	68
Masseria Caposella	Italy	110
Fontanasalsa Biancolilla	Italy	126
Antinori Pèppoli	Italy	74
Badia a Coltibuono Campo Corto	Italy	77
Núñez de Prado Flor	Spain	181
Dauro de l'Empordà	Spain	152
CARM Grande Escolha	Portugal	199
Château de la Tuilerie Fleur de Goutte	France	225
Adelaide Parklands	Australia	261

FOR VALUE		
Name	Country	Page
Olearia San Giorgio L'Ottobrattico	Italy	117
Frantoio Oleario De Carlo, Fruttato Delicato Torre di Mossa	Italy	107
Parqueoliva	Spain	181
Periana Verdial Frutado Dulce	Spain	182
Montebrione	Spain	152
Jacoliva Manzanilla Cacereña Verde	Spain	164
Mélas PDO Lygourgió Asklipíou	Greece	234
Borba Azeite do Norte Alentejano	Portugal	206
Ficalho Azeite Virgem Extra	Portugal	207
Bariani	USA	254

FOOD AND OLIVE OIL Bread is delicious with olive oil, but don't use it to taste an oil; it changes the flavor.

of people who tell you that a particular oil combines well with a fairly long list of foods that includes fish, shellfish, white meats, vegetables, and salads; it is as meaningless as the labels that tell you that a particular wine combines well with roasts, stews, grills, game, and cheeses. The conventional wisdom is that soft, gentle oils are best with light-flavored foods because stronger flavors can overwhelm the taste of the oil so that only its texture remains perceptible. Cooks often have strong views on what sort of oil—often a specific label—is best for a particular dish or type of cooking. But every cook seems to have a different view and to favor a different producer, so it is up to you to decide what you like best. And remember that food always changes the taste of an oil.

TASTING OIL

Some people have a greater sensibility than others. Women, for example, are usually more receptive to smell than men. And our sense of both smell and taste diminishes with age but not until late middle-age and then not equally.

It is best not to accompany a tasting with any food or drink other than water because it will affect the way you perceive the taste of oil. Bread can make the oil taste better than it is. Professional

Trained tasters

Professional tasters make an objective assessment of an oil's qualities and shortcomings. They use a precise vocabulary so that, for example, there can be no confusion between the meaning of "bitter" and "astringent." They usually work in panels, because the composite opinion of several is always safer than that of an individual and lessens the possibility of error. Objectivity is the sum of experience, and they have a wide experience on which to draw. An expert taster is usually an expert only within his chosen field. For example, if his job is to select the oils that will be blended by the large company that employs him, he will have a clear idea of the sort of product he wishes to create.

tasters, however, may use apples to cleanse their palates. It is also a good idea to repeat your samplings, perhaps in a different order, because the sequence may reveal new smells and tastes. Professional tasters tend to test mild oils before those with a more pronounced taste, bitterness, or piquancy. Olive oil is best tasted at an ambient temperature somewhere in the region of 82°F (28°C); the optimum for distinguishing its qualities and

How to taste oil

It is better to taste oils in the morning because this is when your sensory capacity is usually at its best. Make sure at least one hour has elapsed since eating or drinking.

Your sense of taste and smell are strongest when the stomach is empty, in anticipation of a meal. But you should not be so hungry that you cannot concentrate.

1 Hold the glass up to the light. Look at the color. This is not a guide to quality and I would never discard or endorse an oil by its color. It does, however, take a deep golden color, which may be a sign of rancidness. Opaque oils are often young and fruity.

2 Begin by sniffing the oil. This will give you a first impression of its qualities—smell and taste are closely related—and help identify any defects. Good, fresh oil should smell of grass, fruit, or almonds, but not excessively olivey. A bad oil smells immediately rancid.

3 Sip enough to roll around your mouth and cover your tongue; some tasters then suck air into their mouth to aspirate the oil. Now you should notice the flavor of the individual oil. You will also feel its consistency or texture. Finally, you should swallow the oil, or spit it out and swallow what is left in your mouth.

4 Swallowing allows you to taste the pepperiness and bitterness of the oil, which are best sensed at the back of the throat and may take several seconds to develop. A "long" taste is generally considered a quality. Make a note of your findings under different headings: color, smell, texture, and taste.

KEY QUALITIES, TASTES, AND DEFECTS OF OLIVE OIL

QUALITIES

Fruitiness A fresh taste that may remind you of fruit or vegetables, but is lively and attractive.

Bitterness This is normally felt on the back of the tongue and in the throat, and is characteristic of certain olive cultivars. It is an important part of an oil's aftertaste.

Pepperiness This hot sensation is associated with modern oils pressed from immature olives, and may even induce you to cough. It may not be sensed immediately, but form part of the aftertaste of the oil.

TASTES TO LOOK FOR

Grassiness This is both a taste and a smell. It is reminiscent of freshly cut grass and is a characteristic of young oils made from semimature olives.

Nuttiness The taste of sweet almonds is associated with oils made from fully ripe olives. Most oils acquire a nutty taste as they age.

Other positive attributes Artichokes, cardoons, beans, a general herbaceous or "green" taste, citrus, tomatoes (and tomato leaves), dried fruit, fresh almonds, apples, pears, bananas, and tropical fruit.

DEFECTS

Rancidness The most common defect and the result of oxidization. Many people do not recognize rancidness and think it is the "normal" taste of olive oil. Put some oil in a glass on a sunny windowsill for a week, and you will discover how to recognize the smell of rancidness.

"Wineyness" A smell and taste of wine or vinegar, caused by anaerobic fermentation of the olives.

Mold Bacteria and fungi can infect badly stored olives and impart a taste to the oil sometimes called fustiness or mustiness.

Muddiness The sediment at the bottom of the bottle has decayed—usually it has turned brown or black—and the oil tastes putrid.

Flatness This is caused by heating the paste (in the processing), which imparts a flat taste. Nowadays almost all oils are pressed cold.

Other defects Metallic taste from contact with metal; vegetable taste from prolonged contact during processing with the olive paste or extracted water; earthy taste from using olives that have fallen to the ground; the dirty, grubby taste of oils made from olives infested with olive-fly larvae, a common failing in badly managed groves.

---

shortcomings. In cool climates, warming the container in your hands can help release the smells and flavors of an oil.

WHAT TO LOOK FOR WHEN TASTING OIL

You need to recognize the various sensations—smell, taste, and consistency—and then quantify them. Experts mark oil using a scale of 1 to 9. The norm or average is therefore 5.

Look at the color and smell the oil. We tend to mistrust our sense of smell, and allow it to be overridden by sight. Green oils are often more bitter or astringent than yellow ones, but you must not allow your eyes to contradict your nose. Smells are elusive, and hard to define. We often say "I recognize the smell but cannot put a name to it" but, with training, it is possible to identify smells and describe them accurately.

Different oils also have very different textures, from thick and viscous to thin and runny. This has no effect on the taste, but may determine how you use them with food. Thick oils tend to bounce off a salad, for example.

Remember that pepperiness and bitterness, too, are qualities, not defects, although not everyone likes them. People who prefer their tea or coffee sweetened tend not to enjoy bitterness in olive oil. Excessive bitterness is strongly disliked by many. It is not necessary for fruitiness, bitterness, and pepperiness to be present in every oil. Many traditional oils (and those made late in the season) have neither pepperiness nor bitterness, for example. But it is important that none of the tastes should be excessive (bitterness, for example, should never verge on astringent) and that they are harmoniously balanced.

Do not rely entirely on tasting oil by itself. Unlike wine, oil is a condiment, not a food in itself. Its taste changes when it is put with food. Savory flavors mask the bitterness and pepperiness that may otherwise seem overpowering. It is also important to remember that an oil's taste will change as it ages and the same product will differ from year to year. Keep a diary of all the oils you taste, and compare them.

Olive Oil & Health

Many claims are made for the health benefits of consuming olives and olive oil. These are usually associated with studies of the Mediterranean diet, itself based on the dietary traditions of Italy and Greece, see opposite. Olive oil is 98 percent fat, but some of those fats are "healthy" and can help reduce the risk of cardiovascular disease (diseases of the heart and circulatory system). Olive oil also contains the antioxidant vitamins A, C, and E.

PREVENTING HEART DISEASE

There are three types of dietary fat: saturated fats (mostly of animal origin, though palm oil is an exception to this), polyunsaturated, and monounsaturated fats (both mainly of plant origin). Olive oil contains high levels of mono- and polyunsaturated fats, both known to confer important health benefits, while animal fats are high in saturated fats, known to increase the risk of high blood pressure, heart attacks, and strokes.

Blood contains important compounds called lipoproteins, which carry fats and cholesterol around the body. There are two types of lipoprotein: low-density lipoproteins (LDLs), and high-density lipoproteins (HDLs). LDLs are unhealthy because they deposit fat and cholesterol in the body tissues; HDLs are beneficial because they prevent the formation of fatty deposits in the arteries by removing free cholesterol from the tissues and carrying them to the liver to be eliminated. Cholesterol is a major component of every cell in the body, especially the brain and nervous system, but extra, or free, cholesterol accumulates to form a fatty deposit within blood vessels (atherosclerosis). The high monounsaturated-fat content of olive oil helps lower the levels of LDLs and other fats (triglycerides) in the blood, without reducing the HDL levels. There also seems to be a relationship between olive oil and blood pressure. The exact reasons are not understood, but is claimed that the regular consumption of olive oil decreases both systolic and diastolic blood pressure.

Olive oil therefore reduces the risk of developing heart disease, and helps prevent recurrence in anyone recovering from a heart attack. Olive oil helps raise HDL levels, lower triglycerides, and moderate blood sugar, so it can also help prevent the onset of diabetes as well.

AS AN ANTIOXIDANT

Antioxidants are substances that slow down and neutralize the effects of chemicals in the environment that react with, and damage, the body cells. The antioxidizing properties of olives can be transferred to human cells so that they deteriorate more slowly. Antioxidants are also said to increase longevity and slow down skin aging.

Some researchers claim that olive oil has a measurable effect in preventing the cancers that are associated with diet, notably colon, prostate, and breast cancers. This may be explained by the way oleic

TABLE OLIVES
Olives are an excellent source of monounsaturated fat. They also contain important vitamins, minerals, and essential amino acids.

HEALTHY EATING AND OIL The best olive oils need have nothing added to make an ideal salad dressing.

acid lowers the production of prostaglandins or by the effect of antioxidants, phytochemicals such as flavonoids, polyphenols, and squalene found in extra virgin olive oil.

OTHER HEALTH BENEFITS

Olive oil is thought to help calcium absorption and thus act against osteoporosis. More importantly, it is said to insure against memory loss, cognitive decline, dementia, and Alzheimer's disease in the elderly. This may be related to the brain's need for monounsaturated acids to maintain its cell structure and membranes.

A recent study in the United States found that olive oil contained a natural chemical that acts in a similar way to a painkiller. The chemical, oleocanthal, was found to inhibit inflammation in the same way as ibuprofen and other anti-inflammatory drugs.

The evidence is incontrovertible. Olive oil protects against illness and delivers longevity. It should be said, though, that the claims for the beneficial properties of olive oil apply largely to fresh extra virgin olive oil and not oil used for cooking or refined, because heat destroys many of the phenols and other compounds found in olive oil.

The Mediterranean diet

When Professor Ancel Keys, an American scientist, carried out fieldwork in connection with the Mediterranean diet in the 1950s, he noticed that Italians and Greeks, and in particular the people of the Greek Island of Crete, were seen to be long lived and to have a particularly low incidence of cardiovascular disease. Crete was a traditional society with limited economic opportunities. Ancel Keys's research showed that, of all European peoples, Cretans had the most balanced and healthy diet; they ate a diet low in saturated fats and high in monounsaturated and polyunsaturated fats. They ate more grains, fish, and vegetables, and most importantly used olive instead of animal fats in almost all of their cooking.

OLIVE OIL AND SARDINES

MAJOR OLIVE-GROWING COUNTRIES

European Producers

The main olive-producing countries—Spain, Italy, and Greece—all fall within the European Union. The EU has about 12,500,000 acres (5,200,000ha) of land under olive cultivation, which is roughly four percent of the total cultivable area. Nearly one-half of this land is in Spain, and one-quarter in Italy. Two and a half million farmers are involved with olives but the industry also includes cooperatives, mill-owners, refiners, and blenders. Olive oil is big business.

AN EXPANDING INDUSTRY

The latest published estimates (for 1999–2000) indicate that there are about 800 million olive trees in the EU: 44.5 percent in Spain, 26.3 percent in Italy, 18.8 percent in Greece, 9.7 percent in Portugal, and 0.7 percent in France. By now, the figure is probably closer to 900 million trees, because some 60 million were planted between 1995 and 1998, and planting continues. Most of the new trees are intensively planted and actively managed, in very high densities, which means high yields too. Spain has an estimated 5.7 million acres (2.3 million hectares) of olives, mainly in Andalusia (60 percent), Castilla-La Mancha (14 percent), Extremadura (11 percent), and Catalonia (5 percent). Italy has an estimated 2.89 million acres (1.17 million hectares), largely concentrated in Puglia, Calabria, and Sicily. The olive

industry in Greece is strongest in the Chalkdikhi peninsula, Crete, the Peleponnese, and the islands of the Ionian and Aegean seas. Oil producers within the EU are supported by subsidies that aim to secure them a fair return and by a system of promotion that encourages consumption. The main aims of EU policy are to improve the quality of olive oil, encourage diversity, and create the conditions for high pricing. It seeks to prevent large price fluctuations, and offer income security to farmers in the poorer regions where olives are mainly grown.

SMALL OLIVE GROVES PREDOMINATE

Landholdings, or olive-holdings, are generally small, especially in Italy and Greece, where they rarely exceed 5 acres (2ha). The average size of a professional holding is 33 acres (13.5ha)

AN EXPANDING INDUSTRY The larger producers store their oil under insert gas in huge cylinders.

SMALL HOLDINGS Olive farmers manually sifting the leaves and stones from newly harvested olives.

in Spain, 23 acres (9.4ha) in Portugal, 10 acres (4ha) in Italy, and 8 acres (3.2ha) in Greece; but these are professional holdings. The average size of all olive holdings (including the professionals) in Italy, for example, is less than 2½ acres (1ha), but15 acres (6ha) in Spain. One-fifth of owners in Italy produce less than 220lb (100kg) of oil; in Portugal about 40 percent of owners produce less than 220lb (100kg) of oil and in France 65 percent.

Another indicator of the fragmented nature of ownership is to look at the number of owners who make crop declarations to claim the EU production bonus but own less than 50 trees: 37 per cent in Italy, 45 per cent in France and 17 per cent in Spain, Portugal and Greece. These figures do not include those who omit to claim the subvention.

ITALIAN DOMINANCE
The Caparelli olive-oil botting plant in Florence is capable of producing 300 bottles of oil every minute. Their olive oil is sold in supermarkets around the world.

AN EXPENSIVE COMMODITY

Prices differ across the world but, as a general rule, wholesale prices of olive oil are four or five times higher than other vegetable oils. Italian prices are highest, followed by Greek and Spanish. The EU has a growing surplus that needs to be sold in world markets. However, it is hoped that much will be absorbed by an expansion of conmsumption within the new member-states of the EU. These accessions to the EU have had only a small effect on production figures. The allocated quotas are 6,600 tons for Cyprus, 440 tons for Slovenia, and 165 tons for Malta. This is 0.4 percent of the rest of the EU's total.

MAIN PRODUCERS

The EU is also an importer of oil (on average, 181,000 tons in the 1990s). Italy is by far the largest importer and most imports are brought into Italy duty-free for blending and processing, then reexported in the form of finished products. Tunisia has an EU zero-rated import quota of 62,000 tons. Morocco, Lebanon, and Algeria also have special tariff arrangements. Some imports also come from Turkey. Trade within the community of the EU accounts for about 716,500 tons of oil, most of it bought by Italy from Spain, and to a lesser extent Greece. Sixty five percent of Spanish exports (290,000 tons) and 94 percent of Greek exports (132,000 tons) are to Italy. Of all the oil traded within the EU, 78 percent of the total amount is extra virgin.

ITALY

Italy is the world's second-largest producer of olive oil, ranking well behind Spain but consistently ahead of Greece. It is also preeminent in the quality of its oils and produces a wider spectrum of interesting styles and tastes than any other country. Tuscany and Umbria account for no more than 5 percent of the national total.

LARGE INDUSTRY

Italy's annual production of olive oil oscillates between 550,000 and 770,000 tons. Some 40 percent comes from Puglia in southern Italy, the only part of the peninsula where olives are grown to the exclusion of all other crops—followed by Calabria, Sicily, and Campania. Biennial cropping is a constant feature and in Italy in one freak year in the 1990s Italian production actually exceeded Spain's—an event that for a while had rather a destabilizing effect on world markets.

HARVESTING OLIVES
BY HAND

ANCIENT STOCK

Olives were introduced to Italy by both the Phoenicians and the Ancient Greeks.

Some historians consider that very little in the way of breeding or selection has taken place for over 2,000 years. The large-fruited olives developed principally for the table are generally of North African origin and were brought by the Phoenicians, while the small oil-producing cultivars came originally from Greece. Certainly, olive growing was widely established at the time of the Roman Empire. Consignments of olive oil for the imperial city were one of the principal ways in which taxes were levied. Volumes declined during the Dark Ages, but the cultivation of the olive was always important to the Catholic church, for sacramental and medicinal purposes.

TRANQUIL SCENE A view of the countryside from a hilltop near San Gimignano in central Tuscany.
◀ TUSCAN LANDSCAPE The rolling hills of Tuscany are dotted with old farmhouses.

The maturity of taste

Those new to olive oil tend to prefer oils with a light taste. They start with refined oil, then move to soft, mild oils like *Taggiasca* from Liguria and *Manaki* from the Argolis. The next step is to appreciate more fruity oils, like the *Arbequina* oils of Catalonia and *Koroneïki* oils from Greece. Only when their taste has matured do most people come to appreciate the extra body, bitterness, and pepperiness associated with Tuscany and Umbria. This generalisation does not apply to everyone. Some individuals appreciate strong flavors right from the start. In any event, it is important that the fruitiness of an oil should always exceed the degree of its bitterness and pepperiness.

OLIVES FOR PRESSING

NEW PLANTATIONS IN THE 15TH CENTURY

By the Renaissance, olive oil had a premium value among consumers in the fast-expanding towns. Olive planting was encouraged as a way of keeping the countryside economically viable at a time when the Black Death had greatly reduced the population of agricultural workers. Right through until the 1950s, new olive plantations were a way of bringing marginal land into cultivation.

The postwar end of the sharecropping system known as the *mezzadria* led to the widescale abandonment of the countryside from which the industry has never fully recovered. Rising wage expectations, both in farming and in other industries, have made olive growing uneconomic in many areas, especially in such terrain as Liguria's, where the steep terraces are unsuitable for machinery. The biggest production costs are pruning and harvesting; the industry is too fragmented to embrace widescale mechanization. In hilly areas old trees are often more valued for their contribution toward the landscape. On the flat plains and in the valley bottoms, however, olives have to compete with more profitable crops like vines.

POPULAR CULTIVARS

Italy has a rich heritage of local olive cultivars. DNA research has reduced the synonyms from nearly 2,000 olive names, but that still leaves the country with more than 700 different olive cultivars, including more than 100 in each of Campania and Tuscany. Two cultivars are widely grown throughout the mainland. One is *Leccino*, which makes up 15.5 percent of the overall crop. The other is *Frantoio*, which accounts for 11.5 percent. Both are Tuscan in origin, and very hardy. *Leccino* is immensely adaptable, yielding high-quality oils even in hot climates. *Frantoio* is less successful and does not always transfer well to warmer latitudes, such as California, Australia, and Argentina.

The internal market for Italian olive oil is very fragmented. About 65 percent of all holdings yield less than 446lb (200kg) of olives a year—about 9 gallons (35 liters) of oil. One-fifth of the Italian olive oil crop goes for home

SHEEP GRAZING IN SARDINIA
Pecorino cheese is a well known Sardinian foodstuff. It is made from the milk of sheep that graze beneath the olive trees.

PUGLIA'S OLIVE GROVES Puglia accounts for 40 percent of all the olive oil produced in Italy.

consumption. Fragmentation and the Italians' attachment to their own locality mean as much as half the production is consumed locally even in a province like Arezzo. In Isernia, the figure is 90 percent. Italians say that olive oil is considered noble in Tuscany, middle-class in Umbria, and plebian in the south. This explains why much of southern Italy's oil is bought in bulk by big blenders in the north of Italy. Oils from well regarded areas like Tuscany and Liguria, where demand outstrips supply, are often wildly overpriced. Tuscan oils are good, but not as good as the Tuscans believe. For top-quality oils at bargain prices you cannot beat the Sicilians.

Increased education and prosperity has engendered a huge renaissance of Italian interest in their gastronomic inheritance. Traditional foods have been rehabilitated for their distinct local character and wholesomeness. Olive oil is a statement of local and national character. Groups like the movement for Slow Food publish guides to the best Italian olive oils. The quality of Italian oil may vary, but there is a higher general level

of excellence in Italy than in any other part of the world.

REGULATION OF HIGH-QUALITY OILS

Oils of a high quality are not always easy to find. Even Italy's top producers are too small to afford expensive promotion. Fierce competition militates against wide distribution. An oil may win prizes at national and international shows, but be sold in only one or two retail outlets in the area where it is produced. More than anywhere else in the world, seeking the best in Italy means asking the producer where to buy his oil.

In Italy, the areas of high-quality production protected by European Union legislation are known as DOP (Denominazioni di Origine Protetta). There are now more than 30 olive oil DOPs, and more are in the pipeline—the number may even reach 100 by 2015. This is far too many, given that some DOPs are being

TAGGIASCA OLIVES

created for political reasons or to encourage higher standards of production. The percentage of oils that conform to DOP regulations in these areas is usually very low. Other DOPs are governed by such widely drawn rules that there is no knowing what the essential taste of an oil will be. Chianti Classico DOP oils, for example, may be made from any one of four completely different olive cultivars, including *Frantoio, Moraiolo, Leccino*, and *Correggiolo*. Whereas other DOPs permit olives of only one cultivar.

OLIVE TREES More than 700 different olive cultivars are grown in Italy.

STANDARDS OF PURITY

Olive oils are not always what they seem to be at first taste. The Italian ability to blend oil from other places and convert it into a highly priced product is a source of wonder, indignation, and envy to others. Because of this skill, Italy sells much more oil than it actually produces. There is a much greater degree of transparency at every stage than there used to be, but undoubtedly there are still instances where you may be led to believe that an oil has a better pedigree than it has. The secret is to taste before you buy and trust your own judgement.

You will not encounter any discrepancy of this sort when dealing with the great and famous estates, whose integrity is above suspicion. You can also trust self-monitoring brands such as Laudemio in Tuscany. And the DOP mark is everywhere a guarantee of quality. These oils are checked every year against all the criteria (and there are some 30 of them) in the governing regulations. Failure in only one category and the regulator will withhold recognition.

THE RUNNING MAN LOGO OF LAUDEMIO

TUSCANY
Much of the Tuscan landscape features rolling hills with vines, olive trees, and the distinctive cypress trees.

Olive Regions of Italy

The following pages are a guide to the different olive growing regions of Italy. The section starts with Liguria, then follows a sequence from north to south down through the peninsula.

FACTS AND FIGURES

OIL PRODUCED 698,000 tons

LAND PLANTED WITH OLIVES
2,830,000 acres (1,700,000ha)

NUMBER OF DOPs 30

PERCENTAGE WORLD CROP 24.7%

MODERN HARVESTING
Olives are harvested mechanically on the large estates; they are still handpicked on the steep slopes.

National Brands of Italy

Italy's reputation for producing quality olive oil applies not just to single-estate oils, but also to the big brand names. The demand for Italian olive oil exceeds supply. An enormous amount is imported from Spain and Greece, then blended with local oils and sold as "Made in Italy," either at home or abroad.

MAJOR ITALIAN BRANDS

The biggest blenders are mainly based in northern Italy—Lombardy, Liguria, Tuscany, and Umbria—where investment capital and good communications are concentrated. There are five groups with a large share of both the domestic and international olive oil markets: Unilever, Carapelli, Sasso, Monini, and Salov.

Unilever is a multinational company, the second-largest food group in the world. Its main labels are San Giorgio, Dante, and Bertolli. The Bertolli label has been expanding its home market by segmenting its oils into five labels: Classico, Fragrante, Gentile, Riserva and Robusto.

Carapelli is owned by a group of institutional investors including Monte dei Paschi di Siena.

Sasso belongs to Nestlé, the third-largest food group in the world.

Monini is based in Spoleto and has a strong presence in the United States.

Salov belongs to the Fontana family from Lucca. Its main label for the home market is Sabra, and it uses the Filippo Berio label for export.

SMALLER ORGANIZATIONS

In the second rank is a large number of companies, often only with a regional presence, but with a strong position in those markets: **Isnardi** in Liguria, **De Santis** in Puglia, and **Farchioni** in Umbria, for example. Some producers, including **Minerva**, **Olisa**, **Olitalia**, and **Colavita**, are essentially focused on export markets.

Unaprol is the biggest consortium of cooperatives and smallholders (600,000 members) in Italy. But the big brand names have a much stronger market position.

BOTTLING OLIVE OIL The sheer size of Carapelli's bottling plant is impressive.

In addition, there are large food companies that offer many products, including olive oil, under their brand names: for example, Cirio, De Cecco, and Zonin. It is also important not to underestimate the buying power and branding of the large Italian supermarket chains, such as Coop Italia, Conad, and Esselunga. These are often supplied directly by the large blenders such as Carapelli, Minerva, Monini, Olitalia, and Salov.

There is a tradition in Italy of buying oil by mail order or from door-to-door salesmen. The great oil producer Fratelli Carli in Imperia, built its fortune on mail order. Its factory now houses the best oil musem in the world (see p.60).

STORING OLIVE OIL
After extraction, oil is stored under inert gas in enormous sealed stainless steel cylinders until it is ready for bottling.

HIGH-QUALITY BLENDED OILS

The blenders take enormous trouble to produce high-quality oils of dependable taste and character that do not change significantly from year to year. Reliability is the foundation of their commercial success. Critics maintain that their oils are sometimes a little dumbed down, and the essential flavor dulled by too much careful blending. Nevertheless they offer consistency and value for money.

The leading producers of extra virgin oils are Unilever, Carapelli, Monini, Sasso, Farchioni, and Minerva. All place great emphasis upon the traceability of the oils they sell. On Farchioni's website you can enter the bottle's individual number and receive a full report on its origins. Leading producers of low-grade oils are Unilever, Carapelli, and Monini, followed by Minerva, and leading producers of refined oils are Carli, Bertolli, and Unilever (Dante).

CURRENT MARKET TRENDS

The trend in Italy now is for the big companies to introduce DOP-registered (see p.37), organic, and extra virgin oils to their range. Conad, for example, features DOP oils from Umbria, Terra di Bari, and Riviera Ligure in its Sapori e Dintorni collection. It is fair to say that such oils are better than nonvirgin oils, but they are not of the highest quality.

It is the large brands that have given Italy its lead in world markets. Dependable quality is matched by stylish packaging and good promotion. For millions of consumers they remain the embodiment of excellence. Their oils are exactly what customers need and seek. Nevertheless, it is among individual estates that the finest oils and greatest choice are found.

My advice is to use the big-name brands for cooking, and with dishes where the texture of the oil is more important than its taste. The taste of good food is however better complemented by oils that possess a more individual character.

Liguria

The olive oils of Liguria are among Italy's most distinctive, by reason of their late harvest and mild, mellow, almondy taste. The extent of Liguria's olives is not great—some 37,065 acres (15,000ha)—but so steep are the landscapes of this long, thin region that the cultivable land is small. Harvests vary greatly, but usually account for less than one percent of the national total.

IMPERIA, SAVONA, GENOA & LA SPEZIA

The Riviera Ligure is the only DOP in the four provinces of this northwestern coastal region. It is divided into three subzones: Imperia is the Riviera dei Fiori zone (the oil must be a minimum 90% *Taggiasca* olives), Savona forms the Riviera del Ponente Savonese zone (minimum 60% *Taggiasca* olives), and the provinces of Genoa and La Spezia make up the Riviera del Levante zone (65% *Taggiasca* olives—here called *Lavagnina*—in combination with either *Razzola* and/

THE OLIVE REGIONS OF LIGURIA

or *Pignola* olives). The best oils come from Imperia, where olive trees dominate the landscape. Olives are also a typical feature of Savona, but less so of Genoa and La Spezia. There are some excellent producers in these provinces but they lack the intense striving for quality that characterizes Imperia.

TAGGIASCA OLIVES

These are the olives of Liguria, so-called as they were first grown by Benedictine monks in Taggia, in the province of Imperia, in the 12th century. The tall, thick, spreading trees are a major feature of the Ligurian landscape. They are often planted in incredibly steep terraces that run right down to sea level. *Taggiasca* olives are fairly small (.07–.09oz) and are not picked until they are fully ripe, which is usually in December. They give a high yield of distinctive mellow oil. It is a taste much prized by those who like soft, gentle oil—the antithesis of the bitter, Tuscan style, which is more peppery in flavor (*see p.66*). However, some modern producers now prune their olives trees very severely to ensure regular cropping, and then pick earlier to guarantee healthy, pest-free olives; this new-style oil is more robust and longer lasting.

The Museum of the Olive— from Babylon to modern day

The Museum of the Olive in Imperia is the finest in the world. It is housed in old Art Nouveau offices at the headquarters of Fratelli Carli, the largest high-quality producer of olive oil in Liguria. The docks in Oneglia, now part of Imperia, were built to accommodate large export consignments of oil from the Carli factory.

　　The oldest exhibits in the museum are cuneiform inscriptions recording Babylonian olive oil transactions in about 2000 B.C.E. Other areas deal with the olive's expansion from the Middle East into the Mediterranean basin; its use in religious, sports, and political symbolism; the invention of amphoras, ceramic jars, and canning; extraction equipment (from primitive wooden screws to hydraulically powered presses); household articles like oil lamps, fine silver, and crystal table-oil containers.

Museo dell'Olivo

Via Garessio, 13, 18100 Imperia Oneglia
📞 0183 295762　🅆 www.museodellolivo.com
Open daily, except Sundays, from 9a.m. to 12:30p.m. and from 3p.m. to 6:30p.m. Admission free.

Leading producers in Liguria

Abbo – Frantoio del Podere Bevera

18039 Ventimiglia (Imperia)
☎ 0184 211012
🖥 www.olioabbo.it

The Abbo family buys its olives from farmers in the area around Ventimiglia. Their best oil is Abbo Podere Bevera DOP Riviera dei Fiori — well made, pale gold in color, and clear, it has a mellow taste of pears and almonds and a long, warm aftertaste.

Anfosso, Olio

18027 Chiusavecchia (Imperia)
☎ 0183 52418
🖥 www.olioanfosso.it

Oleum Salutis Fructus Anfosso is yellow and unfiltered, with a light, grassy smell and the smooth, soft taste of *Taggiasca*—sweet almonds and pears—followed by a peppery kick that develops slowly and is surprisingly strong. Tumai is pale, unfiltered, cool, and nutty, but not as smooth and gentle as one might also expect from a *Taggiasca* oil.

OLEUM SALUTIS
FRUCTUS ANFOSSO

Benza Frantoiano

18100 Imperia
☎ 0183 280132
🖥 www.oliobenza.it

The Benzas have 35 acres (14ha) of *Taggiasca* in Dolcedo, near Imperia. Primuruggiu is their *affiorato* oil, skimmed from the olive paste before it is pressed. Dulcèdo is a new style of oil, made from olives picked early, with a taste that is greener and gutsier than usual, but still a certified DOP oil. Buonolio is the Benzas' traditional line. It is soft, smooth, and nutty in the best Ligurian style.

Bo, Frantoio

16039 Sestri Levante (Genoa)
☎ 0185 481605
🖥 www.frantoio-bo.it

The Bo family buys olives from their neighborhood (70% *Lavagnina/Taggiasca*) and crushes them young, to produce their atypical (but much praised) Le Due Baie oil. Clear golden yellow, with a hint of green, it smells of cut grass and herbs, and tastes lightly herbaceous, with a hint of apples and especially of almonds, followed by a light (but appreciable) bitter and peppery aftertaste.

Lucchi e Guastalli

19037 S. Stefano Magra (La Spezia)
☎ 0187 633329
🖥 www.frantoiolg.com

This young company buys olives from its neighbors, mostly *Maurino* (here called *Razzola*) with some *Lavagnina/Taggiasca*, to make its excellent Tuscan-style Lucchi e Guastalli Extravergine Riviera di Levante oil. Greeny yellow, clear, cool, and aromatic, its taste is complex but recalls apples, grass, and exotic fruits, and ends with a long warm, bitter aftertaste.

Pria Grossa

17029 Finale Ligure (Savona)
☎ 019 698044

This small producer has acquired a cult following for its Pria Grossa Monovarietale di Colombaia oil, made from an ancient grove of the rare and local *Colombaia* olive, a late-ripening olive long neglected for its poor yields. It is clear golden yellow with a rich and complex vegetable smell and a full taste of herbs, artichokes, and bitter almonds complemented by pepperiness and bitterness.

Raineri

18027 Chiusanico (Imperia)
☎ 0183 529050
🖥 www.olioraineri.com

Raineri Taggiasca has a rich, gentle smooth taste with a hint of grassiness and rather more of sweet almonds. It has only the mildest trace of bitterness in its aftertaste and no pepperiness.

RAINERI
TAGGIASCA

Ranise Agroalimentare

18100 Imperia
☎ 0183 767966
🖥 www.ranise.it

Ranise is one of the best and most consistent of Ligurian oil-makers. Its Riviera dei Fiori DOP oil is pure golden yellow, cool, juicy, and more fruity than usual for a *Taggiasca* oil and has a warm and peppery aftertaste.

GOLD WRAPPING

It is a tradition of Liguria to wrap its fine *Taggiasca* oils in gold paper. This associates the oil with excellence, but not all oils in gold wrapping are good, or even Ligurian. Demand for Ligurian oils is high. They are very popular in Germany and some less reputable companies dilute *Taggiasca* with taste-alikes, such as *Empeltre* from Aragon. Look for a DOP certificate on the label, and remember that high demand for the genuine article means high prices, too.

TUMAI OLIO EXTRA VIRGINE DI OLIVA

Rota, Roberto

18033 Camporosso (Imperia)

☎ 0184 288702

Rota makes high-quality *Taggiasca* oil and sells it under two labels. Taggiasca has a delicate taste of apples and almonds complemented by a warm aftertaste. Crudum is cloudy, fruity, and almondy, skimmed from the unpressed olive paste. Both are good.

Sant'Agata d'Oneglia, Frantoio di

18100 Imperia

☎ 0183 293472

W www.frantoiosantagata.com

Sant'Agata d'Oneglia's excellent Oro Taggiasca oil is clear and golden yellow, with a gentle taste of apples, herbs, and almonds. Cool and smooth, it ends with a soft, well balanced suggestion of pepperiness.

Sommariva, Antico Frantoio

Via Mameli, 7

17031 Albenga (Savona)

☎ 0182 559222

W www.oliosommariva.it

This firm specializes in organic products. Its Extravergine Riviera Ligure Sommariva is a cool, soft oil, with a gentle taste of apples and almonds and a long, delicate aftertaste. Sometimes it is available as Nuovo Mosto, a newly pressed, unfiltered oil that is fruitier, but equally gentle.

RIVIERA LIGURE SOMMARIVA

Taggiasca, Casa Olearia

18011 Arma di Taggia (Imperia)

☎ 0184 486044

W www.casaoleariataggiasca.it

Terre Bormane Riviera Ligure Riviera dei Fiori is a mild and mellow oil, with a light taste of almonds and a hint of warm pepper and gentle bitterness in the aftertaste.

Taggiasca, Consorzio dell'Olio Extravergine dell'Oliva

18027 Pontedassio (Imperia)

☎ 0183 279034

The Cultivar Taggiasca oil from this small cooperative is golden yellow, unfiltered, and lightly fruity with hints of apples and grass, a long, warm aftertaste, and a hint of almonds.

Other producers in Liguria

Gocce d'Olio

18010 Villa Faraldi

☎ 0183 41118

W www.goccedolio.com

The *Taggiasca* oils made by Gocce d'Olio are sold as Goccedolio. Sometimes they are DOP oils, sometimes not.

Olio Roi

18010 Badalucco (Imperia)

☎ 0184 408004

W www.olioroi.com

Several excellent labels come from Olio Roi, including Riviera Ligure Roi and Carte Noire.

Paolo Cassini

18035 Isolabona (Imperia)

☎ 0184 208159

W www.oliocassini.it

This estate makes organic oils under the Isolabona label, including DOP Riviera dei Fiori.

Renato Labolani

18035 Apricale (Imperia)

☎ 0184 208093

This company makes an oil called Albareu that is fruitier than many *Taggiasca* oils.

TAGGIASCA TREES Olives are often seen in a garden setting now that the Italian Riviera has become so developed.

Lombardy to Friuli

Olive growing in the cold, northerly regions of Lombardy, Trentino, Veneto, and Friuli is only possible in the relative warmth of isolated microclimates. This is an area of high mountains, inland lakes, and broad, flat plains. The favored areas include the edges of Lakes Como, Iseo, and Garda. The good quality of the oils and small quantities produced are reflected in high prices.

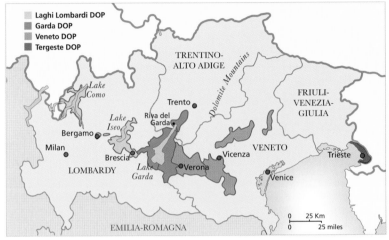

Laghi Lombardi DOP
Garda DOP
Veneto DOP
Tergeste DOP

THE OLIVE REGIONS OF LOMBARDY, TRENTINO, VENETO, AND FRIULI

AN AREA OF CONTRASTS

Olives are grown in four north Italian regions: Lombardy, which includes the provinces of Como and Brescia; Veneto, which includes the province of Verona; Trentino Alto Adige covering the southern tip of the province of Trento around Lake Garda; and Friuli Venezia Giulia, in the east, which borders on the Adriatic and includes Trieste. There are four DOPs: Laghi Lombardi, Garda, Verona, and Tergeste. The Laghi Lombardi DOP area is mainly made up of lakes, which have a mitigating effect on the harsh climate. Olives also grow on sheltered south-facing hills in the Veneto DOP area. The Tergeste DOP on the Adriatic coast owes its existence to warm, karstic soils, shelter from northerly winds, and a long list of hardy local olive cultivars.

LAKES COMO, ISEO & GARDA

Olive growing in Lombardy is small-scale and concentrated around lakes Como, Iseo, and Garda. There are two DOPs— Laghi Lombardi in the west and Garda in the east. The Laghi Lombardi DOP is divided into two subzones: Lario around Lake Como and Sebino around Lake Iseo. Both are greeny yellow and fruity, with a light touch of bitterness and pepperiness. Lario must have at least 80% *Frantoio, Casaliva,* and/or *Leccino* olives; Sebino must have at least 40% *Leccino* and at least 40% *Frantoio, Casaliva, Pendolino,* and/or *Sbresa* olives.

Olives grow all around Lake Garda but the largest concentration is toward the southern end (the Sirmione Peninsula has been famous for its olives for centuries). Nevertheless, a small area around Riva del Garda, at the northern end of Lake Garda also has a mild microclimate that has made it possible for some 1,000 acres (400ha) to be planted with 100,000 olive trees. The contrast between the palm-lined boulevards of the town of Riva and the snowbound mountains on either side is remarkable.

THE THREE SUBZONES OF GARDA

An accident of political geography means that the edge of Lake Garda falls within no fewer than three provinces, each within different regions of Italy— Lombardy, the Veneto, and Trentino Alto Adige. This is reflected in the three subzones of the Garda DOP. Garda Bresciano lies to the southwest, with its epicenter around Polpenazze. Garda Orientale is in the southeast; the part within the province of Verona coincides with the wine area of Bardolino (there is a very good oil museum in Cisano). Garda Trentino occupies a small area at the very northern tip of the lake.

Casaliva is the traditional olive of Garda and its trees produce a heavy crop. Its oils are noted for their fragrance and light, aromatic taste. The tree suffers in the cold winters that periodically affect northern Italy, which has led to its gradual replacement by hardier cultivars.

GARDA OILS

The oils of the Garda Orientale DOP must contain at least 50% *Casaliva* olives (also known as "*Drizzar*"), but in Garda Bresciano the rules allow for the oil to contain up to 55% of the Tuscan cultivars *Frantoio* and *Leccino*, as well as *Casaliva*, and the same applies farther north, in the Garda Trentino area. There is a large number of local cultivars: the rules for Garda Orientale, for example, mention *Lezzo, Favarol, Rossanel, Razza, Fort, Morcai,* and *Trepp* olives as well as *Casaliva*.

Garda oils are noted for their fluidity, their greeny yellow color, and their delicate fruity taste, which has a hint of almonds. They are not cheap, but the best are very good indeed.

VERONA & TRIESTE

The Veneto DOP is divided into three subzones: Veneto Valpolicella, Veneto del Grappa, and Veneto Euganei e Berici, but in practice only Veneto Valpolicella is active. There, the local olives, *Grignano* and *Favarol*, must account for at least 50% of the oil: *Favarol* oils are often of mediocre quality, but *Grignano* is capable of producing oil of good quality and has a very distinctive taste. Around Monte Grappa, the super-Tuscan olives *Frantoio* and *Leccino* constitute 50% of the blend.

OLIVE GROVES AT PUNTA SAN VIGILIO The gray-leaved olive trees in this promontory on the eastern shores of Lake Garda have been celebrated by poets for hundreds of years.

In Vicenza and the Euganean hills, *Leccino* and *Rasara* olives must make up at least 50% of the DOP oils. *Rasara* (a rare endemic olive capable of producing high-quality oils) is one of many local cultivars enshrined in the DOP legislation; others are *Leccio del Corno*, *Drop*, *Marzemino*, *Matossa*, *Riondella*, and *Padanina* olives from the Veneto Euganei e Berici subzone alone. Quality in the Veneto is variable. Much is made in small quantities for local consumption.

AVANZI FAMILY CHAPEL AMONG THEIR OLIVE TREES

Some, particularly the delicate oils of the Euganean hills, commands high prices that reflect upon its scarcity rather than its quality. A fraction of the oil produced reaches DOP standards. The best comes from the alpine foothills north of Verona. It is well made, if not always exciting. Trieste has one small DOP—Tergeste. The leading cultivar here is *Bianchera*—its oils are elegant, delicate, fruity, and well balanced. The Tergeste DOP oils must contain at least 20% *Bianchera* olives.

Leading producers around Lakes Iseo, Como & Garda

De Zinis, Redaelli

25080 Calvagese della Riviera (Brescia)
☎ 030 601001
Ⓦ www.dezinis.it

Extravergine Radaelli de Zinis is made from *Leccino* olives grown in Soiano. Golden yellow with a green tinge, and unfiltered, it has a light, fruity smell, a smooth, almost buttery texture, a fresh taste of grass and tomatoes followed by a hint of almonds, and just a touch of pepperiness and bitterness to round off the aftertaste.

Madonna delle Vittorie

38062 Arco (Trentino)
☎ 0464 505432
Ⓦ www.madonnadellevittorie.it

The oil from Madonna delle Vittorie, Cantina Madonna delle Vittorie, is rather Tuscan in taste (80% *Frantoio*) and

MADONNA DELLE VITTORIE

very good. It is clear, greeny gold, fruity at first (apples, tomatoes, and a herbaceous taste) followed by a good warm pepperiness and a light bitterness. They also make a *denocciolato* version that has an even more intense taste.

Manestrini

25080 Soiano del Lago (Brescia)
☎ 0365 502231
Ⓦ www.manestrini.it

The Extravergine Manestrini DOP Garda Bresciano oil is golden green and fluid, with a light, fruity smell and a taste that recalls grass, herbs, artichokes, and almonds, followed by a light piquancy and bitterness.

Riva del Garda

38066 Riva del Garda (Trentino)
☎ 0464 552133

This cooperative (almost the most northerly in Italy) offers an excellent Olio Garda Trentino DOP. It is clear golden yellow, with a light, fresh smell, and a cool, soft taste of hay and almonds, followed by a very light (but long) aftertaste of bitterness and pepper.

OLIO GARDA TRENTINO

San Felice del Benaco, Coop

25010 San Felice del Benaco (Brescia)
☎ 0365 62341

Brescia's largest producer makes a high-quality DOP oil with a typical Garda color and taste: yellow with a tint of green, fresh, fruity, and smelling of cut grass, its taste recalls apples, herbs, and almonds and is rounded off by a gentle warming pepperiness and a touch of bitterness.

WELL MANAGED ROWS Careful cultivation characterizes olive-growing in the surrounds of Lake Garda.

Turri, F.lli

37010 Cavaion Veronese (Veneto)
045 7235006
www.turri.com

Turri is the largest producer in the Garda area, with a foot in the Veneto, too. Its oils are varied and excellent: San Vigilio is not a DOP oil but is made from local cultivars from Punto San Vigilio, including *Casaliva*, *Lezzo*, *Favarol*, and *Rossanel*. It is clear, dark yellow, grassy, and fruity. A light note of bitterness and pepperiness emerges in the aftertaste. Turri also sells a very successful 100% Casaliva oil, a well made 100% Grignan oil, and a DOP Garda oil. The mill has a collection of antique agricultural machinery.

Uliveti, Cooperativa

37010 Brenzone (Verona)
0456 590002
www.coop-uliveti.it

This is the leading cooperative in the Garda Oriental DOP and its oil is of a very high quality: clear, green yellow, and rather fluid, with a light fruity smell and an aromatic, almost sweet taste. It is cool and smooth, lightly fruity, later grassy, but always gentle and long, with only a hint of bitterness and pepperiness at the end, plus a suggestion of nuts.

Valtenesi, Frantoio

25080 Polpenazze del Garda (Brescia)
0365 654029
www.frantoiovaltenesi.com

The very fluid, pale, greeny gold Mirum is Valtenesi's best oil. It is made from lightly pressed *Leccino* and *Casaliva* olives to give a floral smell and a fruity taste of tomatoes, then cut grass and almonds, and a long-lasting, warm aftertaste. Arzane, also good, is richer and fruitier.

MIRUM

Vanini, Oleificio Osvaldo

22016 Lenno (Como)
0344 55127
www.oliovanini.it

Vanini is by far the best-known producer on Lake Como, established in 1850. Its DOP Laghi Lombardi Lario oil is made mainly from *Frantoio*, *Leccino*, and *Pendolino*, and sold as Vanini Osvaldo Olio Oliva Extra Vergine, with its distinctive labels, which have remained unchanged for nearly 100 years. The oil is golden yellow and very fluid, with a pleasing smell of grass and fruit, and a taste that runs from herbs and apples to almonds, followed by a light pepperiness and bitterness.

Other producers in Lake Garda

Avanzi, F.lli.

25080 Manerba del Garda (Brescia)
0365 551013
www.avanzi.net

Avanzi's DOP Garda Extravergine is golden yellow, smooth, and gentle with a taste of grass and of almonds followed by a light bitterness and pepperiness.

Ca' Rainene

37010 Torri del Benaco (Verona)
045.6296720

Only one oil—Ca' Rainene Garda DOP—but consistently good: fresh, fruity, vegetable, and almondy with a moderate aftertaste of pepperiness and bitterness.

Malcesine, Consorzio Olivicoltori

37018 Malcesine (Verona)
045 7401286
www.oliomalcesine.com

This is a big cooperative (for northern Italy) and produces a fine Garda Orientale DOP oil. It is yellow with a hint of green and fluid, with a fresh, grassy smell and taste, followed by herbs, almonds, and a touch of pepperiness and bitterness.

Montecroce, Frantoio di

25015 Desenzano del Garda (Brescia)
☎ 030 9911504

35 acres (14ha) – a lot for the area – producing DOP Garda Bresciano oil.

Pellegrini Maddalena

37010 Castion Veronese (Verona)
☎ 338 8803078

A small producer known for the quality of its DOP Garda Orientale oil from a mix of *Casaliva*, *Frantoio*, *Pendolino*, and *Leccino* olives.

Rocca Pietro e Rita

25087 Salò (Brescia)
☎ 0365.40646

Soft, delicate, well balanced DOP Garda Bresciano from a leading estate.

Tre Colline

37011 Bardolino (Verona)
☎ 0457 235219

Good DOP oil under the Tre Colline label: golden yellow, fluid, appley, and almondy, lightly bitter and peppery.

Leading producers in Verona & Trieste

Bonamini, Frantoio

37031 Illasi (Verona)
☎ 045 6520558
W www.oliobonamini.com

Bonamini is one of the larger firms in Verona. Its Veneto Valpolicella DOP is an unusual, interesting oil; yellow, with a green tinge and a smell of tomato. The taste is fresh, fruity, and long, with a hint of tangerines and pear drops, followed by a fair measure of bitterness and strong pepperiness that persist over a long time.

Isola Augusta

33056 Palazzolo della Stella (Udine)
☎ 0431 58046
W www.isolaugusta.com

Isola Augusta is a leading Friuli wine producer, with a tiny sideline in estate olive oil (mainly from *Leccino*), that it sells as Fior di Fiore. It is greeny yellow, unfiltered, grassy, and herby with suggestions of sweet almonds and a touch of pepper and bitterness to end with. Delicious.

Livon

33048 Dolegnano (Udine)
☎ 0432.757173
W www.livon.it

Livon is well known as a wine estate, but its Valbuins oil is much prized. Made from *Bianchera*, *Maurino*, and *Pendolino* olives, it has a greeny yellow color, a delicate, grassy smell, and a taste that recalls apples, herbs, and almonds, ending with a neat aftertaste of bitterness and pepperiness.

Parovel, Frantoio Oleario

34018 San Dorligo della Valle (Trieste)
☎ 040 227050
W www.parovel.com

The Parovel family are big suppliers of bought-in olive oil, but their own groves produce an exceptional Triestino oil from 30 acres (12ha) of *Bianchera*, backed by some hardy Tuscan cultivars. The oil is delicate, herbaceous, and appley, with a hint of almonds and herbs, and a light, lingering aftertaste of pepper and bitterness.

Redoro

37023 Grezzana (Verona)
☎ 045 907622
W www.redoro.it

The Extravergine Veneto Valpolicella DOP Redoro is greeny gold and clear, with a light fruity, floral smell, a taste that recalls apples and tomatoes, and a peppery finish. Redoro's Antico Frantoio di Mezzane label is made from *Leccino*, *Frantoio*, *Pendolino*, and *Gentile* olives, and has a fresh, light, "Tuscan" taste.

VENETO
VALPOLICELLA
REDORO

San Cassiano

37030 Mezzane di Sotto (Verona)
☎ 045 8880450

A small-scale, young producer with a good-quality label Monte Paradiso Veneto Valpolicella DOP from *Grignana* and *Favarol*, plus some *Frantoio* and *Leccino*. The oil is fine, fruity, delicate, and well balanced.

Sancin

34018 Dolina (Trieste)
☎ 040 228870

Sancin's Olio Celo is very good. It is dark yellow in color, with a green tinge, and a sound balance of fruitiness, pepper, and bitterness. Cool, mild, and appley at first, it then develops a herbaceous taste and a light nuttiness. Though the oil contains the local *Bianchera* olive, its dominant taste is of *Leccino* olives, which are present alongside *Pendolino* and *Maurino*. The exact proportions of the different olive cultivars vary from year to year.

OLIO CELO

Emilia Romagna

Most of Emilia Romagna lies north of the Rubicon River, traditionally the boundary beyond which olive trees cannot thrive because of the cold winters. The growing of olives here is confined to a few low hillsides and sheltered valleys, usually close to the Adriatic. There are 2,500 acres (1,000ha) in Rimini, 740 acres (300ha) around Forlì and Cesena, and perhaps 500 acres (200ha) in Ravenna.

SMALL OLIVE-GROWING AREA

Most of the olive trees in Rimini are the super-hardy *Frantoio*, *Moraiolo*, and *Pendolino* cultivars, which have been imported from Tuscany. All the older trees, however, are traditional, local specialties like *Correggiolo*, *Rossina*, and *Dondolino*. The newest DOP in this area is called Colline di Romagna. Its oils must contain at least 60% *Frantoio* or *Correggiolo* olives, or a combination of both, plus up to 40% made from *Leccino* olives and up to 15% of other local cultivars. The oils are generally golden yellow in color with green tints, lightly fruity, moderately peppery, and bitter.

The largest plantations in Emilia Romagna are along the coastal hills of southern Rimini, where pasture and vines are the main agricultural activities. Oil production in Forlì, Cesena, and Ravenna is miniscule, but it includes the exquisite oil from Brisighella (*see right*); production is limited to five communes.

THE OLIVE REGIONS OF EMILIA ROMAGNA

Nostrana di Brisighella: rare, expensive, inimitable

Brisighella oil must be made from at least 90% of the indigenous *Nostrana di Brisighella* olive to gain DOP status. This oil is unusually high in oleic acid and low in linoleic acid. It is also high in phenolic and polyphenolic compounds, which means it keeps well and oxidizes only slowly. The oil is green, perhaps with a dark gold tint, medium or strongly fruity, with a light bitterness and a little more pepperiness. Brisighella oil is expensive; the price reflects not just its rarity but also its inimitable quality.

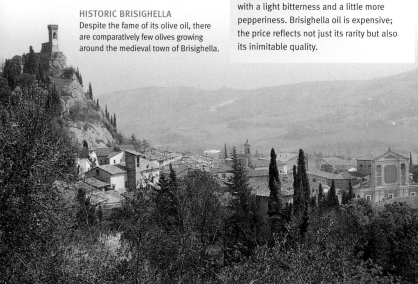

HISTORIC BRISIGHELLA
Despite the fame of its olive oil, there are comparatively few olives growing around the medieval town of Brisighella.

Leading producers in Emilia Romagna

Brisighellese, Coop.

48013 Brisighella (Ravenna)
☎ 0546 81103
ⓦ wwwbrisighello.net

This cooperative produces the unique Nobil Drupa oil, which is dark green-brown, smells of tomato leaves, and provides an explosion of pungent fruitiness in the mouth. The flavor suggests tomatoes, rosemary, and arugula, and is followed by a fairly strong peppery aftertaste, and a lesser bitterness—but all long-lasting, pleasing, and appropriate. Also worth trying is the non-DOP Pieve Tho Terra di Brisighella oil, which is only 80% *Nostrana di Brisighella*, and much lighter (and cheaper) than the Nobil Drupa. Orfanello, made from the even rarer *Orfano* olive, is also excellent.

NOBIL DRUPA

Colli Riminesi, Coop. Oliv. dei

Cà Baldone, 1a
47854 Montescudo (Ravenna)
☎ 0541 983119

This is the largest cooperative in the region, and produces an excellent oil called Arimolio from *Frantoio*, *Correggiolo*, and *Leccino* olives. It has a golden-yellow color, a good olivey smell, and a lightly appley taste, followed by grassiness and a measured bitterness and pepperiness.

TURCHI

Turchi, Antico Frantoio Pierluca

47020 Longiano
(Forlì-Cesena)
☎ 0547 665555
ⓦ wwwturchifarm.com

Antico Frantoio Turchi was founded, it is said, in about 1400 by Amin Saud, the Turkish ancestor of the present owners, who also run a popular restaurant. There are two oils: Oro dei Turchi, made from the family's own olives (mainly *Correggiolo* and *Frantoio*), is herbaceous and almondy with a good measure of pepperiness and bitterness. The plain but softer Turchi oil from their neighbors' olives tastes of cut grass, tomatoes, sweet almonds, and dried fruits, with a warm aftertaste.

Other producers in Emilia Romagna

Il Poggiolo

Fraz. Vallecchio
47854 Montescudo (Ravenna)
☎ 0549 908464

Only one label—Vallechiese —made from *Frantoio* and *Leccino* olives; this oil is lightly Tuscan in flavor.

Lo Conte, Centro

Via Art e Mestieri 2/4
47036 Riccione (Ravenna)
☎ 0541 604260

Lo Conte's DOP Colline Romagnole unfiltered oil from 9 acres (3.5ha) in Misano Adriatico (*Frantoio*, *Moraiolo*, *Pendolino*, and *Leccino* olives) tastes like a light Tuscan— medium fruity (tomatoes, fresh almonds, and apples), with a good bitter aftertaste.

Monsignore (F.lli Bacchini), Tenuta del

47842 S. Giovanni in Marignano (Ravenna)
☎ 0541 955128
ⓦ wwwtenutadelmonsignore.com

Lightly fruity, unfiltered oils from a charming estate in the hills above Cattolica.

San Rocco

Via San Rocco
47824 Poggio Berni (Ravenna)
☎ 0541 625536

Only one oil, Lolibon, made from local *Correggiolo* and *Rossina* olives: grassy, peppery, and bitter.

Sapigni, Oleificio

47827 Rimini
☎ 0541 679094
ⓦ wwwsapigni.com

Three good brands: Il Solatio, Colle Natio, and the new, lightly fruity, bitter Colline di Romagna oil, which qualifies for a Colline di Romagna DOP.

Savignano sul Rubicone, Cantina e Oleificio Soc. Coop. di

Via Emilia Ovest, 93
47039 Savignano sul Rubicone (Forlì-Cesena)
☎ 0541 945183

A well made, lightly fruity oil made from *Correggiolo*, *Frantoio*, and *Leccino* olives, Gocce di Natura tastes of grass and almonds, with an unexpected pepperiness and a lingering bitterness to finish. Well balanced.

Tuscany

Olive trees are an essential part of Tuscany's landscape. Olive oil from the region is consistently good, and commands high prices. The surprise is that it accounts for no more than five percent of Italy's national olive-oil production. Tuscan producers have set a standard for style and quality that many try to emulate. The distinctive Tuscan olive cultivars have been exported all over the world.

THE DEVELOPMENT OF THE OIL INDUSTRY

Tuscan olive growing developed gradually. During the 15th century, in the era of the powerful Medici family, areas of unexploited woodland were handed over to villages on condition they were cleared and turned into olive groves. The motive was economic—olive oil was a valuable commodity.

However, olives were not a major feature of the landscape until the mid-19th century when the scattered plantations were thickened up and new plantings made. Marginal areas like the Maremma in the west and Val di Chiana near Arezzo were brought into cultivation for the first time. Until then lard had been the staple of peasant dishes: Olive oil was aspirational. Nowadays olive oil is fundamental to Tuscan cooking.

The earliest olive plantations were in Versiglia and around Pisa, Livorno, Lucca, and Siena, especially in the Val

THE OLIVE REGIONS OF TUSCANY

d'Elsa; Siena is still the province with the most trees. About 469,500 acres (190,000ha) of Tuscany are planted with olives. A few trees grow on the plains and in the mountains, but most are on the region's rolling hills.

THE TUSCAN CLIMATE

Olives thrive in the long, dry summers and mild winters typical of southern Italy. In inland Tuscany, olive growing is at its limits geographically and climatically. Late springs, short summers, early falls, and cool nighttime temperatures mean there is only a short growing season. Severe winter damage to crops occurs roughly once every 20 to 50 years. Frost occurs every winter, but killer frosts depend on their timing, intensity, and duration. Frozen olives produce inferior oil, so Tuscan olives are picked before they are ripe (ahead of the first hard frosts), resulting in green oils with a typical fruity, peppery, bitter taste.

TYPICAL TUSCAN LANDSCAPE
Olive, cypresses, and umbrella pines are the classic trees of the Tuscan landscape.

TUSCAN OLIVE GROVES Olive trees in Tuscany are most usually grown in rolling hill country.

Admirers describe this taste as proof of quality, like tannin in wine, and they try to copy it (*see right*). The reason is market-driven: Tuscan oils are seen to command high prices. The oils last well thanks to their low levels of acidity and high levels of polyphenols (*see p.36*)— traits forced on them by the climate.

TUSCAN OLIVES

The most important Tuscan olives are *Frantoio, Leccino, Moraiolo, Pendolino*, and *Correggiolo*. *Frantoio* is the Cabernet Sauvignon among olives—an adaptable, dependable cultivar that gives an oil body and structure—while the gentle, softer *Leccino* has a modifying effect like the Merlot grape. Other cultivars, used less, are the *Cipressino, Seggianese, Gramignolo*, and *Maurino* olives. All these cultivars are slightly variable, with many individual clones selected for their special qualities, such as hardiness, disease-resistance, and yield.

BIG ESTATES AND SMALL FARMS

About two-thirds of the olive-growing land in Tuscany belongs to big estates and large-scale farmers. The best known producers are the wine-making estates with a sideline in olive oil, such as Antinori, Frescobaldi, and Melini. The area put to olives on these estates is invariably small but the quality is usually excellent. Some farmers, no matter how small their farm, are members of cooperatives. These

The distinctive taste of Tuscan olive oil

The fame of Tuscan oils is founded not on their quantity, but their quality. Pepperiness and bitterness are positive qualities of this style of oil. They indicate low levels of acidity, high and healthy levels of polyphenols, and good resistance to rancidity. The Tuscan style is one of the universal benchmarks for good olive oil. Is Tuscan oil quite simply the best? Many would say that the oils of Trapani in Sicily or Tarragona in Spain are better.

The taste of Tuscan oils differs from year to year. The droughts of 2003 produced oils of excessive bitterness, even by Tuscan standards. In contrast, 2004 was uncharacteristically light, more delicate and rounded, less definite, and less robust than normal. This was said to be the result of heavy rain. The gutsy Tuscan style is not to everyone's taste. Many prefer a softer, gentler oil like *Taggiasca* from Liguria (*see p.60*), or a fruitier one, like *Nocellara del Belice* from Sicily (*see p.120*). But different oils are good with different foods, and their taste changes too. Much of the bitterness of a Tuscan oil is obscured by the savory taste of the food it accompanies.

groups produce nearly 17 percent of all Tuscan oil, a higher figure than for much of the rest of Italy (which stands at 11 percent). Cooperatives do not have the distinctive identity of the big estates, so cannot sell their oil as readily except on price or quality; much is exported simply as "Tuscan Olive Oil" and is good value.

THE OLIVE-GROWING AREAS

Tuscany extends from Massa-Carrara in the north to Grosetto in the south, and Arezzo in the east. There are three DOPs in the region – in Lucca, Siena, and Florence. There is an additional mark of quality seal for some areas called Toscana Indicazione Geografica Protetta (IGP), which indicates that an oil is from a defined region (*see p.74*).

FLORENCE

Florence, together with Siena, forms the heartland of Tuscan oil-making and this province includes a major part of the Chianti Classico DOP (the rest is in Siena). The rolling hills, often planted with olive trees of considerable age, are a major feature of the landscape of inland Tuscany.

The Chianti Classico DOP, the only one in the province, is also the centre of Tuscan wine production. The DOP area for oil covers the four communes in the Chianti area (Castellina, Gaiole, Greve, and Radda), plus parts of five adjoining communes in Siena (Barberino, Castelnuovo Berardenga, Poggibonsi, San Casciano, and Tavernelle). Chianti Classico DOP oils must be made from

Frantoio, Moraiolo, Leccino, or *Correggiolo* olives, up to 80% alone or together. The oils should be greenish, fruity, peppery, and lightly bitter. In practice, Chianti Classico oils are very strongly flavoured. They have a rich combination of fruitiness, pepper, and bitterness.

DOP recognition is expected soon for the other major olive-growing area in this province, covering the hills south of Florence around L'Impruneta, Scandicci, and Bagno a Ripoli. This new DOP will be called Colline di Firenze.

SIENA

Olive-growing is a major activity in Siena. In the 15th century, every farmer was required by law to plant four olive trees every year. Despite the damage that periodic cold winters do to the trees here and in other parts of Tuscany, there has been a lot of planting of young olive trees in recent years.

In addition to the Chianti Classico DOP in the extreme north of the province, Siena has its own Terra di Siena DOP. The main requirement is that four different olive cultivars *Correggiolo, Frantoio, Leccino*, and *Moraiolo* must each be represented by at least 10% of the crop, and that together they must account for at least 85% of the olives. Terra di Siena oils should also be fruity, with a bitter and peppery note.

THE FLORENCE COUNTRYSIDE Olive trees are an essential element of the Florentine countryside.

SANT'ANTIMO
This abbey in the heart of inland Tuscany is surrounded by small olive groves.

AREZZO

The best Arezzo oils come from the Val d'Arno, close to the boundaries with Florence and Siena. Castelfranco, Valdarno, Cavriglia, Montevarchi, and Mercatale belong more to the Chianti country than to Arezzo itself. Producers believe their oil is distinctive but the oils do not differ significantly from the rest of inland Tuscany.

Oils from Toscana IGP Colline di Arezzo should be made from a minimum of 85% of *Frantoio*, *Moraiolo*, or *Leccino* olives. Any of these three cultivars qualifies, whether alone or together, which means there is little consistency among oils from Arezzo. However, they do have the typical green colour and intense fruitiness, bitterness, and pepperiness that is the hallmark of the Tuscan style and the best are very good indeed.

GROSSETO, LIVORNO & PISA

Grosseto is a large province. Wide-scale olive growing, however, is a new phenomenon. Much of the Maremma area was uncultivated until the 19th century and serious planting did not get underway until the last 100 years.

The area around Monte Amiata – a vast extinct volcano that dominates the landscape of southern Tuscany – is home to an indigenous olive called *Olivastra di Seggiano*. The olive gives a good yield of delicate, fruity oil, characterized by suggestions of artichokes, nuts, unripe tomatoes, and pears. The oil has only a light aftertaste of bitterness and pepperiness, which fades away quite quickly. This makes it very different to the robust and pungent taste of *Frantoio* and *Moraiolo* oils.

Most of the olives in Livorno and Pisa grow on steeply terraced slopes like those in Liguria (*see p.60*). The main olive cultivars grown here are *Frantoio*, *Moraiolo*, *Leccino*, and *Maurino* (here called *Razzola*). Livornese and Pisan oils are light or medium fruity, with a soft rich taste and an attractive pepperiness, but without the strong bitterness that is characteristic of inland Tuscany.

LUCCA, MASSA-CARRARA, PISTOIA & PRATO

This group of provinces includes the oil from the Lucca DOP, an area associated with olives and olive oil for many centuries. Until the middle of the 20th century, Lucca's oils were renowned for their golden colour and sweet, soft, almondy taste, but the modern fashion for early-picked long-lasting oils has changed all that. Lucca DOP oil is made from up to 90% *Frantoio* olives, 30% *Leccino* olives, and 15% other cultivars.

Laudemio oils

This marketing syndicate of about 25 producers was founded in 1990 to promote their olive oil as a premium product. The rules of membership cover geographical boundaries (central Tuscany), soil types, and best practices for planting and cultivating olives. The production cycle is also monitored. Laudemio has a trademark label of a Roman runner and a trademark bottle. The bottles are rectangular and flat and have a spout with an airlock. They are sold in boxes designed to exclude light. The oils are of outstanding quality, but not cheap.

The oil should be greeny yellow, with a light, fruity smell, and a peppery, bitter taste to match the fruitiness. There are several IGP subzones in this area. The Toscano IGP Colline Lucchesi label represents a contrasting style. Here, oils are golden yellow (with a green tint), soft, sweet, lightly fruity, and not too peppery. This can only be achieved by not picking the olives too early in the season. The IGP requires that the oils should be made from *Frantoio* (maximum 90%) and *Leccino* (maximum 20%) olives.

Oils from Massa-Carrara are usually made from *Frantoio* olives but the Toscano IGP Montalbano in Pistoia reflects a more diverse tradition, and permits any one of six different olive cultivars to be used in any proportion. The olives are *Leccino*, *Moraiolo*, *Frantoio*, *Pendolino*, *Rossellino*, and *Piangente* (considered by many to be a synonym for *Pendolino*) and their oils differ considerably, but all are made in the Tuscan style. These oils are fruity with

The IGP seal

Tuscany benefits from a mark of quality seal called Toscana Indicazione Geografica Protetta [IGP]. All oils that bear the IGP Toscana seal must be made from olives grown in Tuscany and the producer must be able to prove this. If a bottle of olive oil says simply "Made in Italy" or "Extra-virgin oil from the Hills of Tuscany," this merely tells you where the olives were pressed—not where they were grown. Only an IGP (or a DOP label) assures you that an oil is made from olives grown in the area from which they claim to come.

a taste of almonds, artichokes, ripe fruits, and green leaves, followed by a pepperiness. The town of Prato falls within the Toscano IGP Colline di Firenze, where the choice of cultivars that can be used, some 30 in all, is even greater. However, the leading estates base their oils on *Frantoio*, *Moraiolo*, and *Leccino* olives (in that order of importance).

Leading producers in Florence

Antinori, Marchesi

Piazza Antinori, 3
50123 (Firenze)
☎ 055 23595
🌐 www.antinori.it

The Antinori are kings of Chianti, and their fine olive oils come from S. Casciano Val di Pesa where the Chiantigiano hills run down to Florence. The Pèppoli estate has 66 acres (27ha) that are organic with 5,500 trees, mainly of *Frantoio*, some centennial, some young. Pèppoli oil is greeny gold in color and fragrant (fresh fruit, grass, and olives) with an herbaceous taste

CASTELLO IL PALAGIO MORAIALE

(beans, herbs, and later, almonds), and an aftertaste that is decidedly peppery and bitter. The estate also produces Laudemio Antinori, which is usually softer and fruitier than Pèppoli, with a long, fresh, vegetable taste that develops a suggestion of apples and almonds before revealing a warm peppery aftertaste and a light touch of bitterness.

Castello Il Palagio

50024 Mercatale Val di Pesa
(Firenze)
☎ 0558 21630
🌐 www.castelloilpalagio.it

Il Palagio, one of the leading oil estates in Chianti, has 136 acres (55ha) of classic Tuscan olive trees. It sells their produce as monocultivar oils and, uniquely, all three of them are recognized as Chianti Classico

DOP oils. All have a Castello Il Palagio label, with the name of the cultivar at the bottom: Frantoiane (*Frantoio*) has a mild, fruity taste (apples, grass) that becomes warmer as the pepperiness and bitterness grow on the taste buds to display its robustness, balance, and excellence; Leccine (*Leccino*) is mild at first, and lightly vegetable, with a long, rounded almondy taste and a growing, warm, gentle pepperiness; and Moraiole (*Moraiolo*) has a strong herbaceous taste of grass, watercress, and bitter almonds, which then develops into a long, smooth, bitter, peppery aftertaste. All are excellent.

Frescobaldi, Marchesi de'

50060 Pelago (Firenze)
☎ 055 27141
🌐 www.frescobaldi.it

The Frescobaldi estates, best known for their vines, have some 494 acres (200ha) of olive trees—mainly *Frantoio*, but there are some *Moraiolo*, *Leccino*, and *Pendolino* too. Laudemio Marchesi de' Frescobaldi is an excellent example of Tuscan oil at its best—clear, greeny yellow with a good grassy smell and an excellent fruity taste of tomatoes, arugula, cut grass, and herbs. It is followed by an appropriate level of pepperiness and bitterness; strong, robust, gutsy, but balanced.

Pruneti

Via Case Sparse 22
50020 San Polo in Chianti (Firenze)
055 855319
www.pruneti.it

This small organic estate offers three excellent oils from its 39 acres (16ha) of olives. Pruneti Moraiolo is a very good example of a traditional, big, early-picked *Moraiolo* oil. It has a good grassy smell, a pronounced herbaceous taste (watercress and olives), and a strong aftertaste of pepper and bitterness that persists for a long time. Pruneti Leccino is milder, fresh, and elegant, with a more complex herbaceous taste (artichokes and endives) and a delicate peppery aftertaste. The Pruneti DOP Chianti Classico oil smells strongly of grass and watercress. It starts with a smooth, delicate flavor but develops a fruity taste with hints of apples, herbs, and almonds. It has a big peppery aftertaste that continues for a long time and reveals an underlying bitterness.

PRUNETI DOP
CHIANTI CLASSICO

MIXED FARMS Most Tuscan farmers combine olives with other crops.

Querce di Massimo Marchi, La

Via Imprunetana per Tavarnuzze, 41
50023 Impruneta (Firenze)
0552 011380
www.laquerce.com

This estate has 32 acres (13ha) of olives, some 2,800 trees, mainly *Frantoio*, *Leccino*, and *Moraiolo* with a few less common cultivars mixed in. La Querce oil is green yellow and unfiltered, with a fresh, grassy smell and a cool, smooth texture. This develops a distinctly herbaceous taste and warms up as a firm pepperiness builds and lasts a long time.

Vetrice, Fattorie di Galiga e

Via Trieste, 30
50068 Rufina (Firenze)
0558 397008
www.grati.it

This estate has 197 acres (80ha) of olives, a large area for Tuscany, with 12,000 trees of *Frantoio*, *Leccino*, and *Pendolino*. Its IGP Toscana Extravergine Villa di Vetrice oil is deep golden yellow with a green tinge, and a good grassy smell. It is cool on the tongue, but strong-flavored (cut grass, beans, and fresh almonds) and well balanced in the Tuscan style. A long, lingering pepperiness develops slowly and gives a rounded edge to the finish.

Zucconi delle Massete, Fattoria

Via Imprunetana per Tavarnuzze, 29
50023 Impruneta (Firenze)
0552 011154
www.agricoladellemassete.it

Fattoria Massete has 15 acres (6ha) and 1,500 olive trees, which produce an oil of consistently high quality. The olives are mainly *Frantoio* and *Moraiolo*, and picked early, so their Olio di San Luca is therefore a "typical" Tuscan oil. The oil is unfiltered, with a strong grassy smell. The taste is thick, rich, strong, and robust—mainly watercress and general "greenness" at first, but with hints of almonds too. It leads to a pronounced peppery and bitter taste, which is very satisfying and well balanced. Excellent.

Other producers in Florence

Basciano, Fattoria di

50068 Rùfina (Firenze)
☎ 055 8397034

The Masi wine-making estate produces small quantities of a high-quality oil (mainly from *Frantoio* olives) under its Fattoria di Basciano label.

Bonsi, Fattoria, I

50066 Reggello (Firenze)
☎ 055 8652118
🖥 www.agriturismoibonsi.it

A large estate with 254 acres (103ha) of mixed Tuscan cultivars, whose well balanced I Bonsi oil is sold under the Laudemio label.

Buonamici

50014 Fiesole (Firenze)
☎ 055 654991
🖥 www.buonamici.it

Produces a nicely balanced organic oil under the Buonamici label. Made from a mixture of at least five traditional Tuscan cultivars.

Cafaggio, Tenuta di

50023 L'Impruneta (Firenze)
☎ 055 2012085
🖥 www.castellodicafaggio.com

Sixty-two acres (25ha) of *Frantoio* (plus a little *Moraiolo* and *Leccino*) produce the rich, fresh Cafaggio oil.

Calcinaia, Fattoria di

Via Citille, 84
Loc. Calcinaia
50022 Greve in Chianti (Firenze)
☎ 055 854008
🖥 www.villacalcinaia.it

Owned by the Capaldi family, top-quality Villa Calcinaia DOP Chianti Classico oil from *Correggiolo*, *Moraiolo*, and *Leccino*.

Casa al Brandi

Loc. Donnini
50066 Reggello (Firenze)
☎ 055 860172

Thick, rich, grassy organic oil from about 20 acres (8ha) of *Frantoio* and *Moraiolo* olives.

Casa Sola, Fattoria

Fraz. Cortino
50021 Barberino Val d'Elsa (Firenze)
☎ 055 8075028
🖥 www.fattoriacasasola.com

Fruity, peppery Casa Sole oil, made from a mixture of traditional Tuscan olives.

Casellino, Il

Loc. Il Casellino, Fraz. Torri
50067 Rignano sull'Arno (Firenze)
☎ 055 83053220
🖥 www.campoditorri.com

Campo di Torri is an excellent, strongly flavored, very Tuscan oil made mainly from *Frantoio* olives.

Collina, Fattoria di

50041 Calenzano
☎ 055 8819935

This is one of the largest estates in Tuscany and produces excellent oils, both blends and monocultivar.

Corti, Le

50026 San Casciano in Val di Pesa (Firenze)
☎ 055 829301
🖥 www.principecorsini.com

This well-run estate produces its fine, balanced Le Corte oil from 158 acres (64ha) of traditional Tuscan cultivars.

Fontodi, Tenuta di

Via S. Leonlino, 89
50020 Panzano – Greve in Chianti (Firenze)
☎ 055 852005
🖥 www.fontodi.com

Sixty-nine acres (28ha) of *Correggiolo* olives, producing fine, filtered, strongly flavored Fontodi oil.

Morello, Fattoria di

50019 Sesto Fiorentino (Firenze)
☎ 0574 69721
🖥 www.fattoriadimorello.it

Classic Tuscan oil, mainly from *Moraiolo* olives, sold as

Fattoria di Morello. It is strong, fresh, peppery, and bitter.

Parri, Fattorie

50025 Montespertoli (Firenze)
☎ 0571 609154
🖥 www.fattorieparri.it

Strong, fruity oil from 99 acres (40ha) of *Frantoio*, *Leccino*, *Moraiolo*, and *Pendolino* olives, sold under the Fattorie Parri label.

Pasolini Dall'Onda, Impresa Enoagricola

50021 Barberino Val d'Elsa (Firenze)
☎ 055 8075019
🖥 www.pasolinidallonda.com

These 62 acres (25ha) of *Frantoio*, *Moraiolo*, and *Leccino* produce a robust, fruity oil sold under the Laudemio label as Pasolini Dall'Onda.

Poggiopiano, Fattoria di

Loc. Girone
50061 Compiobbi—Fiesole (Firenze)
☎ 055 6593020
🖥 www.poggiopiano.it

Stunning full-flavored organic oil from a mixture of Tuscan cultivars, sold as Galardi Olio—Fattoria di Poggiopiano.

Quintole, L'Erta di

50023 Impruneta (Firenze)
☎ 055 2011423
🖥 www.ertadiquintole.it

Rich, fruity oil from 22 acres (9ha) of *Frantoio*, *Leccino*, *Moraiolo*, and *Pendolino* olives, sold as L'Erta di Quintole.

Sorgenti, Fattoria le

50012 Bagno a Ripoli (Firenze)
☎ 055 696004
🖥 www.fattoria-lesorgenti.com

Thirty-two acres (13ha) of *Frantoio* and *Moraiolo* olives produce strong-flavored Fattoria Le Sorgenti oil sold under the Laudemio label.

Leading producers in Siena

Barbi, Fattoria dei

53024 Montalcino (Siena)
☎ 0577 841111
W www.fattoriadeibarbi.it

Fattoria dei Barbi extends to 914 acres (370ha), of which only 20 acres (8ha) are planted with olives—about 1,200 plants of *Correggiolo*, plus a few *Frantoio*. Extravergine Fattoria dei Barbi DOP Terre di Siena is deep gold with a hint of green and a distinctive fresh smell of grass and tomatoes. Green tomatoes are also characteristic of its taste, together with suggestions of herbs and artichokes. The robust fruitiness is well matched by a bitter, peppery aftertaste, which is all in proportion—this oil is especially well balanced.

Cacchiano, Castello di

53010 Gaiole in Chianti (Siena)
☎ 0577 747018
W www.castellodicacchiano.it

The historic estate of Cacchiano has belonged to the Ricásoli family since the 12th century. Its 474 acres (192ha) include 86 acres (35ha)—mainly *Frantoio* and *Moraiolo*, with a little *Leccino* and others. The Extravergine Castello di Cacchiano qualifies as a DOP Chianti Classico oil. It is deep golden yellow and unfiltered, with a strong, fresh, fruity smell of olives. The taste is smooth at first, then strongly herbaceous (cut grass and artichokes) as it opens out to

CASTELLO DI CACCHIANO

reveal a powerful balance of pepper and bitterness. It is very Tuscan and very good.

Campriano

53016 Murlo (Siena)
☎ 348 3827233
W www.campriano.com

The Campriano estate has 20 acres (8ha) and 2,000 trees of *Leccino* and *Frantoio*. Campriano is a powerful oil in the Tuscan mold, but nicely balanced—cool and fruity at first with a fresh, grassy taste, and almonds and artichokes too, followed by a peppery, bitter aftertaste, which is both gentle and insistent.

OLIO
EXTRAVERGINE
DI
OLIVA
DI
CAMPRIANO

CAMPRIANO

Cerro, Fattoria del

53040 Acquaviva (Siena)
☎ 0578 767700
W www.saiagricola.it

Fattoria del Cerro has some 32 acres (13ha) dedicated to olives, mainly *Frantoio* and *Leccino*, with a few *Moraiolo* and *Pendolino*. The Fattoria del Cerro oil has a Terre di Siena DOP label: deep gold in color, with a smell of apples and "greenness," and a taste of cut grass, arugula, and fresh almonds. This develops into a powerful, peppery, and bitter aftertaste. The result is elegant, complex, full, and well balanced.

DECORATIVE OLIVE TREES
Large olive cultivars, ready for planting, are offered for sale at Margheriti's nursery near Chiusi in southern Siena.

Coltibuono, Badia a

53013 Gaiole In Chianti (Siena)
☎ 057 774481
W www.coltibuono.com

Badia a Coltibuono is a famous wine estate on the boundaries of Siena and Arezzo, with 44 acres (18ha) of organically grown olives divided between two holdings called Albereto and Campocorto. Olio d'Ulivo Coltibuono is the "basic" estate oil—but good. Badia a Coltibuono Albereto is greenish yellow and unfiltered, and made mainly from *Frantoio*, *Leccino*, and *Pendolino*. It has a juicy, herbaceous smell and an intense flavor (artichokes, herbs, and bitter almonds), with a peppery aftertaste. Badia a Coltibuono Campo Corto is made only from *Frantoio*. It is usually greeny gold and unfiltered, with a herbaceous smell, (hints of artichokes and herbs), a strong taste, and a typically peppery aftertaste. When, as sometimes happens, it is made later in the season than normal, the taste is of sweet almonds and apples—fragrant, balanced, and fruity, with only a trace of pepper and bitterness.

Felsina

53019 Castelnuovo Berardenga (Siena)

☎ 0577 355117

Felsina is primarily a wine estate—and famous for it—but it also has 116 acres (47ha) and 5,800 trees of *Correggiolo* olives, a close relation of *Frantoio* (also known as *Raggiolo*) and a few *Leccino*, *Moraiolo*, and *Pendolino* too. Felsina specializes in *denocciolato* oils. The Leccino Denocciolato and Moraiolo Denocciolato oils are both excellent, and quite different in character, but the Raggiolo Denocciolato is the most interesting, because it shows just what this unusual olive is capable of when picked early: golden yellow with a hint of green and a fresh, fruity smell of tomatoes and nuts. Its taste is cool and gentle at first, then develops a suggestion of cut grass and bananas before a long, fragrant, peppery, bitter aftertaste develops.

FELSINA MORAIOLO DENOCCIOLATO

Fontanelle

53042 Chianciano Terme

☎ 0578 60125

W www.azfontanelle.it

Fontanelle is a small 136-acre (55ha) estate planted with traditional Tuscan olives—old trees of *Moraiolo*, *Leccino*, and *Correggiolo*. Its unfiltered Agricola Fontanelle Terre di Siena DOP oil is dark yellow with a green tinge. It has a fresh, grassy smell and a good clean taste (green and grassy). This is followed by a light almondy aftertaste and a peppery warmth that is not too powerful but quite in proportion to the other tastes. Fontanelle also

AGRICOLA FONTANELLE

makes an IGP Toscana oil from the same cultivars, picked slightly later.

San Felice

53019 Castelnuovo Berardenga (Siena)

☎ 0577 359087

W www.agricolasanfelice.com

The San Felice estate has 16,500 trees, mainly *Correggiolo* and *Frantoio*. Its main oil is Chianti Classico DOP San Felice, which is golden yellow and clear, with a smell of grass and leaves, and a strong herbaceous taste (artichoke and beans), which takes on a hint of almonds before turning into a peppery and bitter aftertaste. San Felice also sells an agreeable unfiltered new oil called Il Velato, which is fresh, fruity, and cool, with a green, vegetable taste.

IL VELATO

Other producers in Siena

Ama, Castello di

Lecchi in Chianti

53010 Gaiole in Chianti (Siena)

☎ 0577 746031

W www.catellodiama.com

Castello di Ama oil, made from *Correggiolo*, *Leccino*, and *Moraiolo*, is robust, well balanced, and reliable from year to year.

Badia al Guardo

Loc. Capovento

53017 Radda in Chianti (Siena)

☎ 0577 740755

W www.chiantiverde.com

A tiny estate of 10 acres (4ha), it has a big reputation for its Capovento IGP Toscano and Super Etruscan oils.

Banfi, Castello

53024 Montalcino (Siena)

☎ 0577 840111

W www.banfi.it

This American-owned estate is enormous—nearly 7,413 acres (3,000ha). Its low-yielding, mature trees produce a Castello Banfi oil of exceptional quality.

Castagnoli, Rocca di

53013 Gaiole in Chianti (Siena)

☎ 0577 731004

W www.roccadicastagnoli.com

Primarily a wine estate, it has 148 acres (60ha) of pan-Tuscan olives (*Frantoio*, *Leccino*, *Moraiolo*, and *Pendolino*) that produce the fresh, peppery, nutty Rocca di Castagnoli oil.

Cinciano, Fattoria di

Poggibonsi

☎ 0577 936588

W www.cinciano.it

Fattoria di Cinciano DOP oil comes from 123 acres (50ha) of Tuscan olives, mainly *Moraiolo* and *Frantoio*. Fresh, fruity, bitter, and peppery, it is well balanced.

Col d'Orcia, Tenuta

53020 S.Angelo in Colle—
Montalcino (Siena)
☎ 0577 80891
W www.coldorcia.it

The full-flavored Col d'Orcia oil from 74 acres (30ha) of *Frantoio* and *Leccino* olives.

Forte, Podere

Loc. Petrucci, 13
53023 Castiglione d'Orcia (Siena)
☎ 0577 8885100
W www.podereforte.it

DOP Terra di Siena oil Podere Forte is made from *Moraiolo*, *Leccino*, and *Frantoio* olives: fresh and fruity with a strong taste of grass and artichokes followed by a peppery, bitter aftertaste.

La Romita

Via Umberto I, 144
53020 Montisi (Siena)
Tel. 0577 845186
W www.romita.it

The Flos Olei label is a good organic oil with an IGP Toscana certificate.

Panizzi, Giovanni

Fraz. Santa Margherita
Loc. Racciano, 34
53037 San Gimignano (Siena)
☎ 0577 941576

High-quality producer with 12 acres (5ha). The oil is made from *Correggiolo*, *Frantoio*, and *Moraiolo* olives.

Vabro, Frantoio

Loc. Casa del Corto
53025 Piancastagnaio (Siena)
☎ 0577 786677
W www.frantoiovabro.it

This is an olive press, not an estate, but its DOP Terra di Siena oil is excellent.

Volpaia, Fattoria Castello di

53017 Radda in Chianti (Siena)
☎ 0577 738066
W www.volpaia.com

Small estate selling elegant classic Tuscan oil, mainly *Frantoio*, under Volpaia label.

Leading producers in Arezzo

Boggioli

52020 Cavriglia (Arezzo)
☎ 055 9166222
W www.boggioli.com

Boggioli is a small farm, revitalized over many years by the Australian Keith Richmond. Its prize-winning oil is made from a mixture of *Frantoio*, *Moraiolo*, *Leccino*, and *Pendolino* olives, grown without irrigation or artificial chemicals. Podere Boggioli is yellow with a tinge of green, fresh, and full flavored, with hints of apples, artichokes, grass, and exotic fruits, plus a good (not too dominant), bitter, peppery aftertaste.

Borro

52020 San Giustino Valdarno (Arezzo)
☎ 055 977053
W www.ilborro.it

Il Borro is a vast estate once owned by the Duke of Aosta and now belonging to the Ferragamo family. There are 44 acres (18ha) of olive groves with 7,000 trees, mainly *Leccino*, *Frantoio*, and *Moraiolo*. Il Borro Extravergine is golden yellow with a green tinge, full and rich, with a taste of cut grass, artichoke, and herbs, followed by almonds and a gutsy aftertaste of bitterness and pepper.

Casamora, Fattoria

52026 Pian di Sciò (Arezzo)
☎ 0559 60046
W www.casamora.it

Fattoria Casamora is one of the largest estates in Arezzo: 212 acres (86ha) and 12,000 trees, organically managed. It has modern extraction systems and a *denocciolato* plant. There are six Casamora oils, all filtered: Supremum (three

monocultivar oils—*Frantoio*, *Moraiolo*, and *Leccino*); Regale (*denocciolato* monocultivar oils of *Frantoio* and *Moraiolo*); and Florilegium (a blend of *Frantoio*, *Moraiolo*, and *Leccino*, each harvested and pressed on the estate). All good.

REGALE

La Maritana, Podere

52100 Arezzo
☎ 0575 21926
W www.lamaritana.it

La Maritana has 15 acres (6ha) of organically maintained *Frantoio* (50%), *Moraiolo* (25%), and *Pendolino* (25%), picked early to ensure low acidity and high levels of polyphenols. La Maritana oil is clear, fruity, and fresh, with a smell of cut grass, artichokes, and herbs, and a fruity, vegetable taste that recalls tomato and bitter almonds, with a long, strong, lingering bitter and peppery aftertaste, all in proportion to the fruitiness.

Petrolo, Fattoria di

52020 Mercatale Valdarno (Arezzo)
☎ 055 9911322
W www.petrolo.it

The Petrolo estate has 44 acres (18ha) of olives planted with 4,500 trees, mainly of *Frantoio*, together with some *Leccino* and *Moraiolo*. Its best oil is Torre di Galatrona Laudemio, made from *Frantoio* and *Moraiolo* and extracted by the Sinolea system. It is clear, deep yellow with a green tinge, a vegetable smell (grass and herbs), a full, fruity taste (apples and artichokes), and a fine strong mix of bitterness and pepper.

Ristori, Silvio

52044 Cortona (Arezzo)

☎ 0575 603571

This small estate on a north-facing slope is planted mainly with *Frantoio* and *Moraiolo*, but with a little *Leccino* and *Pendolino* too. Its Silvio Ristori oil is very tasty—fresh, green, cool, smooth, olivey, and grassy at first, with a hint of nuts and almonds later, followed by a distinct pepperiness that lasts a long time and overlays the bitterness. A complex and delicious combination.

SILVIO RISTORI

San Fabiano, Fattoria di

52100 Arezzo

☎ 0575 24566

W www.fattoriasanfabiano.it

San Fabiano has 62 acres (25ha) and 4,000 trees of *Frantoio*, *Moraiolo*, and *Leccino*. Its oil is organic and sold under the Laudemio brand, with the benefit of a Toscana IGP certificate. Extravergine San Fabiano Laudemio is clear golden yellow, with a smell of artichokes and apples and a strong, persistent vegetable taste, followed by bitter almonds and a warm aftertaste.

Vitereta, Tenuta

52020 Arezzo

☎ 329 8618500

W www.tenutavitereta.com

Vitereta is a small estate on the hillside below the city of Arezzo, planted mostly with *Frantoio* and *Moraiolo*, and a little *Leccino*. Its Tenuta Vitereta oil is green with a hint of yellow, a smell of green olives and artichokes, which turns to bitter almonds on the palate, and a sustained pepperiness.

Leading producers in Grosseto, Livorno & Pisa

Colle Massari, Castello

58044 Cinigiano (Grosseto)

☎ 0564 990458

W www.collemassari.it

This is a young, mixed estate that includes some 49 acres (20ha) of olives (2,500 trees) mainly of *Frantoio*, *Moraiolo*, and *Leccino*. Its Castello Colle Massari oil is not entirely typical of Grosseto oils, being more bitter and robust than usual—but very good. Green yellow and filtered, it has a fresh, grassy taste (and smell) with suggestions of herbs and almonds before the pepperiness fills the mouth and the bitterness kicks in.

Colombaio di Roberto Delli, Il

58038 Seggiano (Grosseto)

☎ 0585 784630

Il Colombaio is made from ancient trees of the local *Seggiano* olives. It is golden yellow with a green tinge and cool on the palate. The initial smell of grass, tomato, fruit, and nuts is followed by an intense vegetable taste with lesser aromas of bananas and almonds. Its aftertaste is fairly peppery and bitter, but all in proportion to the fruitiness, and pleasantly long lasting.

Franci, Frantoio

58040 Montenero d'Orcia (Grosseto)

☎ 0564 954000

W www.frantoiofranci.it

Franci is the most renowned oil producer in Grosseto, winning top prizes at national and international events year after year. It is much larger than many estates, and buys in olives to make a varied choice of oils. These include: soft, fruity, fragrant, elegant Olivastra Seggianese from local Grosseto olives; and medium-bodied Le Trebbiane, which has an excellent balance of fruit, bitterness, and pepperiness. The super-strong Villa Magra dei Franci is the quintessence of the Tuscan style—greeny gold, with a powerful smell of artichokes and grass, and a similar taste that also develops hints of almonds and citrus before the intense pepperiness and underlying bitterness cut in and confirm the rounded quality of this remarkable oil.

VILLA MAGRA GRAN CRU

Ghizzano, Tenuta di

56030 Ghizzano di Peccioli (Pisa)

☎ 0587 630096

W www.tenutadighizzano.com

This big mixed estate has 74 acres (30ha) of olives, all *Frantoio* and all organically cultivated. They are picked early to produce Tenuta di Ghizzano Extravergine, which has an IGP Toscana label. It is fresh and green with a hint of gold, a taste that recalls cut grass, artichokes, and almonds, and a firm peppery and bitter aftertaste that is nevertheless in proportion to the fruitiness.

Morrona, Badia di

56030 Terricciola (Pisa)
☎ 0587 658505
🆆 www.badiadimorrona.it

Badia di Morrona is a 1,235-acre (500ha) mixed estate with 62 acres (25ha) of *Frantoio, Leccino,* and *Moraiolo.* The olives are picked early, starting toward the end of October, to give an oil that is green with a golden tint. Badia di Morrona is fruity and almondy on the nose but rather more herbaceous in taste. Full and robust, it has a firm, peppery, bitter aftertaste.

OL.MA.

58035 Montepescali Scalo (Grosseto)
☎ 0564 39090
🆆 www.oleificioolma.it

OL.MA. is the largest cooperative in Grosseto and one of the few Tuscan producers to combine top quality with considerable quantity. Its members, all of them growers, provide 500 tons of oil a year from their 500,000 trees. All its oils are extra virgin, and reasonably priced, which has brought considerable export sales. Its best-known labels are Terre Alte (robust and forceful, but smooth, cool, and fruity at first, with

TERRE ALTE DI TOSCANA FROM OL.MA.

hints of apples, almonds, and cucumber, and always very well balanced and tasty), which has an IGP Toscana certificate, and Il Madonnino (fresh and aromatic with a long aftertaste of bitter almonds).

ORNELLAIA

Ornellaia, Tenuta dell'

57020 Bolgheri (Livorno)
☎ 056 571811
🆆 www.ornellaia.it

Ornellaia is primarily a wine estate, owned by the all-powerful Antinori family, but its 2,000 olives (*Frantoio, Moraiolo,* and *Leccino*) also yield an oil of exceptional quality. The olives are picked young to produce a not-too-bitter Tuscan taste. Ornellaia is deep golden yellow with a green tinge and a smell of grass and tomatoes. Its taste is very "green"—of artichokes and herbs —not especially complex, but lasting long in the mouth and gentler than many Tuscan oils.

Pardi, Podere de'

Loc. Il Capitano
Vicopisano (Pisa)
☎ 050 879224
🆆 www.oliodepardi.com

Pardi is an old estate, but its olives (*Frantoio,*

Leccino, and *Moraiolo*) were all replanted after the 1985 frosts. Calìa is made from early-picked olives and qualifies for a Toscana IGP. It is greeny yellow, light-medium fruity (vegetable at first, later more almondy) and with a good warm pepperiness to finish.

Parrina, Tenuta La

58010 Albinia (Grosseto)
☎ 0564 862 636
🆆 www.parrina.it

La Parrina is a historic wine-producing estate, but it also makes a seriously good oil from its 49 acres (20ha) of *Frantoio* (50%), *Leccino* (30%), and *Moraiolo* (20%)—plus a few *Caninese* and *Pendolino* as pollinators. Most of the trees are ancient. The olives are picked early: the unfiltered oil has a greenish gold color and a fruity, herbaceous smell. Its taste is a mixture of artichoke, tomatoes, and almonds, with a good, strong, aromatic bitterness and pepperiness to balance it.

Vigne, Le

58040 Montenero d'Orcia, Grosetto
☎ 0564 954116
🆆 www.aziendalevigne.com

Le Vigne has 37 acres (15ha) of olives on the slopes of Monte Amiata and Le Vigne oil comes from 60% *Frantoio,* 30% *Moraiolo,* and 10% *Leccino.* It is very much a Tuscan oil—fruity, peppery, bitter, and robust. Le Vigne's other label is Olivetaccio, made from 100% *Olivastra Seggianese,* the local olive indigenous to Monte Amiata. It is greeny yellow, unfiltered, with a strong fruity smell of cut grass, olives, and sweet almonds, and a strong peppery, bitter aftertaste.

CALIA

Leading producers in Lucca, Massa Carrara, Pistoia & Prato

Balduccio

Lamporecchio (Pistoia)
☎ 0573 82681

Balduccio produces organic oil, mainly from centennial *Moraiolo* olives (plus a little *Frantoio* and *Leccino*). Its owner is Andreas März, a distinguished Swiss wine-writer. His Balduccio Extravergine is very good— and very Tuscan: greeny yellow, filtered, with a taste of green fruit and almonds, and a fine combination of bitterness and pepperiness to end with.

Camelie, Claudio Orsi alle

55065 Pieve di Compito (Lucca)
☎ 0583 55505
W www.linketto.it/allecamelie

The charming and historic Villa Orsi is surrounded by by ancient camellia bushes and attached to a camellia nursery. There are 10 acres (4ha) put to olives—2,000 *Frantoio*, plus a few hundred *Leccino*, *Moraiolo*, and *Pendolino*, organically grown. Their Extravergine alle Camelie is golden yellow and clear, with a green smell of grass, herbs, and leaves. Its taste is fresh and medium fruity, with hints of artichoke and a fair measure of pepperiness and bitterness.

Capezzana, Tenuta di

59015 Carmignano (Prato)
☎ 0558 706005
W www.capezzana.it

The Capezzana estate, famous for Carmignano wine, also has 345 acres (140ha) of olives—*Moraiolo* (60%), *Frantoio* (30%), *Leccino* (5%), and *Pendolino* (5%), which are picked early, starting from the end of October. Capezzano oil is green, unfiltered, and fruity, with a smell of artichokes, fresh grass, and herbs, and a rich taste of artichokes and bitter almonds. It also has a fine peppery aftertaste and enough bitterness to give body to the whole. Very good indeed.

Farnete, Tenuta Le

59015 Carmignano (Prato)
☎ 055 8719585
W www.enricopierazzuoli.com

The Pierazzuoli estates produce two excellent oils. Tenuta Le Farnete has 25 acres (10ha) of *Frantoio*, *Moraiolo*, and *Leccino*, picked starting in early November and pressed on the same day. Le Farnete Extravergine is green, fruity, and juicy with a vegetable taste and a firm peppery aftertaste. Tenuta Cantagallo, across the border in Florence, produces Laudemio Tenuta Cantagallo from 74 acres (30ha) of *Frantoio*, *Moraiolo*, and *Leccino*. It has a characteristic Tuscan taste of green fruitiness, but is well structured with a matching bitter and peppery aftertaste. Both oils are good.

Marini Giuseppe

51030 Pistoia
☎ 0573 452096
W www.marinifarm.it

The Marini family makes its oil from 15 acres (6ha) of *Frantoio*, *Moraiolo*, *Pendolino*, and *Leccino*, picked starting in late October. The Olio Extravergine di Oliva Toscano IGP is fruity, with a smell of artichoke and a fresh olivey taste, nicely balanced by a fairly bitter-peppery aftertaste. The Marini also have a nursery with olive trees of many different sizes and cultivars.

Valgiano, Tenuta di

55010 Valgiano (Lucca)
☎ 0583 402271
W www.valgiano.it

The Valgiano estate has a very pretty house, surrounded by 3,000 olive trees, mainly *Frantoio*, as well as famous vineyards. Its Tenuta di Valgiano oil has a peppery taste, but fresh and fruity—delicate and floral in some seasons, grassy and reminiscent of artichokes in others. It also has the typical Tuscan bitterness—but never aggressively.

VIEW OF LUCCA The fertile Lucchese plains are thickly planted with olive trees, famous for the soft, mellow oil they yield.

Marche

Olive growing is not a major economic activity in Marche, except in such pockets as Cartoceto and Monte San Vito. The region has little more than 19,800 acres (8,000ha) of olives and produces less than one percent of the Italian crop. It is a landscape of small farms, a patchwork of different crops, each owned and managed by many. It is very beautiful, but not the sort of farming for economies of scale.

THE OLIVE REGIONS OF MARCHE

THE OLIVES OF MARCHE

Half the olives grown in Marche are *Leccino*, and one-quarter are *Frantoio*. The rest are accounted for by local specialties like *Mignola* and *Raggiola*. Oils from this region are generally (and increasingly) of a high quality. They are noted for their light fruitiness, characteristic bitterness, and pepperiness, even in soft-tasting cultivars like *Leccino*. Sometimes the bitter, peppery tastes overwhelm the fruitiness, though this is less apparent when the oil is consumed with food.

CARTOCETO DOP

This is the only DOP in Marche, and it covers a small area around the pretty village of Cartoceto itself. By the 16th century there was a flourishing oil industry here, although it suffered from southern competition following the unification of Italy in 1860. Later on, agrarian depopulation meant that by 1983 Cartoceto had only one mill left.

The successful olive-oil industry seen in the region today is of recent origin. Cartoceto oils were originally made from the local *Raggiola* olive. However, the DOP rules now permit any amount (up to 100%) of Tuscan *Frantoio* or *Leccino* too, or any combination of them. Other cultivars may account for up to 30% of the content of the olive oil. Olives are picked early in the season, so the oils are very similar to Tuscan oils but lighter and less fruity. They are high in polyphenols, and long lasting.

CARTOCETO This village is at the heart of a small area of high-quality olive-oil production.

OLIVE CULTIVARS Young olive trees for sale outside an agricultural supplies retailer in Cartoceto.

Leading producers in Marche

Gabrielloni E. & C., Frantoio Oleario

62019 Recanati (Macerata)
☎ 0733 852498
Ⓦ www.gabrielloni.it

Gabrielloni is one of the few "traditional" producers using old-fashioned extraction presses but offering high-quality, fault-free oil. It has two labels: Laudato is made mainly from its own *Leccino* and *Frantoio* olives, and has a light, fruity taste of green tomatoes and artichokes, with a fair degree of bitterness and pepperiness. The softer Solivo comes from its neighbors' late-picked olives and is medium fruity, with a pleasant citrus smell, an opulent texture, and a more aromatic taste of grass and fresh almonds.

SOLIVO GABRIELLONI

Galiardi

61030 Cartoceto (Pesaro e Urbino)
☎ 0721 899565

Galiardi is Cartoceto's largest producer, with 9,000 olive trees and two labels—

Olio extravergine di oliva

GALIARDI RAGGIOLA

red and gold. The red label is 100% Raggiola and has a grassy smell and a taste of cut grass, herbs, and arugula. The gold label, Blend, is a mixture of the usual five cultivars (*Leccino*, *Frantoio*, *Raggiola*, *Moraiolo*, and *Pendolino*) and has a green, bitter taste with quite a strong pepperiness.

Guerrieri, Luca

61030 Piagge (Pesaro e Urbino)
☎ 0721 890152
Ⓦ www.aziendaguerrieri.it

Guerrieri is famous for its Sangiovese wine, but its 35 acres (14ha) of olives produce prize-winning oils. It has three brands, all unfiltered and all excellent: 100% *Leccino* olive (white label with gold cap); a mix of 60% *Frantoio* and 40% *Raggiola* (white label and green cap); and an organic oil that is 100%

Moraiolo and has a green label. The *Leccino* oil has a nice grassy smell and a "greener" taste than normal, with hints of cut grass, fresh almonds, and herbs, and a long, lingering, bitter, and peppery aftertaste.

La Cilestra, Coop. Olivicola

Strada del Pincio, 70
62012 Civitanova Marche (Macerata)
☎ 0733 892417

La Cilestra is a small, young cooperative, with high standards of production. Its Olio della Cilestra is made from a mixture of local and national olive cultivars and tastes of grass, herbs, and bitter almonds. It is soft and gentle at first until the bitterness and pepperiness cut in.

Moroder, Alessandro

60029 Ancona
☎ 071 898232
Ⓦ www.moroder-vini.it

The Moroders are best known for their Rosso Conero wines; oil is a sideline. However, their unfiltered Moroder oil is soft and fruity, with a "green" taste that is not overwhelmed (as sometimes happens in Marche) by bitterness and pepperiness. It is made from *Leccino*, *Frantoio*, and the local *Raggia* cultivar.

Petrini, Fattoria

60037 Monte san Vito, Ancona
071 740386
W www.organicfood.it

The Petrini family's organic San Vito oil tastes of herbs, artichokes, and almonds, with a lingering bitterness and pepperiness. Sei Colli has a hint of green tomatoes.

Other producers in Marche

Bucci

60010 Ostra Vetere (Ancona)
071 964179
W www.villabucci.com

Aromatic, organic Bucci oils are made from blends and monovarietals from local *Carbonella*, *Raggia*, and *Minerva* olives.

Carmine, Agraria del

60100 Ancona
071 889403
W www.aziendadelcarmine.it

Two labels, Oleo de la Marchia and Olio del Carmine, are made here. Both are fresh and herbaceous, with a bitter and peppery aftertaste.

Falerio Picenus, Produttori Associati

Via Procida, 43
63029 Servigliano (Ascoli Piceno)
0734 710772

Twelve small proprietors combine to produce Falerio Picenus oil from rare local *Falerone* olives: golden yellow, herby, vegetable-like, bitter, and peppery.

Giacani, Frantoio Oleario Gianni

60035 Jesi (Ancona)
0731 64409
W www.frantoio.net

Aroli is the label and comes in three choices—two monovarietals and one blend: soft 100% Raggia, fruity, floral 100% Rosciola, and the fresh Gran Crù, a blend of *Leccino* and other olives.

La Collina

61030 Cartoceto (Pesaro e Urbino)
0721 893001
W www.sangiovese.it

From 17 acres (7ha) in the hills around Cartoceto come several self-explanatory labels: Frantoio, Raggiola, Leccino, and Blend. All are good; the Frantoio, excellent.

La Ripe di Roberto Lucarelli

61030 Cartoceto (Pesaro e Urbino)
0721 893019
W www.laripe.com

The La Ripe label is a typical Cartoceto oil, being light, peppery, and bitter.

Mancinelli, Stefano

60030 Morro d'Alba (Ancona)
0731 63021
W www.mancinelli-wine.com

Three good oils from this top estate: Raggia, Leccino, and Stefano Mancinelli.

Montenovo Oleificio

Via San Pietro, 11
60010 Ostra Vetere (Ancona)
071 964471

Several good labels, including Montenovo, which is mainly *Leccino*, and a Montenovo Raggiola.

Serafini, Frantoio

Via San Michele, 2
61030 Cartoceto
(Pesaro e Urbino)
0721 898127

Try Biologico. It is bitter, peppery, and harmonious.

Venturi Agape, Oleificio

Via Peschiera, 7
61028 Sassocorvaro
(Pesaro e Urbino)
0722 76464

Venturi Agape is milder and softer than many oils from Pesaro-Urbino.

VENTURI AGAPE

MIXED FARMING Olives are a minor crop on the coastal hills of Marche.

Umbria

There are few disappointing oils in Umbria, where olive growing dates back to at least the Etruscans (6th century B.C.E.) and was well regarded in Ancient Roman times. Most of today's industry owes its success to the Popes' incentives to plant olive trees in the 19th century. There are 69,000 acres (28,000ha) of olives in Umbria, which yield 1.5–2.5 per cent of Italy's olive oil. Olive trees are a prominent feature of the landscape, notably around Assisi, Spoleto, and Lake Trasimeno. Moraiolo and Frantoio olives, the main cultivars, are responsible for the outstanding quality.

THE OLIVE REGIONS OF UMBRIA

THE OLIVES IN UMBRIAN OIL

There is one large DOP for the whole region, called Umbria DOP, and the olive oils produced under its name are of a uniformly high quality throughout the entire region. The largest producer by far is Monini, which is based in Spoleto. The Umbria DOP is split into five different subzones. Most of their oils are based on combinations of *Moraiolo*, *Leccino*, and *Frantoio*, but their taste differs not only within subzones but also between producers.

• Colli Assisi-Spoleto, the largest subzone, runs through eastern Umbria from Gubbio to Terni. The oil has a minimum of 60% *Moraiolo* olives, with *Leccino* and *Frantoio* (either or combined) to a maximum of 30%. It is strongly fruity, with strong bitterness and pepperiness.

• Colli Martani, is in central Umbria from Torgiano to Todi. Its oil contains a

OLIVES IN ORVIETO   Olives, vines, cypresses, and grazing are all features of the countryside around Orvieto.

minimum of 20% *Moraiolo* olives, and a minimum 80% *San Felice, Leccino,* and/or *Frantoio* olives. The oil is medium-strongly fruity, with medium bitterness and pepperiness.

• Colli Amerini is the area around Narni and north to Avigliano. Its oil contains a minimum 15% *Moraiolo* olives and a maximum 85% *Rajo, Leccino,* and/or *Frantoio*. It is medium fruity, with only a touch of bitterness and pepperiness.

• Colli del Trasimeno, is in northwestern Umbria, including Città di Castello,

Perugia, and Trasimeno. The oil contains a minimum of 15% *Moraiolo* and *Dolce Agogia* olives, and a minimum of 65% *Leccino* and *Frantoio* olives (either or combined). Medium fruity, the oil has only a touch of bitterness and pepperiness.

• Colli Orvietani, runs from Orvieto, Città della Pieve, and Marsciano. The oils contain a minimum 15% *Moraiolo* and *Dolce Agogia* olives, *Frantoio* olives (maximum 30%), and *Leccino* olives (maximum 60%). It is medium fruity, with medium bitterness and pepperiness.

Leading producers in Umbria

Mancianti, Frantoio Faliero

06060 San Feliciano sul Trasimeno (Perugia)
☎ 075 8476045
🌐 www.mancianti.it

This oil comes from Alfredo Mancianti, the doyen of Italian olive oil. The Mancianti Umbria Colli del Trasimeno label is a gentle, smooth, fruity oil with hints of apple, artichoke, and almond, followed by a mild pepperiness and bitterness. Also good, but not produced every year, are the San Feliciano extra virgin and the unfiltered, super-fruity Affiorato.

MANCIANTI

Marfuga, Frantoio

06042 Campello sul Clitunno (Perugia)
☎ 9743 521338
🌐 www.marfuga.it

This estate has 74 acres (30ha) of organic olives, mainly *Moraiolo*. The extra virgin Marfuga Umbria Colli Assisi Spoleto is an excellent, fresh, green-yellow oil, bursting with fruit and grassiness and ending with a light, slowly emerging pepperiness and bitterness. Simple but delicious. L'Affiorante is also good.

Monini

06049 Spoleto (Perugia)
☎ 0743 23261
🌐 www.monini.com

The largest producer, by far, is Monini whose top-of-the-range oils are very good: look out for their Amabile DOP Umbria Colli Martani and their organic oil Bios.

Montecorona, Tenuta di

06019 Umbertide (Perugia)
☎ 075 9413501
🌐 www.saiagricola.it

Montecorona's 111 acres (45ha) of olives yield a deep green-yellow Umbria Colli del Trasimeno oil called Tenuta di Montecorona. It has a long taste: cool, smooth, and herbaceous at first, then warm and spicy with hints of apples and almonds. Very good.

San Lorenzo

06034 Foligno (Perugia)
☎ 0742 22553
🌐 www.tenutasanlorenzo.it

San Lorenzo is a mixed estate with 98 acres (40ha) of olives. Its only oil is the excellent Millenario: golden yellow with a green tinge and a taste of grass, apples, and exotic fruits, followed by a good peppery aftertaste and a matching bitterness.

Trampetti, Frantoio

06039 Trevi (Perugia)
☎ 0742 78991
🌐 www.trampetti.it

Twenty-two acres (9ha) of organic *Moraiolo* produce the Trampetti Umbria Colli Assisi Spoleto oil—greeny yellow, unfiltered, strongly fruity with a taste of grass, artichokes, and apples, followed by a well balanced aftertaste of bitterness and pepperiness.

Trevi Il Frantoio

06039 Trevi (Perugia)
☎ 0742 391631
🌐 www.oliotrevi.it

Olio Trevi is a good Umbria Colli Assisi Spoleto oil, made mainly from *Moraiolo* olives. Grassy and herbaceous at first, it then develops a suggestion of almonds and a pronounced but pleasing pepperiness, plus some bitterness.

SPOLETO FROM FIELDS Olive trees, wildflowers, Italian cypresses, and the towers of Spoleto.

Viola

06037 Foligno (Perugia)
☎ 0742 67515
W www.viola.it

The Viola Umbria Colli Assisi Spoleto oil is cool, smooth, and fruity, with a strong herbaceous taste and hints of tomatoes, grass, and almonds. It is pleasantly peppery and sometimes rather bitter.

VIOLA

Other producers in Umbria

Bachetoni

06049 Spoleto (Perugia)
☎ 0743 521251

This estate has 210 acres (85ha) of ancient olives (mainly *Moraiolo*) producing tasty, top-quality Umbria Colli Assisi Spoleto oil—big, herbaceous, spicy, peppery, and bitter.

Bartolini, Frantoio Oleario Emilio

05031 Arrone (Terni)
☎ 0744 389142
W www.frantoiobartolini.com

High-quality, strong-flavored, fruity Casale Bartolini oils with DOP or organic certificates.

Batta, Frantoio

06126 Perugia
☎ 075 5724782

Full-flavored, grassy, peppery, balanced oils made mainly from a blend of *Frantoio* and the local *Dolce Agogio*.

Cipolloni, Frantoio Alberto

06034 Foligno (Perugia)
☎ 0742 311436
W www.cipolloni.com

Moraiolo Alberto Cipolloni oil, popular with restaurateurs for its strong, fruity, grassy taste, and its long, lingering, warm aftertaste.

Colonna, Mauro

06035 Gualdo Cattaneo (Perugia)
☎ 0742 920202
W www.lecasegialle.it

A tiny 5-acre (2ha) prestigious producer of fresh, fruity, grassy Le Case Gialle *Moraiolo* oil.

Gaudenzi, Frantoio

06039 Trevi (Perugia)
☎ 0742 781107
W www.oliodopgaudenzi.it

Full-bodied organic and Umbria Colli Assisi Spoleto oils, mainly from *Moraiolo*.

Lungarotti, Cantine Giorgio

06089 Torgiano (Perugia)
☎ 075 9886661
W www.lungarotti.it

This mixed estate is also well known for its wines. Its

olive oils are big, grassy, fruity, and peppery. Umbria Colli Martani oil under the Lungarotti label is a well balanced blend of 65% *Frantoio*, 25% *Moraiolo*, and 10% *Leccino*.

Petasecca Donati, Frantoio

Bevagna (Perugia)
☎ 0742 361900
W www.frantoiodibevagna.com

Gold-green Intero oil with a strong vegetable taste and a long, warm aftertaste.

Spacchetti

06036 Montefalco (Perugia)
☎ 0742 379859
W www.tiscali.it/azagspacchettii

Fresh, fruity, greeny yellow Olio di Montefalco is big and well structured with a lingering aftertaste of pepper and bitterness.

Torale

06065 Passignano sul Trasimeno (Perugia)
☎ 075 829275
W www.torale.com

This large 160-acre (65ha) estate makes its lightly fruity Torale Umbria Colli del Trasimeno oil mainly from *Frantoio* and *Leccino*; it has a grassy, herby, aromatic taste, and quite an aftertaste of pepperiness and bitterness.

LUNGAROTTI

Lazio

Olives have been cultivated on the hills of the Roman heartland for thousands of years, certainly since the time of the Etruscans (8th century B.C.E.). Imperial Rome received tribute in oil from all over the Mediterranean: 321,000 amphoras every year, at the empire's height, equal to 22,500 tons today. Lazio is still an important area; its 188,000 acres (76,000ha) now account for 3–5 percent of Italy's annual olive crop.

RIETI, FROSINONE & LATINA

The Sabina DOP includes 32 communes in the province of Rieti. Sabina was Italy's first DOP. There is an olive tree at Canneto Sabino that is one of the oldest (more than 1,500 years), the broadest (20-ft/6.1-m trunk) and the tallest (43ft/13m) in Italy. The main olive cultivars here are *Carboncella*, *Raia* (*Dolce Agogio*), *Leccino*, and *Frantoio* which, together with some minor cultivars like *Rosciola*, must account for 75 percent of the olives used in the Sabina oils. The high proportion of *Leccino* olives in Sabina oils detracts from the distinctive taste of *Carboncella* olives. In a poor season the oils can be a little ascetic. A good year brings out the fruity character.

Carboncella is the traditional olive of the Sabine hills, though it is being edged out by the inexorable rise of *Leccino* and *Frantoio* olives. It is a vigorous, fast-growing, dark-leaved tree. The *Carboncella* produces a good crop of small purple olives that have a high oil yield.

Itrana is the olive of the province of Latina. Its fruits are medium to large, round, and fleshy, used both for oil and table olives. *Itrana* trees are very hardy and grow to a considerable height. Their oils are very fruity and accessible—and highly prized.

THE OLIVE OIL REGIONS OF LAZIO

Map labels: TUSCANY, UMBRIA, Lake Bolsena, Montefiascone, Sabine hills, Viterbo, Rieti, ABRUZZO, ROME, LAZIO, Frosinone, Latina, 0 30 Km, 0 30 miles, Canino DOP, Sabina DOP, Tuscia DOP

OLIVE HARVEST ON A ROMAN TILE FRIEZE

VITERBO & ROME

These provinces include the southern tip of the Sabina DOP (covering 12 communes in Rome), the Canino DOP, and the new Tuscia DOP. The Canino DOP occupies a small corner of northwestern Viterbo and its oils are based on the local *Caninese* olive, though *Leccino*, *Frantoio*, *Pendolino*, and *Maurino* olives are also permitted. *Caninese* is the olive of northern Viterbo and adjoining parts of Umbria. Its olives are small, round, produced in great quantity, and late to mature. Their oil is moderate in yield but prized: light, herbaceous, and usually fine and delicate but in some seasons rather thin.

Canino oils should be greenish yellow, fresh, fruity, and almondy, with a strong taste and a firm aftertaste of bitterness and pepperiness.

The Tuscia DOP, established in 2004, covers most of the eastern part of the province of Viterbo. It is divided into three subzones, called Colli Cimini, Collina Viterbese, and Lago di Bolsena. The oil must be made from at least 90% *Frantoio*, *Canino*, and/or *Leccino*. It should be greeny yellow and have a fresh, fruity flavor, properly balanced by a peppery, bitter aftertaste.

Leading producers in Rieti, Frosinone & Latina

Agnoni

Loc. Capellara
Cori (Latina)
☎ 069 678668

This estate has 49 acres (20ha) of organically grown young olives (5–20 years old). La Badia is 40% *Leccino*, 40% *Itrana*, and 20% *Frantoio* olives, but the cool, fresh fruitiness of *Itrana* dominates and gives it a "green" taste, with a hint of sweet almonds, until the "greenness" returns and leads into a long, very light, bitter aftertaste.

Billi – La Mola, Anna Maria

02031 Castelnuovo di Farfa, Rieti
☎ 0765 36388
✉ lamola.billi@tiscali.it

This is the leading estate in Sabina with 34 acres (14ha) of *Frantoio*, *Leccino*, and *Pendolino* next to the abbey at Farfa. It has won more prizes for quality than almost any other oil. La Mola is a DOP Sabina oil, greeny yellow and unfiltered, with a fruity smell of olives and a delicate herbaceous taste followed by hints of grass and artichokes, light pepperiness, and a suggestion of bitter almonds.

LA MOLA DI ANNA MARIA RILLI

Carpineti, Marco

04010 Cori (Latina)
☎ 069 679860
✉ www.marcocarpineti.it

This small organic estate in northern Latina has 12 acres (5ha) of *Itrana* olives and a few *Leccino* to pollinate them.

Its Biologica Marco Carpineti oil is thick, fruity, unfiltered, and green, with a taste of grassiness, tomatoes, bitter almonds, and pepperiness—all in proportion to its fruitiness.

Cetrone

04010 Sonnino (Latina)
☎ 0773 949008

This is a large estate with 247 acres (100ha) and over 20,000 olive trees, almost all the local *Itrana*. Cetrone oil is golden yellow, clear, with a fruity smell and a strong herbaceous taste of cut grass and leaves, followed by a hint of almonds and a forceful measure of bitterness and pepperiness to match the intense fruitiness. Delicious.

Fagiolo, Laura (Fagiolo di Laura e Antonella Fagiolo)

02032 Fara in Sabina (Rieti)
☎ 0765 487036
✉ www.laurafagiolo.it

Dr. Fagiolo's Cru de Cures is one of the more flavorsome Sabine oils. Pale gold with a green tinge and a light olivey smell, it has a very upfront fruitiness, a taste of artichokes, cut grass, and sweet almonds and a warm, peppery aftertaste.

Farensi, Soc. Coop. Prod.

03030 Coltodino, Rieti
☎ 0765 387084
✉ www.agricolafarense.com

The cooperative produces a very sound and inexpensive oil: mid-gold with a green tinge, lightly fruity and nicely balanced with a taste of grass and sweet almonds and a good aftertaste—peppery and bitter.

Santarelli, Olivicola Alberto

02038 Scandriglia, Rieti
☎ 06 65771373

Santarelli's 15 acres (6ha) of *Carboncella* (plus a few *Frantoio* and *Pendolino*) yield a fine Extravergine Santarelli DOP

Sabina oil. It is deep yellow with a touch of green. Its grassy smell and herbaceous taste (artichokes and watercress) are complemented by a long-lasting peppery and bitter aftertaste.

Sole Sabino di Pingi Francesca

02031 Castelnuovo di Farfa (Rieti)
☎ 0765 36385

Francesca Pingi is the daughter of Anna Maria Billi (q.v.). Her Sole Sabino oil is made from 44 acres (18ha) of *Leccino*, *Frantoio*, *Raia* (*Dolce Agogio*), and *Pendolino*; greeny yellow, unfiltered, medium fruity, with a nicely balanced aroma of grass and artichokes. Its taste suggests herbs and apples and grassiness again, but this is balanced by a hint of bitter almonds and a peppery aftertaste.

Unagri, Coop. (Unione Agricoltori Itrani)

04020 Itri (Latina)
☎ 0771 27928
✉ www.unagri.com

Unagri is the leading cooperative in the Gaeta area. Unagri oil, from *Itrana* olives, is green yellow, unfiltered, with a luscious fruity taste of apples, tomatoes, and bananas, followed by a warm aftertaste and a hint of bitterness at the end.

Valcomino, Coop. Olearia

03046 San Donato Val di Comino (Frosinone)
☎ 0776 695445
✉ www.olioanticoborgo.com

This small cooperative makes its organic Olio dell'Antico Borgo oil from a very rare endemic olive of Samnite origins called *Marina*. It is green, unfiltered, and delicately fruity (traces of apples and herbs), followed by a long peppery aftertaste and a slightly bitter ending.

Leading producers in Rome & Viterbo

Battaglini, Bruno

01023 Bolsena (Viterbo)

☎ 0761 798847

W www. frantoiobattaglini.it

This organic estate's Extravergine Battaglini oil is made from *Caninese*, *Moraiolo* and *Frantoio* olives. Greeny yellow, fruity, fresh, cool, and rounded, it has a long, grassy, herbaceous taste and a touch of bitterness and pepper. It is very good value and well balanced.

BATTAGLINI

Canino, Oleificio Soc. Coop di

01011 Canino (Viterbo)

☎ 0761 437089

W www.oscc.it

This is the largest oil cooperative in the Canino DOP. It was founded in 1965 and now has 1,200 members who own 8,150 acres (3,300ha) and 250,000 trees. The olives are mainly *Caninese*, but with a small proportion of *Pendolino*, *Leccino*, *Maurino*, and *Frantoio*, too. The greeny-gold, filtered oil is made in the Tuscan style, but is mild and delicate, with a "green" taste of artichokes, cut grass, and herbs, and later of nuts and almonds. The lightness of the bitter, peppery aftertaste is quite in keeping.

COOP DI CANINO

Colli Etruschi, Coop.

01010 Blera (Viterbo)

☎ 0761 470469

W www.collietruschi.it

This well managed cooperative has 90 percent of the small local olive farmers, responsible for some 2,000 acres (800ha). Colli Etruschi oil is 90% *Caninese*: yellow green, fluid, and grassy, with an herbaceous smell and a fruity taste with hints of tomatoes, it is followed by a light, bitter aftertaste.

L'Olivella

00044 Frascati (Rome)

☎ 06 9425656

W www.racemo.it

The 74 acres (30ha) of olives at L'Olivella are mainly *Frantoio*, *Leccino*, and *Moraiolo*, and all organically managed. Their L'Olivella Racemo oil is greeny gold, with a light smell of olives, grass, and herbs, and a smooth taste of "greenness," apples, and bitter almonds, and by a warm aftertaste.

Mosse, Coop. Oleificio Le

01027 Montefiascone (Viterbo)

☎ 0761 824440

Most of the olives Mosse presses (77%) are *Caninese*; the rest are *Frantoio*, *Leccino*, and *Pendolino*. Its oil is golden yellow and fruity, with a rich taste of grass, artichokes, herbs, and bitter almonds, followed by a warm, peppery aftertaste.

Pietraporzia, Tenute di

00044 Frascati (Rome)

☎ 06 9464392

W www.tenutadipietraporzia.it

Tenute di Pietraporzia oil comes from 15 acres (6ha) planted with *Frantoio* and the same area with a mixture of *Leccino*, *Moraiolo*, and *Rosciola*.

The oil has a fresh, fruity smell, a strong, rich taste of apples, grass, and tomatoes, and a long, warm, peppery aftertaste.

San Clemente F.lli Lozzi

00019 Tivoli (Rome)

☎ 0774 411068

W www.oliosanclemente.it

Sevent-four acres (30ha) of *Leccino*, *Carboncella*, and some local rarities. Fons Olei is delicately fruity and aromatic, with hints of grass, citrus, and artichokes, then a definite bitterness and pepperiness that are nevertheless balanced and harmonious. The final flavor is reminiscent of almonds.

Spagnoli, Biologica di Augusto

00017 Nerola (Rome)

☎ 0774 683040

This estate's 99 acres (40ha) of olive groves are put mainly to *Carboncella* (45%) and *Frantoio* (40%). Its excellent oils include: the organic Augusto Spagnoli DOP Sabina (grassy, medium fruity, and aromatic with a light peppery aftertaste); Cru Secolari (medium fruity, smooth, grassy, herby, with a mild aftertaste of pepperiness and bitterness); the rare monocultivar Fecciara (green-tasting, almondy, and spicy with a light bitterness and pepperiness to end); and a pure *Leccino* (light, with a greeny taste of grass and artichokes and a robust pepperiness and bitterness).

Tre Colli Biologica

00010 Montelibretti (Rome)

☎ 0774 608080

W www.trecolli.it

This organic estate has 37 acres (15ha) of *Carboncella*, *Frantoio*, and *Leccino*. Its excellent organic Tre Colli oil has a Sabina DOP. Greeny gold, unfiltered, fresh, and fruity, it has a good structure, a hint of herbs, and a long, peppery aftertaste.

Abruzzo & Molise

Olives are grown throughout the regions of Abruzzo and Molise, but are not the main agricultural activity: producing wine and raising stock are more important in Abruzzo and grain in Molise. Abruzzo has about nine million olive trees producing some 5,283,500gal (20 million liters) of oil a year—somewhat more than the entire output of Tuscany—and Molise has about 2.5 million trees.

MARCHE

Aprutino Pescarese DOP
Colline Teatine DOP
Molise DOP

Teramo
L'Aquila
Pescara
Chieti
ABRUZZO
MOLISE
Iserniia
Campobasso

0　30 Km
0　　30 miles

THE OLIVE REGIONS OF ABRUZZO & MOLISE

HISTORICAL LINKS

Olive oil has been produced in Abruzzo for centuries. The Pretuzi people, who lived in the area of modern-day Teramo, were making oil in the 3rd century B.C.E. To acknowledge this ancient link, a new DOP in Abruzzo will be named Pretuziano delle Colline Teramane.

Archeological excavations recently unearthed an entire 2nd-century oil press. In 1806, one of Napoleon I's officers marching through Abruzzo toward Loreto and Penne referred to its "interminable olive plantations" but admired the silvery effect of light on the leaves.

RAISING STANDARDS

Every province in these regions makes good oil. The leading producers realize that everyone benefits if the perception of the entire area is enhanced. The three DOPs have an important role to play in adding value.

ABRUZZO

Within Abruzzo, 116,000 acres (47,000ha) are dedicated to growing olives. Olives are most important in the warmer, southeastern parts of the region: there are 5,000 acres (2,000ha) of olives in inland L'Aquila, 12,400 acres (5,000ha) in Teramo, 24,700 acres (10,000ha) in Pescara, and 74,000 acres (30,000ha) in Chieti. That said,

more than 40 percent of Abruzzo oil is destined for home consumption.

Teramo oils tend to be imitation Tuscans—greenish yellow and medium fruity, with a bitterness verging on the acrid. The Pretuziano delle Colline Teramane DOP will raise standards further.

Pescara has an active olive industry in the area around Loreto Aprutino and along the Pescara river valley. Aprutino Pescarese was one of the first DOPs in Italy and its oils are medium or strongly fruity. *Dritta* is the local olive in Teramo and Pescara. It is hardy, vigorous, and heavy cropping, with a fair yield of oil.

Chieti's DOP is substyled Colline Teatine, substyled Frentano in the northwest and Vastese in the southeast, each with different proportions of *Gentile di Chieti* and *Leccino* olives. *Gentile di Chieti* is perhaps the best of the indigenous Abruzzo olives. It is related to the Tuscan *Frantoio* olive, and shares many of that cultivar's strengths. Its oil is high quality, fine, and delicate.

Yet despite all the attention given to conserving indigenous olives, by far the most widely grown cultivar in Abruzzo is the Tuscan *Leccino*, accounting for two-thirds of all the olives grown in the area and making for fruitier, softer oils than in Tuscany itself.

COLONNA®
OLIO
EXTRA VERGINE
DI OLIVA

prodotto nel frantoio e imbottigliato
nella Masseria Bosco Pontoni
di proprietà della
Principessa Marina Colonna
86046 San Martino in Pensilis
www.marinacolonna.it
Da consumarsi preferibilmente
entro la data indicata sul sigillo
PRODUCT OF ITALY
N. 00HCB Reg. CE 2815/98
0,25 ℓ e
8,45 fl. oz.

COLONNA—THE BEST OLIVE
OIL PRODUCER IN MOLISE

ABRUZZO COUNTRYSIDE A view of the town of Loreto Aprutino and surrounding hills of olive trees.

MOLISE

There are some 33,360 acres (13,500ha) of olives in Molise—in national terms, about one percent of the total Italian production. Molise has some very skilled oil-makers and interesting indigenous olive cultivars that produce distinctive oils. These olives include *Aurina*, *Gentile di Larino*, and *Rosciola*. Some are said to date back to Roman times, when the oils of Molise were praised by Cato, Pliny, and Horace. The province was granted DOP status in 2003, though rules governing the choice of cultivars are so widely drawn that it is impossible to define a "typical" Molisan oil. The Molise DOP will improve quality (often already excellent), however, and raise the profile of Molise's oils so that they are more highly valued and widely available.

Leading producers in Abruzzo

CAPO (Consorzio Abruzzese Produttori Olive)

65019 Pianella (Pescara)
📞 085 971680
W www.oleificiociocapo.it

CAPO is a cooperative with about 2,500 members in Pescara. Its main brand Antichi Feudi Vestini DOP is one of the best in Abruzzo. The taste is fruity and clean, with a hint of tomatoes, herbs, and sweet almonds, followed by a long, lingering pepperiness. It also comes in an organic version named Biologica. CAPO's other labels include Vestino, a gentle, flavorsome blend of *Dritta* (80%) and *Leccino* (20%) olives.

Di Pasquale, Frantoio

64020 Morro d'Oro (Teramo)
📞 085 895802
W www.frantoiodipasquale.com

Alessandro Di Pasquale is the leading oil producer in Teramo. All his oils are well made and tasty. Some are very unusual, including those made from the Abruzzo olive speciality *Dritta* and the ultralocal *Tortiglione*. Many of the old, stumpy, distinctively twisted trees that are a feature of the Teramo hills are *Tortiglione*, which is valued for its long-lasting oil. The firm sells three main oils in addition to its Classica blend: the monocultivar Tortiglione, which smells of hay and tastes of herbs and fresh almonds, with a light pepperiness and a pronounced bitterness to follow; the organic Biologico (smooth and grassy, with lots of body) made from *Leccino*, *Dritta*, and *Frantoio* olives; and the Denocciolato, which is robust and herbaceous with a long, strong aftertaste, made from *Leccino*, *Dritta*, *Frantoio*, and *Tortiglione* olives.

DI PASQUALE DENOCCIOLATO

Fazia, Frantoio Olive Vito Della

66020 Rocca S. Giovanni (Chieti)
📞 0872 60483
🌐 wwwdellafazia.com

The Della Fazia family produce 10,566–13,200gal (40,000–50,000 liters) of oil every year, under five main labels: Della Fazia is their "basic" extra virgin oil, made from *Gentile di Chieti* and *Leccino*; Fior di Venere is a pure *Leccino* selection, with a soft, delicate, fragrant taste; Nobile di Rocca is a pure *Gentile di Chieti* oil, slightly fuller, with an herby scent and a taste of fruit, almonds, and artichokes; Bio Nostro is their organic label; and Le Menare is their Colline Teatine DOP oil, which has a scent of cut grass and tomatoes, a taste of artichokes and sweet almonds, and a light aftertaste of nuttiness, warmth, and bitterness.

DELLA FAZIA

Plenilia, Cooperativa

65019 Pianella (Pescara)
📞 085 971329
🌐 wwwoliore.com

Plenilia is the largest high-quality oil producer in Abruzzo, with some 300 growers producing more than half a million litres (132,000gal) of oil a year. Its label is Olio Re, and 80% of it qualifies for the Aprutino Pescarese DOP. They also offer a Biologico option. All are made mainly from the local *Dritta* olive and are lightly fruity, smooth, and harmonious, with an herbaceous taste that turns to sweet almonds as it ages and a light touch of bitterness and pepperiness.

SCAL (Società Cooperativa Agricola Loretana)

65014 Loreto Aprutino (Pescara)
📞 085 8291293
🌐 wwwscal.it

SCAL's 500 members own about 19,800 acres (8,000ha) of olives in the Loreto Aprutino area and produce four brands: SCAL and Loretello (both good), and Feronia and San Zopito (both Aprutino Pescarese DOPs, and even better). San Zopito is markedly fruity, a blend of *Dritta* and other olives, with a hint of grass and almonds; Feronia is 95% *Dritta*, with a more delicate fruitiness, a gentle, smooth texture, and a long, light aftertaste of bitterness and pepperiness.

Ursini

66022 Fossacesia (Chieti)
📞 0872 60361
🌐 wwwursini.com

The Ursini family's oil business is growing fast, and now averages over 120,000 litres (31,700gal) annually, mainly from *Gentile di Chieti* olives. But they also offer a wide choice of monovarietal oils, including *Dritta*, *Intosso*, *Toccolana*, *Tenera Ascolana*, and *Gentile di Chieti* itself, each of

TERRE DELL'ABBAZIA

which is marketed under the Solo label (Solo Dritta, Solo Intesso, and so on). Their main label is Terre dell'Abbazia (lightly fruity almondy, mild, smooth, almost bland, but correctly made and nicely balanced). Their Opera Mastra, Albis Ulivis, and Primus labels (the latter from early-harvested olives) are all reliable too.

Other producers in Abruzzo

Azienda D'Alessandro

C. da Mancini, 14
66038 San Vito Chietino (Chieti)
📞 0872 61006

Azienda D'Alessandro makes Rupe del Biancospino, which is typical of the soft, fresh oils made principally from *Gentile di Chieti* olives with the addition of a little *Leccino*. The oil is unfiltered, lightly fruity, smooth, and almost buttery, and has a light aftertaste of bitterness and pepperiness.

RUPE DEL
BIANCOSPINO

Coppini Arte Olearia

65014 Loreto Aprutino (Pescara)
📞 0521 874370
🌐 wwwcoppini.it

Coppini has estates in Sicily (*see* Frantoio L'Albero d'Argento, *p.128*) as well as Abruzzo and, unusually, blends its oils to produce some remarkable hybrids. Novolivo is two-thirds *Gentile di Chieti* olives and one-third Sicilian olives, made early in the season to produce a fruity mouthful with quite an aftertaste of bitterness and pepperiness.

D'Onofrio, F.lli

Via Piana, 85
66010 Villamagna (Chieti)
☎ 0871 300106
🖥 wwwdonofriosrl.it

The Onofrio brothers make some of the best oils in Abruzzo. Scorpius is their "ordinary" DOP Colline Teatine oil, Gemini is their *affiorato* oil (also DOP), and Taurus is their organic oil. All are excellent, with a moderately fruity, grassy, gentle taste, which is followed by a suggestion of bitterness and pepperiness.

Goccia d'Oro snc, Oleificio

65017 Penne (Pescara)
☎ 085 8270631
🖥 wwwgocciadoro.com

Goccia d'Oro makes about 25,000 litres (6,600gal) of oil a year, mainly from *Dritta*, *Leccino*, and *Frantoio* olives. The firm, founded in 1992, is still expanding by buying from small growers to produce its smooth, lightly fruity Goccia d'Oro oil.

Imbastaro, Sapori della Majella Frantoio

C. da Fiorentini, 5/7
66043 Casoli (Chieti)
☎ 0872 982356

Imbastaro DOP Colline Teatine is Domenico Imbastaro's leading oil. It is made from 100% *Gentile di Chieti* olives and is golden yellow and gently fruity, with a scent of tomatoes and a taste of almonds and herbs, followed by a light pepperiness and bitterness.

Magnolie, Agrit. Le

65014 Loreto Aprutino (Pescara)
☎ 0858 289804
🖥 wwwlemagnolie.com

Le Magnolie (The Magnolias) is a youngish estate, whose 24 acres (10ha) are planted with *Dritta* olives and a few *Leccino* and *Frantoio*. Its Le Magnolie label qualifies as an Aprutino Pescarese DOP oil, and has a "green" taste of grass and herbs, followed by a lingering pepperiness and a hint of bitter almonds.

Presutti, Natale

65013 Città Sant'Angelo (Pescara)
☎ 051 334285
🖥 wwwoliodellangelo.com

Natale Presutti has 27 acres (11ha) of *Dritta* and *Leccino* olives within sight of the Adriatic Sea. They are supplemented by ancient specimens of *Toccolana*, *Tortiglione*, and *Nociara*, and new plantations of all of them. The estate sells only one oil, under the Olio dell'Angelo label, which is unfiltered and qualifies for Aprutino Pescarese DOP status. It has a smooth, grassy, herbaceous taste, with an aftertaste of pepperiness, bitterness, and almonds. It is not strongly fruity, but is nicely balanced.

Persiani, Mattia

Via San Martino
64030 Atri (Teramo)
☎ 06 8554830

Professor Persiani has 10,000 *Dritta*, *Gentile di Chieti*, *Frantoio*, and *Leccino* trees on his 81-acre (33ha) organic estate. The olives are picked young, before they are ripe, to make the strongly herbaceous, greeny-gold San Martino oil. It has a strong aftertaste of pepperiness and bitterness.

SAN MARTINO

Leading producers in Molise

Colonna, Marina

86046 San Martino in Pensilis (Campobasso)
☎ 0875 603009
🖥 wwwmarinacolonna.it

This estate has 173 acres (70ha) of olives; its modern plantations are remarkable for the experimental choice of cultivars. The Colonna oil (sold in clear-glass amphoras) gets its fine flavor not so much from the blend of olives (which is dominated by *Leccino*, *Peranzana*, *Frantoio*, and *Coratina*), but from early picking and skillful extraction techniques. It is not cheap, but it *is* excellent, with a fresh, smooth, grassy taste of herbs and artichokes, followed by an aftertaste of almonds, and a long, balanced, lingering pepper and bitterness.

Larinese, Cooperativa Olearia

86035 Larino (Campobasso)
☎ 0874 822697
🖥 wwwdecurtis.it

This leading producer of oil from the indigenous *Gentile di Larino* olives produces some 100,000 litres (26,400gal) a year. Its Gentile di Larino monovarietal oil is gently fruity and herby, with a warm aftertaste. The organic Biologico oil contains a little *Leccino* and *Peranzana* as well as *Gentile di Larino*.

Maresa snc di Maria Teresa Occhionero

86049 Ururi (Campobasso)
☎ 0874 831200
🖥 wwwquartodeigreci.it

Oil sold under the Quarto dei Greci label (typically 90% local *Gentile di Larino* olives) is smooth, rounded, almost rich in texture, with a gentle herbaceous taste, a hint of pears, and a brief aftertaste of pepper and bitterness.

Campania

This region is a major producer of olive oil, the fourth most important in Italy, after Puglia, Calabria, and Sicily. The five provinces that make up Campania are very different in their landscape and the sheer variety of their olive—more than 80 indigenous cultivars. Quality is easy to find, but not always reflected in prices paid. Quantity is equally ubiquitous, especially in Salerno, the largest province.

THE OLIVE REGIONS OF CAMPANIA

GEOGRAPHY AND CLIMATE

The region of Campania is very variable in its topography. Its five provinces are bound together by a shared history rather than geography. Naples, the smallest, is dominated by the vast volcanic cone of Mount Vesuvius; its soils are fertile and draining freely. Volcanoes—but extinct—are a feature of the landscape in Avellino and Benevento too. Some of the region's best oils come from the Irpinia and Sannito areas. The province of Caserta has attractive limestone hills covered in olives right down to sea level. Limestone predominates, too, in Salerno, the largest province. Olive oil is made throughout, from the fashionable peninsula of Sorrento and the flatlands around the city of Salerno itself to the jumble of remote villages that occupy the hills of the Cilento area.

BENEVENTO & AVELLINO

The hills of Avellino and Benevento produce small quantities of top-quality oils from little-known local olives. Avellino's most prestigious area is Irpinia, northeast of the city of Avellino, where a new DOP is in the process of being established. It will be called Irpinia—Colline dell'Ufita (8,650 acres/3,500ha), and be based on the local *Ravece* olives. Venticano and Flumeri are two of the leading centers. In Benevento there are

CATCHING THE CROP Nets are laid out at harvest when trees are knocked or shaken to release the olives.

HILLSIDE GROVE Olive trees silhouetted by the sun near the town of Moiano, Benevento.

moves to establish DOP status for two overlapping areas: Colline Beneventane (12,355 acres/5,000ha) based on the *Ortice* olive (known locally as *Coglioni di Gallo*), and Sannio-Caudino Telesino (14,826 acres/6,000ha) on a mixture of *Ortolana* and *Racioppella*—all local specialties. The best oils already command a good price on the market.

CASERTA & NAPLES

Olives are grown throughout both of these provinces, and most of the oil is sold directly to the public by the producers. The only DOP is the tiny Peninsola del Sorrentina, which includes some of the Sorrento peninsula and the island of Capri. Peninsola del Sorrentina oils are not among Italy's most distinguished, but are well made and pleasant enough. Landholdings are small, and most olives are processed by village cooperatives. However, the oil is valued by local restaurants and some is exported. The steeply terraced hillsides are thick with gray-leaved olives, which are beautiful on a windy day. The local *Minucciola* olive gives the oils their

characteristic light taste. There is also a move to establish a new DOP to be named Terre Aurunche (or possibly Terra di Lavoro) in western Caserta. The oils of this DOP would be based on the indigenous olive cultivars *Caiazzana*, *Sessanella*, and *Tonnella*.

SALERNO

More than half of the olive trees in Campania are grown in the province of Salerno. Many of the cultivars are rare and very local. The stately, large-fruited *Nostrale* olive predominates in the north of the province and the *Rotondella* in the remote, beautiful Cilento area in the south. The oils of Salerno are among the least esteemed of Italy, and yet they also include some of the most interesting and exciting extra virgin oil. The province is also one of the few to have two DOPs. They are called Cilento and Colline Salernitane. There is plenty of bad oil in Salerno, made from poorly cultivated olives and processed in antiquated presses. However, almost everything you see in bottles will be good—and sometimes very good indeed.

Leading producers in Benevento & Avellino

De Marco

83040 Lapio (Avellino)
☎ 0825 985095
🖵 www.oliodemarco.it

The De Marco family buy olives from neighboring villages to supplement their own. Their straightforward Olio Extravergine De Marco is soundly made, cool, and nutty, with a taste of herbs, almonds, dried fruits, and pears, a pleasant warm aftertaste, and a light bitterness to end with. Even better are their Riserva (from *Ravece* olives) and Terre d'Irpinia (a blend), both gentle and fruity, with a lingering, long-lasting taste.

OLIO DE MARCO

I Capitani

83030 Torre Le Nocelle (Avellino)
☎ 0825 969182
🖵 www.icapitani.com

Young groves of *Ravece* and *Ogliarola Avellinese* are the backbone of the Capitani's production, each of them sold as monocultivar oils under the Aurum Silvae label. Turrioro is a blend of oils from a wider area within the province. All are soft, fruity, and dependable.

Oleificio F.A.M.

83030 Venticano (Avellino)
☎ 0825 965829
🖵 www.oliofam.com

FAM stands for Flora, Antonio, and Maria, the three Tranfaglia siblings who make their oil from olives in the area around Venticano.

Dominus Riserva is their top label, made only from *Ravece*, with a taste of herbs, green tomatoes, and apples followed by a long, lingering aftertaste of almonds, pepperiness, and bitterness. Also worth seeking out is their ordinary blend Extravergine dagli Uliveti d'Italia. It is pale gold, nutty, gentle, and very good value.

Rinaldi, Frantoio Oleario

82027 Pontelandolfo (Benevento)
☎ 0824 851072
🖵 www.frantoiorinaldi.it

Rinaldi's Olio Extra Vergine del Frantoio Rinaldi is made from bought-in *Ortice* olives. Their high content of polyphenols makes the oil last long. It has an unusual and delicious taste: herbs, tomatoes, dried fruit, and nasturtium leaves, matched by a well balanced pepperiness and bitterness. It is strongly flavored and harmonious.

San Lupo scarl, Olivicola

82030 San Lupo (Benevento)
☎ 0824 811220
🖵 www.galtiterno.it

The cooperative in San Lupo is the leading producer in the Samnite hills and its Olio Extravergine di Oliva cultivar Ortolana is the benchmark for quality. It is greeny gold, with a smell and taste of grass, artichokes, apples, and tomatoes, followed by strong pepperiness and some bitterness. It is a strong, juicy, Tuscan-style oil, and nicely balanced. San Lupo produces another excellent monocultivar oil from the local *Ortice* olive.

OLIVICOLA SAN LUPO

Terre Stregate

82034 Guardia Sanframondi (Benevento)
☎ 0824 864312
🖵 www.terrestregate.it

The name of this estate means "bewitched land." Their Primo Fiore is a light, grassy oil with a taste of apples and green tomatoes, and a good pepperiness, which adds body. It is skillfully made from local cultivars— *Ortice*, *Ortolana*, and *Raciopella*.

PRIMO FIORE

Titerno, Olivicola

Via Lampione
82032 Cerreto Sannita (Benevento)
☎ 0824 860065

Titerno is a young, go-ahead cooperative that has won great praise for its three monocultivar oils, which celebrate the local distinctiveness of the Samnite hills: early-picked, green-tasting Ortice, almondy Ortolana, and late-picked, appley Racioppella. All excellent.

Zamparelli

82032 Cerreto Sannita (Benevento)
☎ 0824 861117
🖵 www.zamparellifarm.it

Vincenzo Zamparelli is a small producer, but the quality of his ORO blend is very high. He also offers two much-praised monovarietal oils from *Ortice* and *Racioppella*.

Leading producers in Caserta & Naples

Badevisco, Olivicola

81037 Sessa Aurunca
(Caserta)
📞 0823 938761
W www.badevisco.it

This is a young producer with 50 acres (20ha) of *Itrana*, *Frantoio*, *Coratina*, and the local *Sessanella* olive. The Badevisco oil is a blend of *Itrana* and *Sessanella*, with a fresh smell of grass and herbs, a fruity taste (artichokes and bitter almonds), and a peppery aftertaste. It is well balanced and harmonious.

Le Peracciole

80061 Massa Lubrense
(Naples)
📞 081 5330558
W www.donalfonso.com

On the mainland across from Capri, are 15 acres (6ha) of *Minucciola*, *Rotondella*, and *Frantoio* olives. Le Peracciole oil is green yellow, unfiltered, and grassy, with hints of arugula and a firm, peppery aftertaste. Some years they also offer an early-picked Raccolta Anticipata. More peppery and bitter, it is altogether more robust.

OLIVES AND VINES AT S. LUPO
Old olive trees rise out of this young vineyard in the Sammite hills of Benevento.

Monte della Torre di Antonio Marulli

Via Appia km. 184,500
81100 Francolise
(Caserta)
📞 0823 882073

Monte della Torre oil gets its character from 50 acres (20ha) of the local *Pignarola* and *Olivastro di Caserta* olives, backed by a little *Coratina*, *Frantoio*, and *Leccino*. It smells of grass and green tomatoes, but tastes more herby, with a good degree of bitterness and pepperiness.

Other producers in Caserta & Naples

Colline di Sorrento, Coop., Le

80067 Sorrento (Naples)
📞 081 8773793
W www.lecollinedisorrento.com

Le Colline di Sorrento is a DOP oil, with a light taste of herbs, a stronger one of bitter almonds, and a peppery aftertaste.

Ferraro, Frantoio

Loc. Montechiaro
80069 Vico Equense (Naples)
📞 081 8028039

Olio Peninsola Sorrentina is medium fruity, with a grassy smell and soft taste that soon develops a good herbaceous flavor, a light bitter aftertaste, and long-lasting pepperiness. It is well balanced. Equense is also good.

Le Tore, Agricole Lubrense

Via Pontone, 43 80064
Massa Lubrense
(Naples)
📞 081 8080637
W www.letore.it

Le Tore oil has a nice, fresh, grassy smell and a long, herby, bitter taste, but is only lightly fruity.

LE TORE

Russo

80069 Vico Equense (Naples)
📞 081 8028404
W www.larcangelo.it

Small producer with grassy oil from *Minucciola* olives. Some claim to taste bananas.

Solagri, Coop.

80065 Sant'Agnello di Sorrento
(Naples)
📞 081 8772901
W www.solagri.it

Frantoio delle Sirene is a soft, well balanced, fruity oil with a smell of green tomatoes and an unusual taste of herbs, tomato, and nuts.

Sorrentolio

80065 Sant'Agnello di Sorrento
(Naples)
📞 081 8072300
W www.sorrentolio.com

The pale, green-yellow DOP oil Syrenum tastes of artichokes, bitter almonds, and apples. It is made from 90% *Minucciola* olives.

Leading producers in Salerno

Serra Marina, Oleificio

84050 Laureana Cilento (Salerno)
☎ 0974 832573
🌐 www.serramarina.it

Careful cultivation, modern processing equipment, and technical know-how are the basis for Serra Marina's success. The range includes the basic extra virgin Parmenides (the philosopher lived at Elea Velia) and the Cilento DOP oil called Colline del Cilento, which is deep gold with a good gutsy flavor of pears and bananas. It also has a long, aromatic aftertaste and a lingering note of pepperiness and bitterness.

COLLINE DEL CILENTO

Nuovo Cilento, Soc. Coop.

84070 S. Mauro Cilento (Salerno)
☎ 0974 903239
🌐 www.cilentoverde.com

Nuovo Cilento is the leading cooperative in southern Salerno and the country's largest producer of organic oil. Its three extra virgin oils are all well made, fruity, and tasty: Terre del Casale is a

TERRE DI MONACI

high-quality "basic" oil; Terre Antiche is organic; and Terre dei Monaci is its Cilento DOP oil, made from 85% *Rotondella* olives. It has a distinctive taste of artichokes, herbs, and tropical fruits, a good dose of pepperiness, and a pleasingly bitter aftertaste.

Val Calore

84049 Castel San Lorenzo (Salerno)
☎ 0828 944035
🌐 www.valcalore.it

Val Calore is the market leader in northern Salerno. It has 1,200 members and 2,500 acres (1,000ha). Val Calore produces amphora-shaped bottles of a stunning DOP oil under the name Colline Salernitane. It is cool, fresh, gentle, and fruity at first, until a strong note of pepperiness and bitterness develops. It is exceptionally well made and long and balanced in taste. Also good is Nostrolio, made from selected color, it is fruity, with a powerful taste of artichokes, fresh almonds, and bananas, and a long aftertaste of bitterness and pepperiness. Both are predominantly made

from local *Nostrale* and *Rotondella* olives, with a small addition of Tuscan *Frantoio* and *Leccino* olives.

Other producers in Salerno

Agrioil

84020 Roccadaspide
(Salerno)
☎ 0828 943685
🌐 www.agrioil.com

Agrioil's brand name is Stilla. There are three good-quality labels: Stilla d'Oro Prodotto Italiano (soft and fruity), Stilla Biologico (organic and delicate), and DOP Colline Salernitane (full bodied, fruity, and robust).

Apicella, Francesco

Via Palma, 11
84060 Perdifumo
(Salerno)
☎ 0974 845137

Apicella's deep-gold Oro della Tavola label is full bodied and well balanced, with hints of herbs, almonds, and tomatoes, and a warm, slightly bitter finish.

Marino

Agrópoli (Salerno)
☎ 0974 821719
🌐 www.vinimarino.com

Twenty-four acres (10ha) of olives, including *Frantoio* and *Leccino*, which give a fresh fruity edge to the Marino oil and a strong peppery, bitter aftertaste. Sometimes it bears a Cilento DOP label.

Radano, Frantoio Oleario Massimo

84070 Droro di Stella Cilento (Salerno)
☎ 0974 909003

Greenish oil under the Radano label: hints of herbs, fresh almonds, dried fruits, pepperiness, and a strong bitter aftertaste.

VAL CALORE

Puglia

This is the largest oil-producing region in Italy, and accounts for about two-fifths of Italy's national oil crop. It is divided into three main areas of production: the hillier parts of the province of Foggia, (especially in the Gargano Peninsula and in the foothills of the Apennines); the entire province of Bari; and the southern Salentine peninsula, which incorporates most of the provinces of Brindisi, Lecce, and Taranto.

HIGH-QUALITY OILS

Puglia is the one Italian region where olives stretch as far as the eye can see in all directions. There are 915,000 acres (370,000ha) devoted to olives and some 50 million trees. In some years Puglia produces as much as half of the Italian national crop; even in a "bad" year like 2002–2003 the figure was just over one-third. Quantity in this region is often matched by quality. Though disparaged by the producers of northern Italy, Puglian oils can be among Italy's best—often better than the overpriced oils of Umbria, Tuscany, and Garda. With four DOPs in Puglia and a fifth—Taranto—underway, almost every province in the region forms part of a denomination.

Puglia possesses the classic geology of areas where olives grow (*see p.23*); four-fifths of the land is made up of

THE DOP REGIONS OF PUGLIA

cretaceous limestone in its many forms. The rest of the region consists of flat, sedimentary plains like the vast prairies around Foggia, where wheat is grown to the virtual exclusion of all else.

Conical houses called *trulli* are the traditional buildings of the area around Alberobello and Martina Franca, and give the towns and landscapes their distinctive character. They are made like an igloo from a continuous course of flat limestone slabs spiraling up to a distinctive finial.

Underground oil: A Puglian tradition

Underground oil mills, the oldest dating back to the fifteenth century, were a tradition of Puglia, especially in the area of Salento. Cut out of the cool, soft rock 13ft (4m) deep and more, olives were processed here by traditional horse-powered grinders and presses. Men and beasts would spend as many as six months of the year transforming the harvest into oil. At the height of the season, two teams of men would take turns to work continuously around the clock until all the oil was stored in the large ceramic jars, which are still a specialty of such places as Grottiglie. There are fine examples of underground presses, which are open to visitors, in the grounds of the Villa Agreste, in Lamacavallo and Masseria il Frantoio near Ostuni, and Masseria Torre Coccaro near Fasano.

OGLIAROLA SALENTINO TREES AT MASSERIA S. DOMENICO

Affiorato oils

So-called "affiorato" oils are a Puglian specialty. After the olives are crushed, but before the pulp is pressed, a small amount of oil, known as the "flower" of the oil, rises to the surface and runs out of the sides. It is then skimmed off manually. According to its producers, 440lb (200kg) of olives might produce 1/3gal (1.5 liters) of affiorato oil.

L'AFFIORATO

MANY LOCAL CULTIVARS

The oils of Puglia differ enormously, according to the olive cultivar they are made from. There are many local varieties dominated by *Coratina*, supplemented by *Ogliarola Garganica*, *Ogliarola Salentina*, *Ogliarola Barese*, and *Cellina di Nardò* olives. All are noted for the excellent, fruity, rich oils they produce, far removed from the comparatively thin, bitter oils of northern Italy. The oil of Puglia is ridiculously undervalued and underpriced. Far too much is sold in bulk to big companies that blend it and resell it under their own branded names.

The *Coratina* olive comes from Corato near Bari and is the most important Puglian olive. It is found widely throughout southern Italy as well as abroad. The tree is medium-sized with a dense canopy. It has high oil yields (up to 26 percent, when irrigated) and its oil is fruity, bitter, and peppery. It is also strong in polyphenols, so it is very stable and long-lived. Unusually, the strong flavor improves with age and becomes aromatic, gentle, and almondy. The olives weigh up to 0.2oz (6g) when irrigated, and are suitable for table olives.

Ogliarola Barese is a medium-tall tree with long, pendulous fruiting branches. Most trees are ancient and unirrigated, tend toward biennial cropping, and produce fairly small fruits. Modern, irrigated plantations have bigger olives and larger, more constant yields. The oils are gentle and fruity with an aftertaste of almonds.

The *Cima di Mola* olive is said to be the oldest olive cultivar in Puglia. It makes a vigorous broad tree, which is not very tall. It produces small or medium-sized fruits with rather a low oil yield of (18–20 percent) of their weight. It is capable of producing high-quality oils, lightly fruity, and somewhat bitter.

FOGGIA

This is a province of immense geographical variations. The vast, flat, open prairie known as the Tavoliere plain around the city of Foggia is given over to the growing of grain, in particular durum wheat. Most of the olive production takes place in the hilly edges of the province, above all in the Gargano Peninsula. This promontary is a biological island, quite distinct from the rest of Italy.

The entire province of Foggia is entitled to produce DOP oils under the name of Dauno. This ruling is intended to improve standards of cultivation and production, and to raise brand awareness for the whole area. The different traditions within the province are each preserved by the name of a subzone. In the northwest, around Torremaggiore, is the area of Dauno

Alto Tavoliere. Here the oils contain a minimum of 80% *Peranzana* olives. Dauno Gargano is in the northeast; its oils must contain at least 70% *Ogliarola Garganica* olives. Oils produced in Dauno Basso Tavoliere in the southeast must contain at least 70% of the Bari olive, *Coratina*, while the Dauno Sub-Appennino area in the southwest is far less specific. The rules for this area say simply that 70% of the olives must be *Ogliarola Barese* and/or *Coratina* and/or *Rotondella*, which is an olive variety that comes from neighboring Campania. There is also an overlap between the subzones so that, for example, the area around Castelnuovo della Daunia qualifies to belong to both Dauno Alto Tavoliere and Dauno Sub-Appennino.

The northern and eastern sides of the Gargano peninsula are largely devoted to the cultivation of olives. Carpino, Vieste, and Mattinata are all major centers for growing olives. There are five producers in the small town of Carpino alone, which between them produce 2,000 tons of oil every year. Olives are also the major crop on the southern slopes around San Giovanni Rotondo and in the northwest around Sannicandro. *Ogliarola Garganica* is the traditional olive cultivar of the Gargano peninsula, but many modern plantations are devoted to the ubiquitous *Coratina*

OIL-MAKING ARTIFACTS
Old olive presses on display at Masseria Sant'Angelo dei Graecis in Fasano—one of the best olive museums in Italy.

olive, while *Peranzana* and *Rotondella* are also present in mixed plantations. There is little in the way of artificial irrigation, and most olives are picked by hand. However, the private estates in the Gargano Peninsula are usually large enough to be able to invest in modern machinery and methods of production.

The *Ogliarola Garganica* olive is indigenous to the Gargano peninsula, and accounts for 80–90 percent of all the oil produced. Its olives, though small, are sometimes used for the table, and give a soft, pale, fruity oil. Genetic analysis shows it is closely related to the Tuscan cultivar *Frantoio*.

DNA analysis has recently shown that the *Peranzana* olive is the same as the Sardinian *Bosana*, though it behaves differently in the two areas. It suffers from a tendency to biennial cropping. A tree may produce 220lb (100kg) of olives one year and no more than 22lb (10kg) the next. It produces fruity oils with a greenish tinge, which is unusual for Puglia, and an attractive bitter aftertaste.

BARI

The province of Bari is the epicenter of the Italian oil industry; here the cultivation of olives is at its most intensive and extensive. It is divided into three subzones of the Terra di Bari

TRULLI & OLIVE TREES IN ALBEROBELLO
Farmhouses in this olive-growing area are often "Trulli", whitewashed, rounded structures with cone-shaped roofs that are common in Bari.

DOP. Each of the subzones has very different traditions and produces quite different oils. The northwestern area, the largest, is called Castel del Monte. It is characterized by large, thickly planted estates, efficient mechanization, and the use of irrigation to reduce the problem of biennial cropping. There are some 160,615 acres (65,000ha) of olive trees here, mostly of the local cultivar *Coratina*.

Central Bari is known as the Conca Barese. This area has about 173,000 acres (70,000ha) of olives, but most are grown on small, unirrigated, mixed holdings of olives, vines, and almonds. In the center of the Conca Barese is the subzone Bitonto. To qualify for DOP status, at least 80% of the oil must come from either *Coratina* olives or from the very different *Ogliarola Barese* olive (also called *Cima di Bitonto*), or a mixture.

The southeastern corner of the province, the Murge, is also fairly thickly planted with olives, but the industry here

OLD WOODEN OIL
PRESS AT FASANO

is less sophisticated than elsewhere in Bari. The DOP subzone is known as "Murgia dei Trulli e delle Grotte" and available only to oils containing at least 50% *Cima di Mola* olives, but it is not yet fully developed.

BRINDISI

The best olive oils of Brindisi are delicious. They are soft, gentle, rounded, and intensely fruity. Unfortunately, this is considered an old-fashioned taste: it is the very antithesis of the hard, hot Tuscan oils that are currently so popular. Brindisi oil is also excellent value; far too much is sold in bulk to big blenders in the north of Italy.

The best oils are found in the northwest of the province, which has DOP status as Collina di Brindisi. Their quality comes from the *Ogliarola Salentina* olive, which must account for a minimum of 70% of any DOP oil; the rest is made up from whatever else is grown locally, which includes *Cellina di Nardò*, *Coratina*, *Frantoio*, *Leccino*, and even the French olive, *Picholine*. Good producers,

EXTENSIVE PLANTATIONS Olive trees (here in Bari) often occupy the middle ground between vines at the bottom of the valley and pine woods on the surrounding hills.

such as the Balestrazzi family at Il Frantoio, use the remaining 30% to create character and add distinction to their oils.

The coastal soils of the Collina di Brindisi DOP area are extremely fertile. Many of the older trees are very old indeed, some as much as 1,000 years of age—huge, gnarled specimens that grow to 50ft (15m) in height. They are appreciated for their historical significance and landscape importance, and either maintained in a parklike setting or kept as ancient sentinels within new plantations. Part of the Terra d'Otranto in Lecce also falls into this DOP (see below). Brindisi has many large estates, known as *masserie*, with handsome houses at their center. Some were built as baroque palaces, others converted from old abbeys or early Renaissance fortresses. There are cooperatives in every town, some of which produce excellent oil, but the large estates still form the mainstay of the high-quality section of the industry.

Of the local olives in Brindisi, *Ogliarola Salentina* is a medium-tall tree with rather open shape. The olives are usually picked late, when they have turned black, and give a high yield (25 percent) of fruity, soft, and aromatic oil. *Cellina di Nardò* is hardier, and also widely grown in Lecce, Taranto, and southern Brindisi, but flourishes in the most unpromising situations. It grows extremely vigorously, eventually reaching 65ft (20m). The olives are small, hard, and difficult to pick until they have ripened and started to turn black. The olives have a low yield (seldom more than 18 percent), and the oil is fruity, soft, and lightly bitter.

LECCE AND TARANTO

The entire province of Lecce is included in the new Terra d'Otranto DOP, as are adjoining parts of eastern Taranto and

OLIVE JAR AT FRANTOIO
GALATINO

southern Brindisi. The Brindisi part has a distinct denomination named Delle Gravine Joniche, which enables it to use a blend of up to 50% *Ogliarola Salentina* and *Leccino* olives as well as up to 20% *Coratina*. Elsewhere, *Cellina di Nardò* and *Ogliarola Salentina* olives must account for a minimum 60% of the oil, with the balance composed of any other olives in the area. Producers generally choose *Leccino, Coratina,* and *Frantoio* olives. This means that there is quite a difference in taste between the many oils that qualify for Terra d'Otranto DOP status. That said, the oils are usually gentle, fairly fruity, and smooth, with only the lightest touch of bitterness or pepperiness. The best oils are very good indeed.

In Taranto there are some 6,000 olive growers, producing 251,000gal (950,000 liters) of extra virgin oil in a typical year. A small part of eastern Taranto falls into the Terra d'Otranto DOP; the rest of the province is shortly to be accorded its own DOP status with the name Terre Tarentine. This new DOP will cover all the province west of the city of Taranto, plus the northern areas around the towns of Martina Franca, Monteiasi, and Montemesola, which can already qualify for the Terre d'Otranto DOP. The area around Martina Franca is especially well known for its high-quality oils.

The rules for the Terre Tarentine oils are fairly lax. They require that 80% of olives used should be *Leccino, Coratina, Ogliarola,* or *Frantoio,* either individually or mixed, and that the balance of 20% may be composed of other cultivars. This means that the oils will have a very variable composition and flavor. But the purpose of such DOP rules is to improve quality, encourage recognition, and increase the locality's reputation for high-quality oil—and eventually its price, too.

LAGO DI VARANO Olives have been grown for centuries on the limestone hills of the Gargano peninsula.

Leading producers in Foggia

Bisceglia

71030 Mattinata (Foggia)
0884 551003
W www.biologico.it

The 37-acre (15ha) Bisceglia estate is one of the leading organic producers on the Gargano peninsula and its Mattinata Bisceglia oil has a DOP Dauno Gargano certificate. It is medium fruity, fresh, and lightly peppery, with a smooth aftertaste of almonds.

Clemente, Olearia

71043 Manfredonia (Foggia)
0884 543955
W www.oleariaclemente.it

Clemente's principal oils are the extra virgin Re Manfredi (DOP Dauno Gargano) and a non-DOP oil sold under the label Le Zagare. Re Manfredi is very well made, with a long, well balanced flavor. It gives a first impression of smoothness and fragrance, but then develops a soft, fruity taste of cut grass and fresh almonds.

Fortore

71017 Torremaggiore (Foggia)
0882 385111
W www.fortore.it

Fortore is the market leader in northern Foggia. The cooperative was founded in 1960 and now has some 1,500 members. It is a consistent prize-winner at national shows, and its successes have helped raise the profile of the whole Dauno region. Its Terra Maioris oil is first rate, with a deep green tinge and a strong, fruity, grassy taste, followed by hints of herbs and almonds, and enough bitterness and pepperiness to give body to the aftertaste.

Other Producers in Foggia

Associazione Produttori Olivicoli di Foggia

71100 Foggia
0881 721153
W www.aprolfoggia.it

This is a large secondary cooperative with 20,000 individual members and a new DOP Dauno oil.

Coppadoro, Tenuta

Via Tiberio Solis, 128
71016 San Severo (Foggia)
0882 242301
W www.spiavento.it

This wine estate nows makes very promising DOP Dauno oil under its Spiavento label—soft and fruity at first, with hints of herbs, grass, and bitter almonds, quickly followed by a peppery, bitter aftertaste. The Zecchino label is also well regarded, made from 80% *Ogliarola Garganica* and 20% *Peranzana*.

Di Ianni, Francesco

Contrada da Cisterne
71017 Torremaggiore (Foggia)
0882 39293

Produces an organic Dauno Alto Tavoliere oil Èlaion from *Peranzana* olives, in which the powerful finish of the olives is dominant.

GR.A.C.O.

Cda. Pagliaravecchia
71017 Torremaggiore (Foggia)
0882 386505
W www.gracoonline.it

GR.A.C.O produces a stunning, unfiltered, 100% *Peranzana* oil sold as Graco with a DOP Dauno Alto

Tavoliere label. It is greeny gold in color, fresh, cool, powerful, grassy, almondy, and peppery.

Monopoli, F.lli

71042 Cerignola (Foggia)
☎ 0885 422717
W www.giardinodelsole.it

Monopoli are known for their Giardino del Sole label, made from 100% *Coratina* olives, which was the first oil to be registered as a Dauno Basso Tavoliere DOP. They have recently introduced a well made *denocciolato* oil, which is green, intensely flavored, with hints of cut grass, chicory, and dandelions, and a very powerful aftertaste of bitterness and pepperiness—a well made, well balanced oil for those who like their oil with lots of flavor.

Ortore e Figli, Nicola A.

71010 Carpino (Foggia)
☎ 0884 997107
W www.ortore.com

Organic, unfiltered oil made from *Ogliarola Garganica* olives called Castellum Caprelis. It is soft, lightly fruity, almondy, and delicious.

Sacco, Vincenzo

71017 Torremaggiore (Foggia)
☎ 0882 386274
W www.sololio.com

A forward-looking producer of high-quality organic oils from *Peranzana* and *Rotondella* olives, Sololio is its DOP Dauno Alto Tavoliere label.

Trombetta Giovanni & C., Oleificio di

71010 Carpino (Foggia)
☎ 0884 900426
W www.siogargano.com

One of the larger producers in the Gargano, Trombetta make a fine unfiltered DOP Dauro Gargano oil called Siogargano, whose gentle, fruity taste ends with an almondy aftertaste.

Leading producers in Bari

De Carlo, Frantoio Oleario

70020 Bitritto (Bari)
☎ 080 630767
W www.oliodecarlo.com

The De Carlo family were among the first in Puglia to invest not only in modern oil-extraction machinery but also in the know-how to use it successfully. Their stone-ground Fruttato Delicato Torre di Mossa DOP Terra di Bari Bitonto oil is gentle, fruity, grassy, and fresh—Puglia at its best—but their Tenuta Arcamone and Contrada Torre Marina oils are likewise excellent. There are 124 acres (50ha) of olives on their estates—some 7,000 trees. They also sell table olives—*Bella di Cerignola* and the very local *Termite di Bitetto*.

TORRE DI MOSSA

Galantino, Frantoio Oleario F.lli

70052 Bisceglie (Bari)
☎ 080 3921320
W www.galantino.it

Galantino harvests 15,000 olive trees from the 116 acres (47ha) of its La Fenice estate and also buys olives from some 2,000 independent growers in northern Puglia. About 60% are *Ogliarola Barese* and 40% are *Coratina*. The company's oils use different proportions in their blend. One of the best is L'Affiorato, which is smooth and lightly fruity with a long, warm, almondy aftertaste. It

is made from the first skimmings of the press and usually has a preponderance of *Ogliarola Barese*. Also good is the gutsy Terra di Bari oil, made mainly from *Coratina* olives and altogether much more powerfully flavored. It is widely considered the best of all Castel del Monte DOP oils.

Minervini, Ing. Gregorio

70056 Molfetta (Bari)
☎ 080 3974369
W www.marcinase.it

Gregorio and Maria Minervini are the leading producers of organic oils in Bari, and manage to combine a traditional method of cultivating, picking, and processing olives with a modern approach to extraction and storage. All their oils qualify for the Terra di Bari Bitonto DOP and have won innumerable prizes and plaudits in recent years: Fruttato Leggero is largely from *Ogliarola Barese*, and a light, fruity, apple-flavored oil with a gentle hint of almonds; Fruttato Medio is a blend of *Coratina* and *Maiatica*. It has a delicious balance of green fruity tastes, herbs, and nuttiness, without too much pepperiness; Fruttato Intenso is a really big, fruity oil, made largely from *Coratina* olives. It has a strong taste of cut grass and tomatoes, followed by a powerful sensation of pepperiness and bitterness—long lasting and very well balanced, a real mouthful.

Pellegrino, Frantoio Oleario

70031 Andria (Bari)
☎ 0883 569770

A 16th-century *masseria* and 197 acres (80ha) of olive trees are at the heart of this top producer. It offers five different oils, predominantly from *Coratina*, some with a little *Ogliarola Barese* and *Carolea* too. Spineta is the most prestigious. It is grassy, full bodied, and almondy, with a long-lasting aftertaste of pepperiness and bitterness to round it off.

Rasciatano, Tenuta

70051 Barletta (Bari)
☎ 0883 510999
🖥 www.tenutarasciatano.com

Tenuta Rasciatano is a large estate of 370 acres (150ha), of which 197 acres (80ha) are devoted to olive growing —12,000 trees of *Coratina*, each on average 200 years old. There are two Rasciatano labels, red (organic) and green (plain), both good. The red label is golden yellow, grassy, and almondy, with a nicely balanced aftertaste of pepperiness and bitterness.

Rivera, Vinicola

70031 Andria (Bari)
☎ 0883 569501
🖥 www.rivera.it

The Rivera estate near Emperor Frederick II's Castel del Monte is best known for its wines, but 70% of its surface is put to olives, mostly *Coratina*. The Tenute De Corato label has a small addition of *Leccino*, *Picholine*, and *Tonda Iblea*; the result is a lightly fruity oil with a delicious aftertaste, gently bitter and peppery.

Other producers in Bari

ASSO.PR.OLI (Associazione Produttori Olivicoli)

70121 Bari
☎ 080 5539135
🖥 www.assoproli.it

This big cooperative (with more than 40,000 members) offers three Terra di Bari DOPs oils—a Bitonto, a Castel del Monte, and an organic Biologico. All are good examples of their type.

Parisi, Francesco

70032 Bitonto (Bari)
☎ 080 9911568
🖥 www.ilbosco.it

Parisi's *affiorato* oil Gocce del Mediterraneo is creamed from the first pressings on its 197-acre (80ha) estate. Its extra virgin Il Bosco is also good. Both are a blend of *Ogliarola Barese* and *Coratina*.

Santa Croce e Sant'Aloja,

70053 Canosa di Puglia (Bari)
☎ 0883 664536

The well made Santa Croce e Sant'Aloja Terra di Bari Castel del Monte oil is 100% *Coratina* and very fruity with a smell of grass and apple and a taste of vegetables and almonds. It is balanced, bitter, and peppery.

Viterbo, Oleificio Sociale Cooperativo

700013 Castellana Grotte (Bari)
☎ 080 4965617
🖥 www.montaltino.com

This is the leading cooperative in the Murge and an example of what is possible in this traditional corner of the provinces. Its Montaltino label is pale green gold in color, but rich and fruity with a taste of pears and almonds and a pleasant degree of bitterness and pepperiness in the aftertaste.

MONTALTINO

Leading producers in Brindisi

Asciano, Masseria

72017 Ostuni (Brindisi)
☎ 0831 330712
🖥 www.olioasciano.it

Asciano's 173 acres (70ha) are organically run and support about 12,500 olive trees. There are three blends: Amaro (bitter), Medio (medium), and Dolce (gentle), which has a mild taste of herbs and sweet almonds. All are good.

Coopir De Laurentis

72017 Ostuni (Brindisi)
☎ 0831 331140
🖥 www.coopirdelaurentis.com

This cooperative's Collina di Brindisi Coopir "De Laurentis" is very well made from the olives of its 1,500 members. It is medium fruity and fragrant, with a light scent of tomatoes and a taste of sweet almonds, pears, and tomatoes again. It is more full bodied than is usual among Brindisi oils, with more pepperiness and bitterness as the taste develops in the mouth.

Il Frantoio

72017 Ostuni (Brindisi)
☎ 0831 330276
🖥 www.trecolline.it

The *masseria* at the center of the 173-acre (70ha) Il Frantoio estate operates as a private hotel. Some of the Balestrazzi family's *Ogliarola Salentina* olive trees are more than 500 years old, but they are supplemented by young plantings of *Frantoio*, *Coratina*, *Picholine*, and *Cima di Melfi* olives. These are sometimes offered as monocultivar oils too and used to add character to their Collina di Brindisi DOP oils. Their Tre Colline Masseria Il Frantoio oil is yellow, soft, fruity, and easy, with a taste of sweet almonds and just a little pepperiness afterward. But their Monovarietà Leccino has been the greatest success. It is soft, fruity, and nutty, with a gentle hint of vanilla and almonds—an oil of quality and balance.

Sant'Angelo de' Graecis, Masseria

72015 Fasano (Brindisi)
☎ 080 4413471
W www.masseriamati.it

Year after year, this estate produces one of Puglia's best olive oils—the skillfully made, unfiltered, and intensely fruity Tre Colline. But it is a cool, soft, juicy fruitiness, with a taste of pears and a hint of almonds, and almost no trace of bitterness or pepperiness. The oil is the quintessence of Brindisi oils. The beautiful house at the center of the estate is called Abbazia di San Lorenzo, and dates from the 1660s. Near the entrance is a museum of olives and olive oil, the best in southern Italy, with a great variety of ancient presses, implements, and equipment—well worth a visit.

TRE COLLINE

Stasi

72028 Torre Santa Susanna (Brindisi)
☎ 0831 745586
W www.agricolestasi.it

The castle at the center of the Stasi estate is a majestic 16th-century fortress. Some 141 of its 272 acres (57 of its 110ha) are devoted to olive growing and support a total of about 15,000 olive trees. There has been much

CORTI VECCHIE

experimental planting in recent years, so the estate grows an unusually large number of different olive cultivars. Each is harvested separately, pressed within four hours, and stored separately (until it is used for blending) under nitrogen to prevent oxidization. Stasi's Corti Vecchie Extravergine has won many prizes—and deservedly, for it is very well made. It has a sweet smell and a very smooth, soft, rich, almost creamy texture, followed by a light taste of pears and almonds and a gentle, warm aftertaste.

Other producers in Brindisi

Fasano, Oleificio Cooperativo di

Via dell'Artigianato 21
72015 Fasano (Brindisi)
☎ 080 4413446

The dynamic Maria Guarini makes some of the best oils in all Italy on behalf of landowners throughout the Collina di Brindisi.

Frantolio di d'Amico Pietro, Il

72014 Cisternino (Brindisi)
☎ 080 4444671
W www.ilfrantolio.it

Sovrano is their Collina di

Brindisi DOP oil, while Lacrima is a most unusual oil made from seven ancient unnamed cultivars grown on the estate.

Raggio Verde

C. da Pico n.8
72014 Cisternino (Brindisi)
☎ 080 4449198

One of the leading organic producers—and good.

San Domenico, Masseria

72015 Savelletri di Fasano (Brindisi)
☎ 080 4827769
W www.masseriasandomenico.com

Now a luxury hotel with its own golf course, San Domenico has 148 acres (60ha) of stupendously beautiful old olive trees and makes a delicious Extravergine di Masseria San Domenico.

SAN DOMENICO

Serenerba, Biologica

72017 Ostuni (Brindisi)
☎ 0831 330276
W www.meridiano17est.it

Two organic *Ogliarola Salentina* oils: Olio delle Pendici is picked early in the season and has an intense "green" taste, while the late-picked Meridiano is ripe, gentle, and smooth.

Torricella, Masseria

72021 Francavilla Fontana (Brindisi)
☎ 0831 841697
W www.masseriatorricella.com

Excellent monocultivar Coratino and Leccino oils.

Leading producers in Lecce and Taranto

Aprol Lecce

73100 Lecce
☎ 0832 280250
W www.aprol.it

Aprol (short for *Associazione tra Produttori Olivicoli della Provincia di Lecce*) is one of the largest secondary cooperatives in Italy, with 54,000 producers and 68 cooperatives as members. Its Extravergine Aprol Lecce oil (widely sold throughout Puglia) is a high-quality selection made from *Ogliarola Salentina* and *Cellina di Nardò* —gentle, herbaceous, and smooth, with a touch of pepperiness and bitterness that develop later and give character to the blend.

Caposella

Piazzetta Montale 3
73100 Lecce
☎ 0832 354592

The Petrucci family grow olives in two locations in the south of the province. One, near Otranto, has 44 acres (18ha) of *Cellina di Nardò*, whose oil is sold as Masseria Furca: cool and fairly fruity, with a green taste and a light aftertaste, slightly bitter, peppery. The other location

is in the Ugento area, where 62 acres (25ha) support no more than 1,000 very ancient, unirrigated *Ogliarola Salentina* trees growing around the 15th-century *masseria*. The oil from this farm is more complex; it is sold as Masseria Caposella, and has won many prizes. Unfiltered, cool, and very fruity, it is currently the best oil in Lecce, with aromas of apple, pear, almonds, and fresh grass, and a long, warm aftertaste. Both oils are of exceptional quality.

MASSERIA CAPOSELLA

Caricato

73010 San Pietro in Lama (Lecce)
☎ 0832 631160
W www.caricato.it

This 52-acre (21ha) estate has three labels: Lucrezio, made mainly from *Cellina di Nardò* and *Ogliarola Salentino* with a fresh vegetable taste; the rather more robust Caricato from the same olives plus the Sicilian *Tonda Iblea*; and an *affiorato* oil, Di Affioramento, which is intensely fresh and fruity.

Caroli, Frantoio Oleario Stefano (Antico Masseria)

74015 Martina Franca (Taranto)
☎ 080 4490402
W www.caroli.it

The Caroli family own two estates high in the hills above the flat plains of the Tarentine littoral and offer a wide range of oils, each intended to express a different type or style. These include Agricoltura Biologica, which is organic, and the Novello label, made from *Leccino* and *Ogliarola* olives, which is fresh, unfiltered, and best consumed within six months of making. Caroli's premium products are the fruity, grassy Gusto Fruttato (mainly from *Carolea*, *Leccino*, and *Ogliarola*) and the gentler Gusto Delicato, made from *Frantoio* and *Leccino*. Its flagship is Monti del Duca, a fine, Tuscan-style oil, usually made from *Leccino*, *Coratina*, and *Frantoio*. Deep gold, very fluid, and medium fruity, it has a taste of cut grass and herbs, and a strong, peppery aftertaste. Caroli's straightforward Classico and Messapico lines are also high-quality oils.

Guarini, Duca Carlo

Largo Frisari 1
73020 Scorrano (Lecce)
☎ 0836 460288

This is a large estate: the Guarini family say it was founded by Roger Guarini

OLIVE FORESTS Thousands of olive trees grow on flat plains in the province of Taranto.

GUARINI

in 1065. It has at least 18,000 centennial trees (no one has ever counted them), some as old as 500 years. One-fifth are of *Ogliarola Salentina* and the rest are *Cellina di Nardò*. Their oil—the only one—is one of Puglia's best. It is cool and soft with an unusual taste of bananas at first; later come hints of apple and almonds, and an attractive warm, persistent aftertaste.

Monacelli, Tenuta

73016 San Cesario (Lecce)
☎ 0832 382037
🖥 www.tenutamonacelli.com

The Monacelli estate is famous for its restaurant "Il Rifugio del Re" but also offers four different oils with astronomical names: Luna, Sole, Terre del Sole, and Raggio di Luna. Sole is especially robust, not typical of Lecce, but good, with a soft, nutty taste that develops a hint of artichokes, cut grass, and sweet almonds, followed by a forceful, long-lasting, peppery aftertaste and a pleasant hint of bitterness.

SOLE

Piantatella

74010 Statte (Taranto)
☎ 099 4722963
🖥 www.piantatella.it

Piantella grows mainly *Frantoio*, *Leccino*, and *Pendolino*, as well as the Puglian *Coratina* and *Peranzana*. It has about 8,500 trees on 96 acres (39ha). Its two brands are called simply Fruttato Leggero and Fruttato Medio, the latter fuller than the delicate Fruttato Leggero. Both are well made, harmonious, balanced oils, and, as often in Puglia, very good value. Given the rather loose rules for the new Terre Tarentine DOP, we can expect to see more such oils from the province in future.

Vetrere

74020 Taranto
☎ 099 5661054
🖥 www.vetrere.it

Vetrere is a large wine-and-oil estate on the fertile plains inland from Taranto. It includes 356 acres (144ha) of olive orchards, with some 14,200 trees, 70% of which are *Ogliarola Salentino*, with the balance made up of *Coratina*, *Frantoio*, and *Leccino*. Vetrere offers two oils; a fine Olio Extravergine Vetrere and its organic equivalent Biologico. Both have a very green, fruity taste, are smooth and cool, with hints of cut grass, herbs, and green tomatoes, followed by an aftertaste of bitterness and pepperiness as the fruit fades.

Other producers in Lecce

Adamo

73040 Alliste (Lecce)
☎ 0833 584346
🖥 www.ag.adamo.it

Adamo's 123 acres (50ha) of *Picholine*, *Ogliarola*, *Salentina*, and *Cellina di Nardò* produce a prize-winning DOP oil

called Le Chianche and a remarkable, soft, fruity *affiorato* oil called Il Fior d'Olio. Their ordinary Adamo extra virgin oil is also good.

Cito, Dott. Luigi

Via Unità d'Italia 3
73020 San Cassiano (Lecce)
☎ 0836 992076

Tenuta Tresca is a nicely balanced, medium-fruity oil made from a blend of six different olive cultivars.

Gianni Calogiuri

73023 Lizzanello (Lecce)
☎ 0832-651729
🖥 www.vincotto.com

Calogiuri produces an excellent *affiorato* oil, Gianni Calogiuri, which is surprisingly robust.

Santa Venia, Masseria

73010 Veglie (Lecce)
☎ 0832 966467
🖥 www.santavenia.it

One-third of the 790 acres (320ha) here are organic *Ogliarola Salentina* and *Cellina di Nardò* olives. The gentle, fruity oils produced include an organic Bio and a DOP Terra d'Otranto.

Sapori del Salento di Stefanicò

73039 Tricase (Lecce)
☎ 0833 544759
🖥 www.orgoglio.it

The Orgoglia label is soft and nutty, made largely from *Leccino* and *Ogliarola Salentino*.

Tamborino Frisari, Franco

73024 Maglie (Lecce)
☎ 0836 484436
🖥 www.cortededroso.it

The main label here is Corte de' Droso, and it includes an Affiorato oil, a Delicato oil from *Leccino*, *Carolea*, and *Frantoio*, a prize-winning Intenso from *Picholine*, *Tonda Iblea*, and *Carolea*, and a traditional DOP Terra d'Otranto from *Cellina di Nardò* and *Ogliarola Salentino* olives. All are respectable, and often excellent.

Basilicata

There are some 79,000 acres (32,000ha) of olives and five million trees in Basilicata, and the figure is increasing steadily. The most widely planted cultivars are local specialties: Cima di Melfi *in Potenza, and* Maiatica *and* Ogliarola del Bradano *in Matera. All are capable of producing excellent oil—and quality is improving throughout the region. Many of the better producers blend in a measure of "foreign" olives, such as the Tuscan* Leccino *or the Puglian* Coratino.

THE OLIVE REGIONS OF BASILICATA

POTENZA AND MATERA

There are two DOPs awaiting formal recognition in this region: Colline del Vulture in the north of Potenza and Colline Lucane in Matera. The Colline del Vulture covers the foothills and plains to the east of the extinct volcano, Monte Vulture. Here, the terrain is difficult. The plantations tend to be small, as are the trees, which are mainly *Cima di Melfi*. Colline del Vulture oils are medium fruity and pale yellow, with a taste of cut grass and almonds, and a fine bitter and peppery ending.

The Colline Lucane is usually divided into two areas, one around Ferrandina and the other in the hills near Matera. Ferrandina overlooks the Basento valley, whose steep, north-facing slopes are thickly planted with olives. This area is the stronghold of the *Maiatica* olive, a vigorous, heavy-yielding cultivar that tends toward biennial cropping (*see p.27*). The olives are plump and fleshy, (they are often cured black in salt). However, they are susceptible to olive fly (*see p.24*).

The golden-yellow oil of the *Maiatica* olive has a particularly delicate taste. Local producers (often small-scale, intensive, and new) have in recent years used it to create high-quality oils. It may also be treated as a table olive.

On the arid, open hillsides around Matera the local olive is *Ogliarola del Bradano*. The oils produced by this cultivar are greener and fruitier than the *Maiatica* oils of Ferrandina. Throughout Basilicata, irrigation is rare and yields subject to biennial cropping.

OLIVES IN POTENZA *Cima di Melfi* olives dominate the Colline del Vulture landscape near Barile.

Leading producers in Basilicata

Lacertosa, Frantoio Oleario Giovanni

Via Sinisgalli 29
75013 Ferrandina (Matera)
☎ 0835 556098

This is a large estate that includes 148 acres (60ha) of *Maiatica* and *Ogliarola del Bradano*, plus a little *Coratina* and *Leccino*. Its Don Giovanni label is soft, smooth, and mild with a taste of grass, herbs, and almonds—a most elegant, balanced, and harmonious oil.

DON GIOVANNI

L'Orto di Lucania

75024 Montescaglioso (Matera)
☎ 0835 202195
W www.ortodilucania.it

A fraction of this 620-acre (250ha) estate is given to olives, but its L'Orto di Lucania oil (from *Coratina* and *Maiatica*) is good—greeny yellow, soft, fruity, almondy, with a warm persistent aftertaste of pepperiness and bitterness.

Quarto, F.lli

C. da Due Gravine
75100 Matera
☎ 0835 319977

The Quarto brothers have 61 acres (25ha) and 9,000 trees—*Coratina*, *Cima di Melfi*, and *Ogliarola del Bradano*, plus a little *Frantoio* and *Leccino*. Their flagship Tenute Zagarelle has a cool, fresh taste of grass, apples, and almonds, and a long, warm, peppery aftertaste. Due Gravine is milder and less fruity, but no less balanced and well made.

Sapori Lucani, Frantoio Oleario

75010 Stigliano (Matera)
Tel:0835 565461
W www.sapori-lucani.com

The Extravergine Sapori Lucani, made largely from *Maiatica* olives bought in from the area around Stigliano, is greeny yellow with a taste of green vegetables and almonds, then a strong but nicely balanced aftertaste of bitterness and pepperiness.

Valluzzi, Frantoio Donato

75010 San Mauro Forte (Matera)
☎ 0835 674113
W www.lamaiatica.it

Valluzzi buys in most of its olives, but has for many years won prizes for its complex, elegant, unfiltered La Majatica oil, made only from *Maiatica* olives. It has a fresh herbaceous taste of cut grass and green tomatoes followed by a long warm, lightly bitter aftertaste.

Other producers in Basilicata

Cifarelli, Angela

75100 Matera
☎ 0835 312380
W www.oliodeisassi.com

Angela Cifarelli has three estates. Her olives are young plants of *Ogliarola del Bradano*, *Coratina*, *Frantoio*, and *Carolea*—an interesting combination. Olio dei Sassi is full flavored, with herbaceous aromas, a ripe taste of apples and almonds, and a strong, balanced, persistent aftertaste of bitterness and pepperiness. Excellent.

Elaiopolio Cooperativo di Barile

Via Nazionale R.55
85022 Barile (Potenza)

This is by far the best cooperative in the Vulture area. Its Gran Feudo oil is based on *Cima di Melfi* olives and has a light fruity taste of tomatoes, green vegetables, and sweet almonds—well balanced and delicate.

Lucano, Oleificio

S.S. 93 – Km.53
85010 Lavello (Potenza)
☎ 0972 85194

Oleificio Lucano's Rinelli oil is fresh and fruity, with a taste of artichokes, chicory, and cut grass, and a good measure of bitterness and pepperiness to follow. It is made from an unusual blend of cultivars—*Ogliarola del Bradano*, *Scarpeta*, *Coratina*, and *Raccioppella*.

Oroverde Lucano

Via Basentana
75013 Ferrandina,
(Matera)
☎ 0835 754806

LA LACRIMA

This progressive producer has two high-quality labels, both well made and good value. La Majatica is a light, fresh, smooth, green-tasting oil with hints of artichoke and vegetables. La Lacrima is milder but with a similar herbaceous taste and a lightly bitter aftertaste. It has a little *Coratina* in its mix of olives. Both are extracted using the Sineola method

Robbe, Antonio

85020 Montemilone (Potenza)
☎ 0972 99020
W www.masseriaperillo.com

The Robbe estate at the foot of the Vulture hills is organic and irrigated. They use nontraditional olives like *Coratina*, *Leccino*, and *Frantoio*. The result is an oil that tastes like a light Tuscan at a fraction of the price: Masseria Perillo has a rich texture with a taste of new-mown grass and artichokes, and a nice degree of pepperiness to follow.

Calabria

This is the second-largest region in Italy for olive-oil production, with some 470,000 acres (190,000ha) of olives. Two distinct industries exist in Calabria. In the irrigated lowlands and plains, high-quality, modern cultivation produces oils of real distinction. Inland, and in the uplands, old-fashioned ways persist and much of the oil is fit only for refining. The contrast is all the more striking because the best oils of Calabria are very good indeed. As in most of Italy, the leading producers are the large estates whose extensive landholdings justify investment in the means of producing high-quality oil.

THE DOP REGIONS OF CALABRIA

COSENZA & CATANZARO

Carolea is the typical olive cultivar of Calabria and grown in every province, but especially in Cosenza and Catanzaro. The trees produce regular heavy crops of fruits that are about 0.14oz (4g) in weight—more, if the trees are irrigated—and give a good oil yield. They are also cured as table olives. *Carolea* oils are of fine quality. They are medium fruity and have a fresh, succulent taste, and a light aftertaste of pepperiness and bitterness. They are, however, unusually low in polyphenols, and therefore do not keep for very long.

Cosenza has a major DOP called Bruzio, with four subzones all based on local olive cultivars: Fascia Prepollinica and Valle Crati (both *Carolea* and *Tondina*), Colline Joniche Presilane

(*Rossanese*), and Sibaritide (*Grossa di Cassano*). Catanzaro has one DOP, Lametia, whose oils must be made from at least 90% *Carolea* olives.

CROTONE, VIBO VALENTINA & REGGIO CALABRIA

There is one DOP in Crotone—Alto Crotonese—which uses mainly *Carolea* olives. A second DOP, Marchesato di Crotone (based on *Carolea* and *Rossanese* olives) is on the way. In Reggio Calabria, DOPs may also soon be sought for Conca degli Olivi and Geracese della Locride. Three remarkable cultivars grow here and in Vibo Valentia. *Sinopolese* trees reach 82ft (25m). The other two are *Ciciarello* and *Ottobratica*, which has an almond flavor. These three cultivars produce oils that are soft and fruity with delicate and unusual flavors.

TRADITIONAL CULTIVATION Vines are planted on fertile flat land, while olives thrive on the stony hillside.

Leading producers in Cosenza & Catanzaro

De Lorenzo & C.,

88040 S. Eufémia Lamezia Terme (Catanzano)

☎ 0968 51065

🌐 www.tesoridelsole.com

The De Lorenzo family has more than 247 acres (100ha) of olives, almost all *Carolea*, around their handsome house in the flat and fertile plain of Lamezia. Their best oil is Livara, which qualifies for DOP Lametia status and is greeny gold with a fresh grassy smell and a taste that recalls artichokes, cut grass, almonds, and ripe olives. It has a big aftertaste of bitterness and pepperiness, but the oil itself has a "big" taste, too, so the result is balanced and harmonious.

Stancati Maria Vittoria

C.da Padula Inferiore
87047 San Pietro in Guarano (Cosenza)

☎ 0984 838615

This leading organic producer has 49 acres (20ha) of olive trees (both ancient and modern): 29 acres (12ha) are of *Carolea*, and the rest of *Coratina*, *Leccino*, and *Nocellara del Bélice*. *Carolea* is the dominant cultivar in Stancati's powerful Padula oil —greeny gold, with a taste of fresh grass, green tomatoes, and bitter almonds, followed by a strong, long-lasting sense of bitterness and pepperiness.

Gabro, Oleificio

87011 Lauropoli (Cosenza)

☎ 0981 70339

🌐 www.gabro.it

Gabro is one of the most innovative producers in Calabria, with a large following in northern Europe and North America. Its Olio Biologico is made from a wide range of cultivars grown on

GABRO BRUZIO-SIBARITIDE

the firm's own experimental estates. Its Extravergine Bruzio-Sibaritide (one of very few oils to bear that denomination) is a remarkably fruity oil with a strong taste of pears and a buttery texture, which is both unusual and delicious.

Other producers in Cosenza & Catanzaro

Acconia Antica

C. da Favarella
88022 Curinga (Catanzano)

☎ 0968 78057

The Bevilacqua family has 160 acres (65ha) of *Carolea* olives—some more than 500 years old. Its Favarello DOP Lametia oil is greeny gold and delicately fruity, with an aftertaste of almonds, then a light touch of bitterness and pepperiness. Donnavascia is likewise gentle, fruity, and almondy, and, because *Carolea* loses its fruitiness quickly, later acquires a soft, creamy opulence.

Fattorie Greco

87063 Cariati Marina (Cosenza)

☎ 0983 969441

🌐 www.fattoriegreco.it

The Greco family is one of the largest producers of high-quality olive oil in

Calabria—all sourced from organic growers. The Fattorie Greco Biologico and San Tommaso Biologico are both good—gentle, fruity, and well made.

Geraci, Frantoio Oleario Francesco

87064 Corigliano Calabro (Cosenza)

☎ 0983 81969

🌐 www.frantoiogeraci.com

Geraci's Oro Dolce oil bears a Bruzio DOP and is made solely from *Rossanese*. It is golden yellow with a "green" taste of artichokes and herbs, and an aftertaste of bitterness and enough pepperiness to give it body.

Le Conche di Miraglia, Angela

87043 Bisignano (Cosenza)

☎ 0984 941239

🌐 www.leconche.it

This organic estate produces a fruity Extravergine Le Conche DOP Bruzio Valle Crati oil where the influence of *Carolea* dominates. It has a grassy scent, a strong fruity taste, a hint of sweet almonds as it ages.

LIBRANDI

Librandi Pasquale

87060 Vaccarizzo Albanese (Cosenza)

☎ 0983 84068

🌐 www.oliolibrandi.it

This organic estate produces a remarkable oil, mainly from *Rossanese* olives. Librandi is very fruity, with an

OLIVE WHEELS An ancient pair of stone grinders, or "mashers," are put to ornamental use in Roberto Ceraudo's garden.

excellent flavor of cut grass and green vegetables, and a warm, not too powerful aftertaste.

Marchianò, F. Marcello

Via Castritoa 72
87069 S. Demetrio Corone (Cosenza)
☎ 0984 956018

Smooth, cool, creamy, organic Marchianò has an aromatic taste of herbs and a gentle, warm aftertaste.

Romano Angelo

C. Bellezza, 87069 San Demetrio Corone (Cosenza)
☎ 0984 910140

The all-organic Romano estate (30 acres/12ha) is unusual because it has substantial plantings of Sicilian *Nocellara del Bélice* and Puglian *Coratina*, as well as the traditional *Carolea* and *Rossanese*. Romano is golden yellow, with a soft, cool, fruity, grassy, nutty taste, and a light aftertaste of bitterness and pepperiness—very harmonious and smooth.

San Mauro

C. da Mezofato
87060 Cantinella di Corigliano Calabro (Cosenza)
☎ 0983 80533
🌐 www.minisici.it

Three good labels: fruity La Molazza, the DOP Bruzio

Coriolanum, and delicate, aromatic, organic Le Terre del Castello, made from a mix of *Dolce di Rossano*, *Tondina*, and *Carolea*.

Terre Nobili, Tenuta

C. Carigliato
87040 Montalto Uffugo (Cosenza)
☎ 0984 934005

This 37-acre (15ha) estate's oil, known simply as Terre Nobili, is golden yellow, with a taste of grass, herbs, and almonds, followed by a nicely balanced aftertaste of bitterness and pepperiness.

Vulcano Luigi, Frantoio Oleario

87060 Mirto Di Crosia (Cosenza)
☎ 0983 42185
🌐 www.aziendavulcano.it

This beautiful 123-acre (50ha) organic estate runs down to the Ionian Sea, and is planted mainly with *Carolea* and *Rossanese*. Its monovarietal Carolea Biologico is very fruity, with hints of almonds and green tomatoes, and a warm aftertaste. The DOP Bruzio Colline Joniche Presilane is also very fruity with a warm aftertaste (not bitter) but tastes more of ripe tomatoes and herbs, with a soft, almondy edge.

Leading producers in Crotone, Vibo Valentia & Reggio Calabria

Ceraudo, Roberto

88815 Strongoli (Crotone)
☎ 0962 865613
🌐 www.dattilo.it

Roberto Ceraudo has built up a model estate around a 1,200-year-old tree of *Tonda di Strongoli*, a short distance inland from the Ionian coast. Olives are grown on 118 acres (48ha) of the estate and the oil has won many prizes. Ceraudo's unfiltered Extravergine Dattilo Denocciolato is made from roughly equal quantities of *Carolea* and *Tonda di Strongoli*, sometimes with a little *Nocellara Messinese* as well. It is greeny yellow and immensely fruity, with a very fresh, clean, herbaceous taste that eventually develops a lingering suggestion of bitterness and pepperiness. A stunner.

ROBERTO CERAUDO DENOCCIOLATO

Maria Eleonora Acton di Leporano

Fraz. Cannavà (Reggio Calabria)
89020 Rizziconi
☎ 335 6372212

The Acton estates in Reggio are planted with vast and

ancient trees of *Ottobratica* and *Sinopolese*, some as much as 82ft (25m) high—perhaps the tallest in the world. Princess Maria Eleonora Acton di Leprano's husband has also planted extensive new orchards of *Carolea*, *Cassanese*, *Leccino*, and *Nocellara del Bélice*. Their oils are sold under the name La Foresta, but each as a monocultivar extra virgin to bring out the fresh taste of the fruit. The golden-yellow Carolea is full of herby herbaceous tastes, with a strong, persistent aftertaste; the green *Ottobratica* oil is aromatic, almondy—and, if possible, even more delicious.

L'OTTOBRATICO FROM OLEARIA SAN GIORGIO

San Giorgio, Olearia

89017 San Giorgio Morgeto (Reggio Calabria)
☎ 0966 940569
W www.oleariasangiorgio.it

The Fazari family, which owns Olearia San Giorgio, has for many years applied advanced know-how and state-of-the-art equipment to the traditional olive cultivars of Reggio Calabria. The results are stupendous. Their L'Ottobratico is a distinctive oil of the highest quality—golden yellow, cool, and fresh to the taste, later rich, almost buttery, with hints of tomatoes and almonds. Their other oil, L'Aspromontano, is a blend of *Carolea* and *Ottobratico* and much greener in both

color and taste—grassy, with a long almondy aftertaste. It takes its name from the company's 247 acres (100ha) of olives in the foothills of the Aspromonte range. Both oils are quite exceptionally good.

Other producers in Crotone, Vibo Valentia & Reggio Calabria

Librandi

88811 Cirò Marina (Crotone)
☎ 0962 31518
W www.librandi.it

The Librandi family are major wine-makers on their estates in the area around Cirò Marina—olive oil is only a sideline to their main business. Nevertheless, they have 20,000 olive trees, mainly *Carolea*, growing on 229 acres (93 ha). Their Librandi oil is pale gold, fluid, with a smooth and gentle texture and a taste of cut grass, beans, apples, and nuts.

Lucifero e Zurlo

88900 Crotone (Crotone)
☎ 0962 931703
W www.luciferoezurlo.it

Lucifero e Zurlo is one of the largest, modern, estate-based producers in the south of Italy. It has more than 604 acres (250ha) of olive groves on four different sites in Cantazaro and Crotone. Total production in a good year reaches 300 tons. The company produces four excellent, full bodied, fruity oils—Riserva

LUCIFERO E ZURLO

(mainly from *Carolea*), a plain Lucifero & Zurlo (*Carolea* again —but good), an organic Da Agricoltura Biologica, and Le Due Corone (a general-purpose blend).

Mediterranea Foods

89016 Rizziconi (Reggio Calabria)
☎ 0966 503088
W www.mediterraneafoods.it

Mediterranea Foods was one of the earliest producers in Calabria to convert to organic methods. Its Principe di Gerace oil comes from the family's 59 acres (24ha) of olive trees, mainly *Ottobratica* and *Sinopolese*, with a little *Rogianella*. The olives are picked young, so that the oil is green, but instead of the usual grassiness it has an interesting taste of fruit, pepperiness, herbs, and nuts. Excellent on fish.

Torre Marrana, Biologica

89842 S. Calogero (Vibo Valentia)
☎ 0963 367939 – Fax 0963 367939
W www.torremarrana.com

The 67-acre (27ha) Torre Marrana estate offers organic monocultivar oils from ancient trees of two local cultivars: Ottobratica has the rich texture and gentle fruitiness of its type, while Ciciarello, made from young olives, is green with a taste of cardoons and an aftertaste of bitter almonds.

Vaccaro, Leopoldo

Via Marconi 50
88836 Cotronei (Crotone)
☎ 0962 491196

This prize-winning firm produces organic oils from the hillsides north of Crotone. Vaccaro Olio is made from *Carolea* olives, blended with two local cultivars *Pennulara* and *Agristigna*. It is golden yellow, with a cool, fruity taste of pears and tomatoes and a light warm aftertaste of bitterness and pepperiness.

Sardinia

Olive growing in Sardinia goes back to the time of the Phoenicians, and most of the olive groves today are ancient. The industry declined sharply in the 1960s and 1970s when the island was hit by depopulation, high production costs, and competition from seed oils. During the last 15 or 20 years, however, production has enjoyed a renaissance, not least among younger farmers who know how to promote the distinctive character of Sardinian oil.

THE OLIVE REGIONS OF SARDINIA
■ Sardegna DOP

LOW YIELD YET HIGH QUALITY

Sardinia produces a relatively small quantity of oil for such a big island—usually 1.5–2.5 percent of the total national olive crop. Yet there are more than five million trees covering 99,000 acres (40,000ha), usually growing alongside other crops in mixed farms. Most of Sardinia's olive groves are ancient and well established. Quality is mostly good and often excellent. The top producers are among Italy's best. There is a new Sardegna DOP for the whole island.

LOCAL OLIVE CULTIVARS

There are some 35 indigenous Sardinian olive cultivars, some of Spanish origin, and some of very local distribution. *Bosana* is the most widespread: in Sassari

it grows almost to the exclusion of all others, though it is found throughout the other three provinces. *Bosana* olives are small (about .05–.07oz) and freely borne, with a better-than-average oil yield. They tend to ripen late, over several weeks, but are usually picked early to make Tuscan-style oils. *Pizz'e Carroga* is the leading olive of southern Sardinia. The olives ripen early and are medium-large in size. They are used both as green table olives and for oil. *Pizz'e Carroga* oils are elegant, delicate, lightly fruity, and rather floral. Other top indigenous Sardinian olives are *Mallocria*, *Pibireddu*, *Semidana*, *Tonda di Cagliari*, *Manna*, and *Niedda*.

SARDINIAN OLIVES Most of the island's olives grow on well established trees.

Leading producers in Sardinia

Accademia Olearia

07041 Alghero (Sassari)
☎ 079 980394
W www.accademiaolearia.it

Accademia Olearia has 494 acres (200ha) of *Bosana*, with some young *Carolea*, *Biancolilla*, and *Nocellara del Bélice*. Its three main Accademia Olearia labels are all unfiltered. Fruttato is fresh, grassy, fruity, and long, with an easy, rounded, harmonious taste. Biologico is less fruity and more peppery, but light, aromatic, and floral with hints of apples and almonds. Il Riserva is very fruity (apples), flowery, and soft with pepperiness coming through toward the end but little bitterness.

Argei

08030 Gergei (Nuoro)
☎ 0782 808022
W www.argei.it

Argei makes oil from a unique, local cultivar called *Mallocrìa*. Its main Argei label is based on *Mallocrìa*, sometimes with a little *Semidana*, picked early to give an herbaceous taste of artichokes and almonds—fruity, robust, and peppery, with only a little bitterness at the end. Its organic label Bio Argei is a mixture of *Mallocrìa*, *Pizz'e Carroga*, and *Bosana*, and has a complex taste, which is fruity, floral, and herbaceous, ending with a suggestion of tomatoes and almonds, and a warm aftertaste. Both oils are excellent.

BIO ARGEI

Argiolas

09040 Serdiana (Cagliari)
☎ 070 740606
W www.cantine-argiolas.it

Argiolas is Sardinia's leading wine estate: its Argiolas Iolao Extravergine oil is made from early-picked *Tonda di Cagliari* plus a little *Pizz'e Carroga*. The oil is greeny yellow and unfiltered, with a fruity and grassy smell and a gentle taste that evokes apples, tomatoes, eggplant, and almonds. The fine, long aftertaste has a slowly developing touch of bitterness and pepperiness

C.O.PAR.—Cooperativa Olivicoltori del Parteolla

09041 Dolianova (Cagliari)
☎ 070 741329
W www.oliocopar.it

COPAR is one of the most modern cooperatives in Sardinia. Its Extravergine Colline Sarde is unfiltered, yellow (with a hint of green), with a taste of ripe olives, artichoke, and a distinctive floral aroma from *Pizz'e Carroga*—though the blend has more *Bosana* and *Tonda di Cagliari*. The overall impression is of fruitiness and balance, with a warm almondy aftertaste.

Cosseddu

09070 Seneghe (Oristano)
☎ 0783 54247

Cosseddu Sartos (mostly *Bosana*) oil is robust and fruity, with hints of artichokes, herbs, and bitter almonds. It ends with a long-lasting bitter aftertaste, held together by a classy smoothness.

F.lli Pinna

07044 Ittiri (Sassari)
☎ 079 441100
W www.oliopinna.it

The Pinna brothers produce a very fruity prize-winning 100% *Bosana* oil called Antichi Uliveti del Prato—fresh, well balanced, and delicious.

Giuseppe Gabbas

08100 Nuoro
☎ 0784 3374

Solianu is fresh, fruity, forceful, and spicy with a taste of herbs, tomatoes, and grass and a splendid whack of pepperiness and bitterness in the aftertaste.

Manca, Domenico

07041 Alghero (Sassari)
☎ 079 977215
W www.sangiuliano.it

Domenico Manca has 331 acres (134ha) where 20,000 trees of *Bosana* grow, along with some *Frantoio*, *Leccino*, and *Coratina*. The four labels are Fruttato, Biologico, Amabile, and the flagship Primér: Il cru di San Giuliano.

Olea Sardegna

07044 Ittiri (Sassari)
☎ 079 444074
W www.oliosardegna.it

This cooperative produces its excellent Gocce di Coros label from *Bosana* olives, picked young: very fruity and juicy, with hints of artichokes and grass, and a good, long-lasting aftertaste.

San Pasquale, Nuovo Oleificio

07100 Sassari
☎ 260280
W www.sanpasquale.it

This young firm has 296 acres (120ha), mainly of *Bosana*. Extravergine San Pasquale is greeny yellow, clear, fresh, grassy, and fruity with a balanced aftertaste.

Zampa, Giorgio

09073 Cuglieri (Oristano)
☎ 0785 39820

Zampa has 4,000 *Bosana* trees. His organic Extravergine Pirastu Pintu has a fresh fruity smell of olives, grass, and almonds, and an intriguing aromatic taste followed by an attractive, strong peppery aftertaste, which fades to reveal a lingering bitterness.

Sicily

People who only know Sicily in the heat of summer can have no idea of the richness of its landscapes and the fertility of its soils. The intense greens of spring in Sicily are the true measure of this island's agricultural wealth. In Roman times it was known as the granary of Europe. Olives, too, were a major feature of the island's economy. Imperial legislation sought to protect the oils of Rome from Sicilian competition.

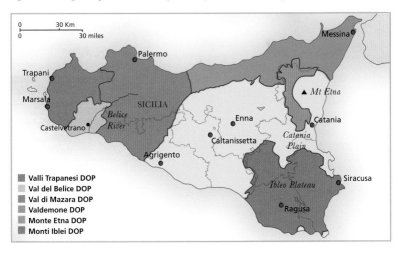

▮	Valli Trapanesi DOP
▮	Val del Belice DOP
▮	Val di Mazara DOP
▮	Valdemone DOP
▮	Monte Etna DOP
▮	Monti Iblei DOP

THE OLIVE REGIONS OF SICILY

HIGH-QUALITY OILS

Modern Sicily has about 20 million olive trees growing on 400,000 acres (160,000ha). After Puglia and Calabria, Sicily produces more oil than any other Italian region—about seven percent of the national crop. Olive trees grow in sparse but dedicated plantations in mountainous areas. At lower altitudes, on fertile hillsides, they flourish alongside almonds, carob-trees, vines, grain, livestock, and sometimes market gardening. Down in the fertile coastal areas where citrus fruit are intensively planted, the olive trees appear along the unirrigated edges. Dedicated intensive

plantations are a new phenomenon—historically, Sicily was a byword for traditional farming. Recent political and social changes have revolutionized the island's agriculture and its olive oil has benefited. New investment in irrigation, improved cultivation, and modern extraction machinery have raised production standards to a high level. Now, Sicily means quality. The oils have a ripeness, fullness, and balance that is often missing in the oils of northern Italy.

MANY LOCAL CULTIVARS

Once efficient cultivation and extraction are assured, the character of olive oil depends most on the cultivars that go into it. One reason for Sicily's pre-eminence is the islanders' attachment to indigenous olive cultivars, and Sicily is supremely fortunate to have so many of superb quality. The pan-Italian olives like *Frantoio* and *Leccino* are unknown on the island. The vast array of olives endemic to Sicily give character to its oils, above all, *Biancolilla*, *Cerasuola*, and *Nocellara del Belice* in the west and *Tonda Iblea* in the southeast of the island. It is therefore no accident that the island has so many DOPs. There are six, with two more under consideration. Three are split into subzones. For example, the Monti Iblei DOP has eight subzones, each with a distinctive character (*see p.125*).

FERTILE LAND
Large areas of inland Sicily are extensively planted with local varieties of olive.

Sicily's top indigenous olive cultivars

It is the olive cultivars that give Sicilian oils their distinctive character. They account for the many different styles of olive oil within the island and form the basis of the DOP rules. They also account for the sheer excellence of Sicilian oils.

BIANCOLILLA

This is the most widely planted olive in Sicily, seen especially in the western half of the island. Its oil combines well with others. It is very hardy and makes a spreading tree, with the unusual habit of producing its olives in bunches. *Biancolilla* oil is lightly fruity, with little bitterness or pepperiness. Cool, smooth, gentle, and aromatic, it tastes of lettuce, apples, almonds, and fruit.

NOCELLARA DEL BELICE

The greatest of all Sicily's olive cultivars, *Nocellara del Belice* is preeminent both as a table olive and for its oil. The oil is aromatic with a distinctive taste. Some liken it to artichokes, green tomatoes, or overripe fruit, but it is more complex than that and is truly the ripe, pungent taste of the olives themselves. It is followed by a peppery, bitter aftertaste.

CERASUOLA

This is an important olive from western Sicily, especially in northern Trapani and western Agrigento where it accounts for about half of all olive trees. The oil is excellent, with a fresh taste of grass, almonds, and herbs. Its intense fruitiness is well balanced by the lightest touch of bitterness and pepperiness. *Cerasuola* also combines well with other Sicilian olive oils.

NOCELLARA ETNEA

This olive is found all over Sicily, but especially in Catania and Siracusa. *Nocellara Etnea* is a vigorous tree with a pendulous habit of growth. Originally grown for green table olives—there are moves to obtain European Union recognition for these—the tree gives large regular yields in fertile, irrigated conditions. In poor soils, where it is usually grown, it is prone to biennial cropping (*see p.27*).

OLIVE TREES IN CASTELVETRANO Nocellara del Belice trees are typically small and pruned severely.

The different olive cultivars and growing conditions give rise to some enormous variations of style within the island. Strongly peppery, intensely fruity oils come from Trapani in the southwest while Messina in the northeast produces gentle, grassy oils.

PRIZEWINNING OILS

Sicilian producers have yet to catch up with northern Italy in their systems of sale, distribution, and pricing. For sheer price to quality ratios, Sicilian oils are unbeatable. It is Sicilian oil (specifically the oils of Trapani) that wins more major prizes at national and international shows than any other Italian oil. The quality of the island's oils can be compared only to those of Tuscany, whose bitter oils are, in any event, very different from the lush, fruity Sicilians. Sicilian oil is now finding its way into stores all over the world. Buy and enjoy them now, before their prices escalate to the heights charged by Tuscan boutique producers. Sicilian oils are ridiculously good value.

NORTH & WEST TRAPANI

Trapani is for olive oil what Bordeaux is for wine. Nowhere else in the world of olive growing is there such a concentration of estates producing uniformly high-quality oil. The plains inland from the towns of Marsala and Trapani are especially blessed. Their good soils and abundant water, produce Sicily's best oils. Quality is linked to enormous new capital investment here in recent years. This has been made possible partly by European Union funding and partly by the sociopolitical changes in western Sicily. Success means that the prices of Trapani oils are rising, but they still represent the best value for money. There is one DOP in this area, Valle Trapanesi. The rules specify that 80% of the olives must be of *Cerasuola* and/or *Nocellara del Belice*.

> ## Val di Mazara DOP
>
> This incorporates all the province of Palermo and much of Agrigento. The legal requirements are widely drawn. Val di Mazara oil may be any mixture of three very different olives (*Biancolilla*, *Cerasuola*, and *Nocellara del Belice*), along with up to 10% of any other cultivar, so the taste of Val di Mazara oils differs hugely. The authorities simply say it should be fruity and smooth with a gentle aftertaste. The oils are usually of a very high standard, often with a taste of cut grass, artichokes, citrus fruit, and green tomatoes, and a bitter peppery aftertaste.

SOUTH & EAST TRAPANI

Nocellara del Belice accounts for 95% of the olive trees in south and east Trapani. Its excellence as a table olive was

recognized by the creation of a
Nocellara del Belice DOP in 1998. Now
its oils have been acknowledged by a
new DOP for Valle del Belice, based
around the town of Castelvetrano.
This is a rundown, more traditional
part of Sicily and does not bustle with
prosperity. The Belice River has carved
out a handsome, broad valley where
olives have grown since at least the times
of the Ancient Greeks. Large olive
crushers have been excavated around the
temples of Selinunte. Many of today's
plantations are young and irrigated. Trees
are pruned low and grown to a single
trunk. *Nocellara del Belice* olives must
account for a minimum 70% of the DOP
oil, with the balance made up of other
Sicilian olives like *Biancolilla*, *Cerasuola*,
and *Ogliarola Messinese*. In practice, most
oils are 100% *Nocellara del Belice*, with the
characteristic pungency of the olive
coming through strongly.

PALERMO

Some of the best-known olive oil brands
in Sicily come from the province of
Palermo, with its 99,000 acres (40,000ha)
of olive trees. It is particularly associated
with the *Biancolilla* olive, which is widely
planted in hilly inland areas. All the
province forms part of the Val di
Mazara DOP, which also covers an area
of Agrigento (*see left*). Palermo oils are
thick, medium fruity, and delicate, with a
gentle long-lasting taste. Sicilians use
them on fish, risotto, tomatoes, salads,
and roasted meats.

AGRIGENTO

There are two types of oil made in
Agrigento: the full-bodied *Nocellara del
Belice* oils in the style of neighboring
Trapani's, and gentle fruity oils made of
Cerasuola and *Biancolilla* olives, which are
delicate and persistent, with a taste of
grass and artichokes. The latter oils are
excellent on fish, salads, and seafoods
and in delicate sauces.

MESSINA, CALTANISSETTA,
ENNA & CATANIA

The new Valdémone DOP covers
almost the entire province of Messina,
about 99,000 acres (40,000ha).

The DOP requirements reflect the
indigenous nature of the olives in the
area. The oil must be 70% of one or
any of three local olive cultivars
(*Ogliarola Messinese*, *Santagatese*, and
Minuta) with the rest made up of
Ottobratica and/or any combination of
four even more local cultivars: *Mandanici*,
Nocellara Messinese, *Brandofino*, and *Verdello*.
Valdémone DOP has five subzones:
Colli di Taormina, Fiumare di Naso,
Halaesa, Mandanici, and Tyndaris—but
they are not yet in use.

Messina oils are harmonious and
delicately fruity, with a definite taste of
fresh grass. They last a long time on the
palate and go well with pasta, soups,
salads, green vegetables, and meat.

Caltanissetta and Enna are less
important provinces for the production
of olive oils. Nonetheless there are
moves to create new DOPs for them,
to be called Colli Nisseni and Colline

Ennesi respectively. The main olive in Enna is *Moresca*. It is also important, alongside *Tonda Iblea*, in Caltanissetta.

The main olive in Catania is *Nocellara Etnea*, which accounts for more than half the olives in the province. The plain around the city of Catania is famous for its oranges, and extraordinarily fertile. Every so often a scattering of black volcanic ash from Mount Etna, whose high cone can be seen all across eastern Sicily, adds new nutrients to the soil. Catania has two DOPs, with totally different characters and histories. Monte Etna DOP has volcanic soil, scattered landholdings, and individual trees of considerable importance to the landscape. It is a small area, with only 17,300 acres (7,000ha) of olives, but extends into the provinces of Enna and Messina. It is split into two geographical subzones: Monte Etna (based on *Nocellara Etnea* olives) and Valle dell'Alto Alcantara (based on the local *Brandofino* olives). Both are still in the early stages of development.

The second DOP in Catania falls within the Monti Iblei DOP subzone Calatino (*see opposite*), where the province runs deep into the Ibleo plateau, with its limestone hills and valley bottoms. Here high-quality olive oil production is already a reality.

RAGUSA & SIRACUSA

Almost all the provinces of Ragusa and Siracusa fall within the area of the DOP Monti Iblei, southeastern Sicily's area for high-quality olive oil. At the heart of the DOP is the Ibleo mountain range, a high limestone plateau with deep fertile valleys. The stony uplands are for grazing, forestry, and prickly pears, while most of the olives are in the valleys and foothills. Even here the land is not dedicated to olive growing, despite the excellence of its oils and the the high price they command in the market place. The Ibleo mountain range is an area of mixed farming that includes vines, tree fruit, almonds, and grain, as well as livestock.

The DOP is divided into eight subzones. By far the most important is Gulfi: this subzone accounts for about half of all the high-quality oil made in the area. The olives are mainly *Tonda Iblea* and *Moresca*.

CHIARAMONTE GULFI This town sits on a rocky limestone ledge in the foothills of the Monti Ibleo plateau.

Tonda Iblea was originally planted for its green or black table olives. The olives weigh about .25oz (5–8g) each, especially when grown in good soil and irrigated. However, the *Moresca* also gives a good yield in oil, which is highly esteemed for its balance between strong fruitiness, medium pepperiness, and light bitterness. The tree is vigorous, tall, and thickly covered with leaves.

The *Moresca* olive is a dual-purpose cultivar. It yields a high-quality oil, which is light and delicate, with a taste of artichokes. It is also the dominant cultivar in much of the provinces of Caltanisetta and Enna, as well as Ragusa and Siracusa.

VIEW OF MOUNT ETNA, CATANIA
The cone of the famous volcano Mount Etna dominates the landscape of eastern Sicily, towering above the olive groves.

Conditions for Monti Iblei DOP subzones

NAME	PROVINCE	COMMUNES	CULTIVARS	STATUTORY DESCRIPTION OF OIL
Monte Lauro	Siracusa	Buccheri, Buscemi, Cassaro, Ferla	90% Tonda Iblea	Green, with a medium-fruity, medium-grassy smell, and a fruity taste, and a medium pepperiness.
Val d'Anapo	Siracuse	Canicattini Bagni, Floridia, Noto, Palazzolo Acreide, Siracusa, Solarino, Sortino	60% Tonda Iblea	Green, with a lightly fruity medium-grassy smell, a fruity taste, and a light pepperiness.
Val Tellaro	Siracusa/ Ragusa	Ispica, Modica, Noto, Pachino, Rosolini	70% Moresca	Green, with a medium-fruity, lightly-grassy smell, a fruity taste, and a medium pepperiness.
Frigintini	Siracusa/ Ragusa	Modica, Ragusa, Rosolini	60% Moresca	Green, with a strong fruity, medium-grassy smell, a fruity taste, and a medium pepperiness.
Gulfi	Ragusa	Chiaramonte Gulfi, Giarratana, Monterosso Almo	90% Tonda Iblea	Green, with a strong fruity, medium-grassy smell, a fruity taste, and a medium pepperiness.
Valle dell' Irminio	Ragusa	Acate, Comiso, Croce Camerina Modica, Ragusa, Santa, Scicli, Vittoria	60% Moresca	Green, with a lightly fruity, medium-grassy smell, a fruity taste, and a light pepperiness.
Calatino	Catania	Caltagirone, Grammichele, Licodia Eubea, Ganzaria, Mazzarrone, Mineo, S. M. di Vizzini	60% Tonda Iblea	Green, with a lightly fruity, medium-grassy smell, a fruity taste, and a light pepperiness.
Trigona-Pancali	Siracusa	Carlentini, Francofonte, Lentini, Melilli	60% Nocellara Etnea	Green, with a medium-fruity, lightly-grassy smell, and a fruity taste, and a light pepperiness.

Leading producers in North & West Trapani

Alestra Staiti, Tenuta

91100 Trapani
📞 0923 21197
🌐 www.alestrastaiti.com

This has 3,500 trees—80% *Cerasuola* 15% *Nocellara Belice*, 5% *Biancolilla*. Its Castellazzo label is excellent: golden yellow with a hint of green, unfiltered and opaque. It has a strong fruity smell and an aromatic taste of grass, apples, and tomatoes, followed by a mild, pleasing pepperiness and just a hint of bitterness. The new Dragonara label qualifies as DOP Valli Trapanesi oil, and may prove even better

D'Alì, Baglio

91027 Paceco (Trapani)
📞 0923 882379
🌐 www.bagliodali.it

The D'Ali have 99 acres (40ha) of olives, with roughly equal quantities of *Cerasuola* and *Nocellara del Belice*, plus a little *Biancolilla*. All three go into their top DOP Valli Trapanesi oil. Pale gold, it has a lively fruity smell. Its taste is cool, aromatic, intensely

VALLI TRAPANESI

fruity (apples and artichokes), and quickly followed by enough bitterness and pepperiness to give the oil its body and substance. Their Don Pepè and ordinary Baglio D'Alì labels are also good.

FONTANASALSA NOCELLARA

Fontanasalsa di Maria Caterina Burgarella

91020 Fontanasalsa (Trapani)
📞 0923 591001
🌐 www.fontanasalsa.it

Fontanasalsa is a charming country house with a palm-lined drive and a commitment to rural tourism. Its monocultivar oils are an essay in Sicilian oliviculture: fresh, delicate, delicious *Biancolilla*, (a mouth-filler); super-fruity *Cerasuola*; and spicy, aromatic, pungent *Nocellara del Belice*. The Valli Trapanese DOP Falconero Az. Agr. Fontanasalsa oil is one of the most coveted in Italy: cool, fruity, grassy, and very good indeed. Fontanasalsa has recently worked with Franci in Grosseto to produce a blend of their oils called Gemini.

Terre di Shemir

91020 Trapani
📞 0923 865323
🌐 www.terredishemir.com

Terre di Shemir is the new name for Case Sparse, the producers of the famous U Trappitu oil. They offer two prize-winning labels.

U Trappitu Delicato is yellow, floral, fruity, gentle, and long lasting. The early-picked U Trappitu Intenso is a powerful and very well balanced oil. Golden yellow with a touch of green, its green herby smell leads into a robust taste of fresh grass, tomatoes, and artichokes. Its rich, intense aftertaste has a strong measure of bitterness and pepperiness entirely in scale with the rich fruitiness.

Titone, Biologica

91025 Marsala (Trapani)
📞 0923 989426
🌐 www.titone.it

Titone is a much-acclaimed organic-oil maker, currently in top form. It has 32 acres (13ha) of *Biancolilla*, *Cerasuola*, and *Nocellara del Belice* olives from which it makes its stunning Titone DOP Valli Trapanesi Bio. The oil has a clear golden color, with a slight green tinge and a delicious fruity smell, and initial taste. A more complex, vegetable taste develops in the mouth, and is then followed by a light, bitter, peppery aftertaste.

Trapanese

91027 Paceco (Trapani)
📞 0923 883500
🌐 www.agricolatrapanese.it

This is a cooperative, with 16 members and 741 acres (300ha) of olives. More than half of the olives are *Cerasuola*, followed by *Nocellara del Belice* and a little *Biancolilla*. There are three labels: Amabile, Rustico, and Zefiro, which carries a DOP Valli Trapanesi stamp. All are excellent—cool, grassy, smooth, and complex— and good value for money. Zefiro is most often praised, but Rustico is especially successful, dominated by the pungent aromas of *Nocellara del Belice* and the fresh fruitiness of *Cerasuola* olives.

Other producers in North & West Trapani

Accomando, F.lli

91026 Mazara del Vallo (Trapani)
☎ 0923 906719

High-quality Accommando oil from 7.5 acres (3ha) of *Biancolilla, Cerasuola,* and *Nocellara del Belice* olives.

Ballotta, Baglio

91100 Erice (Trapani)
☎ 0923 539488
Ⓦ www.baglioballotta.com

Three monocultivar oils *Cerasuola, Biancolilla,* and *Nocellara del Belice.* All sold under the Baglia Ballotta label and all excellent.

Barbàra

91020 Trapani
☎ 0923 864346
Ⓦ www.agricolabarbara.it

24 acres (10ha) of *Biancolilla, Cerasuola,* and *Nocellara del Belice* olives producing Barbara DOP Valli Trapanesi.

Basiricò, Oleificio Pietro

91027 Paceco (Trapani)
☎ 0923 881613

Good Basiricò oil, made from a blend of *Cerasuola, Nocellara del Belice,* and *Biancolilla.*

Colicchia e Figli, Oleificio Michele

91025 Marsala (Trapani)
☎ 0923 981318
Ⓦ www.oleificiocolicchia.it

Olio Colicchia is one of the best in the Marsala area; look out for their SE. IV label.

Cracchiolo, Matteo

91014 Castellammare del Golfo (Trapani)
☎ 0924 39 000
Ⓦ www.olioscopello.com

Two excellent oils: Ceterea from 100% *Cerasuola* olives; and Scopella from *Biancolilla,* and *Nocellara del Belice* olives.

Galluffo

91100 Trapani
☎ 0923 23486
Ⓦ www.galluffo.it

Forty-four acres (18ha) of *Biancolilla, Cerasuola,* and *Nocellara del Belice* olives milled by Fontanasalsa and bottled as Marracco with a DOP Valli Trapanese.

Ingardia, Baglio

91027 Paceco (Trapani)
☎ 0923 881633
Ⓦ www.bagliogardia.it

This estate has 77 acres (31ha) – 66% *Cerasuola* and 33% *Nocellara del Belice* olives producing a very fine Baglio Ingardia oil.

Oddo Filippo

91010 Pantelleria-Khamma (Trapani)
☎ 0923 915500
Ⓦ www.oliooddo.com

The island of Pantelleria's leading oil estate: Feudo Bertolino is made from *Nocellara del Belice* olives and has a DOP Val di Mazara certificate.

Pacheco S.c.r.l. Olearia

91027 Paceco (Trapani)
☎ 0923 409117

Cerasuola, Biancolilla, and *Nocellara del Belice* olives growing on 98 acres (40ha) make prize-winning Crisaole.

Paradiso di Lara

91100 Trapani
☎ 0923 865323
Ⓦ www.paradisodilara.com

Diminutive production of fine Paradiso di Lara oil made from *Biancollila* and *Cerasuola.*

Plaia, Antonella

91100 Trapani
☎ 0923 28128
Ⓦ www.plaia.it

The well made Plaia oils are usually sold as mono-cultivars: *Cerasuola,* and *Nocellara del Belice.*

Safina, Maria

91100 Trapani
☎ 368 692415

Organic oil from *Nocellara del Belice, Biancollila,* and *Cerasuola* olives with the Tenuta Safina label.

Sanacore

91020 Trapani
☎ 0923 864279
Ⓦ www.sanacore.it

Thirty-seven acres (15ha), mainly of *Cerasuola* olives make unfiltered Ogghui oil.

Vallone, Antico Frantoio

91011 Alcamo, Trapani
☎ 0924 25087
Ⓦ www.frantoiovallone.it

Prize-winning Angelicum oil from *Cerasuola, Biancolilla,* and *Nocellara del Belice* olives.

NOCELLARA DEL BELICE OLIVES The old trees in this olive grove have been pruned using modern methods.

Leading producers in South & East Trapani

Biobélice S.c.r.l.

91028 Partanna (Trapani)
☎ 0924 49898
🖳 www.biobelice.it

Biobélice is a small new cooperative committed to organic farming in the Valle del Belice. Its Biobélice oil is fresh and fruity, with a taste that recalls cut grass and ripe tomatoes, followed by a big warm aftertaste of pepperiness and bitterness.

Caruso & Minini, Baglio

91025 Marsala (Trapani)
☎ 0923 982356
🖳 www.capricciodisicilia.it

Capriccio di Sicilia is the label of this leading producer with 86 acres (35ha) and 7,000 trees of *Nocellara del Belice*. Its oil is dark yellow with a touch of green, unfiltered, and fruity on the nose. Its taste is cool, smooth, and intensely fruity with a long taste of grass, apples, and almonds, and a warm aftertaste. Very good.

CAPRICCIO DI SICILIA

TEMPLE OF CONCORD
The valley of temples in Agrigento was once thickly planted with olives that now grow wild.

Consiglio, Angela

91022 Castelvetrano (Trapani)
☎ 0924 904364

Angela Consiglio has 69 acres (28ha) of *Biancolilla, Cerasuola, Nocellara del Belice*, and the little-known *Giarraffa*, and a long list of prizes and commendations for her oils. Baglio Seggio Fiorito comes in two versions, Delicato and the fruity Valle del Belice DOP, both excellent. The stupendous, strong-flavored Tenuta Rocchetta, made from *Nocellara*, is even more highly esteemed. It is intensely fruity, cool, and fresh, with lots of body and a long, lingering aftertaste.

TENUTA ROCCHETTA

D'Alì

91100 Trapani
☎ 0923 28890
🖳 www.tenutazangara.it

The D'Alì sisters make their Tenuta Zangara oil from 79 acres (32ha) of *Nocellara del Belice*. It is greeny gold and cloudy, with a smell of grass and tomatoes and a much richer taste, also of tomatoes, but there are hints of apples, herbs, and exotic fruits.

The long, smooth aftertaste, both bitter and peppery, is particularly pleasing.

Di Benedetto, Carbona di Giuseppe

91022 Castelvetrano (Trapani)
☎ 0924 62611
🖳 www.olioincoronati.it

The Carbona family owns 86 acres (35ha) of *Nocellara del Belice*. Incoronati is its only oil. Rich, fruity, and smooth, it has a green smell and a taste of tomatoes and herbs. It is perhaps a little less pungent than some Valle del Belice oils but ends with a fine warm aftertaste.

L'Albero d'Argento, Frantoio

91022 Castelvetrano (Trapani)
☎ 800 104401
🖳 www.lalberodargento.it

Frantoio L'Albero d'Argento belongs to the Coppini family, who also have an estate in Abruzzo in addition to others in Umbria and Puglia. Their L'Albero d'Argento Terra Gentile oil comes from three estates, which cover 148 acres (60ha) near Castelvetrano. They are planted with *Nocellara del Belice* and *Biancolilla*. Their oil is golden yellow in color with a suggestion of green, and has a fresh, fruity, grassy smell. It has a powerful, pungent taste recalling exotic fruit, tomatoes, and herbs and a good peppery, bitter aftertaste.

Lombardo, Antonino

91021 Campobello di Mazara (Trapani)
☎ 0924 48368

Lombardo is one of the stars of the Valle del Belice, with all 74 acres (30ha) of his olive groves put to *Nocellara del Belice* for olives, not oil. His Fiore del Belice oil is greenish yellow with a fine, fresh smell of herbs, olives, and tomatoes. Cool and soft on the tongue, it soon develops a vegetable taste of grass and artichokes, with hints of ripe fruit, before developing into a firm aftertaste of bitterness and pepperiness.

Olis

91028 Partanna (Trapani)
091 6524711
www.olissrl.it

Olis is in one of the most fertile valleys in Italy, planted with young vines and olives, though the olive mill can only be approached across a ford. Its highly prized Geraci label is pure *Nocellara del Belice* at its most beguiling. The light, fruity smell and bronze-yellow color do not prepare you for the oil's spectacular fruitiness—cool, smooth, appley, grassy, and mouth-filling. There is no overpowering aftertaste—just a hint of warm pepperiness. Wholly delicious.

Peruzza, Oleificio Nicolò

91022 Castelvetrano (Trapani)
0924 905133
www.peruzzaolio.com

Peruzza is the largest producer in the area, with a range of good-value *Nocellara del Belice* oils. They include Nobile di Sicilia, Selinus, and Peruzza Nocellara del Belice. Peruzza Novella has begun to make an impact in foreign markets where its fruitiness is much prized earlier in the year.

PERUZZA NOCELLARA DEL BELICE

Leading producers in Palermo

Disisa

90143 Palermo
091 6255445
www.oliodisisa.com

Disisa's olives grow in the golden valley that leads from Palermo to Monreale and beyond. The estate has 988 acres (400ha), of which 123 acres (50ha) are put to olives. Its "basic" oil is Extravergine Disisa, from 100% *Cerasuola*, picked early—fruity, herby, fresh, and vegetable in taste, followed by quite a strong aftertaste of bitterness and pepperiness. The new DOP Val di Mazara Tesoro is a blend of *Cerasuola*, *Nocellara del Belice* and *Biancolilla*. More complex, it has a more floral smell and an aromatic taste, very well balanced between fruitiness, pepperiness, and bitterness. Both are consistently good.

Frantoio, Coop. Il

90042 Borgetto (Palermo)
091 8782124
www.oliofederic*oll.it

Frederick II, Stupor Mundi, is the trade-mark of Cooperativa Il Frantoio, and a portrait of the great Emperor appears on every label. There are five of them, all unfiltered. The green-labeled Federico II Virgo Novello, from early-picked *Cerasuola*, is green, intensely fruity, herbaceous, bitter and pungent. The yellow-labeled Federico II Cafisù, from *Biancolilla*, is greeny yellow and lightly fruity. It fills the mouth with delicious herbaceous tastes. The red-labeled Federico II Etichetta Rossa, from *Cerasuola* and *Biancolilla*, is greeny yellow, medium fruity with a rounded, satisfying taste. Blue-labeled Federico II Etichetta Blu, from mature *Cerasuola*, is golden green

and medium fruity with an herbaceous taste and a good balancing bitter, peppery aftertaste. The orange-labeled Federico II Elàios, from *Nocellara del Belice*, is golden green, powerfully fruity, and very herbaceous, with a pungent taste of olives, artichokes, and green tomatos. All five are good.

FEDERICO II

Ianello & Manzella

90020 Ventimiglia Di Sicilia (Palermo)
091 8294032
www.biancolilla.sicilian.net

Ianello & Manzella's organic Extravergine DOP Val di Mazara is unfiltered 90% *Biancolilla*, with a fresh fruity, vegetable taste, but always aromatic, smooth, and gentle.

Martusa

90033 Chiusa Sciafani (Palermo)
06 3751 8244

Martusa's Orodichiusa oil comes from 2,000 trees of *Nocellara del Belice* and *Biancolilla*. The olives are picked early to give a greeny-yellow oil with a rich, fresh, vegetable taste of grass, tomatoes, and herbs and a lingering aftertaste.

Tornisia di Federico e Manfredi Caprì

90013 Castelbuono
091 6256970

Tornisia has three labels, all excellent, and especially popular in northern Italy and Swizterland: Tornisia (*Ogliarola Messinese*, *Biancolilla*, and *Giarraffa*); Oleaster (very rare local *Crastu* olive); and Elaion (modern *FS17* olive, a *Frantoio* seedling grown experimentally at Perugia and released commercially.

TEMPLE OF JUNO AT AGRIGENTO The Greek temples are surrounded by ancient olive trees.

Leading producers in Agrigento

Augello

92010 Caltabellotta (Agrigento)
0925 951090
www.suaeccellenza.com

Augello's Sua Eccellenza oil comes from 12 acres (5ha) of organic *Biancolilla* olives and carries a Val di Mazara DOP. It is golden yellow and clear, and smells of cut grass and herbs, but its taste is full of freshness and greenness, ending with a hint of almonds and a light, warm, peppery and bitter aftertaste. Also good is Augello's 1302 Pace di Caltabellotta oil.

Bellapietra, Consorzio

92019 Sciacca (Agrigento)
0925 86963
www.oliocoelium.com

Consorzio Bellapietra is a small, modern cooperative serving about 20 members with 247 acres (100ha). Their main olive is *Cerasuola*, accounting for some 80% of the mix, with *Biancolilla* and *Nocellara del Belice*. Coelium is greenish yellow, with a rich, powerful smell of fresh grass and herbs, which develops into a fruity taste of tomatoes and almonds and ends with a warm, bitter aftertaste.

Borgisi

92019 Sciacca (Agrigento)
0925 24004
www.olioborgisi.it

Borgisi oil is made from 22 acres (9ha) of *Cerasuola* and *Biancolilla*, plus a little *Nocellara del Belice*. It is clear, greenish gold and has a fresh, herbaceous smell. Its taste is delicate, fruity, "green" and olivey, with a fine bitter and peppery aftertaste. Excellent.

Colletti, Giuseppe

92010 Caltabellotta (Agrigento)
0925 951468
www.bioolio.it

Colletti grows 22 acres (9ha) of a local form of *Biancolilla*, organically managed, picked young, and processed speedily. The unfiltered Bio Olio oil has a delicate, herbaceous smell and a taste that recalls grass, artichokes, and herbs and develops a rich, peppery, bitter aftertaste.

Mandranova

92020 Palma di Montechiaro (Agrigento)
091 6120463
www.mandranova.it

The 10 acre (40ha) estate is a mixture of old rare local cultivars and new, modern plantations of *Biancolilla*, *Cerasuola*, and *Nocellara del Belice* olives. Its best label is Mandranova Etichetta Verde (green label), from *Nocellara del Belice*, which is full and fruity, with a taste of green tomatoes, grassiness, and herbs, and a pleasantly bitter and peppery aftertaste. The orange Mandranova Etichetta Arancione (100% *Biancolilla*) is also exceptional—very fruity, simple, and delicious.

Planeta

92013 Menfi (Agrigento)
0925 80009
www.planeta.it

Planeta oil comes from 197 acres (80ha) of *Nocellara del Belice* (about 60%), plus some *Cerasuola* and *Biancolilla*, all picked early to intensify the flavor of their oil. It is greenish with a green, grassy smell, followed by a strong, full taste (grassy, aromatic, and fairly peppery) and a lightly bitter aftertaste.

Ravidà

92013 Menfi (Agrigento)
0925 992483

The Ravidà estate has 128 acres (52ha) of organic olives, (*Biancolilla*, *Cerasuola*, plus a few *Nocellara del Belice*). Ravidà oil is strongly fruity, with a smell of artichokes, herbs, and bananas, and a cool taste of grass and tomatoes, but then develops a very agreeable warm bitter aftertaste. It is available in stores in Sicily and abroad.

Sarullo, Oleificio Gaspare

92010 Calamonaci (Agrigento)
☎ 0925 66024
🌐 www.oliosarullo.com

Extravergine Sarullo comes from
37 acres (15ha) of *Biancolilla*
and has the fresh fruitiness
typical of this olive. It fills
the mouth with grassy,
vegetable, herbaceous tastes,
lingers a long time, and then
delivers a light, bitter, and
warm aftertaste. Delicious.

Scirinda

92016 – Ribera (Agrigento)
☎ 0925 61360
🌐 www.fattoriascirinda.it

Scirinda has 12,000 trees of
Cerasuola, *Nocellara del Belice*,
and *Biancolilla*, organically
managed. The Extravergine
Fattoria Scirinda with its
distinctive burnt-orange
label is deep yellow,
unfiltered, very aromatic
with a taste of ripe olives,
artichokes, and herbs, and
a good mix of delicate
fruitiness, bitterness, and
pepperiness. It usually
carries a DOP Val di
Mazara endorsement.

Val Paradiso, Frantoio

92026 Favara (Agrigento)
☎ 0922 419555
🌐 www.valparadiso.it

Val Paradiso has 247 acres
(100ha) of young, irrigated
Nocellara del Belice, *Biancolilla*,
Nocellara Etnea, and the
Calabrian *Carolea*. Biancolilla
gives Extravergine Val
Paradiso its delicate,
delicious fruitiness.
The oil is pale
greenish yellow
and unfiltered,
with an aromatic
smell of grass and
herbs, a "green"
taste of olives,
herbs, and
vegetables, and a
very light, warm,
bitter aftertaste.
They also offer an
organic Bio label.

VAL PARADISO BIO

Leading producers in Messina, Caltanissetta, Enna & Catania

Aragona

94010 Centuripe (Enna)
☎ 095 7159061
🌐 www.agricolaragona.it

Aragona is a big estate
with 1,482 acres (600ha)
Only 14 acres (6ha) are
planted with olives, mainly
the Tuscan *Cipressino*, with
some local *Nocellara Etnea*
and *Brandofino*—the estate
belongs geographically to
the Mount Etna area.
Extravergine d'Aragona is
golden yellow with a fresh,
fruity smell, and a coolness
that quickly develops an
herbaceous taste (herbs
and almonds) and a long,
complex, warm, peppery,
and bitter aftertaste.
Excellent.

Gerace

94100 Gerace (Enna)
☎ 0935 541666
🌐 www.agrigerace.com

No more than 7 acres (3ha)
of *Nocellara Etnea*, *Moresca*,
and *Biancolilla* produce one
of Sicily's greatest organic
oils. Borgo Antico is greenish
yellow, cool on the palate,
and freshly fruity at first,
then develops a fuller taste
of grassiness and almonds,
and a long, well balanced
aftertaste of bitterness
and pepperiness.

Polizzi, Frantoio Michela

93100 Caltanissetta
☎ 0934 22400
🌐 www.frantoiopolizzi.it

The Polizzi olive
groves are small,
about 14 acres (6ha),
but produce two high-
quality, prize-winning
oils—Extravergine Polizzi
and the organic

Extravergine Biologico
Polizzi—from a mix
including *Nocellara del
Belice*, *Nocellara
Etnea*, and *Moresca*.
Both are excellent:
fruity, grassy,
aromatic, and
well balanced
with a long, warm,
peppery aftertaste.

POLIZZI FRANTOIO

Scalia, Frantoio

95030 Mascalucia (Catania)
☎ 095 7279001
🌐 www.frantoioscalia.com

Scalia's oils are a very good
example of *Nocellara Etnea*
oils. The estate has 24
acres (10ha) of this dual-
purpose olive. Its labels are
Primo Fiore and Borgo San
Rocco. Both are greeny
yellow with a fresh
herbaceous taste and
suggestions of grass,
tomatoes, and herbs. They
then develop, leading into a
powerful peppery, bitter
aftertaste that lingers on the
palate. Excellent.

Other producers in Messina, Caltanissetta, Enna & Catania

Barbagallo

95017 Piedimonte Etneo (Catania)
☎ 095 933580

This producer has 22 acres
(9ha) of *Moresca* and *Nocellara
Etnea*. Its L'Antica Corte oil is
medium fruity, with hints of
artichoke and almonds, and
a fair degree of bitterness
and pepperiness.

Collotta, Tenuta

94012 Barrafranca (Enna)
☎ 0934 467430
🌐 www.tenutacollotta.it

Produces organic oils under
the Antica Goccia label from
Nocellara del Belice, *Carolea*,
and *Biancolilla* olives.

La Uliva

93016 Riesi (Caltanissetta)
C 0934 921619
W www.lauliva.it

Prize-winning fruity, organic oils under the La Uliva label.

Licia Guccione

93013 Mazzarino (Caltanissetta)
C 339 7550308
W www.oliodifloresta.com

Top-quality organic oil from a leading estate made from *Nocellara del Belice*, *Nocellara Etnea*, and *Nocellara Messinese*.

Nixima

95125 Catania
C 095 330485
W www.arance.it

Nixima oil from organic olives on Prince Grimaldi's estate at the base of Mount Etna.

Paparoni

98071 Capo d'Orlando (Messina)
C 0941 916336

Organic oil from local

Santagatese and *Verdello* olives sold under the Contura label.

Poggio Pillé, Olivicola (F.lli Scollo)

95041 Mazzarrone (Catania)
C 0933 28803

This producer's oil is made from *Carolea* olives and is fresh, fruity, and rich, with a taste of green tomatoes.

Leading producers in Ragusa and Siracusa

Avola, Agrobio. Giorgio

97015 Modica (Ragusa)
C 0932 901027
W www.furgentini.it

Furgentini is made from *Moresca* and the local *Verdese* olives and has a greeny yellow,

opaque color. It smells strongly of olives and ripe tomatoes. The smooth taste is also of tomatoes at first, then develops hints of grass, artichokes, and almonds and a light, long pepperiness. Very well balanced.

FURGENTINI

C.O.PA. – Cooperativa Olivicola Pagliarazzi

96019 Rosolini (Siracusa)
C 0932 906523
W www.antheo.it

COPA is a modern cooperative with about 25 members farming some 741 acres (300ha) of olives. Their leading oil is Antheo DOP Monti Iblei Frigintini, made from 80% *Moresca* and 20% *Verdese* olives. It is greeny gold and rather fluid, with a fresh, fruity smell. Its taste is delicate and vegetable (grass, leaves, artichokes, and green tomatoes) followed by a warm aftertaste. Also good are plain Antheo, made from *Moresca* and *Biancolilla*, and Gocce del Tellesimo, from just *Moresca*.

Cutrera, Frantoi

97012 Chiaramonte Gulfi (Ragusa)
C 0932 926187
W www.frantoicutrera.it

The Cutreras have 62 acres (25ha) of *Tonda Iblea*, which makes them one of the largest landowners in the Monti Iblei Gulfi area. Their Primo oil is dark green gold and unfiltered, with a lively grassy smell. The taste is cool, slightly herby, and fruity too, but above all grassy and very long on the palate, ending with a light peppery, bitter aftertaste. Excellent.

RANDOZZA VALLEY Olives thrive in the volcanic soils of this area.

Galioto, Sebastiano

96010 Ferla (Siracusa)
☎ 0931 879710
W www.galioto.it

Sebastiano Galioto has 74 acres (30ha) of olives, two-thirds of them *Tonda Iblea*. His Castel di Lego oil carries a Monti Iblei Monte Lauro label. It is yellow green in color, smells of grass and tomatoes, and has a strong herbaceous taste that, though cool on the tongue, is eventually subsumed by a lightly peppery aftertaste. His Galioto label is also very good.

Modica, Felice

96017 Noto (Siracusa)
☎ 0931 573576
W www.olioevinobufalefi.com/

The Modica di San Giovanni family at Bufalefi combine modern technology with organic practices to great effect. Their Bufalefi DOP Monti Iblei Val Tellaro oil, made mainly from *Moresca* olives has a characteristic deep green-gold color and a fresh grassy smell. Its taste is unusual and delicious. It is fruity and herbaceous, with a distinct suggestion of mint, and later of nuts and almonds, before the long, light, peppery, and bitter aftertaste rounds it off. Excellent.

Nobile, Emanuele

96019 Rosolini (Siracusa)
☎ 0931 856369
W www.giorgionobile.it

Nobile makes an excellent "novello" oil. (*Novello* means *nouveau* as in the wine *Beaujolais Nouveau*.) Nobile is bursting with fruitiness, which creates a cool sensation in the mouth. Its full, fresh, herbaceous taste leads into a

OLIO NOBILE NOVELLO

GNARLED ROOTS The soil has eroded from base of this tree.

lightly peppery, bitter aftertaste. It comes from 24 acres (10ha) of organic *Moresca*, *Verdese*, and *Nocellara Etnea* olives.

Rollo, Giorgio

97012 Chiaramonte Gulfi (Ragusa)
☎ 0932 643804
W www.aziendarollo.it

Giorgio Rollo has 52 acres (21ha) of young olives, mainly *Tonda Iblea*, which means that his Letizia oil qualifies for the Monti Iblei Gulfi DOP. The oil is green, unfiltered, and cool, with a strong grassy smell and an aromatic taste, followed by a peppery aftertaste. It is a very good example of its type, and packs in a lot of freshness.

Rosso, Agrobiologica

97012 Chiaramonte Gulfi (Ragusa)
☎ 0932 621442
W www.agrobiologica-rosso.it

The Rossos have 2,500 trees of *Tonda Iblea* olives. Their Villa Zottopera label carries

a Monti Iblei Gulfi DOP endorsement. The oil is clear golden yellow with an herbaceous smell and a fruity taste of green tomatoes that turns quickly to grassiness. It has a long taste in the mouth, ending with a light hint of pepperiness and bitterness. The organic Villa Zottopera Biologico is also very good.

Team 4 x 4

96010 Buccheri, Siracusa
☎ 0931 880156
W www.oliotereo.it

Behind this strange name lie 37 acres (15ha) of olive trees, mainly *Tonda Iblea*, and a well managed, near-organic undertaking equipped with modern extractors. The main label is Tereo A.D. 2000, made from *Tonda Iblea* with a little *Biancolilla*, and left unfiltered to decant naturally. It has a good, fresh, grassy smell, and a taste of tomatoes, herbs, and "greenness." The bitter, peppery aftertaste is in proportion the fruitiness. Their Kore range from *Tonda Iblei*, *Carolea*, *Moresca*, and *Biancollia* is also very good.

SPAIN

Spain has by far the largest olive-producing industry in the world and also exports more olive oil than any other country. It has more than 300 million olive trees covering more than five million acres (two million hectares), 92 percent of which are grown for olive oil. The rest go to table olives. Two-thirds of the crop is concentrated in Andalusia: almost one-fifth of the world's olive oil comes from the province of Jaén alone.

CENTURIES OF OLIVE GROWING

Olives were grown in Spain before the Roman occupation; the Romans called the River Ebro *Oleum Flumen*, the river of oil. The Arabs were proficient cultivators of olives and makers of oil. The Spanish word for olive oil is *aceite*, which comes from the Arabic *al-zait*, meaning "olive juice". Cultivars like *Farga* and *Cornicabra* date back to the Moorish occupation. The trees that Spaniards took to the New World in the 16th and 17th centuries—*Manzanilla, Gordal (Sevillano)*, and *Cornicabra (Mission)*—still form the basis of the olive industry in California today (*see p.251*).

Spain has always had a spacious and sparsely populated countryside. Olives have long been used as a way of bringing marginal land into cultivation. The vast areas of inland Andalusia and Catalonia that are now devoted to the

VILLAGE OLIVE PRESS
IN PROVINCE OF MALAGA

monoculture of olives had only a few olive trees until the 18th century. But it was from 1913 to 1933 that the greatest ever expansion of planting took place. This "golden age of Spanish olive growing" also saw the first significant national measures to improve quality. Many of the oldest cooperatives date from that period, as well as from the 1950s and 1960s, when the need for more sophisticated methods of extraction became imperative.

SMALL COOPERATIVES

The Spanish oil industry is dominated by village cooperatives. Most are small enterprises, usually with no more than two or three full-time employees. In recent years, these "primary" cooperatives have begun to merge into larger groups, a process that creates economies of scale and critical mass for sales and promotion. These

MIXED FARMING In some parts of Spain olives grow alongside other crops.
◀ GRANADA In much of southern Andalusia enormous olive plantations dominate the landscape.

amalgamated enterprises are known as "secondary" cooperatives. They do not necessarily sell the best oils, but they offer more consistent products. The process of amalgamation continues, and "tertiary" cooperatives that combine the might of several secondary ones are now beginning to emerge. Unlike Italy and France, whose markets are very fragmented, Spain takes the general view that "big is beautiful."

Spanish olive cultivars are infinitely variable. More than 250 are grown commercially, though there are also large tracts where successful olives like *Picual*, *Hojiblanca*, and *Arbequina* are grown to the exclusion of all others. Some have a very local following. The rules for the Rioja local DOP permit no fewer than 13 different cultivars to be used in the mix. Olives of very differing character grow side by side; it is difficult to imagine a greater contrast than between the robust taste of *Picual* oils from Montes de Granada DOP and the soft, fruity oils of *Lechín de Granada* olives made alongside them in the Alpujarras mountains.

THE HOME MARKET

The Spanish home market is locally based and fairly unsophisticated. Olive oil has been slow to develop a gourmet following. It is so plentiful and inexpensive, and used so freely in cooking, that variety and choice are seldom seen as desirable. Most Spaniards go to cooperatives to buy their oil in one-gallon (five-liter) plastic containers. Even some of the best producers—the cooperatives who win prizes at national shows—still sell most of their oil in bulk for blending.

Yet the Spanish olive oil industry has made enormous progress by insisting on high standards of cultivation and harvesting. Spanish and European funds have enabled it to invest heavily in technical education and highly modern extraction and storage equipment. The result is that most Spanish oil is of a very high quality and seriously undervalued.

OLIVE OIL EXPORTS

The olive's tendency toward biennial cropping means that Spanish annual oil production usually varies between 660,000 and 1.1 million tons. It has an excess of 165,000–220,000 tons per year, for which the only possible outlet is foreign markets.

Faith in technical excellence, however, is not matched by investment in marketing, sales, promotion, and distribution. Spain's marketing is often feeble. Where an Italian company would split its production into several different labels, each targeting a different market segment, its Spanish equivalent would offer one oil only. Spaniards do not ask themselves what consumers in other countries want to enjoy and how they can best be satisfied.

ANDALUSIA Most of Spain's oil is from Andalusia and plantations are constantly renewed.

Most of Spain's excess oil is exported to blenders in Italy, who reexport it to North America, Japan, and northern Europe with significantly enhanced prices. Italian companies have invested deeply in the Spanish industry to secure their cheap supplies. Now, in contrast, the larger Spanish companies are investigating the possibility of acquiring Italian subsidiaries through which to access the high margins that Italian exports enjoy. Spanish producers are also working hard to establish themselves in the emerging markets of central Europe, where they can offer a high-quality product at prices that are significantly lower than those of their competitors in Italy.

It is in the private sector that the greatest changes are taking place, notably among estate owners whose marketing skills and management flexibility (plus easier access to capital) have brought success. Their emphasis is on new, intensively managed and irrigated plantations growing non-traditional olive varieties like *Arbequina* to produce high-quality oils that can be sold in the luxury markets and abroad.

IMPROVING AND REGULATING QUALITY

In Spain, only 20 percent of oil sold at retail is extra virgin. The rest is "composed"—a mixture of refined and virgin oils. However, there has been widespread publicity for the superior quality of extra virgin oils, both for their taste and their health-giving properties. As they come to be seen as an added-value product, so their prices have begun to increase.

The areas of high-quality production protected by European Union legislation are known as *Denominaciones de Origen Protegida* (DOP) in Spain; there are now some 20 olive oil DOPs (with more in the pipeline), which vary considerably in size and quality. If you are unable to taste an oil before buying it, the selection in such gourmet retailers as El Corte Inglés is dependable.

Spain's first dedicated oil shop *La Oleoteca* (C/Juan Ramon Jiminez, 37, Madrid, tel: 91 359 18 03) stocks a superb selection of some 80 Spanish oils.

Spanish olive cultivars

There is a rich variety of Spanish olive cultivars, all of which tend to have very local followings. The different cultivars also produce very different oils. The Spanish market should try to emphasize this diversity.

Variety	Area x 1000 acres/hectares	Province
Picual	1.6m/645	Jaén, Córdoba, Granada
Cornicabra	665/269	Ciudad Real, Toledo
Hojiblanca	536/217	Córdoba, Málaga, Seville
Lechín de Sevilla	457/185	Seville, Cádiz
Manzanilla de Sevilla	210/85	Seville, Badajoz
Verdial de Badajoz	183/74	Badajoz
Empeltre	178/72	Zaragoza, Teruel, Balearic Islands
Arbequina	175/71	Lérida, Tarragona
Manzanilla Cacereña	158/64	Cáceres, Salamanca
Picudo	148/60	Córdoba, Granada
Farga	111/45	Castellón, Tarragona
Lechín de Granada	89/36	Granada, Almería, Murcia
Verdial de Huevar	84/34	Huelva, Seville
Gordal Sevillana	74/30	Seville
Morisca	71/29	Badajoz, Cáceres
Morrut	69/28	Tarragona, Castellón
Sevillenca	62/25	Tarragona, Castellón
Castellana	54/22	Guadalajara, Cuenca
Verdial de Vélez-Málaga	49/20	Málaga
Aloreña	42/17	Málaga
Blanqueta	27/11	Alicante, Valencia
Villalonga	15/6	Valencia
Changlot Real	12/5	Valencia
Alfafara	10/04	Valencia, Albacete

Olive regions of Spain

This map shows the main olive-growing regions of Spain. The size of the industry varies thoughout the country and the most important olive region by far is Andalusia. On the following pages are descriptions of each of the regions and their producers. Starting with Navarra and La Rioja, the section works north to south down through Spain.

SOCIEDAD COOPERATIVA DE OLIVAREROS
ELABORACION Y ENVASADO DE VINOS, ACEITES Y ACEITUNAS
FUNDADA EN 1953

TILED SIGN OUTSIDE COOPERATIVE IN
RIBERA DEL FRESNO, EXTREMADURA

SMALL OIL MILL
The pretty entrance of an oil mill in
Zahara de la Sierra in the province of
Cadiz, southern Andalusia.

SCULPTURES OF OLIVE WORKERS IN JAEN
These statues can be seen in the town of Martos, which claims to be at the center of olive growing in the province of Jaén.

ARCHITECTURAL INTEREST
A pupil of the famous architect Gaudi designed buildings for the farmer's cooperative in Gandesa, in Catalonia.

GUADALQUIVIR VALLEY
Olive trees stretch in endless lines across the valley in this view from the ramparts of Ubeda toward the humpback mountains of the Sierra Mágina.

FACTS AND FIGURES

OIL PRODUCED 1,078,000 tons a year

LAND PLANTED WITH OLIVES more than 1,015,140 acres (420,000ha)

NUMBER OF DOPS 17

PERCENTAGE WORLD CROP 38.1%

National Brands of Spain

The Spanish olive oil industry is going through a period of rapid consolidation. Five years ago, there were too many producers and problems with overproduction, undercutting, and narrow margins. Now, as a result of several acquisitions and mergers, the sector is dominated by six leading enterprises.

MAJOR INDUSTRY

Spain's oil industry is the best regulated and most reputable in the world. It is unthinkable that a disaster like the 1981 "Colza" scandal could recur today. Some 700 people died in Spain, and thousands more were blinded, crippled, or disabled, as a result of consuming olive oil that had been deliberately adulterated with car engine oil. The oil was sold by door-to-door salesmen in poor quarters of Madrid and in other Spanish cities. The Spanish oilve oil industry responded by pressing for consumer safeguards, which were rapidly brought into effect and are among the most comprehensive in the world. You may buy from any of the large producers with the utmost confidence in the quality of their oil. The same is true of large cooperatives like Hojiblanca and the high-quality private brands like Mueloliva.

OIL FROM UGIJAR, GRANADA

KOIPE AND CARBONELL

Sos Cuétara is the largest olive-oil producer in Spain by far, and the third largest player in the entire Spanish food industry. It relies on its brand names Koipe and Carbonell to sell its products.

Carbonell is its best-known subsidiary, and has a high profile at retail level. It has been quick to diversify into the market for organic products. It is also the largest exporter of Spanish oil abroad, most of it sold at bargain prices at the bottom end of the market, though its quality is respectable.

Carbonell began in Córdoba in 1866 and, by 1888, had a contract to supply the British navy. Its iconic label showing a gypsy girl was introduced in 1904. By the 1950s, Carbonell was Spain's largest exporter of olive oil. Its top lines, in terms of quality, are its single-variety oils made from *Arbequina, Cornicabra, Picual,* or *Hojiblanca* olives and sold in glass bottles as "Gran Selección."

Koipe sells three monocultivar extra virgin oils—*Arbequina, Cornicabra,* and *Hojiblanca,* as well as its flagship Sublime label. Sos Cuétara is now the largest bottler of olive oil in the world, but until recently only 10 percent of its oil was bottled for sale; the rest was sold in bulk. It recently acquired the Italian Sasso label, which will enable it to export more directly to the fast-growing market in the United States.

MUELOLIVA FACTORY Sign painted on the wall outside the vast olive oil plant at Priego de Córdoba.

has a large presence in the Brazilian market, and the acquisition of Agribética has enabled it to meet demand and continue expansion.

OLIVE MILL
Newly harvested olives are taken by conveyor belts into the processing plant. Then they are crushed to a paste, before oil is extracted.

LA ESPANOLA AND COOSUR

Aceites del Sur has two main brands: La Española and Coosur. La Española has an historic label that is widely recognised; its organic Villa Blanca won a national prize in 2002. Coosur was a state-owned, loss-making company, technologically up-to-date but with no value apart from its brand names. It took several years to find a purchaser, but Aceites del Sur acquired it in 2002. Its main factory is at Vilches in Jaén, but its export office is at Dos Hermanas near Seville. All its oils are sold under the Coosur label. Aceites del Sur offers five monocultivar extra virgin oils. The company also has an agreement with Jaencoop to bottle 5.5 million pounds (25 million kilograms) of oil. Part of that deal involves launching a new Coosur-Jaencoop label for Picual Suave.

AGRIBÉTICA

After passing through several owners in recent years, Agribética was sold in 2002 to Sovena, which is part of the Portuguese Nutrinveste group. Sovena

ACEITES BORGES-PONT

The Lérida-based Aceites Borges-Pont is a Catalonian giant, now rated fourth in size among national brands of Spain. It offers a large number of oils, but its premium extra virgin range includes DOP oils from Baena, Montes de Toledo, and Sierra de Segura, monocultivar oils from *Arbequina*, *Picual*, and *Hojiblanca* olives, and an organic oil as well as several blends. Aceites Borges-Pont has been especially successful in exporting and their oils are now found in more than 60 countries.

MIGASA-YBARRA

The Migasa-Ybarra brand is a recent amalgamation between two producers in Dos Hermanas near Seville: Migasa and Ybarra.

Ybarra was founded in 1842 and its oils are sold in all the major supermarket chains throughout Spain as well as internationally. It was the first to sell its oil in cartons (in 1985), as well as glass, polyethylene, and cans. Migasa has the largest olive-oil refinery in Spain.

TORRES Y RIBELLES

Soon after Torres y Ribelles was founded in 1914 in Seville, it acquired a warrant to supply the royal household of King Alfonso XIII. It claims to be one of the market leaders of Spain, bottling more than 3.9 million gallons (15 million liters) of oil a year. Its leading extra virgin line is Betis, and made from *Hojiblanca*, *Arbequina*, and *Cornicabra* olives.

HOJIBLANCA

The Antequera-based Hojiblanca is now Spain's fifth-largest producer of olive oil (with eight percent of the market) and the largest producer of extra virgin oil. Hojiblanca was the result of a merger of two secondary cooperatives in 2003, Hojiblanca itself and Cordoliva. It is by far the largest olive-oil cooperative in the world, and is committed to further mergers and acquisitions.

Navarra & La Rioja

Wine, rather than olive oil, is the principal agricultural product of this area of northern Spain. Even though olives have been cultivated along the Ebro River for centuries (see p.135), olive growing at the upper end of the Ebro valley has always been a marginal activity. The scattered plantations are often no more than a row of old olive trees along the edge of a cultivated field. Two-thirds of the oil produced in the area is for home consumption.

THE OLIVE REGIONS OF NAVARRA & LA RIOJA

VARIABLE OIL QUALITY

When the French Duc de Saint-Simon was entertained by the Viceroy of Navarre in 1721 he recalled that he was offered "a vast dish of stewed bacalao with oil…utterly worthless," and he added "the oil was detestable." To this day, quality is variable. Some villages still use traditional hydraulic presses. The leading producers listed are young enterprises with modern equipment. The best of their oils are very good.

NAVARRA

The greatest concentration of Navarra's olive trees is in the Ebro valley, south and west of Tudela. Towns and villages like Cascante, Corella, and Ablitas have a long tradition of olive growing and it

is here that there is a frenzy of modern planting, too. Arróniz claims to be Navarra's oil capital, where the local fiesta is dedicated to *tostado*, toasted bread with oil poured over it.

LA RIOJA

There is a new (2004) DOP for La Rioja. Unfortunately, the rules permit any combination of 13 olive cultivars, which means the oil has no consistent taste. The endemic *Redondal* accounts for more than half the trees in Rioja and is almost the only variety around *Arnedo*. Other ancient varieties like *Arróniz*, *Bermejuela*, and *Macho* are also grown. *Empeltre* was only introduced toward the end of the 19th century, and is seen less now than *Arbequina*.

VINES AND OLIVES IN RIOJA Vines are more frequently seen on the plains of La Rioja than olives.

Leading producers in Navarra & La Rioja

Casa del Aceite, La

31520 Cascante
948 85 09 02
W www.lacasadelaceite.com

Most of the oil sold under the label of La Casa del Aceite is made from *Empeltre* olives, whether filtered or unfiltered. But they also offer blends, and a pure *Arbequina* oil—light and sweetly scented of vanilla and citrus, with a very long, mild, smooth, rounded taste, a hint of artichokes, and a lick of pepperiness at the end.

Ebro, Sdad. Coop. Almazara del

31592 Cintruénigo
948 81 10 33
W www.almazaradelebro.com

This cooperative produces monocultivar Almazara del Ebro oils—*Empeltre*, *Arbequina*, and *Picual*—each with an organic Ecológico option.

Ecológica de La Rioja, Almazara

26540 Alfaro
941 18 15 12
W www.fer.es/isul

This was Rioja's first organic estate, with a small production of high-quality *Arbequina* oil sold under the ISUL label—fruity and smooth, with a lingering touch of bitterness.

Mendía, Trujal

31243 Arróniz
948 53 76 51

The extra virgin brand is Villa de las Musas, made mainly from *Arróniz* olives, with some *Arbequina* and *Empeltre* too. It is full bodied, with a lightly bitter aftertaste.

ABBAE DE QUEILES

Queiles, Hacienda

31522 Tudela
948 84 74 95

Abbae de Queiles is a 100% *Arbequina* oil—fruity and aromatic, with hints of green tomatoes and a lightly bitter aftertaste. It is made from young, intensively planted trees and promoted as a high-quality product to the Spanish gourmet market as well as in northern Europe and North America.

Rihuelo

26540 Alfaro
941 18 30 26
W www.rihuelo.com

The Bea family makes its prize-winning organic

RIHUELO

Rihuelo oil from *Arbequina* olives, and sells it successfully in upscale Spanish shops and abroad: it has a gentle, fresh taste of cut grass, green tomatoes, and artichokes, with just a hint of bitterness and pepperiness to finish.

San Isidro, Coop. Frutera

26525 Igea
941 17 58 21

Igea produces an unusual oil under the Cooperativa Frutera San Isidro label, from the local *Macho* olive. The oil is fresh and green, with a lightly peppery, bitter aftertaste. Until recently, all the oil produced went for home consumption; now 15 percent is sold locally in 1-gallon (5-liter) containers.

Other producers in Navarra & La Rioja

Galilea, Trujal de

26144 Galilea
902 45 67 00

Fruity, fresh oil under the Aceite de Galilea label. Mostly for home consumption.

Hejul, Almazara

26144 Galilea
941 48 00 29

A small, private estate at Galilea that produces a long, gentle, smooth, organic oil under the name Hejul.

La Maja

31587 Mendavia
948 68 58 46

At Mendavia, planted with 247 acres (100ha) of *Arbequina* olives with 650 trees per acre (1,600/ha).

Trujal 5 Valles

26580 Arnedo
941 38 33 84

One of the largest, modern cooperatives in Rioja.

Catalonia

This region means beach vacations and stylish living, especially in Barcelona, but Catalonia also consistently produces the best oil in Spain. Quality is excellent and dependable, which means that Catalonian oils represent very good value for money. The region is made up of four provinces: Barcelona, Gerona, Lérida, and Tarragona.

THE OLIVE REGIONS OF CATALONIA

PROMOTING THE REGION

Olive growing has a long history in Catalonia, which now accounts for about 5.5 percent of the Spanish total, and oil production of about 165,000 tons a year. Some cooperatives still sell more than half their crop to the big blenders in Italy. Catalans are aware that they need to promote a distinctive regional profile, especially since the major Italian company Angelini now controls their largest marketing company, Olis de Catalunya.

There have been immense advances in the private sector, where prizes for quality, national recognition, and international sales are consistently won by companies that did not exist as

WELL MANAGED ESTATES

There is a combination of large well maintained olive estates in this part of Spain as well as smaller olive holdings. There is a long history of olive making in this area.

recently as five years ago. The whole Catalan industry is on the threshold of huge, far-reaching changes.

The center of the olive industry here is the province of Tarragona. Production in the provinces of Barcelona and Gerona is miniscule. The industry was almost completely wiped out by the frosts of 1956 and, unlike other areas of southern France and northern Spain, the trees were never replanted.

LERIDA

Catalonia's most northern DOP is called Les Garrigues, in the landlocked province of Lérida. The landscape is austere and hard—a dry, cool upland where spring comes late. The olive-growing and oil-making tradition in this area can be traced back to at least the 13th century. However,

Arbequina olives

Catalonia is the kingdom of the *Arbequina* olive. It is almost the only cultivar in Lérida and Tarragona, and now one of the most widely grown throughout Spain. Its hardiness explains the many new plantations of *Arbequina* in Aragon and Navarre. Its productivity and quality have caused it to be widely planted in Andalusia, and recently in Argentina.

ARBEQUINA OLIVES

Arbequina is a high-yielding, self-fertile cultivar that enters into production early and quickly becomes a regular, dependable annual cropper with little or no tendency toward biennial bearing. The olives are small and turn black as they mature, but gradually, and not all at once.

Arbequina oil is a greenish yellow, and distinguished by its remarkable fluidity and its fruity fragrance—a mixture of almond, apples, and other fresh fruits. Young *Arbequina* oil always tastes very fruity, sometimes with a hint of green grass and almonds, but only lightly peppery and never bitter —just delicious. Its freshness and smoothness remain even when it ages and loses its fruitiness. It is, however, unusually low in oleic acid, which means that it is very short-lived. It is best consumed within a few months of production. Fresh from the press, it is the most delectable of all olive oils.

Arbequina olives, though small, are preserved, ripe and black, as olives to eat, especially as tapas. Their flavor is claimed by some to have a taste that is superior to black caviar.

many of today's plantations date from early in the 19th century when *Arbequina* trees were used to convert the indigenous scrub known as *garrigue* into farmland.

Les Garrigues accounts for 86,500 acres (35,000ha) of olives, slightly less than one-third of the Catalan total. The DOP of Les Garrigues is the oldest in Spain, dating to 1973. The oils must be made from at least 90% *Arbequina* olives, and the balance from *Verdial* olives. The minimum permitted acidity is 0.5% but the average for most producers in the DOP is 0.2%, a good guide to quality. The DOP extends to 45 villages south and east of Les Borges Blanques, which proclaims itself to be the world center of the olive oil industry, and the producers of the best olive oil in the world—an enviable achievement. Most villages have a farmers' cooperative where their olives

The cathedral of olives

Gandesa is the capital of the Terra Alta. Its farmers' cooperative was designed by Gaudí's disciple Cèsar Martinell (1888–1973), the architect who, during the course of his long career, built some 40 Gaudiesque *art nouveau* "cathedrals" for wine and oil producers throughout Catalonia.

The farmers' cooperative at the nearby village of El Pinell de Brai was also built by Martinell. Its roof is supported by vast parabolic arches of the sort Gaudí perfected. Its outside wall is covered in a huge ceramic frieze by the popular Catalan cartoonist and character painter, Xavier Nogués (1873–1941).

THE COOPERATIVE BUILDING IN GANDESA

are processed: 35 cooperatives are registered with the DOP regulators, including a secondary cooperative called Agroles, which handles and markets a large proportion of the oil.

Les Garrigues is one of the poorest areas in Catalonia, and has an aging population. Village cooperatives are often undercapitalized and in debt, which limits their capacity for growth. The *Arbequina* oils they produce have the potential to compete with the greatest in the world, but they are sold on price, not quality. There is great scope for individual marketing and promotion, given the necessary investment. Meanwhile, the oils of Les Garrigues remain good value for money.

BARCELONA & GERONA

Much of the olive population of Catalonia's two most northerly provinces was destroyed in the cold winter of 1956. Subsequent urbanization and rural exodus meant that it was never replaced. Olives survived in a few pockets that still produce interesting oils from very local cultivars, and they have now been joined by modern model farms specializing in high-quality *Arbequina* oils for the luxury market.

FARGA OLIVE TREES

Barcelona also has a tradition of handling oil—refining, exporting, and blending it—but actual production within these two provinces remains very small.

TARRAGONA

There are three DOPs in this province: Siurana, Terra Alta, and Baix Ebre-Montsià. Tarragona has some 178,000 acres (72,000ha) of olives.

SIURANA DOP

By far the best known and most extensive of the Catalonian olive areas is the DOP known as Siurana. It has the highest concentration of reliable, top-class oils in Spain. It includes some 40 primary cooperatives and three secondary cooperatives which buy, blend, and promote the oils from several villages, including Ceolpe (*Centre Oleícola del Penedès*) in the Penedès, and *Unió* and *Olis de Catalunya* in Reus.

Siurana DOP oils must be made from a minimum of 90% *Arbequina* olives; the only other permitted cultivars are *Rojal* and *Morrut*, older varieties, that were common before the great advance of *Arbequina* in about 1700.

The average yearly production in Siurana is 4 million lbs (1.8 million kg)

lines of intensive olive orchards resemble
vineyards more than olive orchards.
These new enterprises are often privately
owned, and well funded. Many have also
applied for organic status, which means
registering with the authorities who can
certify "integrated production." This is a
method of cultivation that seeks to
combine organic, chemical, and bio-
technological management in a balanced
way. The aim is to produce high-quality
oils while respecting the environment.

TERRA ALTA DOP

The Terra Alta DOP is a well defined
area in southwestern Tarragona, better
known for its wine than its olive oil.
Its name, literally "high land,"
distinguishes it from the coastal plains.
The hills are a continuation of the
cordilleras of Bajo Aragón and the
area shares with its olive-growing
neighbors an industry firmly based on
the *Empeltre* olive cultivar.

Buy with confidence, cook with pleasure:

Four leaves. Superbly lush and intense. Syrupy with complex flavors and heady aroma.

Three leaves. Smooth, full-bodied taste. Polished finish with tangy accents.

Two leaves. Round and spirited. Brisk yet vibrantly balanced.

One leaf. Light in flavor and consistency. Sweet and zesty.

This genuine Balsamic Vinegar of Modena adheres to the strict product certification recently established by the Associazione Assaggiatori Italiani Balsamico (AIB). AIB's four grape leaf grading system both informs and guarantees quality levels, so now you can be certain of the graded Balsamic Vinegar you select. Simply refer to the flavor profiles outlined here.

ABANDONED TREES Many olive groves in Gerona were abandoned after the 1956 frosts.

The Terra Alta DOP rules stipulate that oils must be made principally or exclusively from *Empeltre* olives. A proportion may come from secondary cultivars like *Arbequina*, *Morrut*, and *Farga*, but the legislation does not stipulate how much, so oils differ considerably.

The oil of Terra Alta DOP is smooth, transparent, yellow or even golden yellow, with a nutty, almost sweet, taste. Some people detect a hint of almonds, green walnuts, and artichokes. Occasionally you will come across greenish-yellow oils with a fruity taste and a peppery aftertaste. These are made from early-harvested olives. The smoothness of Terra Alta DOP oils is their greatest asset. They combine effortlessly with fish, white meats, cooked vegetables, and salads, and they are unusually stable when used for cooking.

Olive growing has a long history in the Terra Alta. The oldest olive tree in Catalonia, named Lo Parot, is to be found just outside the village of Hort de Sant Joan, where Picasso lived as a young man, close to the road to Gandesa, the capital of the Terra Alta. This tree is thought to be at least 2,000 years old. Its center has long since disappeared, but its vast hollow hulk still fruits regularly. Lo Parot is not an identifiable variety, though it has some resemblance to the ancient *Farga* olive. It is probably one of a number of indigenous cultivars that were grown here before the widespread introduction of the *Empeltre* olive in about 1500.

BAIX EBRE-MONTSIA DOP

Baix Ebre is in the deep south of Catalonia, and includes the extraordinary all-but-island of Montsià, which rises straight from the sea to a height of 2,500ft (764m). The DOP is called Baix Ebre-Montsia. Baix Ebre's capital, Tortosa has been a center for the international trade in olive oil since Roman times. It is here in Tortosa that

CASTLE AT ULLDECONA
Olive trees are planted on the hillside right up to the walls of this imposing castle.

the annual olive oil celebration, the *Fira de l'Oli de les Terres de l'Ebre*, takes place at the end of February.

The olives grown in this most southerly part of Tarragona, around the Ebro River delta and south into Castellón, are quite distinct from those in the rest of Catalonia. There are three indigenous cultivars each of considerable antiquity: *Morrut* (50 percent *Sevillenca* (35 percent), and *Farga* (15 percent). The *Farga* is an ancient cultivar, thought to date back to Roman times. Everyone in this region will tell you that they know of a tree at least 2,000 years old.

Catalan allioli

Garlic sauce—the Catalan allioli—is the most widely used condiment in Catalonia. It is so commonplace and so highly esteemed that it is eaten with almost every foodstuff, from fish and white meats to rice, vegetables, and salads. Allioli is an emulsion of oil and garlic, sometimes with a little raw egg added to guarantee the consistency. It is as old as records relate. When Pliny the Elder was governor of Tarragona in the 1st century C.E., he wrote that when garlic was beaten with oil and vinegar "it is surprising how the foam increases."

Nowadays, allioli is part of any Catalan celebration, and Catalans insist that it is quite distinct from the French provençal aïoli. At the annual celebration called the *Fira de l'Oli* in Tortosa the crowds set out every February to beat their own existing Guinness record for the quantity of allioli that can be made in one day.

◄ MIXED CULTIVATION
The gray-leaved olives grow alongside the greener almonds in many parts of Tarragona, as seen on this unirrigated but well tended terraced hillside.

Leading producers in Lérida

Agroindustrial Catalana

25177 La Granadella
☎ 973 13 30 12
W www.agroindustrialcatalana.com

Agroindustrial Catalana markets the oils of four cooperatives in the Garrigues area. Its brands are Degustus and Gran Degustus. The latter is extracted by the Sinolea method *(see p.35)*—fruity and fresh with sometimes a hint of pepperiness.

Agroles

25400 Les Borges Blanques
☎ 973 14 21 50
W www.agroles.com

This secondary cooperative (about 40 members) markets 70 percent of all Les Garrigues DOP oil. Its brand names are Germanor

PARC TEMÀTIC

The history of olives in Lérida and the rest of Catalonia is well displayed at the museum known as the Parc Temàtic de l'Oli, in Masia Salat near Les Borges Blanques. One of the presses in its collection is considered the largest in the world, with a main beam 39ft (12m) long; it dates from the 17th century and comes from Cambrils in Tarragona. Outside, the museum has 55 millennial trees of the *Farga* cultivar brought from Baix-Ebre. One is said to be 2,500 years old. The museum also displays the processing plant that was used in the village cooperative in Arbeca until 1980, when a modern, continuous system was introduced. Each of the three cones that crushed the olives weighs 5,600lbs (2,500 kilos). Nowadays a visit to the quiet village of Arbeca, from which the *Arbequina* olive takes its name, may be a disappointment: it has kept its rustic simplicity intact for many years.

ROMANICO

and Románico, which also come as top-cru Esència and Ecológico variations. They are all good—fruity, mild, and long lasting, with very little pepper or bitterness.

Casa Pons (Euroaliment)

25124 Rosselló
☎ 973 73 05 25
W www.euroaliment.com

A private company, whose top quality label is Pons, with three excellent lines—"ordinary" Virgen Extra, unfiltered, early-picked Nueva Cosecha, and organic De Agricoltura Ecológico. All are fresh and fruity, with a slight aftertaste of almonds.

Cervià de les Garrigues, Coop. del Camp de

25460 Cervià de les Garrigues
☎ 973 17 80 06

One of the larger and better cooperatives; its brand is Campo de Cervià.

Sant Isidre de les Borges Blanques

25400 Les Borges Blanques
☎ 973 14 29 50
W www.terrall.es

The leading cooperative in Les Garrigues, founded in 1912 and a consistent prize-winner over the years.

Its label is Terall—fresh, light, fruity *Arbequina* at its best.

Veá

25175 Sarroca de Lleida
☎ 973 12 60 00
W www.vea.es

One of the largest private enterprises in the area. Veá comes in squat, square bottles; it has a greenish tinge and an intense *Arbequina* fruitiness. L'Estornell —also 100% *Arbequina*—is usually made with riper olives collected not only from the area of Les Garrigues but also from Tarragona and Alcañiz. The organic Ecológico option has a hint of bitterness in its aftertaste. All very good.

L'ESTORNELL

Vinaixa, S. Coop. de

25440 Vinaixa
☎ 973 17 53 09

This is one of the best cooperatives founded in 1920. Its DOP label is Cooperativa del Camp de Vinaixa, which has a long, fruity taste of tomatoes and artichokes, followed by a gentle hint of bitterness and pepperiness. Half its production is sold in bulk to bottlers and blenders. This is a typical figure for village cooperatives in Lérida.

Other producers in Lérida

Arbeca, Coop. del Camp d'

25140 Arbeca
☎ 973 16 00 00

The village that gave us *Arbequina* olives is dominated by its cooperative, which sells its oil under the Oli d'Arbeca label.

Arp Aliment

25471 La Pobla de Cervoles
☎ 619 74 68 38
W www.oleumflumen.com

Oleum Flumen is delicious unfiltered *Arbequina* oil from Arp's estates in Lérida and Tarragona—incredibly fruity, with a smell of sweet hops and a fresh, herbaceous taste.

Bovera, Coop. del Camp Nuestra Señora de la

25178 Bovera
☎ 973 13 31 43

One of the smallest cooperatives; its prize-winning Or del Terme oil is light, fruity, and smooth, with a gently peppery finish.

Juncosa, Coop. Ag. de

25165 Juncosa de les Garrigues
☎ 973 128 010
W www.coopjuncosa.com

DOP oil with less than 0.2% acidity, sold under the Las Cabanas or L'Or Verd labels.

Maials, Coop. del Camp

25179 Maials
☎ 973 13 00 05
W www.barodemaials.com

Fruity *Arbequina* oil (including DOP) sold under the Baró de Maials label.

MIQEUL FARRE RAIMAT

VALLEY OF CAMP DE CERVIA *Arbequina* olives dominate here.

Olis de Raimat

25111 Raimat
☎ 973 72 40 01
W www.miquelfarre.es

Top-class, unfiltered, early-picked 100% *Arbequina* oil sold as Miquel Farre Raimat, with delicious hints of grass, almonds, and bananas. This estate is best known for its wine but the olives were planted in 1998 and are intensively cultivated.

Vallaserra

25185 La Granja d'Escarp
☎ 610 46 21 04
W www.vallaserra.com

Excellent Vallaserra oil comes from the company's estates in Zaragoza and Lérida, intensively planted with *Arbequina* olives. The main lable is Rincón del Cierno and has the fresh fruitiness that typifies the best made *Arbequina* oils.

Leading producers in Barcelona & Gerona

Pau Roses, Coop. Ag. de

17494 Pau
☎ 972 53 01 40
W www.paurosescooperativa.com

This is one of the few cooperatives in Gerona, dating back to 1954. Most of its olive trees are ancient and of rare endemic cultivars, *Argudell* and *Corivell*. Oli de Pau is 100% *Argudell*—fruity and gentle, with a light, peppery aftertaste.

Rodau

Finca Molí d'en Ballell
Torroella de Fluvia
☎ 972 52 60 63
W www.roda.es

Part of the Bodegas Roda group. Its Dauro de l'Empordà oils are simply delicious—*Arbequina* at its most beguiling.

Leading producers in Tarragona

La Boella, Moli

43110 La Canonja
☎ 977 77 33 09
W www.laboella.com

Moli La Boella sells two outstanding oils: La Boella Premium and La Boella Arbosana. *Arbosana* is a rare endemic Catalan olive cultivar: La Boella uses a selected clone from the agricultural research station at Mas Bové, thickly planted. Its oil is thick, unfiltered, and greenish, with tastes of grass, lemon, almonds— and raspberries.

CEOLPE (Centre Oleícola del Penedès)

43712 Llorenç del Penedès
☎ 977 67 83 34
W www.covides.com

A secondary cooperative that has 16 members in and around Penedès, all within the Siurana DOP and producing a total of about 172,000 gal (650,000 liters) a year. Duc de Foix is its best-known brand— fruity, juicy, and especially popular in France.

Corbera d'Ebre, Coop. Ag. de

43784 Corbera
☎ 977 42 04 32

Smooth, rich, fruity Mirall dels Deus oil has a rich taste of raspberries, arugula, and pepper.

Coselva

43470 La Selva del Camp
☎ 977 84 41 25
W www.coselva.com

Coselva has won prizes at home and abroad for its DOP Siurana oil, sold under its Antara label, which is fresh and fruity with a suggestion of almonds and dried fruit.

Masía Cuatri Camins

43500 Tortosa
☎ 977 58 11 22
W www.masdeladama.com

The Martí family's estate is outside Tortosa near Reguers. Their Mas de la Dama is fruity, with hints of broccoli and artichoke, and richer than many *Arbequina* oils.

MAS DE LA DAMA

Montbrió, Coop. Ag. de

43340 Montbrió
☎ 977 82 60 39

Montebrione is a prize-winning label— golden yellow, unfiltered, fruity, cool, grassy, and long, but mild, with only the

MONTEBRIONE

merest tremor of pepperiness and bitterness to finish. *Siurana* at its best.

Olis Solé

43300 Mont-Roig del Camp
☎ 977 83 70 31
W www.olissole.com

The Solé family makes a fresh, green, robustly fruity *Siurana* oil under the name of Mas Tarrés and an organic version sold as Mas Tarrés Ecológico. Both good.

Riudecanyes, Coop. Ag. de

43771 Riudecanyes
☎ 977 83 40 11

This is a small cooperative, but 90 percent of its land is irrigated and its Escornalbou

SIGN FOR OLIVE OIL FROM ILLDECONA, TARRAGONA

DOP *Siurana* label is outstanding. The oil was used by Sean Connery to season a dish in the movie *Playing by Heart*.

Sant Isidre del Perelló, Coop. Ag.

43894 El Perelló
977 49 00 37

Coperelló, made mainly from *Morrut* and *Farga* olives, is robust, smooth, fruity, and grassy, with a long peppery aftertaste and a trace of bitterness.

Ulldecona, Coop. Ag. d'

43550 Ulldecona (Tarragona)
977 72 00 07

Ulldecona's Arbequina Acomont oil is excellent— golden yellow, fruity, and cool, with a long aftertaste and the mildest suggestion of pepperiness to end.

ARBEQUINA ACOMONT

Unió Agrària Cooperativa

43206 Reus
977 33 00 55
www.unio.coop

Unió is one of the oldest secondary cooperatives in Spain, founded in 1942 and now with some 80 members. Its excellent DOP Siurana oil Unió is widely available in Spain and abroad.

Other producers in Tarragona

ACOBEM

43500 Tortosa
977 58 12 12

Acobem stands for Associació de Cooperatives Olivaires del Baix Ebre-Montsià, a secondary cooperative that promotes

about a dozen cooperatives in the Baix Ebre—Montsià DOP under the Acobem label including that at Ulldecona (*see right*).

Bisbal de Falset, Coop. del Camp de la

43372 La Bisbal de Falset
977 81 90 34

One of the smaller cooperatives, which sells its green-yellow, fruity extra virgin olive oil under the name La Bisbal de Falset.

Escoda, Aceites

43748 Ginestar
977 40 91 19

This well-established family firm uses *Farga* and *Arbequina* olives to make its soft, fruity, filtered Escoda extra virgin olive oil.

Gandesa, Celler Coop.

43780 Gandesa
977 42 00 17

Gandesa's olive oil is mild, gentle, fruity and long, with a light pepperiness to finish.

Gasull, Establecimientos Felix

43201 Reus
977 31 54 14
www.felixgasull.com

This fruity, low-acidity *Arbequina* oil from the Reus area is sold under the Gasull label. Good.

Ideal, Aceites

43500 Tortosa
977 50 02 00
www.idealsa.com

One of the big companies, like Juan Ballester Rosés and Aceites Moncel, that concentrates on lower-grade oil. However, its Ábaco brand offers an extra virgin label.

Olis de Catalunya

43201 Reus
977 34 03 87

This is the marketing arm

OTHER GOOD COOPERATIVES

Other good cooperatives you may come across in the province of Tarragona in the Terra Alta area include Sant Josep in Bot, Terra Alta in La Pobla de Massaluca, and the village cooperatives in Arnes and Sant Salvador d'Horta. Quality in Siurana is uniformly high—disappointing oils are very rare. Good Siurana cooperatives to look for include: Cambrils (prize-winning **Mestral**); La Figuera (**Aubacs i Solans**); Monteroig del Camp (**Coocamp**); and Ulldemolins (**La Llena**). Good estate brands include: **Mas d'Alerany** near Serra d'Almos; **Neus** from Priorat Natur in Pradell de la Teixeta; the young **Olivalls** from near Valls; and **Cervus** from Falset near Montsant.

of about 60 cooperatives in Tarragona and Lérida. Brands are Oleastrum (oil from Siurana) and Oleastrum Verd (Les Garrigues). Both are good.

Pinellense, Coop. Ag.

43594 El Pinell de Brai
977 42 62 34

The cooperative, famous for its architecture and murals, sells its oil as Oli Verge Extra Celler del Pinell de Brai.

Sant Isidre del Mas de Barberans, Coop. Ag.

43514 Mas de Barberans
977 73 90 30

This cooperative's Balcó de l'Ebre oil is made mainly from old trees of *Morrut* and *Sevillenca* olives.

Santa Bàrbara, Coop. Ag. de

43570 Santa Bàrbara
977 71 80 69

This is one of the larger cooperatives. Its main label is Grusco, made from *Farga*, *Morrut*, and *Sevillenca* olives. The oil is golden-yellow, rich, smooth and fruity, with a hint of nuts and pepper in the aftertaste.

Aragón

This region has about 123,000 acres (50,000ha) of olives, of which 64,000 acres (26,000ha) are in Teruel Province, 34,000 acres (14,500ha) in Zaragoza, and 23,500 acres (9,500ha) in Huesca. Most holdings are family owned and few exceed 12 acres (5ha).

THE OLIVE REGIONS OF ARAGON

THE OIL RIVER

Olives have been cultivated in the flat lands of the River Ebro since at least the 6th century B.C.E., when traders sailed up the river to buy the oil of this inland region. The river was called *Oleum Flumen* (oil river) by the Romans. Away from the river banks, the basin of the Ebro valley is dry and barren, with an average annual rainfall of 14in (350mm). The cold, dry, northerly wind, which the Aragonese call the *cierzo*, keeps the olive fly (*see p.27*) at bay and makes it possible to cultivate olives organically.

MOST OLIVE GROWING IN THE SOUTH

There is only one DOP in the Ebro valley, that of Bajo Aragón. The north bank of the Ebro, in the provinces of Zaragoza and Huesca, may soon have its own DOP called Moncayo-Jalon, based largely on blends of *Empeltre* and *Arbequina*. Three-quarters of the olives grown in the region of Aragón fall within the Bajo Aragón DOP (about 91,500 acres/37,000ha), which accounts for about two percent of Spain's production. The DOP covers a large and sparsely populated area in the provinces of Teruel and Zaragoza, up to the southern bank of the River Ebro. Here the dry, stony plains that line the Ebro valley are open and treeless. Olives grow only in the few sheltered fertile valleys such as those around Belchite, where the deep red earth, called *tierra*

OLIVES AT VALDERROBRES Olive growing is a major agricultural activity in the province of Teruel.

roja, has accumulated. Alcañiz is the center of the Bajo Aragón oil industry, an ancient town dominated by its castle. In the hills south of Alcañiz, the land is more fertile and better watered. *Empeltre* is the local olive: its pendulous branches, heavy with fruit, dominate the countryside.

EMPELTRE OLIVES

OILS SOLD FOR BLENDING
Some of the traditional cooperatives produce oils that are a little dull on their own, but are good mixers valued for their smoothness. Much of the Aragonese oil is sold to Italy for blending. The size of secondary cooperatives like Oleoaragon and joint marketing ventures such as Almazares Reunidas del Bajo Aragón enables them to promote the region and sell abroad. Private producers sell their oil in bottles; there are more in Zaragoza and Huesca than in Teruel.

Leading producers in Aragón

Alcorisa, Sdad. Coop. de Labradores de

44550 Alcorisa (Teruel)
☎ 978 84 00 89
W club.telepolis.com/rarias/mestrat/coope.htm

This cooperative was first to install a modern extractor with a continuous system. Its oil is called Alcorcí, and has a hint of green beans and almonds, followed by a gently peppery aftertaste.

Arboleda, Hermanos de Romero e Hijos de

44595 Valjunquera (Teruel)
☎ 978 85 41 28
W www.aceitesarboleda.com

The Arboleda oils come in distinctive clear-glass bottles shaped like an obelisk, and have a scent of almonds and chocolate, followed by a "green" taste, mild and almost creamy, with a gentle pepperiness at the end.

La Calandina, Sdad. Coop.

44570 Calanda (Teruel)
☎ 978 84 62 78
W www.arrakis.es/~lacaland/

One of the best brands in the region, La Calandina smells of almonds and apple and is fruitier than most *Empeltre* oils. With a remarkably long, smooth taste, it is almost sweet, before finally developing a gentle, peppery aftertaste.

LA CALANDINA

Ecostean

22312 Costeán (Huesca)
☎ 974 308 495
W www.ecostean.com

Prize-winning organic oils from the Somontano: Cuarcos de Otto is 80% *Arbequina* and 20% *Empeltre*, while Anigualla also has the very local Verdena. Both are quality oils, skilfully made to a high specification.

San Antonio, Cooperativa del Campo

C/ Ramón y Cajal, 15
44640 Torrecilla de Alcañiz (Teruel)
☎ 978 85 21 35

The cooperative's organic oil Torrecilla de Alcañiz has a whiff of almonds, a smooth, light, fruity taste, and an aftertaste of pepperiness that develops slowly. It is lighter and more fluid than most *Empeltre* oils. One of the best.

San Martín, Coop. Ag.

C/ José Antonio, s/n
50130 Belchite (Zaragoza)
☎ 976 83 03 99

The Oribel oil is smooth and mild, with a smell of almonds and a lightly bitter tang toward the end.

Valdealgorfa Sdad. Coop., Oleícola Aragonesa de

44594 Valdealgorfa (Teruel)
☎ 978 85 70 30
W www.aceitebajoaragon.net/empresa.html

Palacio de Andilla oil of this new cooperative is already a consistent prize-winner.

EMPELTRE OILS

The oils of Bajo Aragón must be made with a minimum 80% of *Empeltre* olives with the balance made up from *Arbequina* and *Rojal*. Nevertheless it is *Empeltre* that gives the oils of Bajo Aragón their distinctive qualities and many are 100% *Empeltre*. The oil is made late in the season, when the olives are fully ripened and have turned black. It is dark yellow or golden, and clear, with a light, fruity taste, a whiff of almonds, a slight piquancy, and a light, bitter aftertaste. However, that bitterness is masked and disappears completely when the oil accompanies cooked food, allowing the rich, smooth texture of the *Empeltre* oil to become its dominant characteristic.

Castilla-La Mancha

La Mancha is Don Quixote country, with wide, dry landscapes and dusty, empty roads. This region is best known for its wines and cheeses, but it is second only to Andalusia in the number of olive trees grown. The flat, open plains are planted with vines and the low limestone hillsides with olives, often topped by the ruins of a medieval fortress.

QUANTITY & QUALITY

Olives are sparse in three of its five provinces—Albacete, Cuenca, and Guadalajara—but the remaining provinces of Ciudad Real and Toledo make up in both the quantity of their trees and the quality of their oil.

The eastern fringe of Albacete has a tradition of producing high-quality oils based on irrigated *Cornicabra* and *Blanqueta* olives. Elsewhere in the region, new experimental owners like J.I.M. Valderrama and Marqués de Griñon are using nontraditional olives to introduce new tastes and new standards of quality for oils, which are then sold to restaurants and gourmet outlets both in Spain and abroad.

TOLEDO & CIUDAD REAL

The Montes de Toledo DOP lies within the part of the region where the most intense cultivation of olives takes place, in southwestern Toledo and northeastern Ciudad Real. Though good oils are made throughout the area, its heartlands

THE OLIVE REGIONS OF CASTILLA-LA MANCHA

are the unprepossessing towns of the windy plain—Herencia, Madridejos, Consuegra, and Mora. In the center of Mora is a famous statue *El Monumento al Aceitunero*, which shows an olive worker posing like a hero in front of a *Cornicabra* olive tree, while his wife and daughter do the work of picking up the olives.

PLAINS OF LA MANCHA Old olives are sometimes overtaken by new vines in this region .

Leading producers in Castilla-La Mancha

Agrovillaserra

13120 Porzuna
926 78 01 00
www.villajos.net

This is a smallish business that produces cheese as well as oil. Both are sold under the Villajos label. Agrovillaserra is unusual among the producers of the region for mixing the local *Cornicabra* olives with the Catalonian super-olive *Arbequina* to produce its unusually fruity and delicious oil.

García de la Cruz, Francisco

45710 Madridejos
925 46 04 96
www.garciadelacruz.com

This is one of the best producers in Toledo. Its devotion to quality even extends to raising young plants of *Cornicabra* for its associates to plant. The García de la Cruz DOP Montes de Toledo oil is clear yellow, with a light appley smell and a richer, fruity taste, followed by an aftertaste with quite a degree of bitterness and pepperiness. The delicious Extra Selección oil is a mixture of *Cornicabra* and *Arbequina* – clear, yellow-gold, apple-scented, cool, fruity and smooth, with no trace of pepperiness of bitterness.

GARCIA DE LA CRUZ

Hacienda de Cañadas

13005 Ciudad Real
926 27 10 53
www.haciendadecanadas.com

This young plantation of *Arbequina* olives near Moral de Calatrava produces a delicious oil —Hacienda de Cañadas—cool, fruity, and appley, with a lightly peppery aftertaste.

HACIENDA DE CAÑADAS

Ifama

45162 Noez
947 17 01 50

Ifama's Arzuaga oil is unusually dark, golden yellow, clear, and apple scented. It has a smooth texture, almost creamy, and a light, rounded taste with a hint of almonds and a suggestion of pepperiness at the end. A high-quality product, it is sold in gourmet outlets throughout Spain.

Jerez, Aceites Hnos.

45249 Alameda de la Sagra
925 50 02 95
www.aceitesjerez.com

Aceites Jeréz makes oil from the area around the Sagra, Bargas, and Olías del Rey. Its DOP label is Jerez. It is greeny yellow, smooth, and fruity with a hint of almonds, and a medium-light bitter aftertaste.

Labranza Toledana, La

45140 Los Navalmorales
925 40 47 11

Labranza Toledana is the leading organic producer in Toledo, and Umbría Oretana is its DOP oil—unfiltered, greeny yellow, fruity, appley, and herby, with an aftertaste of bitter almonds and a light pepperiness.

The olives of Castilla-La Mancha

La Mancha oils are all based on the indigenous *Cornicabra* olive, which is almost the only cultivar in the region. It is thought to date back at least to Arab times (the 12th century), though the extensive plantations around Mora were not begun until the mid-18th century. *Cornicabra* oils are smooth, full-bodied, fruity, and fragrant, with hints of almond and apple and other fruits, and a good measure of bitterness and pepperiness. They are very stable and long lasting, which means that they are good blenders that do not add too distinctive a taste of their own.

Some village cooperatives sell their entire crop to blenders in Italy.

The olive grown in the extreme east of Albacete is *Blanqueta*—also common in the south of Valencia and northern Alicante. It is a small tree that produces a small olive with a high oil content. Its name comes from the pale color of the olives, but they produce an oil that is aromatic and fruity with an aftertaste of tomatoes.

CORNICABRA OLIVES

OLIVE WORKER IN MORA   Notice the olive grower idling while his wife and daughter pick up olives.

Lencina, Aceites R.

02400 Hellín (Albacete)

☎ 967 30 06 27

This family firm, founded in 1860, makes its prize-winning R. Lencina oil from a mix of *Cornicabra*, *Arbequina*, and *Manzanilla* olives. The oil is yellow, with a hint of green, only lightly filtered, and smells of almonds and cucumber. Its taste is smooth, mild, and grassy, with only a little pepper or bitterness.

R. LENCINA

Malagón, Aceites

13420 Malagón

☎ 926 80 00 24

🌐 www.aceitesmalargon.com

Aceites Malagón's DOP Montes de Toledo brand is called Zaitum, which is sold in an inventive range of containers including amphora-shaped pots. The oil is greeny gold, fruity, and fresh, with a taste of apples and almonds, together with hints of ripe bananas, pears, and cherries. It is smooth and delicate on the palate but rich, even opulent, in texture, suggestive of avocados. It also has a hint of bitterness and piquancy at the end. Aceites Malagón also offers a kosher oil.

Marqués de Griñon, Aceite

45692 Malpica De Tajo (Toledo).

☎ 925 59 72 22

This new and much-praised oil, sold as Marqués de Griñon Capilla del Fraile, is made from a somewhat experimental mix of *Picual*, *Arbequina*, and *Manzanilla* olives. All three cultivars are detectable,

though the blend may not be to everyone's taste. The oil is deep, clear yellow, with an almondy smell and a flavor of apples, tomatoes, almonds, and cucumber, ending with a little bitterness and pepperiness. The taste may be unusual, but the oil is unusually well made.

MARQUES DE GRINON CAPILLA DEL FRAILE

Montes Norte, Coop. Oleícola

13420 Malagón

☎ 926 80 26 40

A large cooperative of about 31,400 acres (12,700ha) with 1.8 million trees and a substantial output of 1.06 million gal (4 million liters) a year. Its DOP Montes Norte oil is a regular prize-winner.

Mora Industrial

45400 Mora De Toledo
☎ 925 30 08 58
W www.infonegocio.com/
moraindustrialsa

Produces a good DOP
Montes de Toledo oil under
the Morainsa label, though
much of its production is
also sold in bulk to blenders.

Morlín

45001 Toledo
☎ 925 22 35 91
W www.morlinsa.com

Morlín's estate has 865 acres
(350ha) of *Cornicabra* trees,
the most venerable being
more than 500 years old. Its
leading DOP label is Sierra
De Nambroca, a low-acidity,
unfiltered, greenish-gold oil
with a fruity smell and a rich,
full-bodied taste of tropical
fruits and grass, followed
by a powerful aftertaste of
almonds, pepperiness, and
bitterness. It is widely (and
deservedly) available in
upscale stores throughout
Spain and abroad.

Muñoz, Aceites

45534 La Mata
☎ 925 74 72 35
W www.aceitesmunoz.com

Aceites Muñoz dates from
the 19th century and makes
most of its oils from a 50:50
mix of *Cornicabra* and *Picual*
olives. More than half its
land is newly planted and
irrigated. Its top label is
Herencia Mediterránea, a fruity,
aromatic, and lightly bitter
and peppery oil, but its
100% *Cornicabra* Aceites
Muñoz label is also good.

Palomino Ulla, Aceites

45700 Consuegra
☎ 925 48 09 06

This fairly small company
produces about 600,000lb
(275,000kg) a year from
Cornicabra olives. Its main
label is Palomino—fruity,
almondy, appley, and smooth,
with some bitterness and
pepperiness to follow.

San José, Coop. del Campo

02652 Ontur (Albacete)
☎ 967 32 30 29

This cooperative's well made
Castillo de Ontur oil is 50%
Cornicabra, with the rest made
up of *Picual, Manzanilla*, and
Arbequina. It is clear, bright
yellow, with a green tinge,
and a scent of
ripe olives, lychees,
and other
tropical fruits.
It has a light,
smooth taste
of fruit and
almonds, and
a peppery
aftertaste—
quite bitter,
too. A regular
prize-winner
in regional
shows.

CASTILLO DE
ONTUR

San Sebastian, Sdad. Coop.

45710 Madridejos
☎ 925 460 234
W www.arrakis.es/~quesoman/
oliva/

Founded in 1956 and has
more than 1,100 members.
San Sebastian produces
2,205,000lb (1 million kg)
of oil annually, 95 percent
is extra virgin. Umbrión is
the DOP label. It is golden
yellow, with a hint of green
and a scent of apples, tasting
cool and smooth at first, with
a hint of apples and almonds,
a peppery aftertaste, and a
little bitterness.

San Sebastián, Soc. Coop.

45140 Santa Ana De Pusa
☎ 925 70 30 60
W www.esmipueblo.com/
vallepusa_def/

This cooperative in Santa
Ana de Pusa is small, but
has won prizes for its
Vallepusa DOP oils at
provincial shows.

Subrá, Aceite

45140 Los Navalmorales
☎ 915 11 21 48
W www.aceitesubra.com

Top-quality DOP oil under
the Subrá label made from
ancient *Cornicabra* trees.

SUBRÁ

Tolivir, Expl. Agr.

45400 Mora
☎ 925 30 10 40
W www.aceitestolivir.com

The best of the estate oils
from Tolivir at Mora de
Toledo is Sierra de la Loba y
Arenal. It is fruity, slightly
bitter, and peppery, with
a strong olivey smell.

Valderrama, Aceites

28109 Alcobendas (Toledo)
☎ 916 50 29 19
W www.valderrama.es

José Valderrama has a new
675-acre (273ha) estate in
Pueblanueva in Toledo with
75,000 young *Arbequina*
olives. His family estates in
Córdoba in Andalusia also
grow *Hojiblanca, Picudo*, and
rare *Ocal* olives. He is highly
committed to high-tech
production. Olives are turned
into oil within 45 minutes of
collection. Valderrama offers
four monovarietal oils, all
excellent: the Arbequina is very
fresh and fruity, while the
remarkable Ocal is smooth,
gentle, and olivey with a
lightly bitter aftertaste.

Valencia & Murcia

The regions of Valencia and Murcia are chiefly mountainous, with a fertile coastal plain on which most of the population is centered. Valencia comprises three provinces: Alicante, Castellón, and Valencia. Murcia is both a region and a province. Market gardening and the cultivation of fruit trees are prominent activities.

CASTELLON, VALENCIA & ALICANTE

The three eastern provinces of Castellón, Valencia, and Alicante account for no more than two percent of Spanish oil production, although this is still more than 10 times the total produced by the whole of France. There are many interesting indigenous olive cultivars, and the quality of their oil can be excellent.

The main oil-producing areas in Valencia are Llíria in the Camp de Turia and the area between Millares and Enguera in the Canal de Navarrés. The Camp de Turia produces small amounts of high-quality oils from a combination of the very local *Villalonga* (sometimes called *Manzanilla de Levante*), *Farga*, *Serrana*, and *Morrut* olives. They are golden yellow and very transparent. The Canal de Navarrés area has some 17,300 acres (7,000ha) of olives, mostly *Manzanilla* (70%), the highly local *Alfafareña* (20%), and *Blanqueta* (10%). The oils are a rich greenish-gold, with a light, fruity taste.

The Sierra de Mariola in southern Valencia and northern Alicante has some 22,000ha (54,300 acres) of olives, mainly *Lechín de Granada* (here called *Cuquillo*), *Gordal*, *Manzanilla*, *Farga*, and *Blanqueta*.

There is no DOP in Valencia. The Maestrazgo, in the province of Castellón, lies behind the port of Peñíscola and is best regarded as an extension of the Baix Ebre-Montsià DOP in Tarragona (*see p.149*). The same varieties are grown here as to the north, including *Farga*, *Morrut*, and *Sevillenca* olives, and there is every possibility that the area will be awarded DOP status in due course. The oils of the Maestrazgo have enormous potential for real greatness. The Sierra de Espadán is in southern

THE OLIVE REGIONS OF VALENCIA & MURCIA

OLD OIL CONES AT ALTURA

Castellón, around Segorba. Some of its oils are made from the endemic *Serrana de Espadán* olive.

Important brands are produced by large companies in Valencia and Alicante and include Aceites Soyfonsal in Alacás and Aceites La Canal in Chella. Two big secondary cooperatives are COOVAL (now part of the InterCoop group) at Muro de L'Alcoi and Valsur in Bolbaite, whose **Blanqueta** label is one of Valencia's best.

MURCIA

This region has only a modest olive-growing tradition; the best oils come from the mountains near the border with Albacete. The main industry is citrus fruit and vines.

Leading producers in Castellón, Valencia & Alicante

Alto Palanca, Coop.2º Grado V., Coop. Oleícola

12410 Altura
964 14 60 34
www.aceite-virgen.com

This secondary cooperative promotes oil from 14 primary cooperatives between the Palancia River and the Sierra de Espadán. Its extra virgin Oliespal oil from *Serrana de Espadán* olives is smooth and fruity with a smell of green tomatoes, a taste of almonds, apples, and exotic fruits, with a pleasantly peppery aftertaste but no bitterness. It also sells Dorica and Esmeralda and monovarietal *Arbequina* and *Picual* oils.

OLIESPAL
ACEITE DE OLIVA VIRGEN EXTRA

OLIESPAL

Bodega Ntra. Sra. Virtudes, Coop. V.

03400 Villena (Alicante)
965 80 21 87
www.coopvillena.com

Villena's cooperative produces Tesoro de Villena and a Montañas de Alicante blend of *Manzanilla* and *Blanqueta* sold under the Mariola label. It is lightly fruity, with a slight bitterness and pepperiness.

Casinos, Coop. Ag. Sta. Barbara de

46171 Casinos (Valencia)
962 70 00 56
www.tsc.es/empresa/casinos/

This cooperative makes its Oli d'Oliva Verge principally from *Villonga* olives that impart a soft, grassy freshness and distinct bitterness—a taste Spaniards esteem highly.

InterCoop

12550 Almanzora (Castellón)
964 503 250
www.intercoop.es

A large secondary cooperative with members throughout Castellón, Valencia, and Alicante. Olival, Olidor and Mariola are among its labels. Olidor oils come from all the indigenous cultivars grown by its members (*Serrana de Espadán*, *Blanqueta*, *Villalonga*, *Sevillenca*, *Empeltre*, and others); its top label is Selección Dor. Olival produces two flagship oils: Milenio from 1,000-year-old *Farga* trees and Lágrima de Palancia from *Serrana de Espadán* olives.

MILENIO

J. Montull

12186 Salsadella
964 76 11 74
www.aceitemontull.com

This medium-sized private company uses all the local olive types (*Farga*, *Arbequina*, *Manzanilla*, and *Picudo*) in its Montull Gran Selección blend. The oil has a taste of tropical fruits and artichokes, and a long, peppery aftertaste.

Santísimo Cristo de la Salud, Coop. Ag. V.

46199 Millares (Valencia)
961 80 90 22
www.paralelo40.org/coopmillares

This cooperative promotes an indigenous olive cultivar called *Millarenca* of which no more than 618 acres (250ha) remain. Its oil is fruity, aromatic, dense, and smooth.

Leading producers in Murcia

Herrera, Almazara Luis

30520 Jumilla
968 75 75 73
www.planeta-e.com/AlmazaraLuisHerreraPrincipal.htm

Organic oil made by a traditional press; Aceite de Lágrima is their top label, made from *Manzanilla* and *Cornicabra*.

Lopez De Gea, Juan Antonio

43137 Cehegin
968 74 05 65

Late-picked olives are used for the ACEMUR Aceite de Murcia label. The oil is smooth, cool, almondy, with a hint of green grass but no trace of bitterness or pepperiness.

Murciana, Coop. Oliv. (COOMUR)

30520 Jumilla
968 75 70 20
www.bsi.es

Entrañable oil is made from a variable mix of olives from all over Murcia (*Manzanilla*, *Cornicabra*, *Arbequina*, and *Picual*). It has a complex taste of exotic fruits (passionfruit and mangoes), quite a firm bitterness, and light peppery aftertaste.

Other producers in Murcia

Large producers include Manzano in Beniel, and A. Bernal Romero in Lorca. Both are well established and well regarded. Produna (www.produna.com) specializes in organic oils from the Segura valley. Also well regarded is Aceites de Moratalla (www.moratalla.com) made from ancient trees of Cuquillo (Lechín de Granada) and sold in obelisk-shaped bottles.

Extremadura

This is a region of open plains and dry landscapes, where the historic cities of Zafra, Mérida, and Plasencia are separated by vast empty spaces. Most of Extremadura is sparsely populated and flat, but it has two DOPs that are situated at the edges of its two large provinces, one in northwestern Cáceres and one in southeastern Badajoz, where the monotonous heartlands give way to attractive hilly country.

A REGION OF SMALL PLANTATIONS

There are few intensive olive plantations in Extremadura; most of the olives are spaciously planted and low yielding. This is one of the few regions in Spain where mechanization in olive growing lags behind. Still, in some years it produces more oil than Portugal. It has 117 olive mills (75 in Badajoz and 42 in Cáceres) and 630,000 acres (255,000ha) of olives (432,00 acres/ 175,000ha of which are in Badajoz) and an estimated 65,000 growers. About 124,500 acres (50,000ha) are organically managed, and this area is increasing. Table olives are also a feature in the Tierra de Barros and Monterubbio in Badajoz (*see opposite page*).

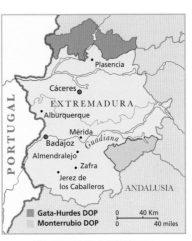

THE OLIVE REGIONS OF EXTREMADURA

CÁCERES

There is one DOP—Gata-Hurdes—in the northwest of the province. The most widely planted olive is *Manzanilla Cacereña*, which also grows in Portugal, especially in Braganca and Vila Real (*see pp.195–199*), where it is known as

Negrinha. In both countries it is used for oil and for table olives. There are about 148,000 acres (60,000ha) of this cultivar in Cáceres and it is the only one permitted in Gata-Hurdes DOP oils. It has a low yield, but its oils are long-lasting and capable of greatness:

CASTLE AT HERQUINJUELAS This grove of ancient trees was planted to provide oil for the estate.

usually fruity with hints of almonds and bananas, and a fairly high degree of piquancy and bitterness.

There are several producers and secondary cooperatives in the larger towns. Among the largest are the Plasencia-based Euroliva and CEXAC (Compañia Extremeña de Aceites y Cereales). CEXAC's main activity is oil refining, but it sells a passable extra virgin oil.

The Gata-Hurdes DOP in the north of Cáceres comprises some 34,500 acres (14,000ha), the size of a village in Córdoba or Jaén, with 2,200,000 olive trees that produce about 11,000 tons (10 million kg) of oil annually. At their best the oils are fruity and aromatic, with hints of banana and green almonds, a certain grassiness, and a piquant and bitter aftertaste.

Quality varies. Some producers offer oils that are not registered with the DOP authorities alongside those that are. The leading firm of Jacoliva says that making extra virgin olive oil is easy with modern equipment, but that a top-quality oil requires much skill, including a meticulous selection of olives, cold pressing, and general knowledge and experience. This is a lesson that more producers in Extremadura should take to heart.

BADAJOZ

Olives are grown in every part of this province, though the best-known areas are the Monterrubio DOP in the southeast of the province, and the Tierra de Barros between Zafra and Almendralejo in the southwest.

The *Morisca* olive is the most widely grown cultivar in the Tierra de Barros and the flat lands called the Vegas de Guadiana. There are some 148,000 acres (60,000ha) of *Morisca* olives across Badajoz; they are chosen for their vigor and drought resistance. *Morisca* oils are soft and pleasant (if seldom distinguished), and lightly fruity, with more than a touch of bitterness and piquancy. Their fluidity and green-gold color are very typical. The *Carrasqueña*

LINE OF OLIVE TREES
The Monterrubio area in southeastern Badajoz has its own DOP, but standards of cultivation and oil extraction are sometimes poor.

olive is also found in the Tierra de Barros area, but mainly as a table olive. Its oils are peppery and bitter, but useful in blends for their resistance to oxidization. The *Verdial* olive is grown in small quantities everywhere in this province, and is the dominant cultivar around Alburquerque. Its oils are fine, fruity, and lightly almondy, with a characteristic pepperiness.

The Monterrubio DOP is in the Sierra Morena, much of which remained uninhabited until about 1800. There are almost no references to olives in the area until the late 18th century. The cultivars planted were *Cornicabra* and *Picual* olives, here known as *Cornezuelo* and *Jabata*. *Cornicabra*, which gives the DOP oils of Monterrubio their characteristic smoothness and whiff of almonds, is complemented by the stronger-flavored *Picual* olive. Monterrubio oil is greenish yellow, very stable, lightly fruity, aromatic, slightly bitter, and rather more peppery than some other olive oils.

The Monterrubio DOP area is small; its 37,000 acres (15,000ha) support 2 million trees and produce about 6,600 tons of oil. Only a small proportion of the oil attains DOP standards. Several of the leading producers, assisted by regional grants to buy modern equipment, are currently updating their extraction techniques. Hitherto, the quality of Monterrubio oils has often been disappointing.

Leading producers in Cáceres

Fejidosa

10664 Mohedas Granadilla
927 67 35 40
www.fejidosa.com

Fejidosa offers two oils that are both of high quality, a DOP brand called Orovic, and the uncertified Urdoliva.

Jacoliva

10813 Pozuelo de Zarzón
927 44 80 11
www.jacoliva.com

Jacoliva offers several first-rate oils. Its fashionable monocultivar 100% *Manzanilla Cacereña* oil is the greenest of all olive oils, with a rich, creamy texture, a grassy, aromatic taste, and a long-lasting piquancy. Its unfiltered organic oil El Lagar del Soto is made from the olives of organic growers all over northern Cáceres and has a green,

CACERES

fruity taste with hints of apples and bananas, balanced by a nice touch of piquancy and bitterness.

Jaraoliva

10869 Torrecilla Angeles
927 67 70 24
www.grupolosangeles.com

This is another market leader, part of the Grupo Los Angeles, which is best known for table olives. It processes about 89,800 tons (8,000,000kg) of olives for oil annually. Its Serie Oro pure *Manzanilla Cacereña* oil is a clear golden color, with a grassy taste, a pleasantly bitter edge, and a degree of piquancy that gives it body. El Ciburnal is also a dependable label.

Jolusa

10900 Arroyo de la Luz
927 27 00 77
www.jolusa.com

The basic marque of this large company is Trajano, a golden-yellow smooth oil made from a mixture of *Manzanilla Cacereña*, *Cornicabra*, and *Verdial*. Their 100% *Manzailla Cacereña* line is Gran Almena, which has a Gata Hurdes DOP. The bright green Almena de Galisteo Barras Verdes is also good.

SIERRA DE GATA

Siglo XXI, Compañía Oleícola (Euroliva)

10660 Plasencia
927 41 79 58

The striking Sierra de Gata label is the best known of the Gata-Hurdes DOP oils and is sold in upscale stores like *El Corte Inglés*. Its fresh fruitiness is well matched by a fair degree of bitterness and piquancy that give it considerable body. Euroliva's La Chinata oil, although based on the *Manzanilla Cacereña* olive, is a blend of oils from all over Spain—pleasant and reliable, if not exciting— fruity and lightly bitter with somewhat more pepperiness.

Secondary cooperatives

Individual producers and cooperatives in Extremadura find it difficult to sell their oil, so the industry is dominated by secondary cooperatives. Much is sold in bulk to blenders and refiners. The leading secondary cooperatives are Viñaoliva in Almendralejo, the capital of the Tierra de Barros, whose main label is **Cortijero**; Acopaex, based in Mérida, with some 15 cooperatives in northern Badajoz, whose oil it sells under the **Acopaex** label; and Indesur

LA CHINATA

(short for Industrias del Suroeste) in Jerez de los Caballeros, whose best-known extra virgin brand is **Jucaro**, made from a mix of *Cornezuelo* and *Manzanilla* olives. All of them deal in other products besides olive oil. Indesur is among Spain's top 20 olive oil producers, as is Compañia Oleícola Siglo XXI (Euroliva) at Plasencia, whose brands include **La Chinata** and **Sierra de Gata**. All produce pleasant, everyday, extra virgin oils.

Leading producers in Badajoz

Aurelio Juzgado Partido

06427 Monterrubio de la Serena
☎ 924 61 06 84

Aurelio Juzgado Partido is a private company with a significant share of the Monterrubio market. Its main label is Juzgado.

Dieta Mediterránea Aceites y Vinagres

06310 Puebla de Sancho Perez
☎ 924 55 14 00

This innovative company near Zafra produces a low-acidity, unfiltered, organic oil, mainly from *Morisca* olives, with a little *Picual*, under its Molino de Zafra label; it has a light taste of apples and delivers quite a peppery punch too.

Marqués de Valdueza

Finca Perales de Miraflores
Mérida
W www.marquesdevaldueza.com

Some of the best producers in Badajoz are privately owned estates with the means to experiment. The oil produced by the Marqués de Valdueza on his 494-acre (200ha) estate in the Guadiana valley near Mérida is a good example. The olives are mainly *Arbequina*, *Picual*, and *Hojiblanca* —none of them indigenous to Badajoz—and great attention is paid to good cultivation, prompt processing and correct storage. Marqués de Valdueza oil is widely available in gourmet outlets throughout Spain and abroad, and

MARQUÉS DE VALDUEZA

makes a most interesting blend—fragrant, fruity, smooth, lightly peppery, and harmoniously balanced between the different cultivars that go into its composition.

Olivareros, Sdad. Coop. de

06225 Ribera del Fresno
☎ 924 53 70 01
W www.olivareros.com

The cooperative at Ribera del Fresno uses the very latest equipment to produce the fruity, peppery Tinajona brand, made almost entirely from *Morisca* olives.

La Unidad', Sdad. Coop. del Campo

06427 Monterrubio de la Serena
☎ 924 61 00 88

The Cooperativa del Campo "La Unidad" at Monterrubio produces on average 422,700 gal (1,600,000 liters) a year and sells its oils in glass and plastic under the names Morubio and La Unidad.

LA MONTERRUBIANA

Ramona García López

06427 Monterrubio de la Serena
☎ 924 61 00 60

Ramona Garcia Lopez has won considerable respect as a woman operating in a traditionally male-dominated business. Her La Monterrubiana label is popular. However, it is

not always registered with the DOP authorities.

San Isidro Labrador, Coop.

06760 Navalvillar de Pela
☎ 924 86 05 66

This cooperative in northeast Badajoz is a national prize-winner.

Sdad. Coop. del Campo La Unión Monterrubiana

06427 Monterrubio de la Serena
☎ 924 61 04 40
W www.aceitel.com

This secondary cooperative offers an extra virgin DOP oil Don Aceitel and an organic DOP Bio Aceitel.

Virgen de la Estrella, Sdad. Coop.

06230 Los Santos de Maimona
☎ 924 54 40 94
W www.maimona.com

The cooperative near Zafra, is one of the region's high-quality producers and regularly wins prizes. It is integrated into Viñaoliva, whose plant at Almendralejo bottles its oil. It was founded in 1963 and now has 700 associates who farm 4,500 acres (1,800ha) of olive trees. Its Maimona label is 100% *Morisca* olive—a pleasant, lightly fruity oil with a fair measure of pepperiness and bitterness.

MAIMONA

Andalusia

Most of Spain's olive oil—some 80 percent—comes from Andalusia. Córdoba and Jaén account for 30 to 40 percent of the world's production and Jaén alone produces more oil than the whole of Greece (the world's third-largest oil-producing country). Row upon row of olives cover every valley and hillside as far as the eye can see. It is a sight to gladden the heart of any gourmet or lover of good food.

MEDITERRANEAN CLIMATE

Andalusia's climate is Mediterranean, with hot, dry summers and mild, wet winters. The Guadalquivir valley is so hot in summer that it is known, even in Spain, as *el sartén*, ("the frying pan"). Andalusia is, however, a region of contrasts. Rainfall in the mountains of Cádiz is high, yet the plains of Almería are a desert landscape. In the uplands of Jaén and Córdoba, snow and frost are regular visitors. But almost every part of the region receives more than 3,000 hours of sunshine every year, which helps to explain the high quality of its olive oil.

CAPITAL INVESTMENT

Massive investment in the infrastructure has revolutionized agriculture in Andalusia. This is a recent phenomenon. Few of the leading oil cooperatives date back before 1950, and many of the most successful producers have only been in business for five years. Their success is the result of investment in

up-to-date extraction machinery and technical know-how. Loans and subsidies come from the EU and regional government.

To attract increased investment, olive-oil producers must have the highest standards of cultivation and harvesting to provide the mills with olives that are fresh, healthy, clean, and unblemished. Once producers begin to gain recognition for quality, perhaps by winning international prizes, they attract more investment, some of which can be channeled into promotion and advertising. Margins should then improve and investors reap the rewards. That, at least, is the theory. Unfortunately, for every successful organization, there are several undercapitalized, badly managed cooperatives selling their indifferent product cheaply for blending or refining.

Generally, Andalusian producers have not been very successful in promoting and selling their oil. Quality has been consistently high now for 20 years, but

THE PROVINCES OF ANDALUSIA

the oil is available in such quantities, and from so many suppliers, that individual producers find it very difficult to promote themselves.

NONTRADITIONAL CULTIVARS
One problem is that too much of the oil tastes the same. There is not the variety and variation among the oils of Jaén and Córdoba that exists in areas with a more fragmented industry. Some of the more adventurous growers have ignored the local traditions and planted the Catalonian wonder-olive *Arbequina*, with excellent results. The superior quality of oils made from *Arbequina* commands a higher price than *Picual* and *Hojiblanca*. What is needed now is more experimentation with cultivars from other parts of Spain and elsewhere.

TOURISM AND AGRICULTURE
The Andalusian olive oil industry was founded on cheap labor. Workers could not afford to seek employment elsewhere. However, the picture is brighter today thanks to tourism. Olive cultivation fits around the seasonal tourist trade on the coast very well. When visitors return home to northern Europe, the workers return to their agricultural pursuits.

OLIVE WASTE
Disposing of olive waste, known as *orujo*, is a problem. It pollutes waterways and smells of rancid olives. In some places it is burned causing malodorous smoke to hang in the air. Oleoliva in Málaga uses *orujo* to produce electricity. It consumes 165,000–220,500 tons (150–200 million kg) of olive waste per year to generate 25m watts.

OLIVE TREES AND POPPIES A view over the countryside near Loja in the Poniente de Granada DOP area.

JAEN

The region of Jaén is the center of the world olive industry. The sheer size of its plantations is staggering. Lines of *Picual* olive trees rise and fall with the lie of the land and crosshatch the hilltops as far as the eye can see. Since the 18th century, olives have been the only crop here, bringing riches to the landowners and social problems to the poor, whose employment is limited to the season of picking and pruning. Cooperatives have brought surer returns to smallholders, and mechanization has improved the quality of their oil.

The heartland of Jaén's olive industry is the gentle hills of the Campiña Sur and Sierra Sur, which are completely clothed in olive trees. The quality of their oils varies from mediocre to good. Northern Jaén is thickly planted with olive trees, especially in the comarque of Campiña Norte. *Picual* is omnipresent so it is not surprising that Jaén produces oceans of identical-tasting oil whose quality is less conspicuous than its quantity. For the most part, however, it is good enough to be sold in bulk to blenders. Aficionados of Jaén oils are spoiled for choice. The best policy is to settle for a DOP oil, or to look for one of the better-known marques with a

THE OLIVE REGIONS OF JAEN

reputation for quality. *Arbequina* oils and single-estate oils also promise above-average quality.

There are three DOPs in Jaén— Sierra Mágina, Sierra de Segura, and Sierra de Cazorla. All are in upland areas, where the oils of *Picual* are thought to be fruitier. The mass-produced oils of lowland areas are perhaps best used for culinary purposes.

The Sierra Mágina DOP is in the south of the province, in the national park. *Picual* is the dominant olive. Olives are only cultivable on the lower slopes of the Sierra Mágina. Higher up, the

SIERRA DE CAZORLA, JAEN The broad valley of the Guadalquivir River is filled with olive trees.

WINTER IN GRANADA Prolonged cold weather is death to olive trees, even well established ones.

hillsides are covered by pine trees and wild rosemary and wild boar roam the forests. There are no large towns in the area, just a federation of villages without a center.

The main requirement of the Sierra de Segura DOP is that the olives should be *Picual* and grown within a small area northwest of the Sierra de Segura. The oil is usually clear yellow with a hint of green, and fruitier than most *Picual* oils.

There are some 79,000 acres (32,000ha) of olives in the Sierra de Cazorla DOP. Production centers on the town of Cazorla itself, on the western slopes of the Sierra de Cazorla mountain range. Olives are certainly the main crop here, though the trees are not so ubiquitously planted as in the lowlands around Jaén. Many of the plantations in the Cazorla area grow a *Picual* clone called *Royal*: *Picual* and *Royal* are the only permitted cultivars.

The La Loma district around Baeza and Úbeda adjoins the Sierra de Cazorla DOP. It is intensively planted. Almost all the olives are *Picual*, producing large quantities of somewhat ordinary extra virgin oil.

GRANADA & ALMERIA

In Moorish times, Granada was the most intensely planted province of Spain and today there are 420,000 acres

(170,000ha) of olive trees in Granada. Olive trees are everywhere, usually as mixed or scattered plantations. The trees dominate the landscape in the north of the province, which is the home of Granada's two DOPs: Poniente de Granada in the west, and Montes de Granada in the east. Geographically and culturally, each belongs to the intensive olive-growing area in Córdoba or Jaén which adjoins it. The oils, too, are similar; Poniente de Granada DOP has many affinities with Priego de Córdoba DOP, as Montes de Granada DOP has with Sierra Mágina DOP. Poniente de Granada is dominated by *Hojiblanca* olives, and Montes de Granada by *Picual* olives. The largest

Montes de Granada DOP
Poniente de Granada DOP

0   10 Km
0   10 miles

THE OLIVE REGIONS OF GRANADA & ALMERIA

Picual olives

During the 17th and 18th centuries, *Picual* olive trees were widely planted as a means of converting uncultivated land to economic use. *Picual* gives fairly fruity and decidedly bitter oils of great body, which are peppery if the olives are picked young. The fruitiness is a green taste—leaves, cut grass, and apples—but never of almonds. Olives from high altitudes are thought to be fresher in taste. *Picual* oils are extremely stable and long lasting.

Picual has two remarkable attributes. It is a very regular, heavy cropper and its olives give a very high yield of oil. Its only shortcoming is the taste of the oil. Spaniards love it, most foreigners do not. The Italian nickname for it is *pipì di gatto* ("cat's urine"). When they are young, *Picual* oils have a distinct smell of bay leaves but take on a nuttier, milder taste as they age.

PICUAL OLIVES

secondary cooperative is Oligra (Oleícola Granadina) with some 30 members; its oil is sold under the Oliveña label.

MONTES DE GRANADA DOP

This is a well established area of olive cultivation north and northeast of Granada city. Its center is the town of Iznalloz, whose small white houses are clustered around the ruins of an old Arabic castle. Gentle, rolling hills, some 2,950 ft (900m) above sea level, fill the upland valley between the Sierra Araña to the southeast and the Sierra de Alta Coloma to the northwest.

Many of the older olive trees in this area are the local specialty, *Loaime*, and up to 500 years old, but most of the olives in Montes de Granada date from 1910–1970. In the 1960s alone, the area put to olives in the province of Granada doubled. There are now 138,000 acres (56,000ha) of olives in the area.

Picual is here known as *Marteño*, and accounts for more than three-quarters of production, with the balance made up largely by *Loaime* (5%) and another local specialty called *Lucio* (11%). Both are strongly resistant to summer drought and winter frost. The addition of these lesser cultivars moderates the bitterness of *Picual* olives. *Loaime* oils are notably stable and resistant to oxidization, especially those made early in the season, which are among the longest lasting. The San Antonio cooperative at Cogollos Vega is the leading producer, and sells a soft, gentle, fragrant oil that is 80% *Loaime*.

The major producers in Montes de Granada are the village cooperatives to which smallholders bring their olives for processing. Quality depends on the skill of the technical manager of the mill and the extent to which farmers adhere to the required standards. It should be said, however, that quality does not lead to smart presentation or sophisticated marketing. Much Montes de Granada oil is sold, on price rather than quality, to large national and international concerns for blending.

PONIENTE DE GRANADA DOP

This is a recent DOP that covers most of the province northwest and southwest of the city of Granada. The three most important centers are the towns of Loja, Montefrío, and Íllora, each of which has an olive-growing tradition going back to at least the 16th century. In the area around Montefrío, 80 percent of the population depends on the cultivation of the olive for its living and olive trees account for 34,500 acres (14,000ha), more than half of which has been planted since 1990. In the 19th century, one of the most famous oil mills, built in 1800, belonged to the Duke of Wellington and Ciudad Rodrigo at Molino del Rey.

There is considerable variation in the style and quality of Poniente de Granada olive oils. The DOP legislation permits three main olive cultivars— *Picudo*, *Picual*, and *Hojiblanca*—together with three local specialties: *Lucio*, *Loaime*, and *Nevadillo de Alhama de Granada*. However, it does not specify the proportions or the preponderance of any variety. The Almazara Casería de la Virgen at Alomartes, for example, produces its oil from 50% *Picual* and 50% *Lucio*, whereas the new (1997) cooperative at Olivajayena produces a 100% *Hojiblanca* oil. The oils are supposed to be light in the mouth, balanced, and rounded, which is DOP-speak for "hard to describe, too much variation among them" and they should have a taste whose "light touches of bitterness are in harmony with the gentle flavors."

NEW VENTURES IN ALMERIA

Almería is the driest province in Spain, with more hours of sunshine than anywhere else in Europe. Rainfall in some parts of Almería may never exceed 4in (10cm) per annum. There is a handful of local cooperatives in villages along the Almanzora valley, such as Tíjola and Albox—the best is at Canjáyar at the eastern end of the Alpujarras—but the commercial edge belongs to young, private estates where olives are intensively planted and irrigated. One of the most successful is Rafael Ubeda's Castillo de Tabernas in the "Desierto de Tabernas," where many spaghetti westerns were filmed. It was

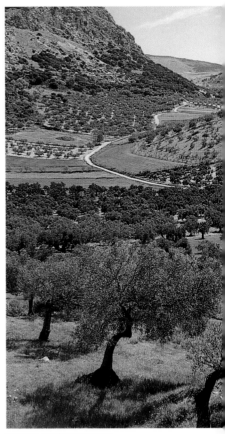

THE HILLSIDES OF MALAGA
Olive trees flourish in the beautiful limestone valleys of the upper Axarquía. This is the heartland of the delicious Verdial oils.

planted with *Picual* in 1993. Nearby is the 1,500-acre (600ha) Jiménez estate of Moraila, planted with *Arbequina*, *Picual*, and *Hojiblanca*. Both take advantage of the constant, dry, sunny weather in the weeks leading up to the harvest to produce a top-of-the-market olive oil whose acidity does not exceed 0.1%.

MÁLAGA

Northern Málaga is thick with olives. Antequera alone has 44,500 acres (18,000ha) and is the center of a new DOP with 10 million olive trees: 90% are *Hojiblanca*, and the rest are *Picual*, *Arbequina*, and *Lechín*. The area is dominated by the Grupo Hojiblanca, a secondary cooperative on the Córdoba

THE OLIVE REGIONS OF MÁLAGA

OLIVES ON THEIR WAY TO PRESSING

road out of Antequera. Grupo Hojiblanca represents 42 primary cooperatives with 23,000 members on 445,000 acres (180,000ha) in Córdoba and northern Málaga, and it sells its oils in 43 countries. It accounts for eight percent of the national product and one-quarter of the extra virgin oil. Grupo Hojiblanca comes in fifth position behind Koipe, Agribética, Coosur, and Ybarra in the general market and first among the sellers of extra virgin oil.

The Axarquía is by far the most distinct olive-growing area within the province of Malaga. Its pretty, Italianate landscape makes it increasingly popular for weekend and out-of-town living. The leading olive cultivars in the Axarquía are two local specialties, *Verdial de Vélez* and, down near the coast, *Nevadillo*: softness and fruitiness are their distinguishing characteristics. There are 23 producers, 14 cooperatives, and 9 private owners, producing about 24.2 million lb (11 million kg) of oil annually. In the Axarquía, as everywhere in Spain, price and bottle-shape are no guide to quality: the local cooperatives sell their extra virgin oil in plastic bottles.

Verdial de Vélez-Málaga is one of many "*Verdial*" olives, but endemic to the Axarquía, where there are about 52,000 acres (21,000ha) of it. Many of the trees are of considerable age, with thick and

twisted trunks. *Verdial de Vélez-Málaga* has larger fruit than most oil-bearing olives, but a smaller oil content. The oil is short-lived but delicious—soft, smooth, and fruity, without bitterness or piquancy. It is greatly in demand for blending with *Hojiblanca*; this "perfect blend" has the fruitiness of *Verdial* and the stability of *Hojiblanca*.

Fifty years ago, olive plantations ran down to the Costa del Sol. Few remain, but many survive a little way inland, around Coín, up the valley toward the Sierra de la Nieves and Ronda. There is talk of possible DOP status for Ronda, which has 7,986 acres (3,232ha) of olive trees, for oils based on *Hojiblanca*, though *Lechín* and *Verdial* are actually more widely grown in the area. At the nearby village of Benalauría the ethnological museum has an 18th-century oil mill.

HUELVA, SEVILLE & CADIZ

Olive growing is not a major industry in Andalusia's outlying provinces of Huelva and Cádiz. Few olives grow in the remote and lightly populated province of Huelva, best known for its cork-oak forests, *jamón serrano* (dry-cured ham), and mining. They are concentrated in the villages around Huelva town and up on the Portuguese frontier beyond the Sierra de Aracena. The most widely grown cultivars are *Verdial de Huévar*, *Lechín de Seville*, *Gordal*, and *Manzanilla*, but these are supplanted in modern

THE OLIVE REGIONS OF HUELVA, SEVILLE & CÁDIZ

OLIVE MILL AT ZAHARA, CÁDIZ Olives, separated from their leaves and stalks, are taken to a hopper.

plantations by *Arbequina* and *Picual*. In Cádiz, 85 percent of all the olives grow in the Sierra de Cádiz, a mountainous area in the northeast of the province, around the small white town of Olvera. Sierra de Cádiz is also a DOP, with some 94,000 acres (38,000ha) of olives in the province of Cádiz and 15,000 in the province of Seville. Most of the traditional olive plantations today are at least 100 years old. Irrigation is unknown; olive fly makes organic cultivation difficult. The dominant olive in this area is a form of *Lechín*, sometimes known as *Lechín de Sevilla*. It gives the oils of the Sierra de Cádiz their character and flavor, which is middling or strongly fruity, with only a touch of bitterness or pepperiness.

Seville is a major oil-producing province, third after Jaén and Córdoba. At Las Hermanas, south of Seville, the large factories—including Coosur, Migasa, Ybarra, and Torres y Ribelles (*see pp.140–41*)—blend, distribute, and sell vast quantities of oil. Extractors, processors, refiners, and bottlers, they serve Spain and its export markets.

The Seville towns with the largest numbers of olives are all in the hilly east of the province. (Cotton is king in the flat, fertile valley of the Guadalquivir.) The figures, representing land planted with olives, are: Osuna (34,500 acres/ 13,970ha), Estepa (30,158 acres/ 12,205ha), Marchena (22,735 acres/ 9,201ha), Morón de la Frontera (19,582 acres/7,925ha), and Carmona (19,256 acres/7,793ha). *Hojiblanca* is by far the most widely planted cultivar for oil, with more than 1.4 million trees in Estepa alone, followed by the native *Lechín*, while *Manzanilla* and *Gordal* are grown for table olives.

Lechín olives

It is the color of their ripe flesh and the texture of their juice that gives Lechín (meaning "milky") olives their name. The fruit has to be picked by hand, because it is very firmly attached to the branches, though it ripens and turns black somewhat early. Its oil is not long lasting because it oxidizes quickly, but it is very attractive when young and fresh. It is also a smooth oil that covers a skillet quickly. Blending is generally thought to improve it, which is why pure *Lechín de Sevilla* oils are difficult to find.

LECHIN DE GRANADA   LECHIN DE SEVILLA

The industry is dominated by one giant secondary cooperative, Oleoestepa, which accounts for 4,000 growers, 113,600 acres (46,000ha) and 6.5 million olive trees. Oleoestepa produces an average of 440 million lb (20 million kg) of oil annually, though the actual figure may be above 66 million lb (30 million kg) in a good year like 2003. This amounts to nearly half the oil produced in the province of Seville. Oleoestepa bottles, promotes, and sells its members' oils: its label is Oleoestepa. Two cooperatives in particular are regular winners of national and international prizes: Nuestra Señora de la Paz at Estepa, and Olivarera San José at Lora de Estepa. The key to Oleoestepa's success is its insistence on the highest standards of cultivation, harvesting, and processing. This is made possible by employing technical experts to advise the individual growers on high-quality management throughout the year. Success has rewards and it is not unusual to see farmers driving their trailers of olives to the cooperative in ATVs. Some 20 years ago they would have made the journey by donkey and cart.

Hojiblanca is by far the most widespread cultivar around Estepa, though *Arbequina* is a feature of Gilena, Écija, and Aguadulce, and the *Lechín* olive is widely grown in Pedrera.

A new DOP for Estepa has recently come into existence, which is, in effect, another measure of Oleoestepa's success. The DOP permits the oil to be made from *Hojiblanca*, *Manzanilla*, *Arbequina*, *Picual*, and *Lechín* (with *Hojiblanca* the most important), and makes the stringent requirement that Estepa DOP oils should have a maximum acidity of 0.3%. Seville may also seek to create a DOP to recognize the traditional cultivar *Lechín*, the olive used in the Sierra de Cádiz DOP (*see pp.172–3*), which includes the Sevillian towns of Coripe and Pruna.

CORDOBA

Córdoba provides some 10–15 percent of the world's olive-oil crop. It is second only to Jaén in the quantity of olives it grows and the oil produced. In parts of the province, olive trees fill the landscape

up to the crest of the hills in all directions. The main olive is *Picudo*, but *Hojiblanca* and *Picual* are also grown, and there is an increasing enthusiasm for *Arbequina*. Córdoba has two denominations, named after the pretty baroque towns of Baena and Priego de Córdoba, both of which are in the southeastern corner of the province. Puente Genil in the west forms part of the new Estepa DOP. In the southwest around Lucena, Benamejí, and Santaella, the province is dominated by

THE OLIVE REGIONS OF CORDOBA

Picudo and *Hojiblanca* olives are thickly planted on the gentle hills around Baena in southeastern Córdoba.

There are also two secondary cooperatives in the Priego de Córdoba DOP—Almazaras de Priego and Almazaras de la Subbética—as well as one very substantial private company, Mueloliva. The permitted olives in the Priego de Córdoba DOP are *Picudo*, *Hojiblanca*, and *Picual*. However, the best oils are made mainly from *Picudo*, which accounts for 60 percent of the olives under cultivation (around one quarter are *Picual* and 15 percent *Hojiblanca*).

BAENA DOP

This DOP is in the central southern part of the province of Córdoba. It includes the towns of Baena, Luque, Doña Mencía, Nueva Cartaya, and Zuheros. In total it covers about 148,000 acres (60,000ha) with 7.2 million olive trees, which produce 66–100 million lb (30–45 million kg) of oil a year. The oil is made principally from *Picudo* olives, but *Lechín*, *Hojiblanca*, and *Picual* are also permitted. Baena DOP oils are robustly fruity, pungent, and aromatic, usually with pepperiness and bitterness in the aftertaste.

the Córdoliva cooperatives, which are part of the Hojiblanca group. This area may yet be included in an expanded Antequera DOP. The small town of Palenciana already belongs. Los Pedroches in the Sierra Morena in the north of the province is a world apart, and a bastion of organic olive growing.

PRIEGO DE CÓRDOBA DOP

This DOP includes the towns of Almendinilla, Carcabuey, Fuente Tójar, and Priego de Córdoba itself. Roughly 111,000 acres (45,000ha) of olive trees are registered with the Priego de Córdoba authorities, producing about 176 million lb (80 million kg) of olives and 37.4 million lb (17 million kg) of oil. It is hilly countryside, sometimes mountainous, and includes part of the Subbética National Park. Priego de Córdoba DOP produces some of the most delicious oils in Andalusia, which are aromatic, fruity, and juicy, with a touch of bitterness and pepperiness. Many cooperatives are national and international prizewinners.

The DOP is dominated by village cooperatives and large private companies. The character of the oil varies slightly, depending on which village it comes from. The best oil comes from Carcabuey, a small white mountain village with a huge cooperative in the valley below.

Picudo olives

The prominent point at its tip gives the *Picudo* olive its name. It makes a vigorous, hardy tree with a very dense canopy. The leaves are rather dark. The olives are large (about .20 oz/4.5–5g) and also useful for serving at the table. The oil is short-lived but fluid in texture and smooth in taste—well balanced, almost sweet, with hints of exotic fruits, apples, and almonds.

PICUDO OLIVES

Leading producers in Jaén

Aceites La Laguna

23529 Puente del Obispo
☎ 953 76 51 00
🖥 www.aceiteslaguna.com

This modern producer's premises are situated at the entrance to the Hacienda La Laguna estate (*see box below*). The company is geared to quality production and worldwide sales. Its main line is Hacienda La Laguna Picual extra virgin oil, but it also offers a Gran Selección

GRAN SELECCIÓN MANZANILLA

HACIENDA LA LAGUNA

Hacienda La Laguna is the best-known private estate in Jaén. It was built by a rich Pole called Bartmanski in the 1920s, and planted with 100,000 olive trees, all irrigated from a 28-ha (69-acre) lagoon. Part of the estate is now occupied by a hotel-school; its restaurant is famous for its olive oil ice-cream. The estate is also home to a very fine Museum of Oil – the best in southern Spain.

Hacienda La Laguna
23440 Baeza
☎ 95376 50 84

Gourmet selection for *Picual, Manzanilla, Arbequina* and a mixture of all three. The Gran Selección Manzanilla is pale greeny gold and unfiltered, with a taste of bitter almonds and vegetables and quite a peppery aftertaste – not a typical *Manzanilla*, but good.

Agrosegura

23360 La Puerta de Segura
☎ 953 486 423

A young firm, with high standards and up-to-date extraction equipment. Its main label is Agrosegura, a fruity, bitter *Picual* oil.

Avirol

23120 Cambil
☎ 953 30 04 11
🖥 www.olivodecambil.com

Good of its kind is Olivo de Cambil oil – clear, filtered, greenish gold, with a light, grassy smell. Its taste is rich, and reminiscent of tropical fruits, but complemented by a grassy bitterness and a warm peppery aftertaste.

Cazorla, Aceite Jienense de

23480 Quesada
☎ 90 23 60 398

Royal Esencial de Sierra de Cazorla is one of the best Jaén oils – clear greeny gold, with a light, smooth, cool taste of greenness and bitter olives, followed by a gentle aftertaste of bitterness and pepperiness. Amargo de Sierra de Cazorla is indeed bitter – even more bitter than most *Picual* oils – but a deep golden yellow colour, with a hint of green, a smell of lemons and artichokes and a touch of pepperiness, too.

Exportadora Andaluza de Aceites (Aceitex)

23001 Jaén
☎ 953 24 31 95
🖥 www.aceitexp.com

Oro Virgen is Aceitex's DOP Cazorla label, but its main

oil, Oleocazorla, comes from the same estates belonging to the Sanchez de la Torre family at Peal de Becerro. It is clear, greeny gold and fairly fluid, with a smell of olives, tomatoes, and almonds and a strong almondy and fruity flavour, followed by a persistent pepperiness and bitterness.

Grupo Proacec

23700 Linares
☎ 953.656990
🖥 www.proacec.com

Proacec is a large company, and Linares is not within the Sierra de Segura DOP, but Caroliva oil comes partly from the Segura area and partly from the Contado. It is a blend of *Picual, Arbequina* and *Hojiblanca*, with a good fruity flavour (apples and herbaceous tastes) and a neat aftertaste of pepperiness and bitterness.

Montabes Vaño (MONVASA)

23100 Mancha Real
☎ 953 350178
🖥 www.vallemagina.com

Valle Mágina is deep, golden yellow, and filtered; it has a strong *Picual* smell, followed by a cool, smooth, fresh taste, lots of body and a long, full aftertaste – an excellent oil, as well as an

VALLE MAGINA

inexpensive one. Dominus is robust, unfiltered, and made from early-picked organic olives, with a strong taste of grass and olives, balanced by a long and pleasing measure of bitterness and pepperiness.

Nuestra Señora de la Encarnación, Coop.

23460 Peal De Becerro
953 730 109
www.scaencarnacion.com

One of the oldest and largest cooperatives in the area. Its DOP label is Castillo de Toya.

Nuestra Señora Esperanza, SAT

23100 Mancha Real
953 372 83 09
www.condeargillo.com

This estate's Conde De Argillo DOP oil is one of the best in the Sierra Mágina – a fruity, fresh *Picual* taste with a lingering aftertaste.

Oleofer

23360 La Puerta De Segura
953 48 61 09
www.oleofer.com

Oleofer's DOP label is Comendador de Segura. Its straightforward extra virgin oil is sold as Segura Oliva.

Olivar de Segura

23350 Puente De Génave
953 435400
www.olivardesegura.es

This is the largest secondary cooperative in the Segura area, representing some 15 local cooperatives. Its brands include: Sierra de Génave, Señorío de Segura, Verde Segura and De Nuestra Tierra. These are widely sold throughout Spain and abroad – they are dependable and inexpensive. Señorío de Segura is dark yellow, with a green tinge, clear and very typical of *Picual* oils – fruity, pungent and bitter.

Piedras Cucas, Aceites Vírgenes de Oliva

23003 Jaén
953 22 05 33
www.piedrascucas.com

The pleasant Esencia de las Piedras Cucas made by the Arjona Cámara family from 100% *Picual* is greeny gold and unfiltered, with a smooth taste of bitter almonds and a long, light pepperiness to finish.

ESENCIA DE LAS PIEDRAS CUCAS

Potosí 10

23380 Orcera
953 48 20 41
www.potosi10.com

The best-known oil produced by this syndicate of private owners is its DOP Fuenroble, which is seen in upmarket shops all over Spain. It comes in the squat, square bottles that are thought by Spaniards to suggest quality. It has a greeny gold, clear colour, and a smell of pears, followed by a taste of bitter almonds and tropical fruits; it is only lightly peppery, but rather more bitter – a very Spanish taste.

Santísimo Cristo del Consuelo, Coop.

23470 Cazorla
953 12 42 23
www.aceitescazorla.com.

A large cooperative with several extra virgin labels,

including Castillo de la Yedra, Cazorla Royal and Cazorla Picual, all in the local style.

Sierra de Génave

23392 Génave
953 49 31 53
www.sierradegenave.com

This cooperative is dedicated to organic production: its leading label is Oro de Génave, marketed by Olivar de Segura. The oil is yellow, very fluid, with a smell of peppers and black olives and a light, greenish taste, followed by a balance of pepperiness and bitterness.

ORO DE GENAVE

Thuelma

Huelma
953 390155
www.thuelma.es

This estate produces Thuelma Oliva oil which is dark gold with a green tinge, a fresh, fruity smell, a strong taste of *Picual* olives and a long, light aftertaste.

Toya, Coop. Aceites

23460 Peal de Becerro
953 716 087
www.aceitestoya.com

Toya is one of the smaller cooperatives (50 members). Its filtered DOP oil is La Almicerana.

Vallejo, Emilio

23650 Torredonjimeno
☎ 953 57 12 82
W www.emiliovallejo.com

The Aceites Vallejo label
is a good "ordinary" *Picual*
oil from an area that
undersells itself. It is greeny
gold, with a *Picual* smell,
a long, fruity, unctuous
taste, a little bitterness and
a solid, peppery aftertaste.
Well balanced.

Viana, Oleo

23539 Garcíez
☎ 953 35 91 21
W www.aceiteviana.com

Viana's main label is Lo Mejor
de Viana – clear, pale green-
gold, with a light olivey
smell and a pleasant taste
of almonds and rocket,
fairly peppery but only
lightly bitter. Viana also
makes oil from centennial
trees on the estate of the
Marqués de la Ensenada
in Garcíez and markets
it as Al-Manzar; this is
unfiltered and rich golden-
yellow, with a smell of
almonds and tomatoes, and
a smooth, mild, almondy
taste followed by a little
pepperiness and bitterness –
very well balanced.

LO MEJOR DE VIANA

Other producers in Jaén

Baeza, Oleícola

23440 Baeza
☎ 953 12 71 33

Oleícola Baeza's principal
brand is Campos de Baeza,
clear golden-yellow with a
greenish hint and the bitter
smell of *Picual*, a taste
of tropical fruits, a warm
aftertaste and a considerable
degree of bitterness.

CAMPOS DE BAEZA

Fedeoliva-Jaén

23210 Guarromán
☎ 953 61 52 00
W www.fedeolivajaen.com

This secondary cooperative's
main brand is Fedeoliva but
it also produces two other
labels – Señorío de Villar and
Lanagrán, which recalls a
strong-flavoured, peppery
blend of bitter almonds and
tropical fruits. The *sabor suave*
version of each brand has a
lower acidity, and lasts
longer, than the *sabor intenso*.

García Morón, Grupo

23750 Arjonilla
☎ 953 52 00 11
W www.garciamoron.com

Greenish-gold *Picual* oils
under the Garcia label: fruity,
bitter and lightly peppery.

La Torre

23620 Mengíbar
☎ 953 37 07 15

Well-made *Picual* oil, sold in
squat, square bottles under
the Oro de Maquiz label and
popular in Germany.

San Felipe Apóstol

23440 Baeza
☎ 953 74 06 05

San Felipe Apóstol's extra
virgin Balcón del Guadalquivir
oil is more golden yellow
and more rounded than
many Jaén oils, with a cool,
smooth taste, mainly of
bitter almonds.

Úbeda SCA, Unión de

23400 Úbeda
☎ 953 75 68 40
W www.uniolixa.es

One of the oldest
cooperatives in Andalusia.
Its main brand is Uniolixa,
but its La Flor de la Loma
label is a high-quality,
prize-winning organic oil –
Picual at its best.

Valderrama, C.B. Hnos. Millán

23300 Villacarrillo
☎ 957 27 10 01

The Valderrama family
make their fine Molino del
Álamo oil at their Finca
El Álamo, using mainly
Arbequina olives, plus a little
Picual. It is golden green in
colour, very fruity, and has
almost no bitterness or
pepperiness – just a mouthful
of delicious fruitiness.

Cooperatives & large producers in Jaén

Alcalá Oliva Distribución

23680 Alcalá la Real
☎ 953 58 38 38

Produces oil under the
Alcalá-Oliva label.

Betica, Aceitera Cooperativa, La

23480 Quesada
953 73 32 82
www.beticaaceitera.com

Cabañas brand.

Casería de Santa Julía, Aceites La

23460 Peal De Becerro
953 243 195

Oleocazorla label.

Conde de Torrepalma, Aceites

23680 Alcalá la Real
953 58 29 07
www.oli-ole.com

Oli-Olé label.

González, Hijos de Bernardino

23192 Carchelejo
953 30 20 55
www.bernardinogonzalez.com
Molino de Aguas Blancas label.

Guadalentín, Aceites

23485 Pozo Alcón

953 738 035
www.aceitesguadalentin.com

Guad Lay and Huesoliva labels.

Nuestra Señora de la Asunción

23370 Orcera
963 48 00 56
Orzeoliva label.

Nuestra Señora de la Cabeza, Coop.

23487 Huesa
953 715 403

Picos del Guadiana Menor label.

Nuestra Señora de Nazaret

23264 Chiclana de Segura
953 466 016

Nuestra Señora de la Paz, Coop.

23477 Chilluevar
953 717 011

Alcoray label.

Nuestra Señora Remedios, Coop.

23530 Jimena
953 35 74 37

Oro De Cánava label.

Oleocampo

23640 Torre del Campo
953 56 79 25

Torres Sur and Fruto del Sur.

Oleo-España

23650 Torredonjimeno
953 57 12 08

Oleo España label.

Oleomartos, S.L.

23600 Martos
953 70 40 40
www.oleomartos.com

Oleo Martos label.

San Francisco

23340 Arroyo del Ojanco
953 42 01 04
Oro Verde, Don Señor, and Fuentebuena labels.

San Francisco de Paula

23538 Albanchez de Mágina
953 35 83 53

Aznaitin and Reino De Jaén labels.

San Isidro, Coop.

23485 Pozo Alcón
953 738 108

Oleo Alcón label.

San Isidro Labrador

23560 Huelma
953 39 01 10

El Santuario de Mágina label.

San Juan de la Cruz

23280 Beas de Segura
953 42 48 03

La Vega de Santo Tomé label.

San Juan, Del Campo

23009 Jaén
953 081 400
www.aceitesanjuan.com

Fuente de la Peña label.

San Marcos

23280 Beas de Segura
953 42 48 05
Natao and Aceites La Ventilla labels.

San Vicente

23447 Chilluévar
953 71 70 16

Cazorliva brand.

Sta. María, Coop.

23110 Pegalajar
953 36 06 82

Fuenterreja label.

Santísimo Cristo Misericordia, Coop.

23500 Jódar
953 78 50 31

La Quinta Esencia label.

Santo Tomás Apostol, Coop.

23311 Santo Tomé
953 736 010
wwwcooperativasantotomas.com

Los Estados de Santo Tomé label.

Sierra Mágina

23539 Bedmar
953 76 05 24

Magnasur brand.

Técnicas Agrícolas Ecológicas e Integradas

23568 Bélmez de la Moraleda
953 39 40 50

Oro Mágina and Verde Mágina labels.

Trujal de Mágina

23120 Cambil
953 30 05 67

Verde Salud label.

Leading producers in Córdoba

Crismona, Aceites

14860 Doña Mencía
☎ 957 67 60 00
🌐 www.crismona.com

Crismona promotes the oil of about 10 producers in the Baena region. It is responsible, for example, for bottling the oils of the cooperative at Zuheros. Its leading label is Crismoliva, a strong-flavored *Hojiblanca* oil. However, Crismona also offers a DOP Baena oil, an organic oil, and a pure *Arbequina* oil. All are of dependable quality.

Germán Baena, Olivarera

14850 Baena
☎ 957 67 01 10
🌐 www.germanbaena.com

Germán Baena is the leading cooperative in Baena. Its 15 members produce large quantities of 8–11 million lb (4–5 million kg) of oil and have won many medals for it. Duque de Baena is its best label, 80% *Picudo* and unfiltered, greenish gold with lots of fruit, followed by pepperiness and bitterness. The everyday Germán Baena extra virgin oil is good, too—also distributed in Spain as La Niña de mis Ojos and in France by Carrefour as De Nuestra Tierra.

Gomeoliva

14800 Priego de Córdoba
☎ 957 70 05 84
🌐 www.gomeoliva.com

This private company produces a fine DOP oil called Molino de Leoncio Gómez, which is greeny gold, fruity, and smooth. Its organic label Olivares de Leoncio Gómez has won much praise in recent years, while their everyday extra virgin Gomeoliva is also

good. All the oils have the characteristically suave texture and robust taste of *Picudo* and *Hojiblanca*, ending with a fair measure of pepper and sometimes a little bitterness.

MOLINO DE LEONCIO GOMEZ

Manuel Montes Marín

14800 Priego de Córdoba
☎ 957 55 30 67

Manuel Montes Marín has two main labels, Fuente La Madera and its flagship Pórtico de la Villa, which is made mainly from *Picudo*, with a little *Hojiblanca*. It is unfiltered, smooth, fruity and rounded with a very long taste of grassiness and almonds, and only a little pepperiness and bitterness toward the end. Excellent.

Morales Morales, Sucesores de

14814 Zamoranos de Priego
☎ 957 70 53 26

A dependable producer, whose Marqués de Priego and Oro del Mediterráneo labels are typical Priego oils—greeny gold, fruity, and full bodied.

Mueloliva

14800 Priego de Córdoba
☎ 957 54 01 47
🌐 www.mueloliva.es

Mueloliva is a giant among Priego producers, employing more than 100 people. Mueloliva is its everyday oil and Venta del Barón its

powerful premium DOP brand made from *Picudo* with a little *Hojiblanca*—clear yellow, fruity and smooth, with hints of bitter almonds and grassiness, ending with a long-lasting warm aftertaste of pepper. It comes in notably handsome, clear-glass bottles.

Nuestra Señora de Guadalupe, Olivarera

14850 Baena
☎ 957 69 08 09

This cooperative sells two fruity extra virgin oils, Fuente Baena and Guadoliva, both with a taste of almonds and fresh greenness, a peppery aftertaste and a trace of bitterness.

Orobaena

14850 Baena
☎ 957 67 07 06
🌐 www.orobaena.com

This young company sells its Orobaena oil all over the world. The oil is fruity, with hints of grass, tomatoes, and bitterness followed by a good whack of pepperiness. Its prize-winning organic OroNovus brand is made only from pitted olives and is even more intensely fruity and smoother. Both are made from 50% *Picudo*, with the balance made up of *Picual*, *Manzanilla*, and *Hojiblanca*.

Priego, Almazaras de

14800 Priego de Córdoba
☎ 957 547 274

One of two secondary cooperatives in Priego: its star member is Olivarera La Purísima, a small, high-quality producer that has won many prizes in recent years for its soft, fruity, well balanced oil. Almazaras de Priego's generic label is El Empiedro, but they also offer an organic Eco Empiedro; both are clear, golden yellow, smooth, robust, and fruity with a well rounded texture and a fair degree of pepperiness and bitterness to end with. They are good representatives of the Priego style.

San José, Almazara

14850 Baena

C 957 67 01 50

One of the smaller producers in Baena, whose unfiltered organic oil bears the label of the Onieva Alcalá owners. It has a rich, fruity taste, a measure of pepperiness, and rather a lot of bitterness in the aftertaste.

Subbética, Almazaras de la

14800 Priego de Córdoba

C 957 547 028

W www.almasubbetica.com

This is the big secondary cooperative in Baena, with

Núñez de Prado, 14850 Baena

C 957 67 01 41,

W www.nunezdeprado.com

six primary cooperatives and 2,000 members, selling 8–11 million lb (4–5 million kg) oil a year. Its members' oils include Fuente de la Salud, Olibrácana, and Bajondillo. Their oils are made mainly from *Picudo* and *Hojiblanca* (40% each, plus 20% *Picual*)—fruity, well made, balanced, and good value.

Virgen del Castillo

14810 Carcabuey

C 957 55 30 14

W www.virgendelcastillo.com

The cooperative in Carcabuey—an enormous building that dominates the valley—is consistently one of Spain's top producers. It has more than 2,500 members, some of whom grow quinces for *membrillo* (quince paste), the other specialty of the area. Its prize-winning extra virgin Parqueoliva is made mainly from *Picudo* olives—unfiltered, pale green gold, fruity, grassy, cool, smooth, lightly bitter, slightly peppery, and simply delicious.

PARQUEOLIVA

Vizcántar, Aceites

14800 Priego de Córdoba

C 957 54 02 66

W www.aceitesvizcantar.com

Vizcántar's DOP oil Señorío de Vizcántar is dark green gold, with a rich fruity taste of *Picudo* olives (though made with some *Picual* and *Hojiblanca* too), balanced, full bodied and well made, ending with firm peppery and bitter aftertaste. The company also sells organic oils under the names Eco-Vizcántar and Bio-Vizcántar.

Other producers in Córdoba

ArteOliva

14700 Palma del Río

C 957 64 90 27

W www.arteoliva.com

ArteOliva was the first producer anywhere in the world to sell its oil in cartons. It buys olives from all over the region, so its extra virgin ArteOliva is a mixture of *Picudo*, *Picual*, *Arbequina*, and *Hojiblanca*. It also offers an organic oil.

Francisco Gómez Reina

14500 Puente Genil

C 957 72 10 46

W www.aceitecortijocanal.com

The remarkable fruity unfiltered Cortíjo El Canal oil is produced using traditional presses. It is fresh, grassy, cool, and smooth, with a light touch of pepperiness and bitterness to finish.

Pedroches, Olivarera Los

14400 Pozoblanco

C 957 77 05 29

W www.olipe.com

The cooperative in Los Pedroches is a beacon of the organic movement, and the uplands around Pozoblanco in the Sierra Morena are now the largest single area of organic-olive growing in Spain—some 24,700 acres (10,000ha). The cooperative's top oil is Olivalle, which comes from a great mixture of olives (*Nevadillo Blanco*, *Picudo*, *Manzanilla*, and *Lechín*) but it is well made and gutsy—grassy, rich, leafy, peppery and bitter. The nonorganic extra virgin Aceite del Valle de los Pedroches is also good. Both are sold in distinctive octagonal bottles. Another good oil from Los Pedroches is Olivar de la Luna from Santa Catalina.

Leading producers in Huelva, Seville & Cádiz

El Agro

11692 Setenil de las Bodegas (Cádiz)
956 13 40 63

In Setenil de las Bodegas, the El Agro cooperative (with 800 members) produces a prize-winning oil from a mixture of *Lechín*, *Hojiblanca*, and *Picual*. It is yellow with a hint of green, and a taste of grassiness, apple, and banana, followed by a light aftertaste of bitterness and pepperiness.

Camacho, Angel

41530 Morón de la Frontera
955 85 47 00
W www.acamacho.com

Angel Camacho (founded in 1897) is a large producer that employs 160 people and releases its oil and table olives under the *Fragata* brand. It offers *Gordal*, *Manzanilla*, and *Hojiblanca* as table olives, and in various treatments and presentations —green, black, or natural, whole, husked, or filled, and so on. Their oils come in a very great range too.

La Campana, Olivarera

41429 La Campana
954 19 95 06
W www.oleocampana.com

The cooperative in La Campana only sells its prize-winning Oleocampana extra virgin oil in ½ or 1¼-gal (2- or 5-liter) containers. It is made mainly from *Lechín de Sevilla* olives.

Nuestra Señora de la Oliva, Almazara Coop. de

21500 Gibraleón (Huelva)
959 30 00 33

Oleodiel is made from *Picual*, *Arbequina*, and *Verdial* and has a long, soft, smooth, fruity taste—a real mouthful— followed by a long peppery aftertaste and just a little bitterness.

Nuestra Señora de los Remedios

11690 Olvera (Cádiz)
956 13 00 83

The cooperative at Olvera is the largest producer in the area, with 3,000 members. Its trademark oil is Dehesa Vieja, the first to be sold with a Sierra de Cádiz *denominación* label. The cooperative also offers an organic oil called Oro Natura with an acidity of less than 0.5%. Both are greeny yellow, fresh, and fruity, with a taste of greenness, herbs, and artichokes, ending with a touch of bitterness and pepperiness.

Oleoestepa

41560 Estepa
902 23 24 05
W www.oleoestepa. com

This highly successful secondary cooperative, founded in 1986, accounts for some 4,000 growers. All its oils are extra virgin and of excellent quality —unusually fresh and fruity.

OLEOESTEPA

San Isidro Labrador (CASIL)

41620 Marchena
954 84 38 25
W www.casil-e.com

The smooth, gentle oil of the cooperative in Marchena is made from *Lechín* and the form of *Verdial* they call *Verdial Real*, plus a little *Cornicabra*, and is called Casil oil. The commune used to process 95 percent of its olives for oil, but now nearly half is grown for table olives, principally *Manzanilla* and *Gordal*.

San José Obrero, S.A.T. 1184

41780 Coripe
955 85 85 75

This village cooperative (200 members) produces about 441,000 lb (200,000 kg) of oil a year, 90 percent of it from *Lechín* olives. A proportion qualifies for inclusion in the Sierra de Cádiz DOP.

Santa Teresa, S.A.T. 1941

41640 Osuna
954 81 09 50
W www.1881.es

The flagship brand of this prize-winning cooperative is 1881: Alta Selección, usually made from 70% *Hojiblanca* and 30% *Lechín*. The company was founded in 1959 and now dominates the area around Osuna. It is also a pioneer in the introduction of ecofriendly cultivation; some 30 percent of its plantations adhere to the principles of sustainability and integrated management.

El Vinculo S.XVII, Almazara

11688 Zahara de la Sierra (Cádiz)
956 12 30 02
W www.arunda.com

The mill in Zahara de la Sierra was founded in 1749. Its El Vinculo oil, made from a mixture of *Lechín* and *Manzanilla*, is greeny yellow, fruity, and grassy with a taste of apples, and a good aftertaste of pepper and bitterness.

EL VINCULO

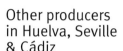

Other producers in Huelva, Seville & Cádiz

Blazquez, Aceites

41670 Pruna
954 85 83 80
www.aceitesblazquez.com

Produces *Lechín* oils with the Blazquez label, some qualifying for the Sierra de Cádiz DOP.

San Juan Bautista

41660 Villanueva de San Juan
954 91 65 71

Produces mainly *Lechín* oils under the Villanoveño label.

San José

41540 La Puebla de Cazalla
954 84 72 33

A large cooperative, whose oil is made from a great mixture of olives. Its label is Pueblaoliva.

San Sebastian

41390 Guadalcanal
954 88 61 11
www.sierradeguadalcanal

The main cooperative in the remote area around Constantina, Cazalla de la Sierra, and Guadalcanal in the Sierra Morena in the extreme north of the province. Sierra del Guadalcanal is the label, made from the indigenous *Verdial de Badajoz* olive, here called *Pico Limón*.

Leading producers in Málaga

Hojiblanca

29200 Antequera
952 84 14 51
www.hojiblanca.es

This secondary cooperative accounts for 90% of the oil in the new Antequera DOP.

Its Malaga labels include Torcaoliva and El Cerro, both good and reliable oils. Torcaoliva has a marked degree of fruitiness and a nice, rich bitterness and pepperiness to balance it.

Labrador, Almazara El

29520 Fuente de Piedra
95 273 50 94
www.satlabrador.com

Almazara El Labrador uses *Lechín* for its La Laguna extra virgin oil. La Laguna is the name of Andalusia's largest freshwater lake, famous for its flamingos. The oil has a grassy scent and a very fruity taste, with hints of celery and tropical fruits, and a warm peppery effect as well as a long, pleasantly bitter aftertaste. In 2004, it won first and second prizes for Spain's finest oils in the "green, fruity, bitter" class.

Ronda, Coop. Almazara de

29400 Ronda
95 287 30 35
www.almazararonda.com

The Ronda cooperative, dating back to 1961, makes its oils from *Morisca, Lechín,* and *Verdial* olives. The unfiltered, deep yellow Aceite de Oliva Virgen Extra is smooth and fruity, but develops an agreeable aftertaste of bitterness and pepperiness.

ACEITE DE OLIVA VIRGEN EXTRA

San Isidro, Cooperativa Aceitera

29710 Periana
95 253 60 20
www.aceiteverdialperiana.com

This cooperative dominates the Axarquía, with 800 growers and two-thirds of the production. About 90 percent of its olives are *Verdial de Vélez*. Its Periana Verdial Frutado Dulce oil is smooth, rounded, pale yellow, and only lightly filtered. Verdior is greener, more peppery, with a hint of tomato and almonds in its taste. A blend of the two types of oil is sold abroad as Oligold or Greengold. All are fruity, fresh, delicious, and excellent value.

PERIANA VERDIAL FRUTADO DULCE

San José Artesano, Olivarera

Barriada Mondrón, s/n
29710 Periana
95 253 79 15

Cosecha Propria Verdial oil from Mondrón is a pale golden yellow, with a scent of lychees and a fruity, aromatic taste, followed by a gentle, lingering bitterness. The cooperative has a small museum attached and is the center of an annual *Día del Aceite Verdial* (Verdial Oil Day), a fiesta held in March.

Other producers in Málaga

Cañero Alfarnate S.L.

29194 Alfarnate
95 275 90 71

The Cañero label from the Axarquía is soft, fruity, and rounded. Excellent value.

Fernandez, Ruiz y Aguilar (F.R.A.)

29400 Ronda
☎ 95 287 13 74
🖥 www.molinodonfelix.com

F.R.A.'s Molino Don Felix oils are made from *Hojiblanca, Picual,* and *Lechín.* The fruity extra virgin oil has a soft taste of almonds and exotic fruits and, eventually, a lightly peppery aftertaste.

MOLINO DE DON FELIX

Guaro, El Molino de

29180 Guaro
☎ 952 11 29 76

This is the leading cooperative in the Sierra de las Nieves, where there is a flourishing industry based on *Lechín* and *Verdial.* The two extra virgin labels are La Guareña and El Molino de Guaro: both are greeny yellow, fruity, rounded with a taste of almonds and apples, a hint of pepper but no trace of bitterness.

Monsalud, Nuestra Señora de

29194 Alfarnate
☎ 95 275 90 52

Aceite de Alfarnate Virgen de Monsalud has a taste of tropical fruit, fairly bodied with a lightly bitter aftertaste. Delicious, and very good value.

Rioliva

29530 Alameda
☎ 95 271 11 44
🖥 www.rioliva.com

This producer makes a reliable extra virgin oil called Rioliva, from *Hojiblanca* and *Picual* olives.

Leading producers in Granada & Almería

Desierto, Cortijo Olivar del

04200 Tabernas (Almería)
☎ 950 27 07 09
🖥 www.cdtabernas.com

Castillo de Tabernas is greeny gold, succulent, fresh, and fruity, with a light peppery aftertaste. It is made only from *Picual* olives, but its juiciness is more reminiscent of an *Arbequina* oil.

CASTILLO DE TABERNAS

Jiménez, Explotaciones Agrícolas

04200 Tabernas (Almería)
☎ 950 52 57 91
🖥 www.moraila.com

The Jiménez label is Los Vergeles de Moraila and its top oil, Selección Gourmet, comes in distinctive Moorish bottles. It is 100% *Picual,* deep golden yellow, cool, and smooth, with a fine taste of tropical fruit, lychees, and tomatoes, a long light pepperiness, and a lingering bitterness.

Maeva Aceites

18220 Albolote
☎ 958 46 61 07
🖥 www.aceitesmaeva.com

Aceites Maeva at Albolote is a medium-sized family-owned company that exports to the U.S., Japan, northern Europe, Italy, and Portugal, as well as supplying the Coviran supermarket chain. It has also made a name for selling its oil in aerosols as a nonstick spray for cooking.

Nuestra Señora de los Remedios

18550 Iznalloz
☎ 958 38 41 79
🖥 www.iznaoliva.com

The Cooperative in Iznalloz is a consistent prize-winner at national oil competitions. Its Sierra Arana is a DO oil with a scent of almonds and tomatoes and a long, full, fruity taste, overlaid by the characteristic bitterness of *Picual* and a lightly peppery finish. The cooperative's Iznaoliva Virgen Extra is also dominated by its *Picual* olives, a full-bodied oil with a hint of almonds and apricots, which is absorbed by its fine pepperiness and bitterness.

Oleosalar Cosecheros

18310 Salar
☎ 958 31 65 43
🖥 www.oleosalar.com

Hojiblanca oils from near Loja, characterized by smoothness, fruitiness, and a hint of almonds. The best is sold in bottles shaped like the Giralda in Seville.

Roldán, Herederos de Francisco

18260 Íllora
☎ 958 46 304 6

The Roldán family (under the marque Castillo de Íllora) offers a fresh, smooth, fruity, unfiltered, pure *Arbequina* oil alongside its traditional, unfiltered, full-tasting blend of *Picual* and *Lucio,* with a fair measure of bitterness and pepperiness, which give it body.

Santa Cruz, Olivarera La

04450 Canjáyar (Almería)
☎ 950 60 83 03
🖥 www.laalmazara.com

The cooperative at Canjáyar in the Alpujarras sells its oil under the label La Almazara de Canjáyar. Their popular, well made Oliverara de Santa Cruz brand is made principally from *Lechín de Granada*, here called *Cuquillo*, with some added *Picual*, *Picudo*, and *Arbequina*. It is deep yellow, cool, lightly fruity and nutty, with a long, well balanced aftertaste of pepperiness or bitterness. They also offer pure *Arbequina* and *Manzanilla* oils; the latter has a taste of grass and bitter almonds, with quite an aftertaste of pepperiness and bitterness.

San Francisco de Asís

18270 Montefrío
☎ 958 33 62 35
Ⓦ www.aceitesmontevilla.com

This is the largest cooperative in Poniente de Granada. It uses roughly 50% *Picual*, 20% *Hojiblanca*, and 30% of the local *Chorreao de Montefrío*. Its oils are sold under the Montevilla and Cortijos de Montefrío labels and have a fresh but complex taste—apples, grass, and almonds.

San Isidro

18570 Deifontes
☎ 958 40 70 29

The Deifontes cooperative is one of the best producers in the Montes de Granada area. Its unfiltered organic oil Ecovir has a long, strong taste of fruit, mixed with almonds and hay, followed by a fair measure of bitterness and pepperiness, while its DOP oil Fuentes de

ECOVIR ECOLOGICA

Dios is filtered, smooth, and fruity, with a milder touch of the bitterness and pepperiness that give such character and body to the oils made from *Picual*.

San Sebastian

18564 Benalúa de las Villas
☎ 958 39 04 02

The San Sebastián cooperative in Benalúa de las Villas offers two *Picual* oils. The organic Conde de Benalúa Ecológico extra virgin and the DO Esencias de los Montes. Both have a fruity, "green" taste, quickly followed by an almondy bitterness and a long-lasting pepperiness. Excellent.

ESENCIA DE LOS MONTES

Other producers in Granada

Montillana, Almazara de

18566 Montillana
☎ 958 39 20 79
Ⓦ www.faecagranada.com/fmontillana.htm

A larger cooperative, with 475 members and 5,000 acres (2,000ha). Full-bodied, green-yellow, fruity oil based on *Picual* olives.

Nuestra Señora de los Remedios

Puerto del Aire
18565 Campotéjar
☎ 958 38 53 71
Ⓦ www.faecagranada.com/fntrasraremedios.htm

Green-yellow, fruity oils made mainly from *Picual* olives with a measure of *Hojiblanca*, and *Picudo*.

Nuestra Señora del Perpétuo Socorro

18180 Diezma
☎ 958 68 03 05

The grassy Diezma Oro is well made and acquires a nutty flavor with age.

Olibaza

18800 Baza
☎ 958 34 22 18
Ⓦ www.altipla.com/olibaza

Picual from the far northeast of the province, outside the Montes de Granada DOP. It is greeny gold, fruity, lightly bitter, and very dense, almost viscous—when poured on a salad it stays put. Typical of the area around Baza, Huéscar, and Guadix, where *Picual* is widely grown.

San Roque

18658 Pinos del Valle
☎ 958 79 31 56

Founded in 1944, now with some 450 members in the valley south of Lanjarón: 60% *Lechín de Granada*— golden yellow, soft, smooth, fluid, and gently fruity.

Santa Isabel

18565 Campotéjar
☎ 958 38 50 65

Extra virgin *Picual* oils sold under the Aceites Campotéjar label and affiliated to the Montes Granada DOP.

Santa Mónica

18568 Piñar
☎ 958 39 45 50

Picual oils sold as Las Ventanas de Pinar or El Castillo de Pinar, sometimes with a Montes de Granada DOP label.

Varaila

18567 Domingo Pérez
☎ 958 39 07 81
Ⓦ www.varaila.com

Respectable oil with the characteristic taste of *Picual*, sold as Montes de Varaila, and endorsed by the Montes de Granada DOP.

Majorca

Olive oil was once Majorca's main export, long before the island's people discovered that more money could be made from tourism, leatherwork, and artificial pearls. In the mid-19th century, olive oil accounted for up to 80 percent of the island's export trade. Majorcans will tell you that its fine quality was especially appreciated by French gourmets; the truth is that Majorcan oil supplied the Marseille soap industry.

THE OLIVE REGIONS OF MAJORCA

LONG TRADITION OF OLIVES

Olives were very widely planted on the island's Tramontana hills throughout the 16th and 17th centuries. The main cultivar was *Empeltre*, here known as *Mallorquín*. The ancient *Empeltre* trees are very impressive—gnarled, gross, bulbous, distended, and twisted. One of the best places to see them is the road between Sóller and Deya, where steep olive terraces crash down the mountainside to sea level. The tightly terraced plantings behind Cai Mari and in the jagged limestone uplands behind Pollensa are equally impressive. Elsewhere on the island, large plantations have been cut down to make way for land development. One byproduct is a flourishing trade in articles made from olive wood.

Olive oil is the foundation of the Majorcan diet. "*Pa amb oli*" (bread with oil) is a popular favorite, eaten both for breakfast and as a snack during the day. Sometimes the bread is rubbed with tomato or garlic before oil is trickled onto it. Tomás Graves, son of the English poet Robert Graves, is Majorca's leading expert on *pa amb oli*; he calls it "Majorcan Culture's Last Stand."

MAJORCAN OIL TODAY

Majorcan oil is expensive because demand for local products is strong. There is a belief that island oil is best, which reduces the producer's incentive to change and modernize. Production costs are also high. Mechanization is difficult and it takes time to get the olives off the terraces and into the mills.

OLIVE TERRACES AT LA GRANJA *Empeltre* olives fill the terraced hillsides of northwestern Majorca.

The minimum weight required to qualify for a separate pressing—the *trullada*—is 551lb (250kg) of olives, and it can take a farmer several days to pick the required quantity. There are still a few traditional presses at work in Majorca but most are now museum pieces in tourist attractions like Son Marroig and La Granja. The quality of oil produced by smaller presses is disappointing. Most olives are picked off of the ground. Traditional oil often has a rancid taste, and its acidity can be as high as five percent.

COOPERATIVE SIGN IN GOLLEN

The Aceites Mallorca DOP has done much to improve quality, and covers the whole island, though the industry is still dominated by the hilly areas along the northwestern coast, especially around Sóller. The DOP rules were widely drawn to accommodate other areas of the island where growers cultivate the high-yielding *Picual* or the Catalonian wonder-olive *Arbequina*. As result, there is no consistent style or quality to the oils, though *Empeltre* still accounts for the major part of the production.

Leading producers in Majorca

Rodau

07500 Manacor
☎ 971 183011

Rodau makes Dauro Aubocassa from *Arbequina* olives. It is intensely fruity, with a long, succulent taste, and a light and pleasant pungency at the end—a proper mouthful. The success of this oil has opened the eyes of the Majorcans to the potential fame and fortune that modern methods of cultivation and extraction may bring.

DAURO AUBOCASSA

Sant Bartomeu, Coop. Ag.

07100 Sóller
☎ 971 630294

This is the main cooperative in northern Majorca, equipped with a modern continuous-extraction plant from Italy. Its Oli d'Oliva Verge Extra is riper than *Empeltre* oils on the mainland, smooth, gentle, rounded, less bitter, and has a hint of almonds as it ages. The cooperative also sells olives, both green and black.

OLI D'OLIVA

Other producers in Majorca

Es Verger

S'Hort d'es Verger s/n
07190 Esporles
☎ 971 619220

Organic DOP oil made from a mix of ancient *Empeltre* olives and a new planting of *Arbequina*.

Josep Campins Reynés

C. d'Arnau Tugores 1, 07360 Lloseta
☎ 971 501970

Small quantities of DOP *Empeltre* oil from this family-owned farm.

Oli Solivellas (Explotadora Agroalcúdia)

07410 Alcúdia
☎ 971 545722

Well balanced blended Solivellas oil, with an Aceite de Mallorca DOP.

Olis Piris

C. Menorca s/n
07630 Campos
☎ 971 650070

A small producer of oil with an Aceite de Mallorca DOP.

BLENDED OILS

Visitors to Majorca are most likely to see the blended oils from Cai Mari and Antoni Mateu. These are based on local olives and have a mild, rounded, pleasant taste, with only a touch of bitterness and pepper—competent, if not as good as those from Sóller's cooperative. A strange anomaly is the ancient firm of Can Det in Sóller, a producer that still uses an old-fashioned stone wheel to grind its olives and hot water to extract the oil. Though popular, this oil is often of poor quality, with a tendency to turn rancid sooner than most *Empeltre* oils.

PORTUGAL

The history of olives in Portugal is a long one. Most commentators believe it to go back at least to the time of the Romans, and probably to the Bronze Age. The Romans praised the oils of southern Portugal, the Alentejo. Olives were widely cultivated in the days of the Arab occupation and the Reconquista. Today, Portugal's olive industry is recovering from years of neglect; it is still the most traditional in Europe.

THE EARLY HISTORY

The first references to olives in the history of Portugal date from the 14th century, when Estremadura and Alentejo were already established as major producers. King João III decreed in 1555 that olive oil, like bread and wine, was an article of sustenance and should never be subject to taxation. Olives were extensively planted in southern Portugal starting in about 1700 as a way of converting marginal land to economic use. At this time, the center of the olive industry was in the province of Coimbra, though Santarém and, later, Castelo Branco were widely considered to produce olive oils of the best quality. Olive trees were not widely planted in northern Portugal, in Bragança and Vila Real, until the 19th century.

EVOLUTION OF THE OIL INDUSTRY

The olive industry was at its peak in Portugal between the years 1874–1957, when the planted area rose from 494,000 acres (200,000ha) to 1,040,000 acres (420,000ha). Most of the new planting was along the coast, in the Tagus valley, in the Alentejo, and on the Guadiana plain. In 1954, the Portuguese crop reached 133,380 tons of oil, whereas today the annual figure is typically 37,500 tons.

THE INDUSTRY DECLINES

Rural exodus started in about 1950 and continued until 1990. Much of the countryside became depopulated as impoverished country people abandoned their traditional way of life and moved to the towns and cities. More

ALENTEJO OLIVE PLANTATION Many of the olive plantations in the Alentejo are old and lightly managed.
◀ OLIVE TERRACES The terraced valley of the Upper Douro is extensively planted with olives and vines.

Galega Olives

Four-fifths of all olive trees grown in Portugal are *Galega*. In the Ribatejo and the Beira provinces it is almost the only cultivar. *Galega* gives Portuguese olive oil its distinctive character and its consistency of taste. The Portuguese are very proud of it, regarding it as part of their cultural patrimony. But some outsiders would say that, as with the indigenous Portuguese wine grapes, *Galega* is not an exciting cultivar. Its great virtue lies in its hardiness and adaptability—it is easy to grow in a wide variety of soils and climates.

Galega trees are naturally short, compact, and ripen their olives early, but are not always productive. The olives are small, their oil content is low, and the trees show a marked tendency to biennial cropping. The tree is very susceptible to *gafa*, a flesh-corrupting infection that gives the oil a dirty, bitter taste. This problem is exacerbated by the tree's tendency to hold onto its fruit when the olives are ripe, and not let them fall. This trait also makes *Galega* difficult to harvest mechanically. *Galega* probably originated in the northern Alentejo, but shows quite a degree of genetic variability in other parts of Portugal. This variability would make a good subject for clonal selection.

Galega oil has a fruity smell and a soft, smooth taste of green fruit and grass, sometimes with a suggestion of almonds. It is usually slightly bitter and has a warm aftertaste. The oil is not very stable and tends to deteriorate quickly, especially if it is made from late-harvested olives. As with all oils, the motto must be "Buy the youngest available."

HARVESTING OLIVES THE TRADITIONAL WAY

significantly, many of the olive orchards were ripped out and replaced by plantations of the fast-growing eucalyptus tree, which changed the face of the Portuguese countryside. Home consumption of olive oil also dropped, because the Portuguese people, always among the poorest of Europe, turned to cheaper corn oils for their daily needs. Average annual consumption now is about 1.8gal (7 liters) per person, much lower than in Spain, Italy, or Greece. Even so, Portugal does not produce enough oil to satisfy its own needs. Most of its imports come from Spain.

THE INDUSTRY TODAY

Nowadays the main olive-growing area is the eastern half of the country from Alentejo to Trás-os-Montes, though Ribatejo still remains important. There are, however, very few producers in any part of the Algarve. Farming is very fragmented. Landholdings are small, especially in the north of the country. Production costs are high, at least relative to the farmers' expectations. There are no dedicated olive farms in Portugal. Olive trees are always part of a mixed farming scheme, which includes vines, fruit trees, or grazing. The Portuguese olive industry faces the common problems of fissiparous landholdings, very low levels of mechanization, and biennial cropping. Many of the olive trees are past their peak and replanting has been slow in recent years. Depopulation and an aging population continue to be problems and many cooperatives are badly run. But sales have not bottomed out. Most oil produced is sold in bulk to the large wholesalers, or retailed locally. Very little is exported. Esporão and CARM (Casa Agricola Robereido Madeira, *see p.199*) are the two most successful exporters of high-quality oil. The potential for export growth is considerable; the quality of the oil of these and other leading estates is very high, and their prices are reasonable.

CULTIVATION PRACTICES

Standards of cultivation and quality differ enormously throughout Portugal,

OLIVE TERRACES, PORTO Olives are planted all over Portugal, except where terrain is too mountainous.

and are often inconsistent even within the same village. Portuguese olive trees give a light yield, partly because they are often badly cultivated, and seldom fed or watered. The growers complain that olives do not bring such good returns as vines. Many of the organic olive farmers in Portugal have embraced the "no-chemicals" mantra not through conviction but through poverty. Most oil is processed by agricultural cooperatives for the benefit of their members. The best oil comes from Alentejo and, to a lesser extent, from Trás-os-Montes, where the leading cooperatives produce oil to a high standard. Many cooperatives are small and are at present unable to invest in up-to-date management and extraction equipment. Some have already closed down or merged; it is to be anticipated that there will be more closures and mergers in future. The quality of the oil in Portugal also depends largely on the caliber of the management, which is determined by the cooperative's constitution and its voting rights.

HIGH LEVELS OF ACIDITY

Many Portuguese will tell you that they prefer their oil to have a higher level of acidity—they believe it gives the oil a stronger taste. Many of these oils have a discernible taste of olive fly or rancidness, but this is sometimes perceived as the traditional flavor of Portuguese oil and therefore desirable. The Portuguese *Denominacao de Origem* (DOP) system has only just begun to make an impression. As recently as 2002, no more than 3 percent of Portuguese oil was registered with one of the DOP authorities, and more than nine-tenths of this came from Moura. The other DOPs have now begun to operate more effectively, with a good number of producers in Norte Alentejano and Trás-os-Montes. The highest prices are paid for single-*quinta* oils (*quinta* translates as estate) from Trás-os-Montes.

THE FUTURE

Olive groves now cover some 741,000 acres (300,000ha) of the country. More than half of the olive oil produced is extra virgin. However, the general standard of Portuguese oils is not up to par with those of Spain, Italy, and Greece. The main problems are low expectations by the producers, poor management at all levels, uncoordinated promotion by the trade, and an unenlightened home market. Efforts are being made to encourage olive-oil tourism, modernize farming practices, plant new olive groves, exercise quality control, publicize the DOPs, encourage organic production, run fairs and competitions, diversify production, and improve distribution.

THE WAY FORWARD

The Portuguese government is actively promoting olive oil as the preferred oil for a healthy, nutritious way of eating. There is moreover a growing interest within Portugal in the organic movement. Higher prices are paid for organic oils, likewise for oils that have a DOP or a low acidity. Organic oils are associated with higher quality, because the oil-makers are commited to the principles of good cultivation. But despite the progress that is being made by quality-led cooperatives and top estates, Portugal remains the least sophisticated producer-country in the European Union.

AZUMBUJEIRA RIBATEJO VINEYARDS AND OLIVE GROVES Ribatejo has a reputation for producing some of Portugal's best olive oil, though quantities are much lower than 50 years ago.

Table olives in Portugal

Table olives are eaten throughout Portugal, and are an important part of its cuisine. Best known, by far, are the black olives from Bragança and Vila Real known as *Negrinha de Freixo*, which are protected by a DOP. They are always of the indigenous *Negrinha* cultivar. It is not a large olive, usually weighing less than 0.25oz (about 3–5g). The olives may be picked and prepared at any stage of their development: green, semiripe, or black. Each stage of maturity involves a different processing and all are sold with both kernel and skin intact. They are used as snacks and in cooking.

Right at the other end of the country, in the Algarve, there are two further culinary traditions: *azeitona britada* (cracked olives) and salted olives. Salted olives are left until they start to turn red or black and are preserved in salt for a couple of months before they are soaked to get rid of the salt. Cracked olives are picked earlier, in September, when they are green, using the Algarve cultivar known as *Maçanilha*. Traditionally they are cracked between two stones and soaked in fresh water every day for one to two weeks. They are then covered in saltwater and infused with pieces of garlic, lemon, and herbs. In the east of Portugal, around Elvas and toward the Spanish frontier in Badajoz, there are two further traditions. One involves picking *Maçanilha* olives when they are still green, or just starting to turn color, and steeping them in fresh water, which is changed every day for two weeks before preserving them in coarse salt with bay leaves and marjoram. The other tradition of this part of Alentejo involves preserving green olives of *Maçanilha* or *Cordovil*, stoning them, and stuffing them with sweet bell pepper, almonds, or capers.

Olive Regions of Portugal

This map shows the four main olive-growing regions of Portugal. On the following pages there is a description of each of the areas, from north to south, and the DOPs that fall within them, together with lists of the most interesting oils I have tasted from the different parts of the country.

ALENTEJO
The beautiful empty plains of central and southern Portugal produce some of the country's best olive oils.

FACTS AND FIGURES

OIL PRODUCED
375,000 tons a year

LAND PLANTED WITH OLIVES
1,040,000 acres (420,000ha)

NUMBER OF DOPs 7

PERCENTAGE WORLD CROP 1%

VIANA DO CASTELO
Viana do Castelo
Braga BRAGA
VILA REAL
Bragança
BRAGANÇA
Matosinhos PORTO
Porto
Vila Nova de Gaia
Vila Real
Douro
VISEU
GUARDA
Aveiro
Viseu
AVEIRO
Guarda
ATLANTIC OCEAN
Coimbra
COIMBRA
CASTELO BRANCO
LEIRIA
Castelo Branco
Leiria
SANTARÉM
Portalegre
SPAIN
Santarém
PORTALEGRE
LISBOA
LISBON
Barreiro
ÉVORA
Setúbal
Tagus
Évora
SETÚBAL
Beja Moura
BEJA
FARO
Faro

WELL MANAGED OLIVE GROVE
This olive grove in the province of Evora is unusual in that it has been plowed. Most Portuguese plantations are put to grazing.

Bragança and Vila Real p.195

Guarda and Castelo Branco p.200

Leiria, Santarém & Lisbon p.202

Portalegre to Moura p.204

National Brands of Portugal

Most oil in Portugal is sold under a major brand name, and competes on price and not quality. The Portuguese consider oil to be a commodity with a specific use, alongside sugar and flour, instead of seeing it as an agreeable condiment.

EVORA MONTE CASTLE, ALENTEJO Olives are planted right up to the walls of the castle.

THE PORTUGUESE MARKET

High-quality olive oil can sometimes be difficult to find. The big supermarkets continue to favor the large, well known brands. These include: **Azeol**, from Torres Vedras; **Azeites Gallo**, now part of FIMA; JC Coimbra (the **Marialva** and **Conímbriga** labels); **Copaz**, which belongs to the Nutasa group; **Nektar**; **Portucale**; Sovena, part of the much larger Nutrinveste; and the Spanish-owned Maeva. Most of the oils are reliable, but they are dull, inexpensive oils for everyday use. The oil sold under the **Castelo de Moura** label by Empresa Fabril de Moura is also widely available and well regarded.

Portuguese cooperatives and the leading estates mostly sell directly to members of the public and to small market traders. Even the best cooperatives and estates are seldom able to persuade the supermarket chains to stock their oils even locally. Nevertheless,

OLIVEIRA DA SERRA FROM SOVENA

despite this, the Portuguese market for olive oils has seen the emergence of a small but growng demand for more choice, notably for organic oils, single-estate, or *quinta*, oils, and oils made from a single, named cultivar. Some of the more upscale supermarkets, such as Modelo and Intermarché are now stocking a number of these new-style oils, which usually carry a Trás-os-Montes DOP. And there is no longer any doubt that the best Portuguese oils, though they are relatively few in number, stand up, in quality, to the best that the rest of the world has to offer.

IMPORTS AND EXPORTS

Portugal exports about one-third of its olive-oil production, mainly to its old colony Brazil. It also imports substantial quantities of oil from Spain to reexport to Brazil. The Brazilians buy most of their table olives, however, from Argentina.

Bragança & Vila Real

This is a land of contrasts: a remote region of dry mountains and fertile valleys, traditionally divided into cold areas ("Terra Fria") and warm areas ("Terra Quente"), such as the upper Douro valley, where olives flourish in microclimates. The region is often referred to as Trás-os-Montes, which is the original name for the area—and now the name assigned to the DOP.

THE GROWTH OF THE OIL INDUSTRY

The cultivation of olives here dates back to at least 1600. It began on a small scale but saw a great expansion in the 19th century when much marginal land was brought into cultivation. There are now about 153,200 acres (62,000ha) of olive trees, roughly one-fifth of the national total, which account for 20–35 percent of the national oil crop. Volumes differ annually but, among the oil-producing regions of Portugal, this region is second in quantity only to Portalegre.

Trás-os-Montes is an area of contrasts. Many of the new olive plantings are irrigated and designed for mechanical cultivation, but innovation and experiment are seldom found among the small, traditional holdings. Here the olives are grown alongside almonds and grapes, both of which are more important crops for the region. This is the only part of Portugal where

THE OLIVE REGIONS OF BRAGANÇA & VILA REAL

you commonly see handwritten signs for "*Vende-se Azeite*" (oil for sale) by the roadside. The schist soils support little or no organic matter so this is an area of low returns but of high-quality oils.

FERTILE VALLEY The valley sites of the Douro River are well suited to olive growing.

DOURO VALLEY Vines and olives are the wealth-creating crops of the Douro Valley.

The main areas of production today are Mirandela, Vila Flor, Macedo de Cavaleiros, and Alfândega da Fé. Mirandela has been a center of the olive industry for several centuries. Its oil is an essential ingredient of the local sausages, known as *Alheiras de Mirandela*. The Trás-os-Montes DOP area comprises the western, southern, and central parts of the province of Bragança, plus small adjoining areas in Vila Real and Guarda (*see p.200*). The DOP accounts only for a small fraction (4–5 percent) of the oil produced, but all Trás-os-Montes DOP oils are highly esteemed in Portugal. They have "perceived value," so that shoppers in other parts of Portugal are willing to pay more for Trás-os-Montes oil. This perception is not yet attached specifically to DOP oils, just to the region as a whole. Trás-os-Montes oils are golden yellow (sometimes with a green tinge), very fruity, sometimes almondy, and possess varying degrees of bitterness and pepperiness.

REGIONAL OLIVE CULTIVARS

The permitted cultivars for Trás-os-Montes DOP certification are *Verdeal Transmontana*, *Madural*, *Cobrançosa*, and *Cordovil*. All of these olives, except *Cordovil*, are specialties of the region. *Verdeal Transmontana* is a medium-sized tree that produces large crops somewhat late in the season. *Madural* is a hardy cultivar that fruits heavily every other year. Some experts consider it a clone of the variable *Galega* olive. The *Cobrançosa* tree is hardy and produces good, regular crops. Its large olives are very resistant to olive fly, which makes it a dual-purpose cultivar for oil and table olives.

To these should be added the *Negrinha* olive (also known as *Azeiteira*), which is a productive and regular cropper that ripens early. Its low oil content and resistance to olive fly make it good for both green and black table olives. Some Spanish authorities consider the olive to be identical to their *Manzanilla Cacereña*.

The remoteness of the region has given rise to local olive cultivars whose distinctness may be developed in future. The indigenous *Santulhana* olive (thought to be a clone of *Gordal Sevillana*) is used, for instance, in Santulhão near Vimioso. The cooperative in Freixo de Espada à Cinta makes a soft, fruity, aromatic, oil from *Negrinha* olives is clear golden yellow in color, with a touch of bitterness and piquancy that lingers in the mouth.

Leading producers in Bragança & Vila Real

Aragão, M. C. Rabaçal

Estrada Nacional 215
5350-022 Alfândega da Fé
📞 279 462 685
🌐 www.casaaragao.com

Maria do Carmo Rabaçal Aragão at Alfândega da Fé is one of Portugal's most successful private estate owners. She makes about 158,500 gals (600,000 liters) of oil every year and is a consistent prize-winner both in Portugal and Brazil. She is also a pioneer of organic oil, which she sells under the name of Alfandagh. It has a good golden color and a very fruity, cool, smooth taste, balanced by a most agreeable medium-strength bitterness and piquancy that develop later on the palate. She also sells two Trás-os-Montes DOP blends as Casa Aragão and Casa da Vilariça, which have a complex, fruity taste of apples, pears, and green grass, as well as offering a fine light bitterness and piquancy that last well in the mouth.

ALFANDAGH

Dão Sul, Soc. Vitivinícola

Quinta de Cabriz
Apartado 28
3430-909 Carregal do Sal
📞 232 960 140
🌐 www.daosul.com

Dão Sul, a very famous name for wine, sells two good estate oils. One is named Quinta das Tecedeiras from *Ervedosa do Douro* olives. It is a clear golden yellow, fruity, and nutty, with a touch of pepperiness and a suggestion of bitterness. The second is Quinta de Cabriz, made from *Galega* and *Cobrançosa olives*. It is a clear, greenish yellow, fruity, smooth, and grassy with a light peppery finish. They are sold in elegantly curved bottles.

AZEITE CASA GRANDE

Freixo de Numão, Coop. de Viticultura e Olivicultura de

Lugar das Olgas, E.N. 324
5155-203 Freixo de Numão
📞 279 789 776

The cooperative in Freixo de Numão was founded in 1957 for wine-growers, but is now more devoted to the production of top-flight olive oil. Its top label is Azeite Casa Grande, which has won many prizes in Portugal and abroad. The oil, which is organic, is well balanced, fruity,

aromatic, and grassy, with a subtle, lingering touch of bitterness and piquancy.

Murça, Coop. Ag. dos Olivicultores de

Lugar do Gueirinho
5090 Murça
📞 259 512 191
🌐 www.coop-olivicultores-murca.pt

Murça's cooperative has some 900 associates from the whole of the Murça district and is equipped with all the latest processing equipment. Its DOP oil Azeite Porca de Murça wins prizes both locally and nationally. It is dark gold in color and clear, with a fruity taste and a good, long-lasting aftertaste of bitterness and pungency.

Prolagar, Carvalhais

5370-081 Mirandela
📞 278 257 368
🌐 www.prolagar.pt

Prolagar was the first producer of oil in the region to introduce a two-phase extraction system in 1995. Ouro do Tua oil is dark yellow, fruity, and grassy, and ends with a suggestion of bitterness and a long, warm, peppery aftertaste. It comes with a DOP certification, but 70 percent of Prolagar's production is sold in bulk.

OURO DO TUA

VIEW ABOVE FREIXO DE ESPADA Rows of olive trees cover the hillside in this remote corner of Portugal.

Its greeny gold Rosmaninho oil is made from *Madural, Verdeal,* and *Cobrançosa.* It has a fruity, greenish taste that is cool and smooth with a light bitterness and piquancy.

VIAZ (Produção e Comercialização de Vinhos e Azeites)

Quinta do Carrascal
5160 Torre de Moncorvo
226 163 9 82

Quinta do Carrascal has 370 acres (150ha), roughly divided between vines (for port) and olives. Its best known oil is Sardeiro Biológico, which is fruity and fresh, with a light, peppery aftertaste.

Other producers in Bragança & Vila Real

Azeites do Côa

Apartado 65
3864-908 Avanca
234 850 817

Azcoa oil is made from *Madural, Verdeal,* and *Negrinha.* It is fruity, cool, and grassy with a refreshing touch of bitterness and piquancy.

Coopa-Freixo

Rua Combatentes Ultramar 5180
Freixo de Espada à Cinta
279 653 876

The new Senhora do Douro oil from the young Cooperative in Freixo de Espada à Cinta, is made from the endemic *Negrinha de Freixo* olive, which also has its own DOP as a table olive.

Norberto Fraga Unipessoal

Quinta das Carvas
5360-909 Vila Flor
917 527 060
www.vilafraga.com

Quinta das Carvas from Vila Flor is made from a mixture of local olives.

Romeu, Quinta do

5370-620 Mirandela
222 001 265
www.quintadoromeu.com

The Clemente Miners foundation in Romeu has 370 acres (150ha) of *Cobrançosa, Verdeal, Transmontana,* and *Madural,* as well as substantial wine-making and cork-growing activities. Its old buildings, gardens, and famous restaurant make it a target for gastrotourism. Quinta do Romeu is an organic DOP oil made with stone grinders but it manages nevertheless to have a maximum acidity of 0.2%. Its taste is delicate, smooth, fruity, attractive, grassy, and almondy, with only a touch of bitterness but a good piquant aftertaste.

Solinor (Sociedade Oleaginosa do Norte)

Av. 25 de Abril, 273
5370-202 Mirandela
278 265 695
solinor@mail.telepac.pt

Solinor is known for its excellent organic oil Ouro Transmontana. Dark yellow and clear, it is fruity and cool, with a light but agreeable pungency and bitterness that linger in the mouth.

Valpaços, Coop. de Olivicultores de

Av. Eng. Luís Castro Saraiva
5430 Valpaços
278 711 256
www.azeite.valpacos.com

The cooperative in Valpaços has more than 2,000 members, two continuous extraction lines, and an ultra-modern storage system.

Casa Agrícola Roboredo Madeira

The achievements of Casa Agrícola Roboredo Madeira (CARM) dominate the recent story of olive oil in Portugal. CARM is a 740-acre (300ha) private estate in the remote village of Almendra, high above the broad, terraced, upper Douro valley. The estate has belonged to Celso Madeira and his family for hundreds of years.

Some 540 acres (220ha) are devoted to olive trees. The rest is planted with vines for Douro Superior wine. The olives grown are the traditional Trás-os-Montes cultivars (namely, *Madural, Cobrançosa, Verdeal*, and *Negrinha*) and the whole estate is managed organically. It is a model of tidiness, order, and good cultivation. Celso Madeira insists that Portuguese olive farmers can make world-class oils by paying attention to good cultivation, quick processing, and temperature-controlled storage. His own olives are milled on the same day they are picked, and his oil is stored under inert nitrogen in stainless-steel vats, where it is allowed to settle out naturally and to clear without artificial filtration. In 2000 he took his best four oils to the annual national oil show in Moura and won the first four prizes, which was an unprecedented achievement.

CARM offers a long list of different oils, each with a distinct character, according to the individual lots that go into the mix from year to year. Some are named after farms on the estate, such as **Quinta da Bispado** (which tastes mild and rounded), **Quinta das Marvalhas** (lightly peppery), **Quinta da Urze** (agreeably bitter), **Quinta do Côa** (middling piquant), and **Quinta de Calábria** (somewhat more pungent). Others are mixes, like **Castello d'Alba**, which is widely available in Portugal and abroad. The top marques are reserved for CARM's **Praemium** and **Grande Escolha** labels, respectively mild and piquant, which are the finest estate oils in Portugal. All CARM's oils are intensely fresh and fruity, and keep this quality for several years, sometimes acquiring a light taste of almonds. Where they differ is in the degree of piquancy and bitterness they offer. There is something here for every taste. They never exceed 0.3% in acidity, and, in fact, some of CARM's oils even achieve an acidity level of less than 0.1%. All are immensely elegant, smooth, long-lasting, nutty, and delicious.

Rua da Calabria, 5150-021 Almendra (Almendra)
📞 00351279718011 🌐 www.carm.pt

QUINTA DAS MARVALHAS   GRANDE ESCOLHAR   CASTELLO D'ALBA   PRAEMIUM   QUINTA DA BISPADO

Guarda & Castelo Branco

These provinces mark the change from the fertile, overpopulated provinces of northern Portugal to the vast empty plains of the south. Both endured depopulation in the 1960s and 1970s. They still suffer from low investment, a shortage of water, and an aging population.

THE OLIVE REGIONS OF GUARDA & CASTELO BRANCO

CULTIVATION PRACTICES

The olive industry within this region is less developed than farther south though there are many olive trees and a large olive-oil industry in Beira Baixa. The dominant cultivar is the *Galega* olive. Its oils are golden yellow, sometimes with a hint of green, a fruity taste, and usually a suggestion of bitterness and piquancy. There are two DOPs in the region—Beira Baixa and Beira Alta—though neither is actively developed. The legislation allows up to four days to elapse between picking and milling, which is far too long to assure quality. The systems of cultivation, harvesting, and processing are now being modernized, often with financial support from the regional government.

BEIRA ALTA & BEIRA BAIXA

At the center of Beira Alta is a high, broad valley. Guarda, at 3,300ft (1,000m) is the highest town in Portugal. Beira Alta covers roughly the province of Guarda, and is an area with cold winters, stony soil, mixed farming, and marginal forestry. Less oil is produced here than in Beira Baixa, although there is an oil museum in Celorico da Beira.

Beira Baixa is an area of large esates and tiny peasant plots. Most of the olives were planted in the early 20th century. Quality is variable but, as throughout Portugal, individual producers have shown that it is possible, with care, to make high-quality oil.

Leading producers in Guarda & Castelo Branco

Cadomate (Coop. Ag. dos Olivicultores de Malpica do Tejo)

Rua de S.Bento
Malpica do Tejo
6000 Castelo Branco

The cooperative in Malpica do Tejo was founded in 1954 and sells its oils (including a DOP Beira Baixa oil) under the label Cadomate. It has modern equipment, an interest in organic oils, and a commitment to quality.

Ferreira Gonçalves, F. Quinta S. Marcos,

6231-000 Fundão
275 74314

This firm specializes in local foods; its Gramenesa oil is an acceptable blend.

GRAMENESA

MIXED FARMING Olives and flowering cherries in Celorico da Beira.

Fundão, Coop. Ag. dos Olivicultores

Apartado 55
6230-909 Fundão
275 752 317
www.olivicultoresdofundao.org

The cooperative in Fundão offers several extra virgin oils, including a DOP Azeite da Beira Interior oil called Cova de Beira, named after the very pretty, lush valley north of Castelo Branco. It has also begun to offer monovarietal oils.

Penazeites

Apartado 39
6090 Penamacor

The oils of Penazeites are all made from *Galega*, and all good. A recent introduction is its kosher oil, the first to be made in Portugal. It is called Ribeiro Sanches Kosher and is also certified as kosher for Passover. Most of this oil is exported to the U.S.

Quinta da Tojeira

Tapada da Tojeira
6030 Vila Velha de Rodao
272 545 314

The organic Azeite Tojeira oil is an international prize-winner.

Rodoliv (Coop. dos Azeites de Rodão)

Z.I.
6030 Vila Velha de Rodão

The cooperative in Rodão, called Rodoliv, makes a small quantity of oil with the DOP of Azeite da Beira Baixa.

OLIVE GROVES IN BEIRA BAIXA There are some very large olive-growing estates in this part of Portugal.

Leiria, Santarém & Lisbon

This area, covering three provinces of central Portugal, was previously known as Ribatejo, the name now given to the only DOP in the region. It is an area of great fertility, where olives are steadily losing ground to vines, cereal crops, and tree fruit.

THE INDUSTRY TODAY

The Ribatejo was once the leading region for the production of Portuguese olive oil. Santarém has been known for its oil since at least the 13th century and Tomar is famous for its *bolos de azeite*, or oil biscuits. Today, however, the area accounts for no more than 5.5 percent of the national production.

The dominant olive cultivar is *Galega*, and it is the only one permitted in the oils of the Azeite do Ribatejo DOP. There is one exception to this, which is that a proportion of the *Lentisca* olive (a very hardy cultivar thought to be a form of *Picudo*) is permitted in one small area. *Galega* is not universally popular because of its marked tendency to biennial cropping and its resistance to mechanical picking. There is therefore a move to allow growers to include a proportion of *Cobrançosa* olives.

RIBATEJO DOP

The area covered by the Azeite do Ribatejo DOP comprises a large chunk of western and central Portugal and includes the districts of Abrantes, Alcobaça, Ourém, Santarém, Tomar, and Torres Novas. It overlaps at its eastern end with the DOP of Beira Baixa, so that Vila de Rei and Mação belong to both DOPs. Azeite do Ribatejo is not a well developed DOP

THE OLIVE REGIONS OF LEIRIA, SANTAREM & LISBON

and has very few registered producers. There were five in February 2003, which produced no more than 1,320gal (5,000 liters) of DOP oil in 2002–2003. It is still one of the least active DOPs in Portugal. The oils should be lightly thick, fruity, and yellow gold, and sometimes slightly greenish. The market leaders in Ribatejo are producers who offer single-estate (*quinta*) or single-cultivar oils. These show the potential still inherent in the oils of this region.

OLIVE TREE IN RIBATEJO There are many small producers with lightly managed olive groves in this region.

Leading producers of Leiria, Santarém & Lisbon

Casal das Sarnadas, Soc. Agr.do

S. Miguel do Rio Torto
2200 Abrantes
☎ 218 439 572

This estate is intensively planted in the modern way and makes a soft, fruity, delicious filtered DOP Ribatejo oil, which it sells as Ourogal. Its taste has hints of grass, tomatoes, and artichoke, followed by a light, warm aftertaste. It won first prize in the Portuguese National Oil Competition. in 2005.

OUROGAL

Dias Bairrão, José

R. das Fortunatas, 25
Vale das Mós
2200 Abrantes

Small estates often offer good quality and value for money. José Dias Bairrão's unfiltered Zéz Bairrão is extremely fruity with a nice touch of piquancy and a long, lightly bitter aftertaste.

ZÉZ BAIRRÃO

João Vitor Reis Gomes Mendes

Comeiras de Baixo
2000-694 Pernes
☎ 243 449 698

Quinta do Juncal oil is unfiltered, fruity, and smooth with a mild, citrus taste and only a light touch of bitterness and pepperiness. Professor Mendes is one of the most go-ahead forces in the world of Portuguese agriculture. He is a pioneer of super-intensive olive growing and holds a teaching position at the agricultural university in Santarém.

SANTA OLAIA

Luís Manuel Gonçalves da Silva Mendes

Quinta do Vale Pequena
R.Arcebispo de Évora, 122A
2350-174 Olaia Torres Novas
☎ 249 981 351

The old hydraulic press, which is still in use at Quinta do Vale Pequena, was installed by the present owner's great-grandfather in the 1920s. The estate's oil, called Santa Olaia, is organically produced, unfiltered, fruity, cool, and smooth. It possesses a smell of green grass and very little in the way of pepperiness or bitterness.

AZEITE VIRGEM EXTRA

Ribeirinha, Quinta da

Rua Bispo D. António Mendonça
2000-533Póvoa de Santarém
☎ 243 428 200
🖳 www.quintadaribeirinha.com

Quinta da Ribeirinha is mainly a wine estate, but its fine, unfiltered Azeite Virgem Extra oil is fruity, cool, and grassy, with only a light touch of bitterness and pepperiness.

Vale de Lobos, Quinta da

Azoia de Baixo
2005-097 Santarém
☎ 243 429 264
🖳 www.valedelobos.com

Vale de Lobos is a model estate. As well as a few old trees of *Galega* there are 32 acres (13ha) of intensively planted *Cobrançosa*, *Picual*, and *Blanqueta* olives and 202 acres (82ha) of young, super-intensive *Arbequina* and *Cobrançosa*. Quinta de Vale de Lobos oil is fresh and fruity, with a light aftertaste of pepperiness and bitter almonds. It won a prize in Los Angeles when it first came out in 2004. Other labels will follow in due course. The point to note is that super-intensive plantations are now producing high-quality oil in Portugal from nontraditional, non-Portuguese, olive cultivars.

Portalegre to Beja

Southeastern Portugal greatly resembles the Spanish region of Extremadura, across the border. The old political name for the region was Alentejo, the name given to two the main DOPs. Its landscapes are expansive, empty, and often monotonous. Olives are an important crop.

Beira Baixa DOP
Azeites do Norte Alentejano DOP
Aziete do Alentejo Interior DOP
Aziete de Moura DOP

THE OLIVE REGIONS OF PORTALEGRE TO BEJA

CULTIVATION OF THE LAND

Most of this part of Portugal is an open, rolling plain where wheat is the main crop. In some places, however, large smooth stone boulders sit on the surface of the land, relics of distant glacial times. These areas have traditionally been planted with olives or cork oaks, and used for grazing. Two thousand years ago, the Roman writer Strabo praised the oil that came from these plains. In fact, much of the area was scrubland until cleared for agriculture in the 19th century. Now it accounts for nearly 358,295 acres (145,000ha) of olive trees (43 percent of the national total), and about one-third of the annual national production of oil. If more water were available for irrigation, this region could be very productive, closer to Andalusia in its landscape than Extremadura. There are three DOPs within these provinces: Azeite do Norte Alentejano, Azeite do Alentejo Interior, and Azeite de Moura.

PORTALEGRE & EVORA

Two of this regions DOPs are in this area: the DOP of Norte Alentejano covers most of the province of Portalegre and part of Evora. It was slow to develop, but came to prominence in 2003 when a joint marketing campaign brought producers together

OIL MILL An advertisement for San Pedro oil on the wall of the cooperative in Portel.

under the "AVE Azeites do Norte Alentejano" logo. Until then, only a few producers made oil to the standards required for recognition by the DOP authorities. Now the branding has led to higher quality and substantially improved sales across the region.

The Azeites do Norte Alentejano DOP covers a large area in the northeast of the province, and is especially strong around Sousel, Estremoz, Redondo, Borba, Vila Viçosa, and Elvas. The main olives here are *Redondil*, *Carrasquenha*, and *Cordovil*, but large areas are dominated by the *Galega* olive. The stipulated DOP cultivars, in contrast, are *Galega*, *Blanqueta*, and *Cobrançosa*, of which *Galega* must predominate. The criteria for a DOP oil are unusually widely drawn: "light, fruity, with a yellow-gold color, sometimes slightly greenish, with a smooth smell and taste, very typical and agreeable."

The DOP of Azeite do Alentejo Interior is still somewhat undeveloped. It covers a large area of southern Evora and northern Beja, or what was central southern Alentejo. The oil must be made from a minimum of 60% *Galega* olives, and the balance of *Cobrançosa* or *Cordovil de Serpa* olives, or a combination of the two. A small addition (no more than 5%) of other cultivars is permitted, but with an absolute ban on the Spanish cultivars *Picual* and *Manzanilla*. The oils of Alentejo Interior DOP are golden or greenish yellow, smooth and fruity, with hints of apple and fig, and a great sensation of softness.

CARRASQUENHA OLIVES

BEJA

The Moura DOP covers most of this province and is the most successful in this region. It lies hard against the Spanish border, partly in the districts of Mourão and Serpa, and partly around the town of the same name. The origins of the olive industry in this area go back hundreds of years. Until quite recently,

DISTINCTIVE LANDSCAPE OF EVORA
Olives were once widely planted near rocky outcrops and boulders; many have naturalized.

it is said, workers' wages were paid partly in oil. The oils of Moura are greenish gold, with a fruity smell and taste, and bitter and pungent when young. Moura has long enjoyed a reputation for good olive oil. In fact, there is a Portuguese saying "*tão fino como o azeite de Moura*," which translates, "as fine as the oil of Moura."

The Moura DOP olive oils are made from *Galega*, *Cordovil*, and *Verdeal* olives. These are sometimes referred to as the "left bank" (of the Guadiano River) cultivars. *Cordovil* olives also grow on a large tree that produces a good, steady crop of olives with a high oil content. *Verdeal* makes a tall, spreading tree that produces fair quantities of olives with a good oil content.

All three cultivars have a tendency toward biennial cropping, so the DOP regulations are fairly flexible about the proportion that each should have within the final blend. The rules of the Moura specify no more than 15–20% *Verdeal* olives, at least 35–40% *Cordovil*, and the rest made up of *Galega*. The characteristic taste comes from the combination of *Galega* and *Verdeal*, while the mild-flavored *Cordovil* imparts a rounded texture and a low level of acidity.

Leading producers in Portalegre & Evora

Almeida, Fundação Eugénio de

Apartado 2001
São Manços
7001-901 Évora

The huge, historic, wine-making estate of Cartuxa has recently started to invest heavily in the production of high-quality olive oil. Its Cartuxa oil is made of 100% *Galega* olives. It is rich, clear yellow, and softly fruity with only a little bitterness and piquancy, and a hint of almonds as it ages.

Borba, Coop. de Olivicultores de

R. Convento das Servas
S. Bartolomeu
7150 Borba

The star producer in the Norte Alentejano DOP is the cooperative in Borba, which runs away with top prizes for quality year after year at national shows. It was founded in 1951 with some 100 members, and now has more than 1,100, all small-scale farmers. Insistence on the highest standards of cultivation and harvesting has brought them widespread renown, especially for the quality of their Azeite do Norte

ACEITE DO NORTE

Alentejano label. This dark golden oil is unfiltered and intensely fruity, with a long, cool, green flavor and only the merest hint of piquancy. For people who prefer a gentle taste without a trace of bitterness, Borba's oil is the best in Portugal—and very good value.

Estremoz, Coop. Ag. dos Olivicultores de

Campo da Mata
Évoramonte-Santa-Maria
7100 Estremoz

This major cooperative's Norte Alentejano DOP oil is called Lavrador. It is dark golden yellow, fruity, grassy, mild, and smooth.

Fonte do Pinheiro, Herdade da

S. Vicente e Ventosa
2054-909 Azambuja
☎ 263 401 178
🖳 www.fontepinheiro.pt

Quinta (or Herdade) da Fonte do Pinheiro sells its Ouro de Elvas oil in distinctive octagonal bottles. It is fruity, smooth, and aromatic.

Gravia Grande, Herdade da

7800 Salvada
☎ 964 768 784

This is a private estate near Beja. Its fruity Herdade da Gravia oil tastes of apples, walnuts, and herbs, as well as having a pleasant touch of piquancy that lingers in the mouth.

Olidal (Olivicultores do Alentejo)

Santo Amaro
7470 Sousel

The little Olidal cooperative sells a high-quality "modern" DOP oil under the label Lagar do Monte. It is dark yellow, smooth, and fruity, with a delicious "green" taste and only a trace of bitterness and pepperiness.

Redondo, Coop. de Olivicultores de

Estrada Nacional 254
7200-107 Redondo
☎ 266 909 246

This cooperative's Redondo label is a Norte Alentejano DOP oil. It has a rich, mild, fruity taste that recalls fresh peaches. The cooperative also has an organic oil made with the olives of some 20 growers committed to integrated production.

REDONDO

Vidigueira, Coop. Ag. de

Rua Eng. Aires da Fonseca, 2
7960 Vidigueira

Relíquia Azeite Virgem Extra Vidigueira oil is made from *Galega*, *Cobrançosa*, and *Cordovil* olives. Golden yellow in color, it is fruity, with a suggestion of cut grass and almonds, and just enough bitterness and pepperiness to give it character. This ultramodern cooperative also offers an oil made from organically cultivated olives.

RELIQUIA

Leading producers in Beja

Brinches, Coop. Ag. de

Monte Acima
7830 Brinches
☎ 284 800 100

The Cooperativa Agrícola de Brinches, founded in 1969, mixes the "left bank" cultivars with *Cobrançosa*. This makes its excellent oils, sold with Flor do Alentejo labels, ineligible for DOP status. The cooperative serves 1,400 members farming 54,000 acres (22,000ha) of olives, of which some 7,400 acres (3,000ha) are organic.

Casa Passanha

Herdade da Charneca
7830-014 Vila Nova de S. Bento
☎ 284 588 112
🆆 www.casapassanha.com

This estate was founded as recently as 1999, but is already a frequent prize-winner at national shows. Its Azeite Passanha oil, made from *Cobrançosa* and *Cordovil*, is intensely fruity, bitter, and fairly pungent.

Coopole (Cooperativa de Olivicultores do Enxoé)

Rua dos Lagares, 7
7830-520 Vale de Vargo
☎ 284 865 110

Coopole is a reliable producer of oils (and wines) whose label is Encostas de Enxoé. Its oils are clear, golden yellow and have a fresh, fruity smell and a green, grassy taste with a light touch of pepperiness and bitterness.

Cortes de Cima

7960-909 Vidigueira
☎ 284 460 060
🆆 www.cortesdecima.pt

This leading wine estate makes first-class oil from its *Cobrançosa* olives under the label Cortes de Cima. It is yellowy green and unfiltered with a fresh, grassy flavor, a light, warm pepperiness, and a long aftertaste.

Ficalho, Azeites

Rua Nova do Outeiro, 25
V. Verde de Ficalho
7830 Serpa

Ficalho Azeite Virgem Extra is one of the most consistently excellent of Moura DOP oils. It is fruity, lightly pungent, and almost without trace of bitterness. Its light scent of citrus is followed by a long, cool, smooth, grassy taste. Azeites Ficalho also produces a non-DOP oil called Pé da Serra, which is of an equally high standard. Both come from the Serra do Ficalho and are based on cold-pressed *Cordovil*, *Verdeal*, and *Galega* olives, with some extra *Cobrançosa* in the case of Pé da Serra. Azeites Ficalho is now starting to export to America and northern Europe.

Herdade do Esporão

Apartado 31
7200-999 Reguengos de Monsaraz
☎ 266 509 270
🆆 www.esporao.com

Herdade do Esporão, part of the Lisbon-based Spaza group, is a huge, modern, irrigated estate, given mainly to wine. It started making oil in 1998, buying olives from some 20 farmers in the Serpa and Moura area. The 100% Galega oil was the first single-cultivar oil to be sold widely in Portugal and shows this typical cultivar at its best. Delicate, fruity, and fresh, the oil has just a touch of bitterness and pungency.

GALEGA

Esporão also offers a greenish-gold, single-variety *Cordovil* oil that is medium fruity and slightly peppery, with a long-lasting aftertaste. Esporão's range of oils also includes a greenish Esporão Moura DOP. This oil has a long and complex taste with a marked measure of fruitiness, pepperiness, and bitterness in harmonious combination. Esporão is seriously committed to gastrotourism. The visitor reception area, with its wine bar, restaurant, and store set above a landscaped lake, is reminiscent of a New World winery. It would not look out of place in Napa Valley or Yarra Valley in Victoria, Australia.

AZEITE DE MOURA DOP

Moura e Barrancos, Coop.

R. das Forças Armadas, 9
St Agostinho
7860-034 Moura
☎ 285 250 720

The 1,000 members of Cooperativa Agrícola de Moura e Barrancos own about 74,000 acres (30,000ha) of olive trees. They produce an award-winning Azeite Moura DOP oil and a non-DOP oil with the same name. Both are a clear golden-yellow color, fruity and smooth, and possess only a touch of pungency and bitterness.

FRANCE

The French oil industry is very small compared to other European countries. The total area put to olive growing is probably little more than 34,600 acres (14,000ha), roughly the same as a single Andalusian village. Olive growing is concentrated mainly in the southeastern corner (see p.211). France produces only 3,300–5,500 tons of olive oil each year, though the French consume more than 88,000 tons.

DECLINE & RECOVERY

French olive growing was hit hard by the frosts of 1929 and 1956, whose effects were exacerbated by rural depopulation, as well as the promotion of sunflower oil as a less expensive alternative to olive oil. Cheap imports from French Algeria led to olive oil being regarded as a food of poor immigrants. It was not until the early 1980s that the industry began to recover, though the area of land put to olives is still less than half what it was 50 years ago—vines and almonds offer greater, short-term returns. The industry now promotes olive oil as a high-quality product, and the strong demand for it is supplemented by Spanish and Italian imports, although French oil is perceived as better. Some of it is; much of it isn't.

FRENCH OIL PRODUCERS

Production is also very fragmented, with the smallest average size of landholding in the European Union: 92 percent of olive growers have fewer than 250 trees and less than 2.5 acres (one hectare). One result is that France offers an extraordinary number of oils from small producers, many of them made from unusual olive cultivars. It is a market of wonderful diversity.

THE QUALITY OF FRENCH OILS

Alain Ducasse, the celebrated French chef, once described French oil production as "very small, and generally of low quality." Indeed, French olive oil is not as good as the French believe it to be. There is a handful of absolutely world-class oils, and one or two areas where the leading producers are reliable from year to year, but there are also many overrated oils. These could only exist in such a curious structure as the French domestic market. Most French oils are overpriced. If French oils had to compete on quality in Spain or Greece, they would fetch only a fraction of the price they command in France. There are, of course, exceptions. For example, in 2004, Moulin du Castelas won first prize in the Mario Solinas international competition in Madrid.

The *Fruité Noir* oil

The French have a particular affection for oils made from late-harvested olives, which are allowed to undergo a controlled fermentation before being pressed. This style is known as *fruité noir* and has none of the green fruitiness that you might expect of an oil. The length of the fermentation—an anaerobic action—depends upon the cultivar, the olives' maturity, and the temperatures at which they are held. The skilled oil-maker will assess all these factors when deciding the optimum length.

Fruité noir oil is said to be characterized by smells of leafmold, mushrooms, hay, and walnuts; it is sweet and gentle, with very little pepperiness and no bitterness whatsoever. It is, however, extremely difficult to make well, and many of the oils I have tasted were unpleasantly musty or winey. The *fruité noir* style is especially associated with Corsican oils.

◀ SOUTHWESTERN FRANCE
Olive trees are grown singly and in small groves throughout Provence and Languedoc, as here, near a village in the Aude.

Olive oil from Corsica

Corsican olive oil was granted a French AOC in 2004 as *"Huile d'Olive de Corse—Oliu di Corsica."* The rules reflect its unusual nature. It must come from the island's little-known indigenous olives with names like *Sabina*, *Zinzala*, *Ghjermana di Balagna*, *Ghjermana d'Alta Rocca*, *Capanacce*, *Curtinese*, and *Raspulata*, picked late, when they are black. Seven days may pass before they are milled and acidity may be up to 1.5% (the EU stipulates that only 0.8% or below is extra virgin). Corsican oil is soft, without pepperiness or bitterness, but tastes of cocoa, glacé fruits, mushrooms, and dried herbs. You either love it or hate it.

CORSICA'S FERTILE LAND

It is difficult to know how to distinguish good French olive oil from bad. You should always seek out an oil that is certified as AOC or AOP. Any bottle that bears a medal from the current year's Paris Concours Agricole (the leading show for agricultural produce in France) also starts off with a guarantee of quality. Avoid anything that claims to be *artisanale*. Apart from a few exceptions, these oils are expensive and of poor quality, often tainted by mold or fermentation from

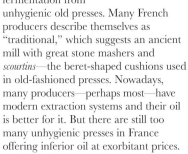

BASKET OF OLIVES

unhygienic old presses. Many French producers describe themselves as "traditional," which suggests an ancient mill with great stone mashers and *scourtins*—the beret-shaped cushions used in old-fashioned presses. Nowadays, many producers—perhaps most—have modern extraction systems and their oil is better for it. But there are still too many unhygienic presses in France offering inferior oil at exorbitant prices.

QUALITY CONTROL

The basis of the European system of protection for products of specified origin is known as the AOP (*Appellation d'Origine Protégée*) in France. Originally the French had their own system of

Appellations d'Origine Contrôlée (AOC). The first olive oil area to be awarded AOC status was Nyons (*see p.212*). The French often describe their AOP oils (those that are recognized by the European Union) as AOC oils because the French national grant of an AOC predated recognition by the EU. Not all French AOCs are recognized by the EU, however. For example, the French government created an AOC on August 27, 1997 for all the olive products of the Vallée des Baux de Provence, meaning [1] split olives, [2] black olives, and [3] oil. Only the oil is recognized by the EU legislation and that recognition did not come until June 6, 2000.

THE PACKAGING OF OILS

Far too many French producers sell oil in clear-glass bottles. These are popular with customers, because the contents can be seen and appreciated, but the oils deteriorate fast if at any stage they are exposed to light. French oil bottles often have thin plastic caps that allow the contents to leak and let in air. Producers say that these are not problems because they can never produce enough oil to satisfy demand. In short, they expect their oils to be consumed young and quickly.

Olives in France

Olives grow in three regions of France: Rhône-Alpes, Languedoc, and Provence. However, they flourish in only a small area of each: consult the individual maps that follow.

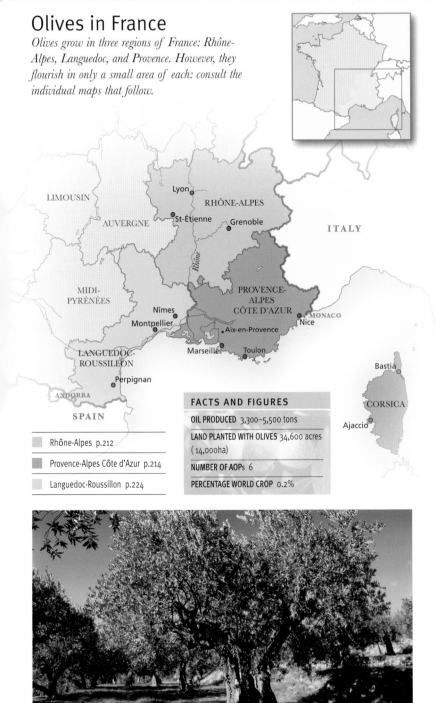

LIMOUSIN

Lyon

RHÔNE-ALPES

AUVERGNE   St-Étienne   Grenoble

ITALY

Rhône

MIDI-PYRÉNÉES

PROVENCE-ALPES CÔTE D'AZUR

Nîmes   MONACO

Montpellier   Aix-en-Provence   Nice

LANGUEDOC-ROUSSILLON   Marseille   Toulon

Perpignan

Bastia

ANDORRA

SPAIN

CORSICA

Ajaccio

▨ Rhône-Alpes p.212

▨ Provence-Alpes Côte d'Azur p.214

▨ Languedoc-Roussillon p.224

FACTS AND FIGURES

OIL PRODUCED	3,300–5,500 tons
LAND PLANTED WITH OLIVES	34,600 acres (14,000ha)
NUMBER OF AOPs	6
PERCENTAGE WORLD CROP	0.2%

OLD OLIVE TREES IN PROVENCE Very few olive trees survived the big frosts of 1956.

Rhône-Alpes

Nyons is the only part of this cold, inland region where olives flourish. The sheltered microclimate has its own AOC, with 57 communes in the south of Drôme, and a few communes across into Vaucluse in Provence. It includes about 2,720 acres (1,100ha) of olives, all growing in small and scattered plantations. The area is characterized by poor soil, hot summers, cool winters, and low rainfall. The olives are the unique Tanche *cultivar, also known as "le perle noir," best known for producing black table olives.*

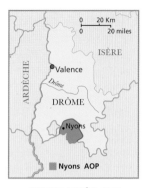

THE OLIVES OF RHÔNE-ALPES

NYONS AOP

Tanche olives are not picked until December (or January, depending on the season) when they are completely ripe. They are black and wrinkled but produce as much as 25–30 percent of their weight in oil, an average of 7 gallons per 220lb (25 liters per 100kg) of fruits. The AOP rules require olives to be delivered to the mill for pressing within four days of picking. The best producers process them within 24 hours. No other French AOP oil is invariably made from such late-picked olives.

The oils are golden yellow and soft, with a delicious aroma of green apples, a taste of almonds, sometimes a hint of walnuts, and hay. Since all are made only from *Tanche* olives, they show a consistency of taste, though considerable variations in style and quality arise from the different methods of cultivation and processing. Producers with modern equipment win more prizes for quality than the traditionalists.

Tanche are the best table olives in France. They are not at all fleshy but have a strong meaty flavor and never the slightest hint of bitterness. Tapenade and pistou are sold widely, while local specialties include *croquettes d'olive* from the Cooperative in Nyons. Across the road from here is France's best olive museum.

Though most of the olives here are *Tanche,* Nyons has a few trees of *Verdale, Cayot,* and *Sauzen* olives planted as pollinators and rootstocks. The *Sauzen* trees are so hardy that they have endured for hundreds of years. Most even survived the famously cold winter of 1709. One venerable specimen on the old road out of Nyons toward Orange is thought to be 800 years old.

HISTORIC MONUMENT
The bridge in the center of Nyons dates back to Roman times.

Tanche olives

The *Tanche* olive makes a dense, compact tree, somewhat erect in habit. Its leaves are large and broad. *Tanche* is resistant to both cold and drought, and is a moderate cropper with a pronounced tendency toward biennial cropping (*see p.27*), so well tended trees are usually pruned annually. The olives are a distinctive shade of violet before turning black and wrinkled when fully ripe. Larger fruits that are at least ½in (14mm) in diameter are sold for eating, smaller fruits are turned into oil. Nyons olives are dense in texture, with a meaty taste.

TANCHE OLIVES

Leading producers in Rhône-Alpes

Autrand-Dozol, Moulin

26110 Nyons
☎ 04 75 26 02 52
W www.moulin-dozol.com

The Autrand-Dozol mill is next to the fine old Romanesque bridge at Nyons. Next door, in the 19th century, a small factory used olive oil in the manufacture of soap. Autrand-Dozol oil is a dark, clear, golden-yellow color, with a smooth texture. It is almost buttery, with a light taste of almonds and apples and a long aftertaste with the merest hint of pepperiness and bitterness.

AUTRAND-DOZOL

Chameil, Moulin de

26110 Mirabel aux Baronnies
☎ 04 75 27 17 22
W www.moulin-de-chameil.com

René Bayle was the youngest oil-maker in France when he took over from his father in 1994. In some seasons, his smooth, sweet, and almondy René Bayle AOC oil is the best in the Nyons area. He also offers a nonappellation *Tanche* oil and one made from *Verdale*, which is very different, being fruity, grassy, peppery, and bitter. Bayle is still planting more, mainly *Tanche*, olive trees on his rich alluvial soil near the Eygues river.

Mathieu, Philippe

26110 Montaulieu
☎ 04 75 27 40 44

Philippe Mathieu is new to Nyons and has only been making oil since the mid-1990s. But his oil is already winning prizes regularly at the annual Paris Concours. The estate is high in the hills behind Nyons' mixed farming. All Mathieu's production is organic, but the oil is made with modern machinery and always filtered. His oil is rich, smooth, and more intensely flavored than many in the area, and sometimes has a trace of bitterness as well as pepperiness.

Nyonsais, Coopérative du

26111 Nyons
☎ 04 75 26 95 00
W www.coop-du-nyonsais.fr

The cooperative is by far the most consistent producer of high-quality oil and olives in the Nyonsais, as well as being the largest producer. Its Nyonsolive oil—the cooperative has only one label—is golden yellow and clear, with a smell of nuts and artichokes, a very smooth texture, a light taste of grass or apples, and a long, almondy aftertaste.

NYONSOLIVE

Ramade, Moulin

26110 Nyons
☎ 04 75 26 08 18
W www.moulinramade.com

Ramade was founded in 1904. Its olives are picked from December onward, after the first frosts. Some are preserved with sea salt and the rest turned into Moulin Ramade oil, which is soft, rich, and lightly fruity. In some years it tastes of apples, but more usually of nuts and almonds.

Provence-Alpes Côte d'Azur

It is Provence which produces the best French olive oils, and in the greatest quantities. Here, too, is a remarkable diversity of flavor, as varied and attractive as the landscape itself. Olives flourish on the limestone Alpilles near Les Baux, the flatlands of the Camargue and the wooded slopes of Var and Alpes-Maritimes. The French have a special fondness for Provence; its olive oils are among the most expensive in Europe.

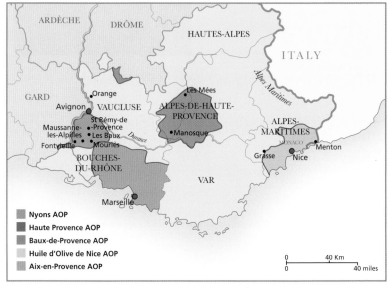

THE OLIVE REGIONS OF PROVENCE-ALPES CÔTE D'AZUR

BOUCHES-DU-RHÔNE

This is the only department in France where olives sometimes dominate the landscape. There are thought to be about 7,000 acres (2,800ha) of olive trees in the department of Bouches-du-Rhône, mostly on light, alluvial, or calcareous soil. There are two AOPs in this department: the Vallée des Baux-de-Provence, in which there are about 4,200 acres (1,700ha) of olives, and the Aix-en-Provence AOP in the east, which has 69 communes in Bouches-du-Rhône, and three in the province of Var.

VALLEE DES BAUX-DE-PROVENCE AOP

This appellation has the greatest concentration of high-quality oils in France. Most of the producers are found along the D17 between Fontvieille, Maussane-les-Alpilles, and Mouriès and north toward Les Baux

and St. Rémy-de-Provence. Here are the famous domains, the aristocrats whose names resound through the great French kitchens—Mas des Barres, Moulin du Mas Saint-Jean, and Mas de Fléchon among them. Most of the domains are mixed farms with a significant proportion of vines, but they have won fame and renown because of their olives. The plantations are often hedged with long lines of tall Italian cypresses, grown from seed and therefore of infinitely variable shape. These protect against the cold winds of the mistral.

In the 19th century, more than half the agricultural land in this area was devoted to olives. Now the figure is nearer to one-quarter: there are about 600,000 olive trees, producing two-thirds of the province's olive oil. The rules of the Vallée des Baux-de-Provence AOP require 85% of the oil to be made from two or more of four olive cultivars: *Salonenque*, *Aglandau* (here called *Béruguette*), *Grossane*, or *Verdale*. *Salonenque* is the principal olive, on which other tastes are built up, and gives the highest yield. The *Grossane* olive is a specialty of the Baux area. The hardy, vigorous tree does yield a fragrant, short-lived oil but its sweet-tasting, freestone fruits are better used for table olives.

There is quite a variation of style among the different producers. Most start picking when the olives are changing color and produce a peppery oil that tastes of grass, fresh almonds, green tomatoes, and artichokes. Others leave the olives until they are ripe, and offer a smooth oil tasting of almonds, apples, and—some say—truffles.

Les Baux-de-Provence itself is an abandoned town high on a rocky limestone pinnacle. These limestone outcrops, known as *alpilles*, occur all over the area. Most of the older trees have three or four separate trunks spreading out from the edge of an ancient rootstock, cut to ground level in the great frosts of 1956.

AIX-EN-PROVENCE AOP

The regulations of this AOP require that a combination of *Salonenque*, *Aglandau*, and *Cayanne* olives should account for at least 60% of the olives used. Other cultivars often seen are *Bouteillan*, *Verdale*, and *Grossane*. The AOP oils therefore vary, with no single established style, though they are based on the interaction of gentle *Salonenque* olives and fruity *Aglandau*. Typical Aix-en-Provence oils are fresh and fruity, with a wide palette of tastes, including apples, grass, artichokes, and almonds. The oils of Château Virant, Château Calissanne, and Margier are among the best anywhere.

VAUCLUSE

Olive growing is scattered throughout the lowland areas of Vaucluse, the department best known for its Gigondas and Beaumes-de-Venise wines. Fifteen communes in the north belong to the Nyons AOP, where oils are made from *Tanche* olives (*see p.213*). The producers in the south of the department have more in common with their neighbors in the Aix-en-Provence AOP. Oils here are

ROCKY TERRAIN Olive trees and spring flowers thrive in Maussane, Bouches-du-Rhône.

High-yielding *Salonenque* olives

These olives take their name from the town of Salon-de-Provence. They are widely planted in the Bouches-du-Rhône where they account for about two-thirds of all plantations. The value of *Salonenque* olives is their high yield and steady production, little affected by biennial bearing. The tree is also very hardy, drought-resistant, and healthy. It is fairly short, with a low, spreading shape. The olives are medium-sized and freestone, which makes them suitable as split green olives.

made from *Aglandau* and *Salonenque* olives. The oil cooperative in Beaumes-de-Venise is a beacon of excellence.

ALPES-DE-HAUTE-PROVENCE

Olives are not a major crop in this French department. It is only on the approach to the beautiful village of Lurs that they dominate the landscape. There are no more than 200,000 olive trees in the department, which is fewer than grew in the area around the town of Manosque alone 100 years ago. The main concentrations today are still around Manosque and, more particularly, around Les Mées, where the parish church is dedicated to Notre Dame des Oliviers. There is one AOP, the Haute-Provence AOP, and this covers 83 of the communes in Alpes-de-Haute-Provence, six in Vaucluse, four in Var, and two in Bouches-du-Rhône.

Manosque is an unusual small walled town, threaded with narrow streets impassable by modern traffic. The French poet Jean Giono was born in a house on the narrow main street. His *Poème de l'olive* begins: "Ce temps des olives. Je ne connais rien de plus épique."

The olive of Haute-Provence is *Aglandau*, which has grown here since at least the 13th century. Nine-tenths of the trees in the Durance valley are

Aglandau olive. The AOP legislation requires that the oils of Haute-Provence should be at least 70% *Aglandau* olive until 2014, and 80% thereafter. The *Aglandau* olive is very firm, which means that it stands up well to picking and transportation, and does not decompose before milling. The oils have a green taste of artichoke and cut grass— vegetable rather than fruit—if, as is usual, they are made early in the season, but are fruitier, fuller, and richer, even unctuous, if harvesting is delayed until later. Both develop a slight hint of almonds and have a good, light aftertaste of pepperiness and bitterness.

Throughout Haute-Provence there are pronounced differences in quality between the best and the worst olive oils. If in doubt, avoid the traditional presses and seek out oils from the larger, modern ones. The three I have listed here are dependable (*see p.221*).

NICE & ALPES-MARITIMES

The department has some 7,500 acres (3,000ha) of olive groves and 400,000 trees. These include modern plantations —the industry is currently expanding—with a dense planting of up to 160 trees per acre (400ha), but most trees are traditionally grown on steep, terraced, calcareous hillsides, protected from the mistral by the Alpes-Maritimes. The main areas of production are around Nice, Grasse, and Menton. Most producers are very small scale, and often run out of oil by early summer, but there

Table olives from Baux

The *Grossane* olive is a specialty of the Baux area. It produces a large, round, black freestone olive used mainly for eating. Cracked green olives are another specialty of the Baux valley. They are picked green, in September or October, from *Salonenque* or *Aglandau* olive trees. The olives are cracked with a wooden mallet and immediately rinsed with fresh water, then placed in an alkaline mix to remove their bitterness. The brine is infused with fresh fennel. These olives are a seasonal product, at their best for only a few months.

OLIVES IN THE HAUTE-ALPES
Olives fill the hillside and valley below the village of Lurs in Alpes-de-Haute-Provence.

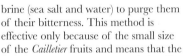

are many of them, and their oils are fairly uniform in taste. All the olive-growing communes within the Alpes-Maritimes – some 99 of them—qualify for inclusion within the Huile d'Olive de Nice AOP.

The olive of Nice and the Alpes-Maritimes is the *Cailletier*, a vigorous, tall-growing cultivar with downward-drooping branches. It is closely related to the *Taggiasca* olive from neighboring Liguria (*see p.60*). The olives are very small (typically .035oz/1.5 gr each), and usually not picked until they are ripe, between January and March, but they give a good yield. The oils are yellow, smooth, and only lightly fruity, with a delicate taste of almonds, walnuts, artichokes, and apples. Occasionally the olives are picked early, from mid-November onward, and produce an oil with a "green" taste of grass and fresh almonds, as well as a good pepperiness and light bitterness.

The Alpes-Maritimes has a second AOP for table olives, also known as "Olives de Nice," which are treated with

OLD PRESS AT GERVASONI, VAR

brine (sea salt and water) to purge them of their bitterness. This method is effective only because of the small size of the *Cailletier* fruits and means that the essential taste of the olives does not become altered by the process of curing. The olives may be green-brown, black, or intermediate—half-ripe *Cailletier* are a winey red—but the flesh comes away cleanly from the kernel.

VAR

Olive growing in the province of Var in the south is on a small scale but widespread and a small part of this department is included in the Haute-Provence AOP (*see p.217*). The principal olives are *Aglandau, Bouteillan* (a local specialty that gives a strong, grassy taste when picked young, and an equally strong pearlike taste when ripe), *Grossane, Picholine,* and *Petit Ribier.* The *Ribier* olive is one of many local and ancient cultivars grown in a small way throughout the department. This promotion of local diversity shows the way forward not only for the oil industry in France, but also for producers in places like Andalusia where far too much oil is produced which, though of good quality, is insufficiently distinct. Quality in Var depends upon having modern extraction equipment and the know-how to use it well. Immense variation and choice are characteristic of the department, but quantities are small, supplies are limited, and many lines sell out early in the season. That said, it is a fascinating area in which to search for olive oil.

FRENCH OLIVE GROVE
Well established trees near the ancient fortified village of Gilette in Alpes-Maritimes.

Leading producers in Bouches-du-Rhône

SIGN FOR MOULIN DE MAS DES BARRES, MAUSSANE, LES ALPILLES

Barres, Moulin du Mas des

13520 Maussane les Alpilles
☎ 04 90 54 44 32

René Quentin makes Mas des Barres from a mixture of *Salonenque*, *Aglandau*, *Grossane*, *Verdale*, and *Picholine*, each separately milled using a Sinolea system. It is then blended, to include early, mid-season, and late-harvested oils. It is unfiltered, golden yellow, and fairly fluid, with a lightly fruity scent (tomato and apples) and a mild, green taste. Its taste is less fruity than redolent of grass and artichokes, with a good, long, peppery aftertaste.

Calissanne, Château de

13680 Lançon de Provence
☎ 04 90 42 63 03
www.calissanne.fr

Château Calissanne is a large estate of 2,500 acres (1,000ha), mainly put to vines but including 123 acres (50ha) of organic olives spread over three plantations. The only cultivars are *Salonenque* and *Aglandau*, but they are combined differently to create two distinct blends—Les Merveilles and L'Olivaie—both with AOP status. They also differ in the state of maturity at which the olives are culled and processed. Les Merveilles is an equal blend of *Salonenque* and *Aglandau* made from 37 acres (15ha) of old olives that survived the 1956

CHÂTEAU CALISSANNE

frosts. It is pale, fluid, unfiltered, and very "green" tasting, fresh, and lively, with hints of cut grass and almonds and a good balance of fruitiness, pepper, and bitterness. It is popular with the French restaurant trade. L'Olivaie is made from 86 acres (35ha) of younger trees, picked during November. It is lemon yellow, aromatic with a green taste of tomatoes and almonds, and is long, harmonious, and only lightly peppery.

Castelas, Moulin du

13520 Les-Baux-de-Provence
☎ 04 90 54 50 86

Moulin du Castelas is a delight. Golden yellow and filtered, it has a good fresh smell, a big grassy taste, lots of *ardence* (the French word for pepperiness) and a light bitterness. It comes from 42 acres (17ha) of ancient *Salonenque*, *Aglandau*, *Verdale*, and *Grossane* olives.

Cornille, Moulin Jean-Marie

13520 Maussane les Alpilles
☎ 04 90 54 32 37
W www.moulin-cornille.com

This is the cooperative at Maussane, a bastion of traditional oil-making with *scourtins*, hydraulic presses, and natural decantation—no filtration. The oil is pale greeny gold and rather fluid, with a good, fruity nose and velvety texture. It is smooth on the tongue and lightly fruity, with a hint of

almonds and a mild warm aftertaste. The cooperative's 600 members produce 200–300 tons of oil a year.

Coudoux, Coopérative Oléicole de

13111 Coudoux
☎ 04 42 52 05 04
W www.huiledecadoux.com

The cooperative at Coudoux is one of the leading "traditional" presses in France. Olives from its 300 members are used to make some 50 tons of unfiltered oil. Their *fruité noir* oil is dark yellow and nutty, with very little pepperiness or

MOULIN DE COUDOUX

bitterness—the result of storing the olives for a few days before pressing them. Devotees describe it as long and harmonious, with a taste of dried fruit, toast, and mushrooms.

Dame, Mas de la

13520 Les-Baux-de-Provence
☎ 04 90 54 32 24 67
🌐 www.masdeladame.com

Mas de la Dame is a late-harvest oil made at Moulin Cornille from 62 acres (25ha) of *Salonenque, Grossane, Aglandau,* and *Verdale,* using traditional granite wheels and *scourtins*. It is smooth, nutty, almondy, and only lightly peppery. Some say the texture reminds them of melted butter.

Estoublon, Château d'

13990 Fontvieille
☎ 04 90 54 64 00
🌐 www.estoublon.com

The AOP oil of Château d'Estoublon is light golden yellow and clear, with a pleasant, light, green-fruit taste of apples and almonds and a long, gentle, peppery aftertaste. Estoublon is a fine house, with some 6,700 olives trees on 118 acres (48ha) that produce about 15 tons of oil a year.

Fare-les-Oliviers, Coopérative Oléicole La

13580 La Fare-les-Oliviers
☎ 04 90.42.61.51

The village of La Fare sits among olive orchards, and became La Fare-les-Oliviers in 1919. Some 800 small producers belong to the cooperative, whose La-Fare-les-Oliviers Huile d'Olive Vierge Extra AOC oil is 60% *Salonenque* and 40% *Aglandau,* picked at the start of November. It is pale yellow, with a green tinge, fruity (apples and almonds), but soft and almost buttery. It is *very* mild and gentle, with a long aftertaste and only a hint of pepperiness.

Fléchon, Mas de

13520 Maussane les Alpilles
☎ 04 90 54 34 59
🌐 www.masdeflechon.com

Mas de Fléchon AOP oil is made mainly from old trees

of *Salonenque, Grossane, Aglandau,* and *Verdale.* Each cultivar is pressed separately, and the blend assembled at the end of the harvest. The oil is pale golden yellow, lightly grassy, fresh, and unctuous at first, then smooth and almondy with a slight pepperiness that lasts long on the palate.

Margier, Moulin à huile

13390 Auriol
☎ 04 42 04 74 09

The Margier family processes the olives of 2,500 producers, using the most modern extraction equipment. The two main oils are both made from a blend of 50% *Aglandau,* 20% *Cayanne,* 20%

MOULIN À HUILE MARGIER

Salonenque, and 10% miscellaneous olives. Domaine La Michelle is mid-gold, clear, fruity, peppery, and bitter. It is smooth and well balanced, with more body than most French oils. It tastes of greenness and tomatoes, and has a long aftertaste. Moulin à Huile Margier Huile d'Olive Vierge Extra is also very good and comes in two forms—the early-picked oil, which is cool, smooth, and gentle, with an appropriate pepperiness and a distinct, pearlike taste, and the *fruité noir* oil from ripe olives, which have undergone a controlled anaerobic

fermentation to give a more complex, mushroomy taste. Margier also offers some interesting monovarietal oils, including one from *Cayanne* (aromatic, with a hint of quinces), and a mix of rare local cultivars. These are popular and tend to sell out early in the season.

Mouriès, Moulin Coopératif de

13890 Mouriès
☎ 04 90 47 53 86

The mill in Mouriès dates back to 1626, but has been a cooperative since 1920 and used electricity since 1923. The present installations date from 1999 and include a continual extraction system. It has won many medals at the annual Paris Concours. Its unfiltered Huile d'Olive Vierge Extra L'Ardente is fruity, green, and soft, with the sort of pepperiness and bitterness more commonly found in Italian olive oils. It has lots of grassy tones, plus hints of apple, artichoke, and exotic fruits.

Saint Jean, Moulin à huile du Mas

13990 Fontvieille
☎ 04 90 54 72 64

The Sourdon family in Saint Jean have 62 acres (25ha) of *Salonenque, Grossane, Aglandau, Verdale,* and *Picholine* as well as milling the olives of some 250 smaller producers. They make about 50 tons of oil a year. It is yellow with a tinge of green, unfiltered, with a good, fruity taste (tomatoes and apples), and a hint of almonds. It then develops a complex aftertaste and a long, warm, peppery ending.

MOULIN MAS DE
SAINT JEAN

CHÂTEAU VIRANT

Virant, Château

13680 Lançon de Provence

☎ 04 90 42 44 47

W www.chateauvirant.com

Château Virant has 44 acres (18ha) of old (pre-1956) olives and 272 acres (110ha) of vines grown on rocky, calcareous soil. Its oils are made from *Aglandau* and *Salonenque* olives, picked in early December. It also mills the olives of 700 small-scale growers, producing some 150 tons a year. The main label is Château Virant AOC Huile d'Olive Vierge Extra, which is mid-gold, full flavored, and fruity, with hints of beans, pears, and tomatoes. It has good body and a nicely balanced pepperiness. The estate also offers two monovarietal oils under the Moulin de Château Virant label. The pure Aglandau oil smells of lettuce and green tomatoes, and has a strong green, grassy taste. It is rather more substantial —fruity and peppery—than most French oils, partly as the olives are picked very young. The milder Salonenque oil is golden yellow with a very slight green tinge and is equally good. It is soft and lightly fruity, with a taste of greenness, fresh almonds, and arugula. With only a trace of pepper and bitterness, it is altogether very harmonious.

Leading producers in Vaucluse

Balméenne, Coopérative Oléicole La

84190 Beaumes-de-Venise (Vaucluse)

☎ 04 90 62 93 77

The leading producer in Vaucluse is the cooperative at Beaumes-de-Venise (best known for its wines), which consistently wins prizes at the Paris Concours. The coop's store has a display of old presses and oil jars. La Balméenne oil is clear yellow, with a touch of green, and is made from *Verdale* olives picked rather early in the season. It has a strong, fresh taste of grass, artichokes, herbs, and almonds, with a gutsy pepperiness and a hint of bitterness, all well balanced and in proportion to each other.

LA BALMÉENNE

Comtat, Moulin à huile du

84330 Caromb (Vaucluse)

☎ 04 90 62 42 05

The Haut family in Moulin du Comtat offers a strong, grassy oil (unfiltered, green gold, and sold only in two-pint/one-liter bottles) with a flavor of ripe apples and a good measure of bitterness and pepperiness.

Vieux Château, Moulin du

84360 Merindol (Vaucluse)

☎ 04 90 72 86 76

Right in the south of the department, near the area of Les Baux, the Boudoire brothers make an oil that is mostly of *Aglandau* with a little *Salonenque*. Moulin du Vieux Château oil is green yellow, unfiltered, with an interesting taste that is both rich and herbaceous, with quite a whack of bitterness and pepperiness to balance it.

Leading producers in Alpes-de-Haute-Provence

Arizzi, Ets.

04190 Les Mées

☎ 04 92 34 04 80

Moulin Fortuné Arizzi lies in a most attractive olive grove above the edge of the Durance valley and, at 81 acres (33ha), is one of the largest olive holdings in France. Many of the olive trees are set in grass, which is watered and mown to resemble an English lawn. Arizzi sells only one oil, called Pur Terroir, which is very smooth, almost sweet at first, until a strong pepperiness develops. It is made from an unusual blend: 60% *Aglandau*, 20% *Picholine*, and 20% *Frantoio*, the Tuscan olive *par excellence*. It is *Frantoio* that gives the oil its unusually dark green color and makes it a Franco-Tuscan hybrid of character and individuality. Its excellence is attested by many prizes won at national and international shows.

PUR TERROIR

Olivette, Le Moulin de l'

04100 Manosque

☎ 04 92 72 00 99

The cooperative at Manosque has 1,600 members and is the largest in the department. Its Le Moulin de l'Olivette AOP oil is medium fruity in the modern, grassy style, and fresh, with a hint of bitter almonds and a pleasant, light-to-medium pepperiness to the aftertaste. Le Moulin de l'Olivette also produces monovarietal oils; its Tanche oil has a rich taste of apples and almonds, and is fresher and less smooth than the great *Tanche* oils from Nyons.

MOULIN DE L'OLIVETTE

Pénitents, Moulin des

04190 Les Mées

☎ 04 92 34 07 67

Moulin des Pénitents is the cooperative at Les Mées and also has a small olive museum. Its AOP oil is fuller, richer, and smoother than many, more fruity and less vegetable, but equally well balanced with a long, lingering pepperiness and a pleasing touch of bitterness. Moulin des Pénitents also produces monovarietal oils; its Bouteillan oil is said to taste of truffles and its Tanche Déssert resembles a ripe oil from Nyons. Its Fruité

MOULIN DES PÉNITENTS

Noir is very successful. It is unctuous, full bodied, and well balanced, with no trace of unpleasant fermentation.

Leading producers in Nice & Alpes-Maritimes

Alziari, Moulin à huile

06000 Nice

☎ 04 93 44 45 12

W www.alziari.com.fr

Alziari is the most famous oil producer in the Alpes-Maritimes, and the only one still functioning in the old city of Nice itself. It is a traditional press, with cold water and *scourtins*. Alziari oil is noted for its mild, gentle, nutty flavour, a smooth texture, and a complete absence of bitterness. It is sold in handsome blue and gold tins.

Gilette-Val Estéron, Coopérative de

06830 Gilette

☎ 04 93 08 54 48

Gilette is on a precipitous slope above the Var valley; many of its members' trees are of great antiquity. The cooperative's oil is smooth and gentle, with a taste of almonds and a hint of apples and pears.

Levens, Coopérative Oléicole de

06670 Levens

☎ 04 93 91 61 16

The AOC oil of the cooperative at Levens is sold as Concept Vert. It is cool, soft, and full, with a light taste of cut grass and sweet almonds, and a warm, peppery aftertaste. It is notably smooth, almost unctuous—and delicious.

Opio, Huilerie d'

06650 Opio

☎ 04 93 77 23 03

W www.moulin-opio.com

This is the largest mill in the province. It is also known as Moulins de la Brague and it is equipped with both modern and traditional systems of extraction. Its oil is soft and smooth, fruity and mild, and has a light, herbaceous taste and nutty, almond finish. Its olives are sourced from a wide area.

Other Producers in Nice & Alpes-Maritimes

Yann Véran

06670 Levens

☎ 04 93 79 77 77

Young Yann Véran has won the top gold medal for his Yann Véran AOC Nice oils at the Paris Concours. The oil was also given by President Chirac to all heads of state attending the Nice Summit in December 2000.

Château de Vignal

2566 route de Berre les Alpes

06390 Contes

☎ 04 93 79 00 11

Henriette and Pierre Chiesa Gauthier's Château du Vignal oil is a fine example of Nice oil—gentle, almondy, and delicious. Their garden, classified as a historic monument, is surrounded by beautiful silvery olive trees.

Leading producers in Var

Callas, Moulin de

83830 Callas
☎ 04 94 76 68 05
🌐 www.moulindecallas.com

The Bérenguier family offers different Moulin de Callas blends from year to year. One prize-winning mix of *Aglandau* and *Bouteillan*, usually in roughly 50/50 proportions, is a very good, grassy, fruity oil with a nutty aftertaste and a long, warm pepperiness. Another is known simply as Mélange Variétés d'olives (including *Cayet Roux, Picholine, Ribier, Cayon, Bouteillan, Aglandau, Cailletier, Grossane,* and *Moncita*) and is usually softer and fruity, with hints of almonds and apples. A regular favourite is their monovarietal Petit Ribier oil, a local speciality, which is gentle, soft, lightly fruity, and smooth, with a taste of artichokes, sweet almonds, and apples.

MOULIN DE CALLAS

Combette, Moulin de la

83780 Flayosc
☎ 04 94 84 63 69
🌐 www.moulindelacombette.fr

This cooperative has about 330 members. The main olive cultivar is the local *Cayet Roux*, but there are many others in their Moulin à

OLD STONE CRUSHERS AT GERVASONI

Huile de la Combette oil. It is mid-gold, unfiltered, and well made, with a light fruity taste of cut grass and apples that persists on the tongue and is followed by a pleasant peppery aftertaste. Demand for this delicious oil is always strong.

MOULIN DE LA COMBETTE

Gervasoni, Moulin

83630 Aups
☎ 04 94 70 04 66

This producer offers two well made oils: one called simply Fruité is 80% *Bouteillan*, a clean, "green" oil tasting of grass and artichokes with a light, long pepperiness; the other (in a slimmer bottle) is a mixture of *Aglandau* and *Salonenque* with a little *Bouteillan* added, and is gentler, with a taste of nuts and pears.

Pierre Plantée, Domaine de la

83120 Ste-Maxime
☎ 04 94 96 65 65

Domaine de la Pierre Plantée is a young plantation high on the hillside above

Sainte-Maxime. Its only oil, which is very well made, bears the name of the owner Olivier Thierry and comes from a blend of *Bouteillan, Aglandau,* and *Grossane* olives. It is gentle, cool, and fruity at first, with a grassy taste, then develops a delicious long aftertaste with a nice balance of pepperiness and bitterness.

OLIVIER THIERRY

Solidarité, Coopérative Oléicole La

83570 Entrecasteaux
☎ 04 94 04 44 08

The Huile d'Olive Vierge Extra of this 250-member cooperative situated in the woodlands of inland Var has a light, herbaceous smell and a soft, pleasing, almost unctuous texture, until you detect its decided pepperiness. It is medium fruity, with a taste of beans, sweet almonds, and red peppers. It won a gold medal at the Paris Concours in 2004.

Languedoc-Roussillon

Languedoc has a more sheltered, warmer climate than Provence, but fewer olive trees. Gard accounts for by far the largest volume of olive oil in Languedoc, around 70 percent, followed by Hérault, Aude, and Pyrénées Orientales. Quality is uneven, but can be excellent. Its best olive oil is recognized by the new AOP for Huile d'olive de Nîmes in Gard and Hérault.

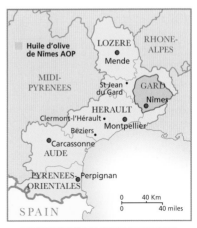

THE OLIVE REGIONS OF LANGUEDOC-ROUSSILLON

GARD, HERAULT, AUDE & PYRENEES ORIENTALES

Languedoc now has a French AOP called "Huile d'olive de Nîmes," covering 223 communes in Gard and Hérault. The permitted olive cultivars are *Picholine*, *Négrette*, and *Noirette*, of which *Picholine* should account for a minimum 60%. *Picholine* gives a strong, hearty oil with a good measure of bitterness and pepperiness. *Négrette* (originally from the Cévennes) produces small, early-ripening olives on a very hardy tree. The oil is golden, fine, soft, and fruity, with hints of walnuts and almonds. *Noirette* is lighter and gentler. The *Lucques* olive is associated with Hérault, and yields a soft, unctuous, and

delicate oil. It is a biennial cropper unless carefully pruned and irrigated.

Table olives are important in Languedoc, especially *Lucques* and *Picholine*. The *Picholine*, a long olive with a smooth skin and fine, firm flesh, is gathered green in October. It keeps well and retains its color. The *Lucques* olive has lopsided fruit and a strongly curved stone with a pointed end. The olives are darker than *Picholine*, with firm, oily flesh and a unique, delicate flavor.

GARD Ancient olive trees surround the Roman Pont du Gard.

Leading producers in Languedoc-Roussillon

Clermont-l'Hérault, Huilerie de

34800 Clermont-l'Hérault (Hérault)
C 04 67 96 10 36

This is the largest cooperative in the Hérault, with nearly 4,000 members producing 80 tons of oil a year. Its only oil is labeled Huilerie Coopérative de Clermont-l'Hérault. It has a soft, ripe flavour of nuts and tropical fruits—well made, well balanced, and delicious.

HUILERIE COOPÉRATIVE

Lacassagne, Domaines

66100 Perpignan (Pyrenées Orientales)
C 04 68 50 25 32
W www.lacassagne.net

Henri Lacassagne, a retired hauler, planted 99 acres (40ha) of *Picholine* olives in 1930; the area cultivated by his grandson Edouard Raymond now includes *Lucques* olives and extends to 148 acres (60ha)—the largest holding in France, close to the Spanish border. The olives are late-picked, and the Henri Lacassagne oil is soft, gentle, clear golden yellow, with a smell of hay and apples, a taste of sweet almonds, and a long, warm, gentle aftertaste.

Oulibo, Coopérative Oléicole l'

11120 Bize-Minervois (Aude)
C 04 68 41 88 88

L'Oulibo is the only olive cooperative in the Aude, and one of the larger producers in Languedoc, with more than 1,500 members and an annual average production of 50 tons. It offers unfiltered monovarietal oils of *Picholine* (surprisingly peppery), *Lucques* (gentle), and the ultralocal *Olivière* (a specialty of Roussillon, it is complex and fruity, with hints of almond, hazelnut, tomatoes, and citrus fruit).

Paradis, Moulin de

30360 Martignargues
C 04 66 83 24 52

Roger Paradis's family has owned Moulin à Huile Paradis since 1929 and produces some 70 tons of unfiltered oil a year. His main line is a *Picholine* oil. It is elegant, nutty, fruity, and buttery with a light pepperiness, but balanced, rich, and complex too. His Négrette oil is also buttery, almost sweet, with an herby smell and a smooth taste of almonds followed by a gentle, long-lasting pepperiness. It probably has some *Noirette* in it too.

MOULIN DE PARADIS NÉGRETTE

Soulas, Ets.

30190 Collorgues
C 04 66 81 21 13

The Soulas family at Collorgues claims to have one-quarter of the whole production in the Gard and offers three different oils, all of them Extra Virgin. Their main label is the excellent Picholine du Gard, with a creamy texture, a "green" taste of herbs and almonds, and a long, pronounced pepperiness. Their other labels are an organic oil, and a blend of *Picholine* and many other cultivars (including *Ascolana, Rougette, Noirette,* and *Verdale*) sourced from over a wide area.

Tuilerie, Château de la

30900 Nîmes
C 04 66 70 07 52
W www.chateautuilerie.com

Château de la Tuilerie is a neat wine estate south of Nîmes, with roses planted at the end of the rows of vines. It offers small quantities of two oils, both unfiltered, stylishly presented in clear glass bottles, and expensive—but good. Larme de Lune is pure *Bouteillan*, a Varois olive that imparts a taste of green apples and tomatoes. Fleur de Goutte is mainly of *Picholine*, with a little *Aglandau*, and *Verdial*. It is cool, smooth, and rich at first, with a taste of artichokes, almonds, and pears—instantly charming and accessible.

Vieilleville, Moulin du

30250 Sommières
C 04 66 80 03 69

This cooperative was founded in 1929 and now has 1,400 members. Its oils are mainly monovarietals—*Picholine, Négrette, Bouteillan, Aglandau,* and *Tanche*. The *Bouteillan* oil is remarkably mild, creamy, and aromatic. The new AOC oil is called Le Nectar d'Athéna, a blend of *Picholine* and *Négrette*.

GREECE & THE GREEK ISLANDS

Olive oil is of great importance historically, culturally, and economically, to Greece. However, while Greek oil is usually of acceptable quality, there is little in the way of variety or choice. Most of Greece's oil comes from the Peloponnese, the Chalkidikí peninsula, Crete, and Delphi in central Greece. Some of the smaller islands, including Zante, Lesbos, Samos, and Rhodes also have extensive plantations.

A LANDSCAPE OF OLIVES

Greek history, literature, and mythology —both ancient and modern—are all bound up with the olive. Sophocles referred to "the gray-leaved olive, the nurturer of children." In modern Greek, the word for olive also means inheritance, and the Greeks have a saying, "He and I ate bread and olives together."

Olive trees are a much more persistent feature of the landscape in Greece than in Italy or Spain. The total area planted with olives is more than 2.4 million acres (1 million ha). There are some 150 million olive trees, 2,800 mills, and over 100 olive cultivars. The Greeks themselves consume more olive oil than any other nation.

STRUCTURE OF THE INDUSTRY

Greece produces around 440,000 tons of oil annually (harvests fluctuate considerably from year to year as a result of biennial cropping). The Greek tradition has always been to buy oil in bulk from farmers. About 40 percent of Greek olive oil is produced for home consumption. Of the rest, much of it is sold in bulk either to middlemen, big blenders, or Italian companies. Greek oils are good for blending because they do not have a strong, distinctive taste, unlike Spanish *Picual*, for example.

The Greek section of this book should be almost as long and detailed as those devoted to Spain and Italy, but the Greek oil industry is structured in such a way that it has led to a lack of choice. Olive oil is not widely perceived by the Greeks as a prestige or luxury item; much of it is sold by cooperatives directly to customers who bring containers to fill. Very little Greek oil is bottled at source. Most producers who do bottle oil do so for export only. Local demand is not yet sufficient to justify the expense of bottling and labeling in small glass containers.

MERCOURI ESTATE A Pithos jar stands at the entrance of the Mercouri estate in Pyrgos.
◀ MONI ARKADIOU The olive trees growing inside this monastery were planted for sacramental use.

ANCIENT PRESSES Museum pieces today, these presses were once integral to the production of olive oil.

Koroneïki and other Greek olives

What is unusual about Greek oil is that almost all of it is made from one olive cultivar, *Koroneïki*, which is found all over the country. *Koroneïki* oils are noted for their fruitiness and their stability, which means that they keep their flavor and freshness for a long time. Other cultivars have only a local following: the *Valanoliá* olive is popular in the northern Aegean islands; *Megarítiki* in southern parts of the mainland; *Kalamón* in the Peloponnese; *Prassinoliá* in Chalkidikí; and *Mastoïdès* (also known as *Áthinoliá* or *Tsounáti*) in parts of Crete. However, there is nothing to match the extensive plantations of *Koroneïki*, nor—some would say —to match the quality of its oil.

FINDING HIGH-QUALITY OILS

The problem when buying Greek oil is to know where it comes from. Much of the market is in the hands of brokers who simply see an opportunity for buying oil and selling it on to larger companies or directly to consumers at a profit.

Quality control for Greek olive oil production is regulated by the European Union (EU) in the same way as France, Spain, Italy, and Portugal. Greece has 20 Protected Designations of Origin (PDOs) and Protected Geographical Indications (PGIs) for olive oil and 10 for table olives, but the system of verifying and validating PDO oils is in its infancy and not properly supervised.

KORONEÏKI OLIVES

There are many single-producer PDOs that were registered in the early years of European Union legislation, when Brussels was inviting the establishment of special areas of excellence. Many PDOs/PGIs were created by sales managers in an attempt to elevate the status of their company.

MARKETING & PROMOTION

All producers of olive oil believe theirs to be the best oil in the world but, in the case of the Greeks, this is an incontestable truth, an article of faith. They do not believe that any oil from Italy or Spain could be as good as theirs. That said, most Greek olive oil is sold on price rather than quality.

The olive oil market in Greece is characterized by bad management and an antiquated sales and marketing culture. At the retail level there is not the equation of quality between wine and oil found in other countries. In France, Spain, and in Italy it is easy to spend 10 euros (about $12) on a 17fl oz (50cl) bottle of extra virgin oil. No Greek producer has yet to charge such a price. Secondary cooperatives

OLIVE HILLSIDE, NEAPOLI, CRETE

sell a proportion of their oil in local supermarkets, usually in 2-pint (1-liter) plastic bottles. The Agricultural Cooperative of Préveza, for example, sells its oil in two Enosis supermarkets in the town itself. Some of the big national producers now offer luxury lines for sale in upscale stores. A local producer will sometimes bottle some of his oil and sell it in retailers for tourists the following summer: the Sirène label in Parga is an example.

Most of the Greek oils found in northern Europe or the United States usually come from large cooperatives like Sitía and Pezá Union (*see p.238*) who can afford the advertising and promotion. A few smaller operations have also taken advantage of local connections or special markets: Blaüel in the Mani has Austrian connections; Tóplou in Crete sells widely to the German organic market. Only recently has the Greek government started to promote Greek olives and olive oil; it remains to be seen whether the initiative will be sustained.

RENEWAL PRUNING, CRETE New styles of training and pruning are almost universal now in Greece.

OLD OLIVE TREES IN CRETE

Olive Regions of Greece

About 36 percent of Greece's oil comes from Crete, 36 percent from the Peloponnese, 6 percent from Lesbos, 7 percent from the Ionian islands and 15 percent from elsewhere, mainly central Greece, Epiros, Thessaly, and Macedonia. The provinces, or prefectures, with the largest industries are Heraklion and Messinía.

- Peloponnese p.232
- Crete p.238
- Rest of Greece p.245

FACTS AND FIGURES

OIL PRODUCED 446,500 tons

LAND PLANTED WITH OLIVES
2,400,000 acres (1,000,000ha)

NUMBER OF PDOs/PGIs 20

PERCENTAGE WORLD CROP 15.8%

MONASTIC OLIVE GROVES
Olives are often associated with old monasteries like Moní Toploú in Crete
(*see p.240*).

MINOAN SETTLEMENT ON CRETE Olive presses found in Minoan settlements date back to 1500 B.C.E.

National Brands of Greece

There are many national brands in Greece. All will improve their sales in years to come as consumers buy more from supermarkets and less directly from farmers, but competition is tough, and some well known names are likely to fall victim to mergers and takeovers.

MAIN GREEK BRANDS

Altis is probably the most common brand of olive oil in Greece. It is owned by Elais, which is part of the multinational Unilever. Elais says that "judicious blending of olive oil from disparate areas results in an end product in keeping with the brand image."

Hellenic Fine Oils is also big, part of the Soya Mills Group. Its home label is Elaidon; its export label is Sparta Gold.

Trofotechniki in Salonika is a general food company with a strong line in oils including an organic one called Xenios.

Minerva (the Greek company, not to be confused with the Italian company of the same name) is part of the Paterson Zochonis group and claims to be the largest Greek exporter of olive oil. Its lines include a Mountain Regions oil and a Horió Koroneïki oil.

ELAIDOLADO
MINERVA
KLASIKO

Eleourgiki is Greece's only tertiary cooperative. It represents 350,000 growers and acts as a clearing house for surpluses and shortages of production and demand.

Gaea offers a PDO oil from Sitía and another from Kalamáta, but its "basic" brand comes from *Koroneïki* olives from the Makinina region around Delphi. Gaea also offers a Lakonia oil sold as Gaea PGI Lakonia Biologiko Extra Virgin, a smooth, golden yellow, buttery oil with a light mild taste and a hint of almonds.

Nutria's lines include the Ionia brand; it does not blend other producers' oil, but buys in olives to make its own oil. It also offers PDO oils from Kalamáta, Lakonía (Sparta brand), and Kolymvári and an extra virgin oil from Chalkidikí called Mount Athos. Likewise, **Kalaméa**'s oils come from Sparta, Lygourio, and Sitía.

Peloponnese

*The Peloponnese in southern Greece
accounts for about 40 percent of the total
Greek olive production and 36 percent
of Greek olive oil. It is a countryside of
stunning natural beauty where olive trees
are a dominant feature of the landscape.
There are a few PDO- and PGI-registered
olive areas but there is no detailed
mapping available. I have described the
provinces, known as prefectures, where
PDOs are based, on the following pages.*

THE OLIVES OF THE PELOPONNESE

MAIN OLIVE-PRODUCING AREAS

The largest concentration of olive trees
is in the southern provinces, or
prefectures, of the Peloponnese, namely
Lakonía and Messinía. The towns of
Kalamáta and Sparta are major
production centers for both oil and table
olives. *Koroneïki* is the ubiquitous cultivar.
There are pockets of interesting, older
olives, such as *Manaki* cultivars in the
province of Argolis and *Mastoidès* in the
Taygétos mountains.

OLYMPIA & PYRGOS

There is also a PGI based on the
Koroneïki olive in the area around
Olympia and Pyrgós in the
western side of the
Peloponnese. But oils from
this PGI, although good,
are not distinctive. This is a
particularly fertile area
where grain, citrus fruit,
and vines are a more
important crop than olives.

KALAMON CULTIVAR

THE ARGOLIS

Some of the olive
plantations in this region
of the eastern Peloponnese date back to
the 13th century, when much of this
part of Greece belonged either to the
Franks or to the Venetians. Indeed,
cultivation of the modern olive owes its
prominence to Greece's former
conquerors, who subsidized the planting
of olives throughout their Greek
colonies. When Venice's power declined

in the 18th century, the French came to
dominate the Ottoman oil trade. Most
of the olive oil went to the soap industry
in Marseilles.

The reputation of Argolid oil was
already well established by the 19th
century, when it was exported to the
Ukraine and Russia. Oil from the region
won first prize at the Paris World Fair in
1890. There are two PDOs in the
Argolis—Lygourgió Asklipíou in the
west and Kranídi Argolídas
in the east. Both of
these PDOs are based on
the local *Manaki* olive,
though the *Koroneïki* olive is
also permitted in Kranídi
PDO oils. The Lygourgió
Asklipíou area has about
450,000 olive trees on
some 9,400 acres
(3,800ha) of which about
one-tenth is organically
cultivated.

The *Manaki* olive gives a very smooth,
gentle oil, without the bitterness that is
sometimes found in other oils. The olives
are late to mature. Many are still green
in the middle of February. Some tasters
claim to detect a taste of apples in the
finished oil, but it would be truer to
describe this oil as gentle, almost sweet,
with a hint of grassiness and nuts.

OLIVES AND FLOWERS IN KALAMATA Daisies are allowed to grow beneath the trees.

Manaki oil appeals especially to those markets where mild flavors are most appreciated.

MESSINIA

Messinía has about 15 million olive trees, producing about 66,000 tonnes of olive oil annually. Most of the oil is made from *Koroneïki* olives, which came originally from Koróni on the western side of the Gulf of Messinía, and have now spread all over Greece. The oil for the Kalamáta PDO must be produced from *Koroneïki* and/or *Mastoidès* olives. The latter is the dominant olive in the foothills of the Taygetos mountains, northeast of Kalamáta.

This province is famous for its *Kalamón* table olives from Kalamáta, as well as its olive oil. *Kalamón* olive trees are easy to identify because they have long, broad, soft leaves. The olives yield an excellent oil, though it is seldom seen because they are so highly prized for the table. Kalamáta oil and the olives each have their own PDOs.

LAKONIA

This province occupies the southeastern Peloponnese, which is its most remote corner and perhaps also its most beautiful. Olive growing is a major industry throughout the prefecture. There is one very loosely defined PGI that incorporates all the different olive cultivars from which oil is made within this province. These are *Koroneïki*, *Koutsoreliá*, *Mastoidès* (here called *Áthinoliá*), and *Ásproliá* olives. *Áthinoliá/Mastoidès* is the dominant olive cultivar in Sparta. The olives grown on the upper Mani Peninsula are almost entirely *Koroneïki*.

Sparta also has an excellent new Museum of the Olive and Greek Olive Oil. The museum has not yet been completely finished. It is, however, already the best by far in Greece and well worth a visit. (129 Othonos-Amalias St., 23100 Sparta 🄲 27310 89315 🅆 www.piop.gr)

Leading producers in Olympia & Pýrgos

Merkoúri Estate

27100 Korakohóri
26210 41601
W www.greekwinemakers.com

The Merkoúri estate near Pýrgos is a rare Greek example of a famous wine producer also offering a premium olive oil made from its own trees—commonplace in Tuscany, but not yet in Greece. The oil comes from 22 acres (9ha) of 100-year-old *Koroneïki* trees on the 74-acre (30ha) estate. The organic Domaine Mercouri or Ktíma Merkoúri Extravirgin is an early-picked oil with a fresh, refreshing "green" taste of cut grass, beans, and tomatoes, followed by a good aftertaste.

Olýmpia-Xenía

14568 Kryonerí
21062 20065
W www.olympia-oliveoil.com

Olýmpia-Xenía is a company of national importance with offices in the north of Greece, but its production is locally based in the lovely limestone hills just north of Pýrgos, near Douneïka in the Ilía prefecture. Its products include extra virgin Xenía and premium Olýmpia PGI, both made principally from *Koroneïki* olives, pressed the day they are picked. Olýmpia PGI is very good, with lots of fruit and a pleasant herbaceous taste, followed by a hint of almonds. Both are found throughout Greece and exported worldwide—sound, dependable oils from a market leader who combines quantity with high quality.

Leading producers in Argolis

Dimarákis, Stylianós

21051 Ermióni – Argolídos
27540 31448
W www.hermes.gr

Evángelos Dimarákis is the leading producer in Kranídi, and his olives are all organically grown. His two labels are the "basic" Kálliston (2,200 tons per annum) and the organic Authentikón (77 tons per annum), which also has a PDO Kranídi designation. Authentikón is fresh and fruity, with a smooth, mild, almondy taste at first, before developing green, herbaceous hints and a warm aftertaste—a very good oil indeed.

AUTHENTIKÓN

Fakláris Bros

21200 Skafidáki
27510 47554
W www.argolis.com.gr

This producer sells *Koroneïki* extra virgin oil under the Fakláris and Árgolis labels. Their sales are oriented toward export. They make a superb Kaléma Lygourgió PDO oil, which is made from the *Manaki* olive of the Argolia peninsula and is widely available.

Mélas, Evángelos

7 El. Venizélou
21052 Lygourgió-Argolída
27530 22974
W www.melasoil.gr

Mélas makes oil from 9,800 acres (4,000ha) and 500,000 trees. Its four main labels are: PDO Lygourgió Asklipíou in both a standard and an organic form, a non-PDO organic oil called Mélas Product of Organic Farming and a "basic" oil called Ólon that comes from a wider area of the Peloponnese and has *Koroneïki* and *Mastoidès* (here called *Áthinoliá*) olives in its makeup as well as *Manaki* olives. The excellent PDO Lygourgió Asklipíou oils are fruity, with hints of pears, tropical fruits, and almonds, and a mild, warm, buttery aftertaste.

Leading producers in Messinía

Agro.Vi. M.

P.O. Box 134
24100 Kalamáta
27210 69269
W www.agrovim.gr

This successful company is behind the Iliada and Erato brands, well known both in Greece and abroad. It handles about one-fifth of the production in Messinía. Its top oils, both made from *Koroneïki* (and both excellent), are Iliada Kalamáta PDO (a smooth and easy oil with a hint of apples and almonds and a mild, gentle aftertaste—good with light-flavored foods) and Iliada Organic (smooth, fresh, and fruity). Agrovim is also one of the largest producers of Kalamáta table olives packed in extra virgin oil.

ILIADA KALAMÁTA

Argyrópoulos, G.B.

12 Idras St
24100 Kalamáta
☎ 27210 22307
🖥 www.finooliveoil.gr

Argyrópoulos are processors and packagers who sell extra virgin olive oil under the Fino and Eleatis labels. Fino is mainly for the home market and Eleatis for export. They are gently fruity, smooth, and cool to the taste, with a nutty aroma and a light aftertaste.

Avía & Mantínea, Coop.

24100 Kalamáta
☎ 27210-58410
🖥 www.kalamata-oliveoil.gr

This Kalamáta-based cooperative was founded in 1924 but now produces its Avia brand oil with a PDO Kalamáta. They also sell PDO Kalamáta olives.

Dragónas Bros

12 Kladá St
24100 Kalamáta
☎ 27210 23172
🖥 www.dragonas.gr

Respectable packers and exporters, founded in 1905, who sell their extra virgin oil under the Angel label.

Gargaliánoi, Ag. Coop.

15a El. Venizélou
24400 Gargaliánoi
☎ 22718 23191

The Agricultural Cooperative of Gargaliánoi was founded in 1940 and now has nearly 1,000 members, who are expected to abide by detailed management specifications for cultivating and harvesting olives. The leading brand is Pithári

PITHÁRI

and its labels carry a drawing of an old oil jar. It is 95% *Koroneïki* and very good —cool, clean, and fruity at first, with a fresh green taste, then a warm pepperiness and a hint of bitterness—the sort of oil that appeals to a wide market.

Kalamáta Foods Ltd.

P.O. Box 153
60100 Kateríni
☎ 23510 47000
🖥 www.konstolymp.gr

A subsidiary of the northern Greek firm Konstantópoulos, best known for its Olymp table olives, made from *Chalkidikí*, *Conserviolá*, and *Megarítiki*. Its olive oil is sourced from Messinía and sold abroad under the Koronis and Platon labels. Koronis also comes with an organic option, popular in Germany.

Messinía, Union of Ag. Coops.

10 Iatrópoulou
24100 Kalamáta
☎ 27210 29880
Fax: 27210 84693

This is one of the more successful cooperatives in Greece. Its top-of-the-range Danáe label is very good, with a deep green color, a full, fruity flavor (*Koroneïki* to the fore), a lively grassiness, and enough of an aftertaste to make it a big oil.

DANÁE

FRIEDRICH J. BLÄUEL

The Austrian Friedrich (Fritz) Bläuel set up in business as a promoter of organic olive oil products some 30 years ago. Today, this tall, athletic figure dominates the market with his prize-winning oils and olives. Bläuel, whose father owns one of the grandest hotels in Austria's Wienerwald, first visited the Mani as a young medical student in search of vacation sun. He was so taken by the lifestyle and opportunities there that he abandoned his studies and stayed on. Organic farming was unknown in Greece when he started his business; now he has five full-time employees who educate, encourage, and monitor the small farmers who work for him—some 300 growers with 200,000 trees of *Koroneïki*—and a total staff of around 40. Bläuel has a strong emotional and spiritual commitment to the organic movement. He is proud of his achievement, which does not rest on purely commercial success, but promotes good food and health, wholesome agriculture, respect for the environment, and

the protection of rural society. His oils are regular prize-winners all over the world. The nonorganic **Mani Olivenöl Bläuel** is more green than gold, with a fruity, herby smell and a delicious, rounded taste— gentle and fruity at first, later grassy and herby. His **Mani Olivenöl Bläuel Bio** is also excellent: cool, clean, and strong-flavored—apples, grass, and herbs —with a good balance of upfront fruit and later warmth, but always smooth and harmonious.

Pýrgos-Lefktrou, 24024 Messinía
☎ 27210 77711 🖥 www.blauel.gr

Plemménos Ltd.

22 Daváki St
15121 Pefki
☎ 21061 40434
🖰 www.oliveoil.gr/plemmenos/

This Athens-based producer sells oil from its own estates in Kalamáta under the labels Plemmémos and Chrysso.

MANIÁTISSA

Skarpalézos, G. Stavropígio

24016 Kámpos
☎ 27210 71280

This traditional producer has something of a following both locally and in Germany for its sweet, gentle, light oil sold under the Maniátissa label.

Leading producers in Lakonía

Krokeés, Ag. Coop.

23057 Krokees
☎ 2735071654

This is a small village cooperative that has its own PDO; its oil is made from *Mastoidès* and the local *Myrtoliá*. Its main brand is Órganon, which has a strong grassy smell and a gentle, soft, grassy taste at first, before developing a richer texture and a surging pepperiness that lingers for a very long time—excellent.

KROKEÉS

The cooperative sells a little to Canada and Sweden, but otherwise only locally, and in bulk to Minerva (the Greek one), which is a pity. It also offers an organic oil.

Lakonía, Union of Ag. Coops.

Leonídou 113
23100 Spárti
☎ 27310 26556
🖰 www.easlakonia.gr

Made mainly from *Koroneïki*, plus some of the milder *Mastoidès*. This secondary cooperative manages the PGI for Lakonía. Its main label is Dorikó, and it also offers an organic Dorikó Biologikó. As with many cooperatives, its oils are of variable quality but, at their best, fruity, herbaceous and buttery, with a light, bitter, peppery finish.

DORIKÓ BIOLOGIKÓ

Medolio

602 Vouliagménis Ave.
22100 Trípolis
☎ 27102 21450
🖰 www.medolio.com

Medolio are dealers ("we select olive oil very carefully from the best producing areas in the Southern Peloponnese") with a plant in Scála Lakonía from which it produces the acclaimed Mystrás label.

Méga

14 km Spárti – Gíthio
23054 Spárti
☎ 20731 35050

Part of the Karachnídis group, but the olive-oil business goes back nearly a century. Their labels include Karachnidi and Petra's Farm.

Mistra Estates Ladópoulos

21 Sarantapíchou St
11471 Athens
☎ 21036 15497
W www.mistraestates.gr

Unfiltered oil from unirrigated estates around Sparta, made mainly from *Mastoidès* and *Koutsorelia* olives and sold (much of it in the U.S.) under the Villa Serenissima, Phanouris, and The Duke labels, as well as Mistra Estates Ladopoulos.

Papadákos, Nikólaos

23100 Soustiánoi
☎ 27310 98253

Organic oil made from young *Mastoidès* and sold under the Líthos label. Soustiánoi is 2,000ft (600m) up in the Taygétos Mountains.

Petrina, Ag. Coop. of

23200 Petrína Lakonías
☎ 27330 92204
W www.peloponnissos.net

Founded in 1907, this cooperative has its own PDO of Petrína Lakonías oil and produces 66-79,000gal (250-300,000 liters) per year. Much is taken up by its members, but some is exported in cans to the U.S. and sold under the Petrina label. It is 100% *Koroneïki*.

Spárta Kefalás

23100 Kefalás
☎ 27310 77181
W www.therapni.com

A cooperative of organic growers in and around the village of Kefalás. They have about 600ha (1,500 acres) between them,

CARPET OF COLOR
Greek olive groves are seldom plowed, so are usually full of wildflowers.

and 100,000 trees, and they also sell organic Kalamáta olives. Their Therápni oil is commonly seen in organic and healthfood stores in Greece. The oil is cool and smooth, with a light herbaceous taste, developing a warm and buttery aftertaste.

THERÁPNI

Crete

Olives and olive oil were the foundation of the Cretan economy. The Minoan villa in Vathypétro, near Archánes, in the province of Heraklion, dates back to about 1500 B.C.E. and includes a stone oil press. Some experts maintain that a press in Phaistós is even older. Even today, two-thirds of the island's cultivable land is put to olives and there are around 40 million olive trees. Crete produces an average of 165,000 tons of olive oil a year.

ROCKY OLIVE ORCHARDS Most of the older olive trees in Crete are ancient cultivars like these *Chrondroliá* near Rethýmnon.

THE OLIVE OIL REGIONS OF CRETE

CONSISTENTLY HIGH-QUALITY OIL

Olive farming in Crete is based mainly on small plantations. It is estimated that some 95,000 families own fewer than 200 trees each. Cretan farmers are committed to quality. Strict disciplines ensure that the olives are healthy, picked at the optimum moment, and delivered to the processors at the end of each day's harvesting. In a good year, as much as 95 percent of Cretan oil can be classified as extra virgin. The leading producers are consistent prize-winners at international contests, notably the Union of Agricultural Cooperatives at Sitía, Botzákis, and the Pezá Union in Heraklion, and the Kolymvári Cooperative in the province, or prefecture, of Chanía.

The quality of Cretan oils depends not (as the islanders believe) on the dry climate and long hours of sunshine, but the intrinsic excellence of *Koroneïki* olives used. *Koroneïki* oil from the mountains is said to be the fruitiest and to have the best flavor. That said, the reliance on this particular olive creates a sameness among many Cretan oils. And *Koroneïki* has its weaknesses, too. It may be nicely fruity and neatly balanced, but it is also lacking in real flavor. It cannot match Catalonia's *Arbequina* or Sicily's *Nocellara del Belice* for taste —or for their intensity of fruitiness.

An average of 165,000 tons of olive oil are produced every year, and this figure is rising as irrigation is introduced. Some 40 percent of all plantations are now irrigated, which also helps to even out the yields, so that there is less of a difference between a year of plenty and a year of light cropping. Most Cretan oil is exported to the rest of Greece or, more significantly, to Italian blenders. Cretans say that their oil is used to improve dull Italian oils.

CHANÍA

This is the most western of Crete's four provinces and the city of Chanía was, until recently, the capital of the whole island. The Mediterranean Agronomic Institute at Chanía houses the Institute of the Olive Tree, which is the leading center for education and research into olive growing in Greece.

There is a PGI for the olive oil from the whole of Chanía prefecture, run by the Union of Cooperatives of Chanía, and two PDOs. The Apokóronas

Haníon Krítis PDO was registered by the Union of Agricultural Cooperatives of the Apokóronas area. The Kolymvári Haníon Kriti PDO is centered on the Union of Agricultural Cooperatives of Kolymvári in the northwest of Chanía prefecture and extends to the whole of the district of Kolymvári. Both are based on *Koroneïki* and, to tell the truth, most of their oils taste somewhat similar, though some are better than others.

HERAKLION

The rolling hills of Heraklion province are perfect for olive growing. Unlike the prefectures of Chanía, Rethýmnon, and Lasíthi, Heraklion has no mountains. Many would say that Crete's best oil is made here in the Messará plain. Heraklion has no fewer than four PDOs: Viánnos Iráklio Krítis PDO, based on the *Áno Viánnos* olive in the south, is fairly dormant; Thrapsanó PDO is very small and based on *Koroneïki* olives. Archánes Iráklio Krítis PDO is

better known for its wine, but the PDO for Pezá Iráklio Krítis is of major importance. *Koroneïki* is the ubiquitous olive cultivar in all of them.

RETHYMNON

This province has a PDO for the oil of Vórios Mylopótamos Rethýmnis Krítis, which must contain at least 90% *Koroneïki* olives with up to 10% of *Chondroliá* olives. Its villages are all in the northern part of the Mylopótamos area of the prefecture. Chondroliá is a local synonym for the *Throúmba* table olive, which has its own PDO called Throúmba-Ambadiás Rethýmnis Krítis.

LASITHI

This is the most remote of Crete's four provinces. It is also the driest, which makes the modern success of its agricultural industry all the more remarkable. Olives are grown throughout, but flourish especially in the lowlands around Sitía; on the

TREES AT TOPLOU, LASITHI Violent Theltémi winds have swept through and bent these olive trees.

WHITE-PAINTED OLIVE TRUNKS, CHANIA White paint improves the visibility of these trees for drivers.

windswept moorland around Moní Toploú in the extreme east, the olive trees are bent sideways by the fierce *meltémi* wind, a cold mistral that blows in from the north. Olives cover three-quarters of the cultivated land around Sitía. There are 27,200 acres (11,000ha), of which about two-thirds are irrigated, and 2.5 million trees. The olives are all *Koroneïki*, which means that the well made oils all taste fairly similar. One hundred years ago, all the olives in eastern Crete were *Tsounáti*.

The Sitía-Lasíthi PDO is a fiefdom of the Union of Agricultural Cooperatives of Sitía and covers about 35 villages in northeastern Lasíthi. Success and recognition in international competitions has enabled the Union to grow stronger and avoid the tendency toward fragmentation, which comes so naturally to Greeks.

THE CRETAN DIET

Professor Ancel Keys's fieldwork in connection with the Mediterranean diet was begun in the 1950s at a time when Crete was a traditional society with limited economic opportunities. It showed that, of all European peoples, Cretans had the most balanced and healthy diet.

Today, Cretans consume almost 60lb (27 kg) of olive oil per person per year, almost double that of their fellow Greeks, who consume 35lb (16 kg) per person per year (the highest figure of any country in the world). Modern Cretans cannot expect the same benefits as their ancestors; they are as addicted to unhealthy foodstuffs as the rest of us. But the experiments have been done, and the data is incontrovertible. Olive oil is an essential part of a diet that protects against illness and delivers longevity. Cretans call it "The Cretan Diet" (*see p.47*).

Island of ancient trees

There are two trees on Crete claimed to be the oldest in Greece. One is in Kolymvári, near Chanía, and the other is in Kavoúrsio in Lasíthi. During the 2004 Olympic Games in Athens, it was agreed that the winners of the Marathon would be crowned with wreaths of olives from the oldest tree. No one could agree which was the oldest, so leaves from the Kolymvári tree were used to crown the winner of the men's race and those from the Kavoúrsio tree the winner of the women's.

GREEK SHRINE ▶
Wayside shrines are a feature of the Greek countryside. This one in Rethýmnon stands at the foot of a slope planted with old olive trees.

Leading producers in Chanía

Agía Triáda, Moni

Akrotíri
Chanía
☎ 28210 63310

This monastery produces some of Crete's best organic oil from its *Koroneïki* trees in the sunny, limestone hills of the Akrotíri peninsula. Its label is AgíaTriáda and its oil has a gentle, rich, herby taste with a hint of artichokes and grass, followed by a long, warm finish.

AGÍA TRIÁDA

Apokóronas & Sfakiá, Union of Ag. Coops

73008 Vámos
☎ 28250 41480
🌐 www.easap.gr

The cooperative's "ordinary" oils are called Lióstoma and Anthós. The PDO label Apokóronas is best; it also comes with an organic option. All are based on *Koroneïki*.

Chanía, Union of Coops.

17 Gerásimou Pardáli
73131 Chanía
☎ 28210 96071
🌐 www.abea.gr

ABEA is the basic label of this important secondary cooperative. Others include Kreta Premium (their top line) and Anatolí. Like most Cretan cooperatives, it also sells a non-extra virgin oil, a pomace, a refined oil, table olives, and soap.

Cretan Taste Co.

VIOPA Soúda
Chanía
☎ 28210 80234
🌐 www.cretantaste.gr

This company operates in the markets for organic and quality products. It sources a soft, smooth "basic" extra virgin oil from northwestern Crete called Cretan Taste, a PDO oil under their Kolymvári label and a PDO Kolymvári Organic oil. It also sells organic olives, both *Koroneïki* and *Tsounáti*.

Daskalákis, Ktíma

Kontomari
Chanía
☎ 28210 62375

Yiánnis Daskalákis sells his organic farm oil under the label Elaionas Daskalaki. It is fresh and grassy, with an opulent texture and a warm pepperiness that lasts well.

ELAIONAS DASKALAKI

Dimitriádis & Co., G. Astrikas

73006 Kolymvári
Chanía
☎ 28210 40575
🌐 www.biolea.gr

The Astrikas estate is planted with 2,000 *Koroneïki* trees, unirrigated and certified organic. Biolea is the main label, of variable quality. The owners call it "delicately fruity with a sweet, rich, nutty flavor."

Kolympari (I. Mihelakis)

73006 Rapanianá Kissámou
☎ 28240 91691
🌐 www.kolympari-sa.gr

The Michelákis family buys in olives and presses them at their own mills. They produce a Mihelákis Family Kolympari PDO oil from Kolymvári. Other labels include Mihelákis and the light, pleasant, 100% *Koroneïki* Liohimo.

Kolymvári, Union of Ag. Coops.

73006 Chanía
☎ 28240 22448
🌐 www.kriti.net/kolymvari

This secondary cooperative (29 village cooperatives and 4,000 members) produces 7,700 tons of oil a year, about one-twentieth of Crete's total. Its "basic" label is Kolymvári, but it also offers a PDO Kolymvári and a premium oil called Athena.

KOLYMVÁRI CRETAN TASTE

OLIVES ON CRETE

At least 85% of the olive trees on Crete are *Koroneïki*, also known locally as *Ladoliá* or *Psiloliá*. One hundred years ago, *Koroneïki* was confined to Apokóronas in Chanía and a few villages in western Rethýmnon. The traditional cultivars are now planted as pollinators or have only a local following—*Mastoidès* (here called *Tsounáti*) in Chanía, where some of the trees are more than 1,000 years old, and *Throúmbi*, known as *Throumboliá* in Rethýmnon and *Chondroliá* in Heraklion. There is an important olive research institute in Chanía, and two small museums—one in Kapsaliana Arkadí and the other within the Psaltákis Folk Museum in Heraklion.

Koumadorákis

73001 Sarakíía
Paleochóra
☎ 28230 31250
🖥 www.olivenoel.gr

The Koumadorákis family own about 2,000 *Tsounáti* trees in the southwest of Crete. Some of the trees are more than 1,000 years old. They grow very tall and are difficult to harvest, so the olives are not collected until they are ripe, any time between December and May. The family has Austrian connections, and all its oil is bottled and sold in German-speaking markets as Koumadorakis Kreta Natives Olivenoel Extra. It has a taste of fresh olives, before developing a soft, gentle smoothness with a hint of almonds and a light, well balanced aftertaste. This is olive oil as it was in the time of the Venetians.

Kouridákis

Voukoliés
73002 Chanía
☎ 28240 31326

Kouridákis are growers and dealers in the Kissámos area. Cool, smooth, rich, almondy Fedra is their top label, but they also offer Zoeforon (PDO Kolymvári), Kalliston (PGI Chanía), and the organic Cretan Emerald.

Roubedákis Bros

Chanía
☎ 28250 71300

Cool, soft, green-tasting oil from the Apokóronas area, sold under the Roubes label.

ROUBES

Psillákis Estate

Zymbrágos
73006 Kolymvári
☎ 28240 41301
🖥 www.psillakisestate.gr

Good, grassy, organic oil sold with a Kolymvári PDO under the Biojoy label—smooth, cool, and accessible, with a green fruitiness and a light, warm aftertaste.

KORONEIKI

Terra Creta

VIOPA 1603
73200 Chanía
☎ 28210 23512
🖥 www.terracreta.gr

This is one of the best producers in Chanía: Terra Creta is also its brand name. Its labels include Koroneïki and The Tradition of Crete. Both are among the best—robust and fruity with a long, warm afteraste.

Leading producers in Heraklion

Botzákis

Alágni
Iráklion
☎ 2810 743132
🖥 www.creta-oil.gr

Botzákis are major growers, producers, and suppliers—and very dependable. Their pan-Cretan labels (all extra virgin, and all very good) are Cretan Prince and Ousia, which also comes with an organic option. Botzákis also sells excellent PDO oils from Pezá Iráklion (individually numbered bottles), Kolymvári (sold in Germany, also in numbered bottles), and Sitía.

Iráklion, Union of Ag. Coops. of

62 Martíron Ave.
71110 Iráklion
☎ 28102 54502
🖥 www.agrunion.gr

This big secondary cooperative has 166 member cooperatives. Its oil is sold in cans and bottles under the Knossos label throughout Greece and abroad.

Messará, Union of Ag. Coops. of

70400 Moíres
☎ 28920 27619

This secondary cooperative was founded in 1928 and now represents 44 primary cooperatives and 5,500 farmer-members. Its main label is Primolo.

Pezá, Union of Ag. Coops. of

Kalloní
71110 Iráklion
☎ 28107 41945
🖥 www.pezaunion.gr

Pezá is perhaps the most successful producer in Crete. Its oils are widely available at home and abroad. It handles some 80 percent of the area's olive oil production. Its "basic" extra virgin labels are Elaia and Union, but look for the organic Elixir (maximum acidity 0.5%) and the PDO Pezá Iráklio Krítis oil. Pezá has won more international prizes for its oils than any other Cretan producer except the cooperative in Sitía. It is one of the few Cretan producers whose factory may be visited by tourists.

Leading producers in Rethýmnon

Brahmino

Pérama, Mylopótamos
Rethýmnon
☎ 28340 23180

Brahmino make Agía Fotiní from locally sourced olives. Agía Fotiní is a village south of Arkadi. The oil is fruity when young, but acquires a nutty taste as it ages— smooth, well balanced, and lightly peppery.

Latzimás (Giórgios Kotzampasákis)

Pánormas, Rethýmnon
☎ 28340 51466
🖳 www.latzimasoil.gr

This organic oil comes from around the village of Latzimás. The best label carries a PDO from Vórios Mylopótamos Rethýmnis Krítis—cool, smooth, aromatic *Koroneíki* oil, with a mild, herby taste and a gentle aftertaste of almonds and pears.

Natural Hellenic Foods

Pérama, Mylopótamos
Rethýmnon
☎ 28340 23563

Mistato oil, made from *Koroneíki*, has a fresh, fruity taste of green olives when young, later more almondy.

Rethýmnon, Union of Ag. Coops.

Tría Monastíria
74100 Rethýmnon
☎ 28310 86101
🖳 www.easreth.gr

This is the big secondary cooperative in Rethýmnon, representing more than 100 cooperatives with some 9,000 members. Its main label is Rithi, but it also offers an organic option and a Vórios Mylopótamos Rethýmnis Krítis PDO version under the Rithigold label.

Leading producers in Lasíthi

Biokalliergetes Siteias

I. Moní Toploú
72300 Sitía
☎ 28430 023249

This producer makes organic oil under the Moní Toploú label. Its taste is cool, gentle, and soft at first, until a gentle grassiness asserts itself and a light, bitter aftertaste comes through. Good, and deservedly popular, especially in Germany.

TOPLOU

Casa dei Mezzo

72055 Makrígialos
Sitía
☎ 28430 29183
🖳 www.casadeimezzo.gr

Boutique *Koroneíki* oil from a small estate in the southeastern corner of the prefecture in the process of going organic. Its label is Casa dei Mezzo and the oil has the typically elegant taste of Sitía. It is cool and fruity at first, then somewhat more grassy, until a warm, peppery aftertaste develops and lasts for a long time.

Lyrákis

Síssi
Lasíthi
☎ 28410 89870

Lyrákis oil is one of Crete's best. It is smooth, cool, and lightly fruity, with a hint of pears and almonds, and a light, peppery aftertaste.

Merambélo, Union of Ag. Coops.

Theotokópoulou 2
Neápoli
Lasíthi
☎ 28410 32216

This producer's top label is eleon lama (lively and fruity—delicious), with less than 0.3% acidity, but their "ordinary" extra virgin chrysalis is also good.

Sitía, Union of Ag. Coops.

74 Misónos St.
22300 Sitía
☎ 28430 22211
🖳 www.sitiacoop.gr

Sitía's secondary cooperative is Crete's most consistent prize-winner at international exhibitions. It represents 30 primary cooperatives and some 9,000 farmer-members. Its main labels include Sitía 0.3 (excellent— cool, fresh, and grassy, with hints of apples and pears and a good, warm aftertaste—elegant and well balanced), Sitía 0.7 (good, but Sitía 0.3 is better). The figures 0.3 and 0.7 are percentages that refer to the maximum acidity level of the oils. Another important label is Bio Sitía Organic (soft, cool, gently fruity, and good). All these oils are very good value.

SITIA 0.3

The Rest of Greece

Olives are grown throughout northern and central Greece, except in the high mountains. There are also extensive olive plantations in the Aegean Islands, particularly on Lesbos, which has a long tradition of olive growing, and also on the Ionian Islands of Corfu, Cephallonia, and Zante. It is here that local olive cultivars are most resistant to the omnipotent Koroneïki.

EXTRA VIRGIN

The Greeks are proud of the claim that a higher proportion of their olive oil is classified as extra virgin than reaches the required standard in Spain and Italy. However, the classification "extra virgin" is only a measure of the acidity of the oil, not a guarantee of superior taste. The highest standards are found in Crete and the Peloponnese. Quality is more variable in northern mainland Greece and the islands of the Ionian and Aegean seas.

VALANOLIA CULTIVAR

CENTRAL & NORTHERN GREECE

The classical sites in Delphi and the Frankish castle in Ámfissa, both in Central Greece, are famous for the vast seas of olives that surround them. In some rural parts, however, many olive groves have reverted to *maquis*, their branches crowded out by seedling evergreen oaks. The coastal areas of Fthiótida and Vólos are famous for their table olives—as is the Chalkidikí peninsula. Thássos has its own PGI, for oil made from the *Throúmbi* olive (known locally as *Thassíki*), which has a separate PDO as a table olive.

THE AEGEAN ISLANDS

The island most completely given to olive growing is Mytiléne—better known outside Greece as Lesbos. It has 11 million olive trees, covering about four-fifths of the cultivable land. This amounts to 126 trees for every inhabitant of the island—more than anywhere else in the world, they say. The people of Lesbos claim that an ancient oil press found at Thermí dates back to 2800–2000 B.C.E. However, the great frost of January 1850 destroyed all the island's olive trees and the inhabitants decided to replant with hardier cultivars from elsewhere. Now the island's olives are 65% *Valanoliá* (here called *Koloví*) and 30% *Ádramytianí* and have their own Lésbos PGI. Lesbos oil is yellow and fluid—and much prized for its soft, smooth, ripe taste.

Olive oil is made on Naxos, Chios, Samos, and Ikaria—Samos has its own PGI based on *Throúmbi* (90%) and

OLIVE TREES IN PARAMOS
Carpets of bright flowers provide fodder for sheep. Olive oil and sheep's cheese—*feta*—come together in Greece.

ABANDONED COAST & OLIVES, MITIKAS Rural depopulation is a big social problem in Greece, but has preserved much of its stunning coastline from exploitation and overdevelopment.

Koroneïki (10%) but the industry is underdeveloped, and the oil is not bottled for sale elsewhere. There is less olive growing in the Dodecanese, but the archipelago has its own Ródos PGI, also based on *Koroneïki* and *Throúmbi*.

THE IONIAN ISLANDS
The Venetians encouraged the cultivation of olives in the Ionian islands. Venice dominated the Adriatic, supplied much of northern Italy with olive oil, and controlled the trade with northern Europe. There are beautiful ancient olive trees throughout the Ionian islands. Corfu's groves in Epikepsí, Nýmfes, and the Rópas valley are particularly fine. High rainfall guarantees good regular cropping for the endemic *Lianoliá Kerkýras* olives. This handsome cultivar is also known as *Prévezas* or *Kérkyras* because in some parts of Greece *Lianoliá* is a synonym for *Koroneïki*. There are PGIs in Kefallonia and Zakynthos.

Leading producers in Central & Northern Greece

Dimítris Próedrou

Limenária, Thássos
☎ 25930 52235

There is a tradition of organic cultivation on Thassos. These producers make a leading organic oil called Bio-Agros from unirrigated *Throúmbi*. It is popular in Germany.

Kavála, Union of Ag. Coops.

18 Ýdras Street
65302 Kavála
☎ 25180 36536
W www.users.otenet.gr/~egs-kav/prodo2.htm

This is the leading secondary cooperative in northern Greece, founded in 1927 and representing some 47 primary producers in Thássos, Kavála, and Néstos. Most of the olive oil comes from Thássos, and it is sold under the Thasos label. It has a light, mild taste. Quality is variable (olive fly can be a problem for farmers), and the oil is better (and cleaner) in some years than others.

THASOS

Préveza, Union of Ag. Coops.

Leofóros Irínis 13
48100 Préveza
☎ 26820 22227

The secondary cooperative in Préveza represents some 70 primary cooperatives with nearly 8,000 members throughout western Greece. Olive oil is only a small part of its business, but sold under the Kioúpi and Athína labels. Préveza has a PGI based on the local *Lianoliá Kerkýras* olive.

Statér

45 Michalakópoulou
11528 Athens
☎ 21072 58394
🖥 www.greekartisans.com

Státer's Greek Artisans brand offers an early-harvest *Agourélaio* oil (gentle and grassy, with a hint of walnuts and almonds), an organic Biologikó oil, which is a blend of *Koroneïki* olives from the Mani and *Koutsourelia* olives from Trichónidas in Aetoloakarnanía, and *Vottikí* from Olýnthos in Chalkidikí.

CARDIÓFILO

VI.EL.THA.

Prínos
Thássos
☎ 25930 71950
🖥 www.vieltha.com

Vieltha's owners—a family firm—include four doctors. Their main oil is Chrysólado, but they also offer a popular organic oil called Cardiófilo, the name chosen to emphasize that olive oil is beneficial to the cardiovascular system. Both oils are made from *Throúmbi* olives and have a good fruity taste followed by a pleasant pepperiness and bitterness.

Leading producers in the Aegean Islands

Catsacoulis

81100 Mytiléne
☎ 22510 47007
🖥 www.oliveoil.gr/members/ catsacoulis

Catsacoulis was founded in 1863 and claims to be the oldest olive oil company in Greece. Its Irína oil is made principally from *Koloví* olives —soft, fruity, and gentle.

Elpa

43 Kountouriótou St
81100 Mytiléne
☎ 22510 28493

A leading producer of olive oil in Lesbos, under the Mytilána label.

Lesel (Union of Ag. Coops. of Lesbos)

21 Alkéou St
81100 Mytiléne
☎ 22510 29224
🖥 www.lesel.gr

Lesel is the big secondary cooperative in Lesbos— well organized and a constant winner of prizes for its soft, rich, delicious oil. Its leading labels are the PGI oil Mytilinió and Theófilos. Both have a smooth texture, a gentle taste of dried fruits and butter, and a very mild, warm aftertaste.

LESEL THEÓFILOS

Soroní, Ag. Coop.

Kameíro
85106 Paradeísi
Ródos
☎ 22410 41061

This cooperative is the leading producer in Rhodes. Its *Koroneïki* oil is sold under the label Roditíko—light, fruity, and nicely balanced. Most is consumed locally or sold to satisfy the demand of tourists from northern Europe for gastronomic souvenirs of the island.

Leading producers in the Ionian Islands

Ionian Enterprises

Paleokastrístas
49100 Kérkyra
☎ 20661 36057
🖥 www.alfa.gr/ionian

Ionian Enterprises is one of the few producers in Corfu to bottle its oil, which is sold as Staliá or Dióni.

Zakínthos, Union of Ag. Coops

42 Lomvárdou
29100 Zakínthos
☎ 26950 27611

Zante's oil is available abroad under such names as Gold of Zante (in Switzerland and Germany) and Levante (in the UK). The oil is based on *Koroneïki* olives, with the addition of some older Venetian cultivars. Here, and throughout the Ionian islands there is a need to conserve the rich heritage of unusual ancient olive types.

OTHER OLIVE-GROWING COUNTRIES

UNITED STATES OF AMERICA

The industry that produces olive oil in the United States is very small, accounting for less than 0.1 percent of world production. However, the U.S. is the largest consumer of olive oil outside Europe and the biggest importer too. Nearly all the olive trees in the U.S. grow in California.

FAST-EXPANDING INDUSTRY

Ever since Italian exporters began to introduce North America to "light" olive oil (usually a mixture of refined and extra virgin oils) in the 1980s, Italian producers have dominated the market. Bertolli, Filippo Berio, Monini, and Carapelli are leading brands. Consumption has grown quickly and although the North American taste is still mainly for these none-too-tasty imports, a minority taste for real extra virgin oils has also evolved.

In California, the olive business is taken very seriously. The state produces more than one-tenth of the world's table olives, although that share is shrinking in the face of Spanish competition. In Sonoma and Napa in particular, the olive oil industry is busy, experimental, and expanding fast.

OLIVES BROUGHT BY SETTLERS

California was first settled by Europeans starting in 1769, when Spanish Franciscans made their way up from Baja California and established a series of missions there. They brought the first olive trees with them, primarily to supply oil for sacramental use but also for soap, food, and lighting. These olive trees (a few still survive at such missions as San Jose) were descendants of those brought from southern Spain to central America in the 16th century. The most common cultivars are *Manzanillo*, *Sevillana*, and *Cornicabra*; the latter came to be known here as the *Mission* olive.

Starting in 1900, olives were widely planted in the newly drained Central Valley to produce table olives—now a great American tradition.

In the 1930s, some Italian immigrants started to make oil, largely for their personal use, from old trees of *Sevillano* and *Manzanillo*. In 1936, Sciabica became the first company to sell its oil and it is still trading. Starting in about 1990, olive oil came to be seen as a high-quality product, a symbol of

WELL MANAGED ESTATES Olive trees are well tended and checked regularly by the growers.
◀ **OLIVES AND VINES** In the United States, as well as Europe, olives and vines are planted side by side.

Mediterranean civilization, and a desirable status symbol. Its health benefits too were widely praised. Wineries in Napa and Sonoma began to plant a few olives as an adjunct to their main business. The first grower to import Italian olives was Ridgely Evers of Healdsburg in 1990. He was followed by Nan McEvoy and Roberto Zecca, owner of Frantoio Olives. Lila Jaeger of Rutherford Hill opened a cooperative olive press in Glen Ellen in 1996. Olive growers now proliferate. Some are enthusiasts who want to live in the country and have an interesting lifestyle. Some are farmers seeking to diversify. Others are serious investors hoping for a good return. Many are amateurs and almost all operate on a small scale.

TYPES OF OIL

Three main types of oil are made and sold in California. The most popular are the Tuscan copycats made from *Frantoio* and *Leccino* olives, though it may be argued that these cool-climate olives will never give a proper Tuscan-style oil in the hotter climate of northern California. Second, there are the *provençal*-type oils, for those Americans who do not like the strong, bitter, peppery, Tuscan style. These are made from gentle French olives like *Picholine* and *Bouteillan*. Some

are excellent. Finally, there are the mild, smooth, late-picked oils made from traditional Spanish table olives like *Mission* and *Sevillano*. This is the most authentic American taste, and some producers are achieving oils of remarkable complexity and deliciousness. Others have had good results picking these olives young to make full-bodied, pungent oils.

Californian table olives

The California Black Ripe Table Olive is an all-American specialty. There are about 1,000 growers and 35,000 acres (14,000ha) dedicated to California black olives. Two-thirds of the crop is *Manzanillo*, followed by *Sevillano*, *Ascolano*, and *Mission*. The olives are picked green and soaked in aerated lye to eliminate their bitterness, which also turns them black. They are then washed and color-stabilized with ferrous gluconate. The main producers are Musco of Tracy (**Black Pearls** brand) and Bell-Carter in Corning (**Lindsay** brand), but they are both operating in a difficult and declining market.

MANZANILLO CULTIVAR

YOUNG OLIVE TREES, LIVERMORE There are many young plantations in northern California.

Because the making of oil is such a recent phenomenon in the U.S., technical expertise is still in short supply. The quality of olive oils is uneven. It is not unusual for them to be spoiled by fermentation or mold. Problems are now exacerbated by the appearance of olive fly. When choosing California oils, it is essential to taste them before buying, and fortunately most estates allow you to do so. If buying from a store, you need to know which olives were used and when the oil was made (its year and season of picking). Be wary of producers unwilling to tell you.

The paradox is that Californian producers are charging expensive prices for oils that are seldom as high in quality as the leading European products, especially the top Tuscan oils many seek to emulate. If they could improve the quality and lower the price, they might compete better, and in quantity, with imported extra virgin oils. The Spanish-owned California Olive Ranch has planted 600 acres (240ha) of new-style *Arbequina* olives in Corning. The small growers are worried, but the future lies with this sort of operation.

Olive growing in the USA

Olive growing in California is concentrated in the northern part of the state. When you choose a Californian olive oil, look for the California Olive Oil Council (COOC) seal of quality, which is backed by chemical analysis and the approval of a tasting panel.

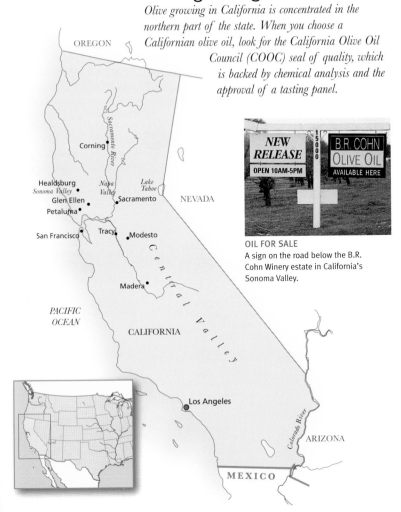

OIL FOR SALE
A sign on the road below the B.R. Cohn Winery estate in California's Sonoma Valley.

Leading producers in California

Apollo Olive Oil

P.O. Box 1054, Oregon House, CA 95962

☎ 530 692 2314

W www.apollooliveoil.com

Apollo's owners are experimenters and they grow nearly 40 different olive cultivars from the northern Mediterranean. They are also committed to organic production and to using a traditional press with woven mats. Their oils come in beautiful, enameled bottles. Fruity Sierra comes from the California tradition—made from *Mission*, with a little *Picholine*, and *Ascolano* to soften it and add complexity. Mistral is more *provençal*: mild and gentle with a buttery taste—rich and light—and made from *Salonenque*, *Picholine*, and *Aglandau*. Both are good.

APOLLO

B.R. Cohn Winery

15000 Sonoma Hwy, Glen Ellen, CA 95442

☎ 707 938 4064

W www.brcohn.com

Cohn's best oil comes from a small grove, thought to be *Picholine*, planted in the 1870s on its Olive Hill Estate in the Sonoma Valley, and sold in exquisite enamelled bottles. B.R. Cohn Estate Picholine is cool, smooth, mellow, almost buttery, with a light, rich texture and a mildly herbaceous taste, followed by nuts. It is delicious, but very expensive—by far the most expensive oil in this book. Cohn's other two oils

—both good—are blended from bought-in, local oils. One is an organic mixture of *Mission* and *Manzanillo* and the other is a California blend of *Arbequina*, *Mission*, and *Manzanillo*.

Bariani Olive Oil

1330 Waller St., San Francisco, CA 94117

☎ 415 864 1917

W www.barianioliveoil.com

The Bariani family have a holding near Sacramento, with 5,000 *Mission* and 12,000 *Manzanillo* trees planted in about 1950. They make their unfiltered oil traditionally, with *fiscoli*. It is remarkably fresh and fruity, with an Italian taste of chicory and grass, lots of body, and a big aftertaste. Good value.

BARIANI

California Olive Ranch

2675 Lone Tree Road, Oroville CA 95965

☎ 530 846 8000

W www.californiaoliveranch.com

This is the future of Californian olive growing: 700 acres (280ha) and 300,000 high-density trees planted since 1999—selected dwarf-growing clones of *Arbequina* and *Arbosana* from Catalonia. Cultivation and harvesting are highly mechanized and the olives are sent immediately to the on-site mill. Freshness and fruitiness are hallmarks of the oils and an acidity as low as 0.01%. California Olive Ranch is by far the largest U.S. producer and is now winning international prizes. It offers three oils: fruity Arbequina, powerful Arbosana, and delicious Estate Reserve Blend. All are excellent.

DaVero Sonoma Inc.

1195 Westside Rd., Healdsburg, CA 95448

☎ 888 431 8008

W www.davero.com

Unfiltered, peppery, Tuscan-style oil from Tuscan olives—50% *Leccino*, 25% *Frantoio*, 15% *Maurino*, and 10% *Pendolino*—but perhaps a little more delicate than real Tuscans.

Frantoio Ristorante & Olive Oil Co.

152 Shoreline Hwy, Mill Valley, CA 94941

☎ 415 289 5777

W www.frantoio.com

Zedez is the trademark of these traditionally made oils. The two main labels are: Frantoio Zedez Estate Blend Green Label California Unfiltered (80% *Arbequina*—fresh, fruity, clean, and delicious) and Frantoio Zedez Estate Proprietor Select Red Label (80% Tuscan olives—lightly fruity with a measure of pepperiness and bitterness).

Jordan Vineyard & Winery

1474 Alexander Valley Rd., Healdsburg, CA 95448

☎ 800 654 1213

W www.jordanwinery.com

Tuscan-style oil from 24-acre (10ha) of *Frantoio*, *Pendolino*, *Leccino*, and *Cipressino* planted in 1995. Jordan Estate is lightly fruity, grassy, and almondy, with a good balance of pepperiness and bitterness—powerful when young, but keeping well.

Lila Jaeger

4325 Big Ranch Road, Napa, CA 94558

☎ 707 255 4937

Lila Jaeger sought to produce "an elegant Napa Valley olive oil in the European tradition." Her Napa Valley oil is Tuscan-style, with a grassy, vegetable taste and a lively mixture of pepperiness and bitter almonds to follow; one of California's best.

Lunigiana Estate

8189 Sonoma Mountain Rd., Glen Ellen, CA 95442

C 707 939 8190

Lunigiana makes organic Tuscan-style oil from Italian cultivars—*Frantoio, Leccino, Maurino*, and *Pendolino*—and sells it in long, slender bottles, stylishly packaged. Lunigiana Estate Certified Organic oil is cool, grassy, and fruity at first, until the pepperiness and bitterness cut in and offer a long, warm aftertaste. Good.

McEvoy of Marin

P.O. Box 341, Petaluma, CA 94953

C 707 778 2307

W www.mcevoyranch.com

Nan McEvoy's ranch in Marin County has 80 acres (32h) of *Frantoio, Leccino, Pendolino, Maurino, Coratina*, and *Leccio di Corno*—a total of 18,000 trees, which is big for the U.S.

MCEVOY RANCH OLIO NUOVO

The estate is certified organic and the oil left unfiltered. McEvoy Ranch Olio Nuovo is a light Tuscan-style oil, with a cool taste of grass and a hint of almonds, followed by a warm, peppery aftertaste. It is sold in somewhat squat, square, clear-glass bottles with a cork.

Oliodessa

P.O. Box 5329, Napa, CA 94581

C 707 252 9038

W www.oliodessa.com

Oliodessa is based on late-picked *Mission* olives, with a touch of *Arbosana, Arbequina*, or *Koroneiki. Mission* predominates. The oil

OLIODESSA

is cool and smooth until a warm pepperiness kicks in, and has only a light flavor, a hint of fruitiness, and almonds.

Olive Press, The

14301 Glen Ellen, CA 95442

C 800 965 4839

W www.theolivepress.com

One of the better producers in Glen Ellen. The Olive Press has three main labels, all unfiltered. California Mission is rich and full bodied. Glen Ellen Blend is mainly *Ascolano*, which gives it a fruity, peppery taste. Sevillano is cool and smooth, with a taste of fresh olives and grassiness, followed by a persistent crescendo of warm pepperiness, reminiscent of watercress.

Poplar Hill

3250 Spring Mountain Road, St. Helena, CA 94574

C 800 676 7170

Poplar Hill is planted with *Lucca* olives, a clone of *Frantoio* selected for late picking. Poplar Hill oil is soft, smooth, rich, and buttery, with very little fruitiness or aftertaste, but not at all dull; a good choice for those who appreciate gentle tastes.

Silverado Vineyards

6121 Silverado Trail, Napa, CA 94558

C 707 257 1770

W www.silveradovineyards.com

Rich, smooth Silverado's Soda Creek Ranch Olive Oil is made from 100-year-old trees of *Mission, Picholine, Santagetese*, and *Manzanillo*. One of the best.

Stone Edge Vineyard

19330 Carriger Road, Sonoma, CA 95476

C 707 938 2110

W www.oliveoilsource.com

This wine estate is also famous for the small quantities of fine Manzanillo Extra Virgin oil it produces from 50-year-old trees.

Stonehouse

675 Cedar Street, Berkeley, CA 94710

C 415 765 0405

W www.stonehouseoliveoil.com

Stonehouse oil comes from the 98-acre (40-ha) Silver Ridge Ranch at Oroville. Its most expensive oils are its own Estate Organically Grown oil and its Sevillano Single Varietal. The fruity unfiltered Novello oil is also made from *Sevillano*. Stonehouse's House Oil (also known as Silver Medal Blend) is a blend of several varieties, mainly *Mission* and *Barouni* plus *Arbequina, Manzanillo, Sevillano, Ascolano*, and *Arbosana* bought in from local farmers.

Storm Olive Ranch

4320 Chiles Pope Valley Road, St. Helena, CA 94573

C 707 965 1544

Tuscan-style oil made from *Frantoio, Leccino, Maurino*, and *Pendolino* and sold as Storm Olive Ranch.

Val di Luna Farms

12800 Sonoma Hwy, Glen Ellen, CA 94574

C 650 726 5392

Careful cultivation (the owners are nurserymen) and a new *denocciolato* machine are producing first-class oils at Val di Luna. Its Field Blend of *Manzanillo* and *Mission* olives is cool, fresh, fruity, and smooth, with a taste of artichokes, beans, and herbs, followed by almonds and a long, warm aftertaste. Val di Luna's Tuscan Blend of *Frantoio, Leccino*, and *Pendolino* is cool, smooth, and grassy at first, with hints of celery and artichoke until a mounting pepperiness comes in, followed by a long and pleasing bitterness that grows and expands.

AUSTRALIA & NEW ZEALAND

Olive oil is a completely new phenomenon in both Australia and New Zealand. In both countries, olive-growing has been very fragmented and on a small scale, although the potential for quality is remarkable. Investment companies in Australia have recently planted vast tracts of olives. These will change the nature of the industry exponentially.

AUSTRALIA

The olive-oil industry in Australia is expanding rapidly even though it is still in its infancy. Australians have discovered that they can make a product that competes on taste and quality with the rest of the world—just as they did with their wines some 30 years ago. South Australia accounts for more than half of Australia's small-scale olive-oil production while the remainder comes from Western Australia, New South Wales, Victoria, and Tasmania.

Olives were among the first exotic trees to be planted in Australia. One specimen in Parramatta, Sydney, dates back to 1793. There are nearly 2,000 old olive trees still to be found in the Adelaide Parklands and more in Renmark, on the Murray River, planted in the 1880s by irrigation experts William and George Chaffey. In Renmark, the Barossa Valley, and parts of New South Wales and Western Australia, wild olives have become a menace to the native ecology. There are those who say that the best oils come from these wild seedlings.

Until recently very little olive oil was made in Australia. Whatever was produced was on a small scale, usually by families of Italian or Greek origin simply for themselves and their friends. In the 1990s, a growing interest in Mediterranean food led some of the wine estates to start growing olives as a sideline and inspired would-be farmers to plant small acreages. Then the big investors got going: Dandaragan, Australian Harvest, and Boort Estate are names that will change the whole industry (see p.263).

The industry is still fragmented but also experimental and innovative. Young plantations and small presses are multiplying, most notably in traditional wine-producing regions like Western Australia's Margaret River, and South Australia's Clare Valley, the McLaren Vale, and the Barossa Valley.

OLIVE TREES ON OLIVEWOOD ESTATE These trees were planted by the Chaffey brothers in the 1880s.
◄ **YOUNG PLANTATIONS** Major investment in Australia has resulted in many new olive plantations.

Olive growing in Australia

Olives are grown throughout Australia except in the tropical north, where conditions are too wet. High-altitude plantations generally produce better-quality oils, but standards everywhere are respectable.

LATER HARVESTS

With a few exceptions, Australian oils are free from defects. There is no olive fly and the naturally dry climate means that fungi and bacteria pose less of a problem than in much of Europe. Olives may safely be harvested later in the season and their oils often have a very low acidity. But late picking and the hot climate also affect the flavor. Many small-producer oils taste somewhat alike—mellow, gentle, soft, smooth, full, and nutty but lacking in freshness and fruitiness. They are very accessible, but perhaps rather too bland—even flabby. Australians like these easy oils and Verdale is popular precisely because of its mildness. So it is to Australia that we should look to discover what Italian olive oil tasted like before the Tuscans started to pick so early in the season. When producers pick their olives young, they avoid the dumbing-down effect that the warmth of the fall season may have on the olives, but often end up with an unbalanced bitterness. Some of the early-picked oils from Western Australia are reminiscent of early-picked Australian Riesling wines—all tartness, with none of the delicious floweriness found in Europe.

OIL QUALITY

The quality of South Australia's oils is variable. Some oils, especially the late-picked ones, are so smooth and gentle as to be almost tasteless. Others have an extraordinary intensity of flavor. The aromas they suggest are exotic and unusual, offering a distinct and

AUSTRALIAN MIXED PLANTING Olives and vines thrive in the hot, dry climate of southern Australia.

QUEENSLAND

SOUTH AUSTRALIA

Brisbane

Darling River

Inverell

NEW SOUTH WALES

Clare Valley

Great Australian Bight

Renmark
Boundary Bend
Adelaide

McLaren Vale

Barossa Valley

Murray River

Parramatta

Sydney

CANBERRA

Kangaroo Island

Bendigo

VICTORIA

Barfold

Melbourne

Tasman Sea

TASMANIA

Hobart

competitive market opportunity. As with Australian wines, so with their oils. It is noticeable how much more flavor the Australians extract than their European counterparts.

BIG INVESTORS IN AUSTRALIA

There are large-scale olive-oil producers in Australia who believe that the potential for quality-led export is enormous. This is seen in the large, new olive groves that

have been planted over the past 10 years. These entrepreneurs are convinced that they can make olive oil more economically than producers in Europe. They have an "import replacement strategy" for the home market and hope to export fresh, new-season olive oil to the northern hemisphere during the European summer. It is fair to say that the character of the oils produced by the new megafirms has not yet fully developed and stabilized. Brands need to be built. It is all still very much at the experimental stage.

The confidence of the Australians is impressive. They do not know which cultivars will prove the best in the very varied conditions created by different soils, climate, and altitude within the vast subcontinent. There is a surprising reliance on the new and untested *Barnea* olive from Israel. They do not know what yields they can expect and, above all, they cannot say whether it will all be profitable. The huge industries will certainly affect the prices and viability of the smaller producers but will they be able to sell what they produce? Much more marketing is needed—and there has never been a market that is changing and developing so quickly.

Leading producers in New South Wales

Gwydir Olives Pty Ltd

35 Brissett Street, Inverell, NSW 2360

☎ 02 6721 2727

🖥 www.gwydirolives.com.au

Gwydir Grove has an interesting fruity taste of pears, bananas, and something more exotic, followed by a good peppery, bitter aftertaste. It is more complex than many Australian oils.

Lakelands Olives

Cremorne, NSW 2090

☎ 02 9953 6649

🖥 www.lakelands-olives.com.au

Organic Frantoio from a dedicated German-Australian couple. Lakelands is more robust than many Australian oils, with a hint of real grassiness and a balanced aftertaste of warm pepperiness and bitterness. But it also has the smooth texture of hot-climate oils.

Ridgeback Park

Pipeclay Lane, Mudgee, NSW 2850

☎ 6373 3119

🖥 www.ridgeback.cc

Ridgeback calls itself "a small boutique operation," but it has 4,000 young trees of *Frantoio*, *Leccino*, *Pendolino*, *Koroneiki*, and *Verdale* olives and sells their pressings as monocultivar or "varietal" oils. Frantoio is rich and opulent, with a hint of herbs

FRANTOIO

and almonds and a light, warm aftertaste—too smooth and full to be a good Tuscan imitation, but good in its own right. Their Leccino is softer, with a hint of exotic fruits.

Leading producers in Victoria

Cobram Estate Pty Ltd

Cobram, VIC 3644

☎ 03 9561 7222

🖥 www.cobramestate.com.au

Cobram has 25,000 trees of *Frantoio*, *Correggiolo*, *Nevadillo Blanco*, *Leccino*, *Manzanillo*, *Koroneiki*, and *Arbequina*. Its oil is endorsed by Victor Chang and celebrity chef Gabriel Gaté. The Première label is an early-season selection, fresh and lightly fruity at first, becoming more nutty, smooth, and appley with age. Nevadillo Gold is a big, ripe, bitter oil whose taste recalls the *Picual* oils of Andalusia.

Kyneton Olive Oil

Barfold, Victoria 3444

☎ 03 5423 4240

🖥 www.kynetonoliveoil.com.au

Gourmet Blend is fresh and fruity (they say "sweet and delicate," with tropical fruit aromas and only a mild pepperiness) in the Tuscan style; Kyneton Family Selection is more robust, with a taste of grass and tomatoes, followed by almonds, and a good peppery aftertaste. Now winning prizes internationally.

Leighgrove Olives

104 Peel Road, Inverleigh, VIC 3321

☎ 03 5265 1526

Leighgrove Classic Cool Climate oil is lightly fruity, with a tangy taste of herbs, tomatoes, and sweet almonds and somewhat

more fruitiness than usual in Victoria, though essentially rich, smooth, and full.

Lyric Olives

172 Up River Road, Rutherglen, VIC 3685

☎ 02 6032 8442

Opulent, smooth, rich, unfiltered oil from ripe *Frantoio* (here called *Paragon*) and *Correggiolo* olives, though with somewhat more body than many Australian pseudo-Tuscans. Walnuts, almonds, and herbs are all detectable in the taste.

Mount Zero Olives

Horsham, VIC 3401

☎ 03 5383 8280

🖥 www.mountzerolives.com

Mount Zero organic oil is lightly fruity, rich, and smooth, with a more complex taste than usual, which includes a suggestion of herbs, dried fruit, almonds, and apples.

Olive Grove Trading Co. Pty. Ltd.

Robinvale, VIC 3549

☎ 03 5026 3814

🖥 www.robinvaleestate.com.au

Robinvale Estate is on the Murray River and dates back to 1924, but has recently (under Italian ownership) increased its trees from 6,000 to 22,000, and the planting includes two oils: Murray Gold Blend (from *Verdale*, *Correggiolo*, *Manzanillo*, and *Sevillano* olives), which has a mild, ripe taste of almonds and herbs, and Verdale Blend, which is also a soft, gentle oil, with a balance between light fruitiness, bitterness, and pepper.

Ridge Estate Olive Oil

404 Main Creek Road, Main Ridge, VIC 3928

☎ 03 5989 6555

The plantings of *Frantoio*, *Pendolino*, and *Leccino* olives on the Ridge Estate are still young, and the oil has yet to develop a distinct personality, but it has been very good so far: smooth, soft, and gentle, with a lightly warm aftertaste and enough fruit—even a suggestion of grassiness—to make it interesting.

Victorian Olive Groves

Bendigo, VIC 3550
📞 03 5441 5399
🌐 www.victorianolivegroves.com

Victorian Olive Groves sources its olives from every part of Victoria and its VGO oils are endorsed by celebrity cook Stefano de Pieri in Mildura. Its premium labels are the Early Harvest Frantoio, a mild, fruity, gentle, lingering Tuscan-style oil and its stupendous Black Harvest Manzanillo whose complex pungent taste recalls dried fruits, bananas, lychees, and butterscotch.

Leading producers in South Australia

Coriole Vineyards

Chaffeys Road, McLaren Vale, SA 5171
📞 08 8323 8305

This well known wine estate has been making olive oil and preserving Kalamáta olives since 1989. Its top Diva oil, 100% *Koroneïki* olives, is full and fruity, genuinely grassy in taste, with a long, green, bitter aftertaste— excellent. Its standard Coriole Extra Virgin and the young, fruity, unfiltered First oil are also good.

DIVA

Diana Olive Oil

Malpas Road, Willunga, SA 5172
📞 08 8557 1037
🌐 www.dianaoliveoil.com.au

Diana Extra Virgin Olive Oil is an interesting example of a late-picked, hot-climate Tuscan oil. The main cultivars are *Frantoio* and *Leccino* and they give a light taste of grassiness and fresh almonds, but this is overlaid by the rich, almost sweet, character of the oil itself. Despite the owners' reliance on old hydraulic presses, the oil is quite acceptable.

Dominic's Barossa Valley Olive Oil Co.

Eden Valley Rd, Mt. McKenzie, SA 5353.
📞 08 8565 3393
🌐 www.edenvalleyshiraz.com.au

Dominic Torzi makes several oils and blends them well. Vat 1 is the freshest, with a hint of grassiness. Una is made from "*Barossa Wild*," a cultivar planted in the Barossa Valley in the 19th century but not yet identified. Its oil is rich, fruity, and peppery. Synergy is softer, milder, and pleasant, but less exciting.

HOMEWOOD

Homewood

P.O. Box 32, Saddleworth, SA 5413
📞 08 8847 4184

Homewood comes from a small, 130-year-old grove of French cultivars in the Gilbert Valley. It has an

intense and unusual taste of fresh and exotic fruit, including pears and mangos.

Olive Vale Estate

Strout Road, McLaren Vale, SA 5171
📞 08 8323 8721

Olive Vale Estate organic oil is made principally from early-picked *Kalamáta* and *Verdale* olives. Its taste recalls cut grass, herbs, and fresh almonds and is followed by a robust, peppery, bitter aftertaste.

Talinga Grove

Strathalbyn, SA 5255
📞 08 8536 3911
🌐 www.talinga.com.au

Talinga Grove Extravirgin is a big oil, with hints of almonds and vanilla alongside the peppery, bitter aftertaste.

Torrens Valley TAFE

505 Fullarton Road, Netherby, SA 5062
📞 08 8372 6800

David Angwin makes this oil from the historic olive groves planted in the Adelaide Parklands in 1862. Adelaide Parklands has an interesting and exotic smell of banana, mint, and pineapple, but the taste is very strong, complex, and concentrated, with a little pepperiness and bitterness. The taste is of tropical fruits—lime and lemon, sometimes with pear, strawberry, and blackberry too, but always of banana. The exact combination of flavors differs from year to year, but the quality is consistently outstanding.

ADELAIDE PARKLANDS

Willunga Olive Farm

Giles Road, Willunga, SA 5172
☎ 08 8556 2588

Willunga Olive Farm has 15 acres (6ha), planted in 1997 with 1,000 trees of *Frantoio*, *Manzanillo*, *Leccino*, and *Mission*, and organically cultivated. The Frantoio oil, perhaps the best, is medium fruity, with a peppery aftertaste, while Willunga's Leccino is soft and unctuous in the Australian style, with a suggestion of almonds and olives and a long, gentle aftertaste of pepperiness and bitterness.

WILLUNGA LECCINO

Other producers in South Australia

Bird in Hand

Woodside, SA 5244
☎ 08 8232 9033
🔲 www.olivesoilwine.com

Three good oils from a top wine estate. 1st Reserve is fresh, green, and fruity. Gourmet is smoother and nuttier, still with some fruitiness and Late Harvest is made when the olives are black to produce a smooth, warm, soft and lightly nutty oil.

Kangaroo Island Olive Oil Co.

RSD 14 Flinders Chase Service, Via Kingscote, Kangaroo Island SA 5223
☎ 08 8559 2284

North Coast Extra Virgin, from olives grown at Stokes Bay, is smooth and nutty with good body and a bitter, peppery aftertaste.

Olive Di Olive Casalingo Pty Ltd.

345 Rogers Road, Sellicks Hill, SA 5174
☎ 08 8557 4350

Mild, sweet oil under the Olivet Estate label made by Italian-Australians from *Verdale* and *Koroneïki* olives in the Fleurieu Peninsula.

Olives 2000

Andrews Road, Munno Para Downs, SA 5115
☎ 0417 830 947

Smooth, soft oil with a gentle taste of almonds and grass.

Primo Estate Wines

PO Box 77, Virginia, SA 5120
☎ 08 8380 9442
🔲 www.primoestate.com.au

This famous wine estate buys in olives from the Italian-Australian network in McLaren and Willunga. They have several Joseph labels, including a 100% Frantoio, the powerful, fruity Foothills, and the fresh, young First Run. All good.

Russo Olive Oil Pty Ltd

PO Box 775, Willunga, SA 5172
☎ 08 8556 4122

Tuscan-style Russo Grove oil is made from *Correggiolo*, *Frantoio*, and *Leccino* by an Italian-Australian family. It is rich and smooth with a more pronounced taste than many.

Leading producers in Tasmania

Evandale Estate

Pleasant Banks Farm, Leighlands Road, Evandale, Tasmania 7212

Evandale Estate extra virgin oil has a freshness and complexity that come from the cooler climate of Tasmania. The olives are picked early, which gives the oil a green tint. It is fruity and lightly peppery, with a pleasing hint of bitterness in the aftertaste.

Leading producers in Western Australia

Kailis Organic Olive Groves Limited

14 Neil Street, Osborne Park, WA 6017
☎ 08 9201 9066
🔲 www.koog.biz

Kailis Organic Extra Virgin Olive Oil is the leading organic oil in Western Australia, and an international prize-winner. It is based mainly on *Frantoio*, with a little *Leccino*, *Coratina*,

RUSSO GROVE

WELL ESTABLISHED TREES Many of the older Australian olives are planted alongside the vineyards.

and *Mission*, but is softer than Italian *Frantoio* oils.

Olio Bello

PO Box 243, Cowaramup, WA 6284
☎ 08 9755 5684
🖥 www.oliobello.com

Olio Bello has some 6,000 young trees in 14 different cultivars and is constantly experimenting to select the best for local conditions. Its organic estate-pressed range includes Kurunba, Romanza, and Kalamata labels. More widely available is its Margaret River Premium Blend made from olives in the surrounding area, which has a light, gentle "green" taste and a warm aftertaste.

Major investors in Australia

Australian Olives Project

PO Box 1041, Fortitude Valley, QLD 4006
☎ 07 3250 0600
🖥 www.olives.net

Australian Olives Ltd. is one of Australia's leading agribusiness investment managers. More than 312,000 olive trees are planted on their Yallamundi plantation.

Barkworth Estates

PO Box 13347, George St., Brisbane QLD 4003
☎ 07 3211 0066
🖥 www.barkworthestates.com

Barkworth has over 9,884 acres (4,000ha) in New South Wales and 3,954 acres (1,600ha) in South Australia. Its Viva label was the first of the new brands to be seen in Australian shops and supermarkets.

Boundary Bend Estate

8533 Murray Valley Highway, Boundary Bend, VIC 3599
☎ 03 5026 8380
🖥 www.boundarybend.co

The Boundary Bend Estate has 1,235 acres (500ha) of *Barnea*, *Frantoio*, *Leccino*, *Picholine*, and *Picual*, and is trialing *Arbequina*, *Coratina*, *Hojiblanca*, and *Koroneiki*. Its first release was a prize-winning *Barnea-Picual* blend.

Frankland River Oil Company

Wingebellup Road, Frankland, WA 6396
☎ 08 9855 2380
🖥 www.froc.com.au

Frankland River has 1,063 acres (430ha) and 100,000 olive trees, of mainly Tuscan types, planted since 1999. The brand is Jingilli.

Olea Australis

Level 14, BGC Center, 28 The Esplanade, Perth WA 6000
☎ 08 9322 5011
🖥 www.dandaraganestate.com.au

The Dandaragan Estate in the Moore River region has 215,000 trees (in seven different cultivars) on 988 acres (400ha). It offers several different labels, each aimed at a different market taste, including Delicate, Fruity, Robust, and Chef's Choice.

DANDARAGAN ESTATE

Timbercorp Limited

Level 8, 461 Bourke Road, Melbourne VIC 3000
☎ 03 8615 1206
🖥 www.timbercorp.com.au

Timbercorp is Australia's largest agribusiness investment company. Its Boort Estate is the biggest single olive grove in the world: 6,845 acres (2,770ha) (soon to be 8,650acres/ 3,500ha) with 950,000 trees and 12 different olive cultivars. Its trademark oil is Australian Harvest.

Olive growing in New Zealand

New Zealand's olive industry is very new and still diminutive. However, the quality of its olive oils, like its wines, has surprised the world. The future is assured.

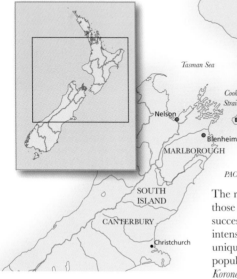

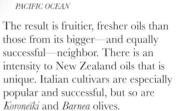

Auckland

Hamilton

Tasman Sea

NORTH ISLAND

Cook Strait

Nelson **WELLINGTON** Martinborough

Blenheim

MARLBOROUGH

SOUTH ISLAND

CANTERBURY

Christchurch

PACIFIC OCEAN

FRESH AND FRUITY OILS

Commercial olive growing is a very recent phenomenon in New Zealand. The first olive grove was planted in Blenheim in 1986. The industry is small, currently extending to about 6,170 acres (2,500ha). There are about one million olive trees in New Zealand. The oil is of very high quality, both chemically and in its taste. Costs are high, so producers operate at the top end of the market, both nationally and internationally.

What makes New Zealand oil so exceptional is the climate in the main areas where it is made, especially the wine-growing Marlborough region, on the North Island. Here, as in Martinborough and Canterbury on the South Island, the climate is cooler than the olive-growing regions of Australia.

The result is fruitier, fresher oils than those from its bigger—and equally successful—neighbor. There is an intensity to New Zealand oils that is unique. Italian cultivars are especially popular and successful, but so are *Koroneïki* and *Barnea* olives.

All the following oils have won prizes at international competitions in the northern hemisphere—a remarkable achievement in so short a time.

NEW PLANTING Almost all New Zealand's olive plantations are very young. It will be interesting to watch the industry develop over the coming years.

Leading Producers in New Zealand

Blumenfeld

PO Box 876, Blenheim
☎ 03 577 9834
🌐 www.blumenfeld.co.nz

Gidon Blumenfeld planted New Zealand's first commercial olive grove in 1986. Blumenfeld oil is now made by a consortium of small growers in Marlborough, and is New Zealand's largest producer. Most of the olives are Tuscan, but there is some *Picholine*, *Koroneïki*, and *Barnea* too. Blumenfeld oil has a fresh aromatic taste of grass, a long, smooth, warm aftertaste—balanced by a light bitterness.

Creekside Olives

774 Rapaura Road, Marlborough
☎ 03 570 5372

A tiny, boutique producer that has won many prizes for its oils, usually blends of *Koroneïki* and *Barnea* olives in varying proportions, sometimes with *Leccino* and/or *Frantoio* as well. All its oils are fresh and fruity, with hints of grass and apples, and a warm, balanced

pepperiness at the end. The *Koroneïki* blends are richer than they would be in Greece, and have a distinctively perfumed taste and a hint of apricots and rosewater—delicious.

Moutere Grove

R.D.2, Upper Moutere, Nelson
☎ 03 543 2232
🌐 www.mouteregrove.co.nz

Moutere Grove produces an organic Tuscan-style oil called Tuscan Blend from *Leccino* and *Pendolino* olives, with some *Frantoio* and *Moraiolo*—gentle, grassy, and almost sweet until the long, warm aftertaste takes over. Excellent.

Serendipity Olive Estate

Waihopai Valley, Marlborough
☎ 03 572 4119
🌐 www.serendipityolives.com

Serendipity is one of New Zealand's largest olive estates, with some 80 acres (32ha) and 10,000 trees. These include *Frantoio*, *Leccino*, *Barnea*, and *Koroneïki* olives. Serendipity oil is an amazing green color, with a real grassy taste, followed by hints of nuts and almonds, and a fairly powerful (but beautifully balanced) aftertaste of pepperiness and bitterness.

Tussock Ltd.

Waihopi Valley, Blenheim RD6
☎ 03 572 4066

Twelve acres (5ha) of *Frantoio*, *Leccino*, and *Minerva* olives, a selected clone of *Leccino*. Minerva is sold as a single-cultivar oil, somewhat more robust and peppery than in Italy. Tussock Blend is a blend of all three cultivars. Both oils are stunning: fresh, fruity, moderately peppery, and very well balanced, right up with the best that Tuscany can produce.

TUSSOCK BLEND

Other producers in New Zealand

- Albany Olive Press
- Akrotiri Estate in Martinborough
- Awatere River
- Clayridge Estate
- Frogs End
- Muratai Olive Oil Co.
- Seresin Estate
- Tasman Bay Olives
- Villa Grove Estate in Marlborough

THE REST OF THE WORLD

Spain, Italy, and Greece are the three top countries for the production of olive oil, both in quality and in quantity. Nevertheless, olives are grown and oil is made in every part of the world where conditions are suitable, from the Middle East to South America, Australia, and Japan.

MIDDLE EAST & NORTH AFRICA

All the countries of the southern and eastern shores of the Mediterranean have long traditions of olive growing and some produce large quantities of olive oil. With few exceptions, however, these are countries with low economic expectations that will not support the kind of high-quality oil industry that the markets of Europe and North America demand. Low wages, a lack of investment, and, in many cases, cumbersome government control of production and sales all point to the same result—poor quality. My travels in these second- and third-world countries in search of good oil have, with a few notable exceptions, been a great disappointment. Yet the potential for excellence remains. There is no doubt that with better cultivation, harvesting, and processing, the countries of North Africa and the Middle East could equal the northern Mediterranean in quality while adding enormously to the choice and variety available to enthusiasts of good olive oil.

BEYOND THE MEDITERRANEAN

Outside the Mediterranean area, the picture is very different. Olive growing is expanding exponentially in such countries as Argentina, the United States (*see p.250*), and Australia (*see p.256*). Here, where the olive tree is not a fundamental part of people's history and culture, the problems are inexperience and even ignorance. People do not know which cultivars to plant or when to pick them. A surprising amount of bad oil is made, and sold (often at high prices) to a public that cannot distinguish good oil from bad. On the other hand, there is great potential in these countries to satisfy a fast-growing demand for high-quality olive oil in the home markets and perhaps to compete in the world markets as they do with their wines.

HARVEST TIME Olives are still picked by hand in many of the smaller countries that produce olive oil.
◀ OLIVE GROWING AROUND THE WORLD (Clockwise from top), Tunisia, Israel, Croatia, and Morocco.

Adriatic Countries

Olive growing is as ancient on the coast of Dalmatia as on the Italian side of the Adriatic. Trees are planted all along the coast from Slovenia through Croatia to Montenegro and Albania but, to date, only Croatia produces oils of reasonable quality.

ANCIENT OLIVE GROVES

Groves throughout this region are often neglected and, from time to time, laid low by a hard winter, but olives are an ideal crop for the rocky limestone soils that predominate. In Croatia, on the island of Brioni, there is a tree that is said to be 1,630 years old. During and after the Second World War, many olive plantations were abandoned for a generation, or longer. Slowly these are being taken in hand again, though at least one-third of Croatia's olive groves are still uncultivated, and slightly more in Albania. Quality is patchy.

CROATIA

Croatia has some 68,000 acres (27,500ha) of olives and 4.5 million trees. A sprig of olives fills the reverse of Croatia's 20-lipa coin, but war, land reform, and economic upheaval have slowed down the renaissance of its olive oil industry.

Croatian oils tend to be made either by the old communist cooperatives, now privatized, or by new companies that buy up stocks of oil made by individual farmers and bottle the resultant blend. Single estates on the Italian or French models are almost nonexistent. The best oils come from Istria, where the main olive is *Bianchera*. Also important are *Lastovka*, which accounts for more than half of the olives on the island of Korula, *Levantinka* (widely grown on Solta), and the dual-purpose *Oblica*.

SLOVENA & ALBANIA

Olive-oil production in Slovenia is tiny. The stores are full of Italian imports. But the limestone hills of northern Istria are home to some 2,470 acres (1,000ha) of *Bianchera*, which makes fine oils in the Tergeste DOP across the border in Italy, so there is potential for quality oils.

Montenegro has 8,460 acres (3,500ha) of olives and the principal cultivar is called *Zutica*, but no oil of any quality has emerged yet. Albania has 108,700 acres (45,000ha) of olives and six million trees concentrated in the south of the country. *Kalinjot* is the main olive, a dual-purpose cultivar with a good taste. At present, a little Albanian olive oil is sold in organic outlets in Switzerland and Germany. The leading brand is Shkalla (Lunder Rruga "Qemal Stafa," 7466 Tirana. Tel.: 06 9229 8924).

Leading producers in Croatia

Agrolaguna

M. Vlašiča
Poreč

Agrolaguna comes from a privatized co-operative in Porec – Istria's largest, whose members have 65,000 trees. Laguna Histria Djevičansko

LAGUNA HISTRIA

Extra Maslinovo Ulje is fresh and fruity with an herbaceous taste and an aroma of olives, followed by a good, peppery aftertaste.

Zvijezda

M. Čaviča 1,
Zagreb
Ⓦ www.zvijezda.hr

Zvijezda is a large food producer, whose Zvijezda Extra Djevičansko Maslinovo Ulje Sortno is a blend of oils from the whole country.

It is smooth and cool at first, until a "green" taste emerges—herbaceous and fruity, too—and is followed by a sensation of bitter almonds and a long, hot aftertaste.

Torkul

20270 Vela Luka
Korcula

Djevičansko Maslinovo Ulje Extra Torkul is fresh and green-tasting, but soft and gentle until the warm aftertaste develops and reveals a pleasant touch of bitterness.

South Africa

Olive growing does not have such a strong tradition in South Africa as it has in other parts of the southern hemisphere, perhaps because Cape Province was largely settled by northern Europeans. Most South African olive oils are produced as a sideline by the big wine estates but they are also beginning to win prizes in international competitions.

Leading producers in South Africa

Cape Olive Trust

Off Swawelstert Road, Klein Drakenstein, Paarl
C 021 868 3120

This is the largest producer of table olives in South Africa. Its Buffet Olives include *Manzanilla*, *Sevillano*, *Kalamáta*, and *Mission*.

Costa & Son, F.

Nervi Farm, Klein Drakenstein Road Huguenot (Paarl) 7645
C 021 872 6700

The Costas are of Ligurian origin; their estate dates back to 1904. Costa Premier Extra Virgin is medium fruity, with hints of grass and tomato, and a peppery aftertaste.

Hildenbrand Wine & Olive Estate

Rhebokskloof Farm, PO Box 270, Wellington 7655
C 021 873 4115
W www.wine-estate-hildenbrand. co.za

This German-owned estate makes its Hildenbrand Estate Extra Virgin Olive Oil from 400 trees planted in the 1890s and 3,500 new plants.

Kloovenburg

PO Box 2, Riebeek Kasteel, 7307
C 022 448 1635
W www.kloovenburg.com

This mixed estate has 74 acres (30ha) of *Leccino* and *Mission* olives. Kloovenburg Extra Virgin is a big, strong-flavored oil—very fruity, peppery, and bitter.

Morgenster Estate

P.O. Box 1616, Somerset West 7129
C 021 852 1738
W www.morgenster.co.za

South Africa's leading olive-oil estate is Italian owned and Italian inspired. The blend is mainly *Frantoio*, *Leccino*, *Coratina*, and *Perenzana*, which produces a robust, Tuscan-style oil—very fruity, peppery, and bitter but wonderfully harmonious and well balanced.

MORGENSTER

Rhebokskloof Estate

PO Box 7141, Noorder Paarl 7623
C 021 869-8386
W www.rhebokskloof.co.za

A wine estate with a small production of Rhebokskloof Extra Virgin Olive Oil—the olives are 80% *Frantoio* and 20% *Mission*.

Vesuvio Estates

PO Box 3295, Paarl 7620
C 021 869 8571
W www.vesuvioestates.co.za

This estate was founded by Italians in the 1950s and is still Italian owned. They are seriously big producers with 1,087 acres (440ha)—and still expanding—of *Frantoio*, with a little *Mission* and *Leccino*, mostly unirrigated. Vesuvio is usually fresh and medium fruity, with slight bitterness and pepperiness, though this varies according to the season.

Willow Creek Farm

Nuy Valley, Worcester
C 023 342 5793
W www.willowcreek.co.za

This producer is now winning prizes in Europe and the United States. It has 247 acres (100ha) of high-density planting and is still expanding. Its Willow Creek Gourmet Intense Fruity is 50% *Frantoio*, 30% *Coratina*, 20% *Leccino* olives, and is grassy and peppery with a fine, lightly bitter aftertaste.

Other producers in South Africa

Bianco Fine Wines

PO Box 103
Tulbagh 6820
C (023) 231 0350
W www.bianco.co.za

Bianco has 73 acres (30ha) of trees, mainly for table olives, but the oil is also good.

Eikendal Vineyards

PO Box 2261
Stellenbosch 7601
C 021 855 1422
W www.eikendal.co.za

This well known wine estate is now producing small quantities of olive oil.

South America

The geography and climate of much of South America are well adapted to olive growing. The wines of Chile and Argentina are already famous internationally, and their olive oils are following on. The South Americans have close links with Spain and Italy and access to the skills and traditions of the Old World. The first results are very promising.

ARGENTINA

Until recently, most of Argentina's olive trees were grown in the foothills of the Andes, and especially in the provinces of Mendoza, San Juan, Córdoba, and La Rioja. Immigrants from Spain and Italy were the major planters of olives, most of them traditionally cultivated *Frantoio*, *Picual*, and *Empeltre* olives. Since the early 1990s, however, there has been an expansion of the area put to olives with intensive irrigated plantations of *Arbequina* olive trees tripling the total acreage. This has put other parts of the country on the olive map—Catamarca, San Luis, Salta, and Tucumán, though the main areas for producing oil are still Córdoba, Mendoza, and San Juan, while table olives grow in Mendoza and La Rioja. About 70 percent of Argentina's oil production came from Mendoza in 1999. The table olives are mainly of the local *Arauco* cultivar—related to *Manzanillo* but little known outside Argentina.

The olive oil market is fairly evenly split between producers who aim for quality and bulk and producers whose oils are sold on price, sometimes mixed with seed oils. Both types of oil are exported to other South American countries, principally Brazil.

CHILE

Until the mid-1990s, the main olive cultivars in Chile were old *Sevillano* trees, grown for their table olives. Then winemakers and agro-investors realized that the same conditions that were benefiting the wine industry—altitude, water, dependable summer heat, and low production costs—would also favor the cultivation of olives. Investment over the last 10 years has been exponential, and the results are the best in South America. Almost all the leading estates are young, large, irrigated—and innovative and experimental too.

URUGUAY

This country has one famous, historic olive estate called Los Ranchos, which succeeds in producing acceptable olive oil despite the subtropical climate. The olives are processed within two hours of picking and the estate is equipped with modern extraction machinery.

ARGENTINA Many olive trees were planted by the early settlers from Europe, as here beside a vineyard.

Leading producers in Argentina

Geier, Az. Mario

Ruta 14, Villa de Las Rosas,
Traslasierra – Córdoba
☎ 03544 494658
Ⓦ www.formandorutas.com/olium

Prize-winning organic oil called Olium.

Plantaciones Catamarca S.A.

Ruta Nacional 38, 4726 Capayán –
Huillapina, Catamarca
☎ (03833) 496070
Ⓦ www.fincalabonita.com.ar

Main label is Romero di Gangi, made from a cocktail of imported olive cultivars, including *Arbequina*, *Picual*, *Barnea*, *Frantoio*, and *Hojiblanca*.

San Juan De Los Olivos S.A.

Fray Justo Sarmiento 2350, Olivos (BA)
☎ 01141 067150
Ⓦ www.sjolivos.com.ar

The main labels are Conde Duque de Olivares and San Juan de los Olivos.

Leading producers in Chile

Olivares de Quepu S.A.

Apoquindo 3669 of. 502, Las
Condes, Santiago
☎ 02 5604982
Ⓦ www.olivaresdequepu.cl

Olivares de Quepu has 593 acres (240ha) in Pencahue and offers several labels, but the main ones are Oro Maule and 1492, made from *Picual* or *Arbequina*. They are trying out other cultivars.

TerraMater

Camino Lo Sierra 1500, Cerrillos
☎ 02 5579121
Ⓦ www.terramater.com

This large and expanding

BOUNTY HUNTER A young olive picker in Uruguay climbs the highest branches of an olive tree to reach its furthest fruits.

producer has several labels. The most common is Canepa, but sometimes you see TerraMater Special Selection, and Petralia. Their latest (2005) selection is Novello—fresh and fruity, made from *Coratina* (here called *Racimo*).

Valle Arriba, Ag. Com.

Av. Kennedy 5146 Piso 7
☎ 02 2190080
Ⓦ www.vallearriba.cl

Valle Arriba has two farms. One is in Pelequén in Malloa, with 618 acres (250ha) and the other in Los Lirios in Ovalle covers 494 acres (200ha), growing young trees of *Arbequina*, *Picual*, *Frantoio*, *Leccino*, *Nocellara del Belice*, and *Biancolilla*. Their first labels are blends called Mestre and Kardamili.

Valle Grande Ltda., Ag.

Balmaceda 1500, Isla de Maipo
☎ 02 8193517
Ⓦ www.olave.cl

The new-style Olave oil is

made from a mix of *Frantoio*, *Leccino*, *Arbequina*, and *Coratina*. It is fresh and fruity, with a peppery aftertaste and a light, lingering bitterness.

Leading producer in Uruguay

Los Ranchos

Zorrilla de San Martín 1347, Fray
Bentos.
☎ 0562 4054
Ⓦ www.guiaindustrial.com.uy

Los Ranchos has 222 acres (90ha) of olive groves, planted in the 1950s with *Leccino*, *Manzanilla*, *Taggiasca*, and *Arbequina*. Los Ranchos oil is unfiltered, smooth, and soft, with a light grassy taste and a rich texture. Half of its production is exported, mainly to France but also to the United States.

Smaller Olive Oil Producers

Olives have been grown in North Africa and the Middle East for centuries. They are a relatively recent (mid 19th-century) introduction to Japan. Most of these countries are capable of producing high-quality oil but lack the technical expertise, machinery, and/or investment to match high western European standards. The most these industries can hope for is to export their oil to Italy for blending or rectification.

KRISTAL RIVIERA OIL
FROM TURKEY

TURKEY

Turkey accounts for 10 percent of the world's land surface committed to olive growing—some 2,216,487 acres (897,000ha) and 100 million trees. It is an important producer of table olives, of which one-quarter is exported. About 75 percent of Turkey's olive groves are in the Aegean region, 11 percent in Marmara, and there are small areas of cultivation in southeastern Anatolia and on the Black Sea coast.

Turkey has a large number of indigenous olive cultivars. The country's best oil comes from the northern Aegean area, where the olive grown is *Ayvalik*, a high-yielding cultivar that is also used as a table olive. In the drier south, the leading cultivar is *Memecik*.

Crops suffer from biennial cropping *(see p.27)* to a very marked degree— much more than in the major producing countries—which impacts on the industry's ability to sustain an export-led expansion. As a result, Turkey's oil production is still relatively unmodernized and its oil is of uneven quality. Home consumption of olive oil is low—roughly two pints (one liter) per person per year. In years of plenty, a large proportion is refined and sold in bulk, principally to Spain and Italy. However, the industry has also been dogged by a scandal involving the adulteration with hazelnut oil by one of the country's largest olive-oil producers.

Retail exports are dominated by the giant secondary cooperative Tariş, which is based in Izmir and has 33 cooperative members representing 27,000 farmers. Its oil is of variable quality. The best brand for dependable, high-quality olive oil is Laleli. Look for the word *Sizma* on a bottle's label—it means extra virgin— but remember that extra virgin is a technical term, a guarantee of low acidity levels, not of good taste.

MALTA

The Wardija Estate in Malta's San Paolo a Mare has 30 acres (12ha) of olive trees and the island's only modern press. The estate is owned by Matty and Salvatore

OLIVE GROVES IN TURKEY
In the warmer coastal areas of Turkey, such as the Meander valley, gray-leaved olives are grown alongside citrus fruits with dark green leaves.

Cremona, who have led the renaissance of Malta's ancient olive industry. Matty is Malta's best-known writer on cooking and the author of *Cooking with Maltese Olive Oil*. Salvatore manages the estate and advises neighbors whose olives he presses. The oil is organic, fruity, and peppery. There are moves to identify old olive groves—and individual trees—and apply to the European Union (EU) for a DOP.

CYPRUS

There are about 20,000 acres (8,000ha) of olive trees in Cyprus, which produce about 14,330 tons of olives a year, though this fluctuates between 11,000 and 22,000 tons according to the season. Table olives account for about 2,755 tons of olives and the rest is made into oil.

Europe's most easterly nation is far behind the rest of the continent in the management of its olive industry. Until recently, most aspects were controlled by the Cyprus Olive Products Marketing Board. The board paid fixed prices for olives, which were compulsorily sold into

intervention, and fixed the price of the finished olive oil in the stores. It also controlled the sales. Home consumption is low—8lb (3.5kg) of olive oil per person a year (as opposed to 33lb/15kg a year for seed oil)—and the island needs on occasion to import oil to make up the shortfall in supply.

The dominant olive cultivar is known simply as *Local* and attempts to establish higher-yielding foreign types like *Koroneïki* and *Picual* have hitherto met with little success. Olives are usually grown in mixed plantings alongside vines, cereals, and forage crops. Irrigation is in its infancy. Quality—never high—is improving, and Archontikó oil from near Limassol won an international prize in Madrid in 2003.

THE MIDDLE EAST

Growing olives and making olive oil have a very long tradition in the Middle East. Archeologists believe that it was in northern Syria that olives were first grown as a domestic crop. Syria is the region's most important producer of olive oil—now the world's fourth largest —with more than 1,235,500 acres (500,000ha) of trees. Lebanon, Israel, Jordan, and Palestine have about 692,000 acres (280,000ha) between them.

The industry in the Middle East is many years behind western Europe in quality, perception, efficiency, and marketing. It is plagued by shortcomings at every stage. Cultivation is poor, pests are rampant, mechanization has scarcely begun, and investment is minimal. All the main olive cultivars grown in the Middle East are capable of making high-quality oil, and a scattering of producers now sets out to do so, but the general picture is of antiquated incompetence and oils that are at best dull, at worst disgusting.

SYRIA

The Syrian government is committed to increasing funding to the industry so that olive growing can be further expanded and modernized. Replanting and irrigation are major projects, but only just begun. Olive-oil production is about 165,000 tons per annum and

ISRAELI OLIVE GROVES Ancient groves are left for sheep to graze while new plantations are intensively cultivated.

at the time of writing is expected to reach 220,500 tons by 2010.

Syria's olives are concentrated in the coastal regions and the north of the country. Most of the country's oil is sold internally at comparatively high prices but Syria now exports its growing surplus. That said, the Syrian industry is very fragmented, and the traditional export markets lean eastward to Iran and Saudi Arabia. Syria has decided to build up a high-quality sector within its industry—*Zaiti* and *Sorani* are both capable of producing high-quality oil—but standards of production and storage need improvement before it can compete in western countries on anything other than price. Zirtoon, al-Motawasset, Tazco, and Sofra are some of the most common brands.

LEBANON

Two-thirds of Lebanon's olive trees are in the north of the country. Olives tend to be picked late and to produce a mild, gentle oil, not always free from defects. Problems include biennial cropping *(see p.27)*, the high cost of labor, the

fragmentation of landholdings, and a lack of government support. Competition from cheaper imports, notably from Syria, has caused the Lebanese industry to shrink. It has also impelled the Lebanon to negotiate a low-tariff quota (1,100 tons) of exports to the European Union (EU). Much of this is sold in France. A few individual producers export directly, often promoting themselves on the basis of being organic, but it is difficult to find high-quality oils among them. There are links to French retailers like Olivier and Italian blenders like Monini, but these have not benefited the Lebanese industry to any great extent. Nay (part of the Massaya group), Second House Products, and Olive Harvest are the main brands.

ISRAEL

There are some 45,000 acres (19,000ha) of olive trees in Israel. The traditional cultivar for oil is the *Souri* olive, which predominates in the unirrigated areas (29,600 acres/12,000ha), most of which still belong to Palestinians. Modern Israeli plantations are intensively or semi-intensively cultivated and irrigated: there are 7,500 acres (3,000ha) of the locally raised *Barnea* olive for oil and 10,000 acres (4,000ha) of *Manzanillo* for table olives.

Although Israel is a net importer of olive oil, there is a market for kosher oil from Israel, especially in the U.S., where several brands claim to be the only one available in North America. The organic oil from Makura Farm near Zichron has won prizes abroad.

JORDAN

The kingdom of Jordan is a major producer of olive oil and its industry is more advanced than those of its neighbors, but little is made to western European levels. The country has some 16 million olive trees and the figure grows by about one million trees every year. There are about 222,000 acres (90,000ha) of young, irrigated olives and 62,000 acres (25,000ha) of traditional plantations. The leading marques, all based in the north, include Ajloun Food Processing Co., Al Jazzazi, Jordan Modern Industrial Co., Jordan's Treasure, and Zaitt. Not all produce oil free from defects. The oils in the Terra Rossa range produced by Jordan Modern Industrial Co., however, can be recommended for their fresh, clean, fruity taste.

TERRA ROSSA
OIL FROM
JORDAN

PALESTINE

The state of Palestine was a major producer and exporter of olive oil but has seen its industry suffer in recent years. It has a small export market in northern Europe and North America, especially among Christians, for whom the idea of oil from the Holy Land is attractive. The industry is fragmented and most oil is made by small farmers for home use, but several cooperatives now promote their oil more widely. Leading exporters include Zaytoun and Holy Land Olive Oil.

NORTH AFRICA

Olive trees have been grown along the North African coast for as long as on the other side of the Mediterranean. Morocco has a thriving oil industry, but it is Tunisia, with one-quarter of its cultivated land put to olives, that has the largest and best organized industry in North Africa.

Visiting North Africa's olive groves is like stepping back 100 years to a pre-industrial economy, when traditional producers stored their olives for several weeks before pressing them, entrepreneurs were starting to distill and purify the oils, and only a few courageous producers promoted a better quality of oil—virgin, if not extra virgin. The contrast is striking but no more than a measure of the difference between relative riches in the northern Mediterranean and relative poverty in the south.

Much of North Africa is based on subsistence farming. Traditional presses are wasteful, unsanitary, and unscientific. Olive oil is considered a food of the poor—even of the extremely poor. Low production costs make the industry competitive, but returns are feeble and poor-quality oil is difficult to sell. Many medium-sized enterprises still follow the old processes with hydraulic presses and hot water.

Main olive cultivars grown in the Middle East

COUNTRY	ACRES/HA	NO. OF TREES	CULTIVARS
Israel	47,000/19,000	3,000,000	Souri, Barnea, Manzanillo
Lebanon	128,500/52,000	13,000,000	Souri
Palestine	235,000/95,000	10,000,000	Nabali Baladi
Jordan	285,000/115,000	16,000,000	Rasi'i
Syria	1,334,000/540,000	66,000,000	Sorani, Zaiti

Most countries encourage investment in modern systems of continuous extraction but poor road communications mean that many olives are spoiled before they arrive at the mill.

The easy availability of abundant, cheap, seasonal labor also means that olives are picked by hand. There is very little mechanization of either the picking or the pruning of olive trees. Technical education in agronomy, at all levels, is available only to the few. The cooperative movement is weak, and strengthening it would in any case have the undesirable effect of weakening the private sector. Until quite recently, most countries had nationalized olive-producing industries.

ALGERIA AND EGYPT

About half of Algeria's olives grow in the area around Constantine, and one-quarter around Algiers itself. Many consider that the best oil comes from Kabylie. The National Agriculture Development Plan has expanded the area put to olives and built new processing plants, but the oil is not of high quality. It is sometimes exported to North America and France.

Egypt is a net importer of olive oil. Egyptian olive oil is generally of poor quality and seldom seen abroad. The better brands include Al-Neama, Baraka, Domaine Horus, El Salheya, Golden Field, Isis, Mina, and Pioneer.

TUNISIA

Olive growing was well established in the Carthaginian period. In Roman times, present-day Tunisia was one of the Empire's major suppliers. Today, Tunisia has about 4 million acres (1.6 million ha) dedicated to olive growing and some 60 million trees. One-third of the total is accounted for by young plantations that are only now beginning to come into production, which means that the volume of Tunisian oil will grow significantly over the next few years. The country is also fast adopting modern farming methods, irrigation, and processing equipment.

The two most important areas of production are around Sousse and Sfax, where more than two-thirds of the agricultural land is put to olives. Tunisia's annual oil production varies considerably, but now averages about 165,000 tons—the crop reached 264,000 tons in 2004. The home market absorbs about 66,000 tons per year; the rest is exported. Most of it goes to blenders in Italy and Spain: Tunisia is entitled to reduced duties for 55,000 tons every year entering the European Union (EU) under trading agreements dating back to 1987. The oils are lightly fruity, soft, and gentle, and good mixers, too.

In the deep south, where annual rainfall is about 10in (25cm), olives are planted at a density of no more than 50 per acre/20 per hectare. *Chetoui* is the most common cultivar in the north, and *Chemlali*, which is resistant to drought, in the center and south of the country. Other important cultivars are *Oueslati* and *Gerboui*, both dual-purpose. The industry was denationalized in the mid-1990s, and the market is now much more varied than before. Nevertheless, it is dominated by large-scale producers, including Sfax Huile, Socohuile, Ben Yedder, and Zit Z'men.

MOROCCO

This country has a thriving olive oil industry, run mainly by large processors and refiners who buy their olives from all over the country. Since 98 percent of the olives come from a dual-purpose cultivar called *Picholine*

Main olive cultivars grown in North Africa

COUNTRY	ACRES/HA	NO. OF TREES	CULTIVARS
Algeria	408,000/ 165,000	15,000,000	Chemlal de Kabylie, Siguase
Egypt	86,500/35,000	400,000	Aggezi Shami
Morocco	1,360,000/ 550,000	64,000,000	Picholine Marocaine
Tunisia	4,013,000/ 1,624,000	60,000,000	Chemlali de Sfax, Chetoui, Ouesleti

Marocaine, the source does not affect the taste of the oil. Despite major agricultural improvements (water supplies to irrigate new plantations, changes to the laws of land tenure, and encouragement for processors to invest in equipment) quality of the oil remains poor. As in much of North Africa and the Middle East, poor cultivation and delays in transporting olives to the mill are at the root of the trouble.

There is nothing to match Morocco's reliance on *Picholine Marocaine*. No other country has such a large proportion of its crop dedicated to one cultivar, nor grown over such an extensive area. *Picholine Marocaine* has its advantages. It is very adaptable, though the size of the individual fruit depends, more than most cultivars, on the standards of cultivation and availability of irrigation. It has disadvantages. The traditional yield is low, never more than 18 percent, and usually closer to 12 percent.

USING OLIVE WASTE
A Moroccan worker bags up the leftovers from olive pressings to be used as fuel.

However, the National Agronomic Research Institute at Meknès has been working on clonal selection and has introduced two variants, *Haouzia* and *Menara*, which represent an improvement on the type. The Institute is also trialing foreign cultivars to see whether some might have a commercial potential in Morocco. Recent changes in cultivar distribution, such as a large-scale introduction since 1980 of *Arbequina* olives in Andalusia and *Leccino* trees in Puglia, have had a great impact on European production. Here may lie the future of the Moroccan oil industry.

A few private estates are making olive oil to European standards. Look for the first-rate oils of **Domaine de la Zouina** and Volubilia from the Meknès area. These give an idea of the excellence of which *Picholine Marocaine* is capable, given careful cultivation, harvesting, and extraction.

OLIMAROC

JAPAN

Olives were first introduced to Japan from France in 1862. Oil was first made in Mita, in Kobe province, in 1881 and was popular in the early 20th century as hair oil. Japan is a major importer of olive oil. Two-thirds comes from Italy and most of the rest of the oil comes from Spain.

Shodo Shima in the Inland Sea is known as the "olive island." It has approximately 2,400 acres (1,000ha) of *Mission* olive trees, planted as the result of a government initiative in 1908 and now a tourist attraction with a scaled-down imitation of the Parthenon.

The island also has an agricultural experimental station where about 50 cultivars are being trialed. The olives are harvested late when they are ripe. Their oil is soft and smooth but not very exciting. The industry has declined since about 1970 as a result of inexpensive imports and a failure to modernize. Quality is now improving but the oil is expensive, difficult to find, and not always of a high standard. Shodo Shima is also known for its olive oil candies.

There is a second Japanese olive grove in Ushimado, in the Okayama prefecture, opposite Shodo Shima. Its olive trees came from Greece.

INDEX

ACKNOWLEDGMENTS

The publisher would like to thank: Hilary Bird for the index; and the following for their kind permission to reproduce their photographs:

(Key: a-above; b-below/bottom; c-center; l-left; r-right; t-top)

1 **Alamy Images:** images-of-france / Mike Blenkinsop (t). **Corbis:** Envision (b). 2 **Corbis:** PhotoCuisine. 3 **Getty Images:** Stone / Oliver Benn. 4 **Cephas Picture Library:** Dario Fusaro. 5 **Alamy Images:** Wilmar Photography.com. 6-7 **Getty Images:** Photographer's Choice / Trevor Wood. 8-9 **Alamy Images:** Cephas Picture Library / Ted Stefanski. 10 **Charles Quest-Ritson.** 11 **Alamy Images:** isifa Image Service s.r.o.. 12 **Chianti Classico.** 14-15 **Getty Images:** Botanica / Anthony / Masterson. 16 **Charles Quest-Ritson.** 17 **Alamy Images:** Israel Images / Yasha Mazur. 18-19 **Charles Quest-Ritson.** 20 **DK Images:** The British Museum, London / Nick Nicholls (tr). **The Picture Desk:** Art Archive / Biblioteca Nazionale Marciana Venice / Dagli Orti (bl). 21 **akg-images:** (b). **www.bridgeman.co.uk:** Bibliotheque Nationale, Paris (ca). 23 **Charles Quest-Ritson.** 25 **Robert Copeland:** (bl). **Charles Quest-Ritson:** (t). 26-27 **Charles Quest-Ritson.** 28 **Alamy Images:** Jon Bower. 29 **Charles Quest-Ritson.** 30-31 **Charles Quest-Ritson.** 32 **Alamy Images:** Olivier Digoit. 33 **Corbis:** Stephanie Colasanti. 34 **Photo by Marco Luethi:** (bl). 34-35 **Charles Quest-Ritson:** (t). 36 **Charles Quest-Ritson.** 38-39 **Corbis:** Carmen Redondo (b). 43 **Corbis:** photocuisine. 46 **Alamy Images:** images-of-france / Dennis Palmer. 47 **Corbis:** Owen Franken (br) ; PhotoCuisine (t). 48-49 **Cephas Picture Library:** Dario Fusaro . 50 **Corbis:** Sygma / Patrick Landmann. 51 **Corbis:** Sygma / Patrick Landmann (t, c). 52 **DK Images:** Kim Sayer. 53 **Alamy Images:** Cephas Picture Library / Dario Fusaro (c) ; Andre Jenny (b). 54 **Corbis:** Owen Franken (tr) ; Philippe Giraud (bl). 55 **Alamy Images:** Cephas Picture Library / Mick Rock (tr). **Charles Quest-Ritson:** (b). 56 **Alamy Images:** Nick Higham (tr). **Charles Quest-Ritson:** (b). 57 **Corbis:** David Lees. 58 **Corbis:** Sygma / Patrick Landmann. 59 **Corbis:** Sygma / Patrick Landmann. 62 **Charles Quest-Ritson:** (bl). 64 **Charles Quest-Ritson.** 65 **Charles Quest-Ritson:** (t). 66 **Charles Quest-Ritson:** (t). 68 **Charles Quest-Ritson.** 70 **Alamy Images:** Bildagentur Franz Waldhaeusl / Ernst-Georg Kohout. 71 **Alamy Images:** imagebroker / Harald Theissen. 72 **Alamy Images:** Maximilian Weinzierl. 73 **Charles Quest-Ritson:** (tl). 75 **DK Images:** Kim Sayer (tr). 77 **Charles Quest-Ritson:** (tr). 82 **Alamy Images:** CuboImages srl / Federico Meneghetti (br). 83 **Charles Quest-Ritson.** 84 **Charles Quest-Ritson:** (t). 85 **Charles Quest-Ritson:** (br). 86 **Charles Quest-Ritson.** 88 **Alamy Images:** Ace Stock Limited (t). 89 **akg-images:** Musée des Antiquités / Erich Lessing. 93 **Charles Quest-Ritson:** (t). 96 **Corbis:** Vince Streano. 97 **Alamy Images:** CuboImages srl / Enrico Caracciolo. 99 **Charles Quest-Ritson:** (b). 101 **Charles Quest-Ritson.** 102-103 **Charles Quest-Ritson:** (b). 103 **Charles Quest-Ritson:** (tr). 104-105 **Charles Quest-Ritson.** 106 **Alamy Images:** Robert Harding Picture Library Ltd. 110 **Charles Quest-Ritson:** (b). 112 **Charles Quest-Ritson.** 114 **Charles Quest-Ritson.** 116 **Charles Quest-Ritson:** (tl). 118 **Alamy Images:** John Ferro Sims. 120-121 **Alamy Images:** CuboImages srl / Alfio Garozzo (b). 122 **Charles Quest-Ritson.** 124-125 **Charles Quest-Ritson.** 127 **Charles Quest-Ritson.** 128 **DK Images:** John Heseltine (tc). 130 **Charles Quest-Ritson:** (t). 132 **Alamy Images:** Bildarchiv Monheim GmbH / Schütze / Rodemann (bl). 133 **Cephas Picture Library:** Mick Rock (tr). 134 **Alamy Images:** Ken Welsh. 135 **Charles Quest-Ritson.** 136 **Alamy Images:** Michael Hilton. 138-139 **Charles Quest-Ritson.** 139 **Harriet Lord** (br). 140-141 **Charles Quest-Ritson.** 142 **Alamy Images:** Keith Lewis. 144-145 **Alamy Images:** Cephas Picture Library / Mick Rock (b). 145 **Charles Quest-Ritson:** (tr). 146 **Charles Quest-Ritson.** 147 **Alamy Images:** Sean Burke. 148 **Corbis:** Francesc Muntada. 149 **Charles Quest-Ritson.** 151 **Charles Quest-Ritson:** (tr). 154-155 **Charles Quest-Ritson.** 156 **Charles Quest-Ritson.** 157 **Charles Quest-Ritson:** (br). 158 **Charles Quest-Ritson:** (t). 160 **Charles Quest-Ritson.** 162-163 **Charles Quest-Ritson.** 167 **Charles Quest-Ritson.** 168-169 **Charles Quest-Ritson.** 170-171 **Charles Quest-Ritson.** 172-173 **Charles Quest-Ritson.** 174-175 **Charles Quest-Ritson.** 186 **Charles Quest-Ritson.** 188 **Charles Quest-Ritson.** 189 **Alamy Images:** bildagentur-online.com / th-foto. 190 **Alamy Images:** Geopix. 191 **Getty Images:** Pascal Perret. 192 **Alamy Images:** Cephas Picture Library / Mick Rock (bl). **DK Images:** Joe Cornish (tr). 193 **Alamy Images:** Bildagentur-online.com / th-foto (bl). **DK Images:** Paul Harris (cla). 194 **Alamy Images:** Sean Burke (t). 195 **Charles Quest-Ritson.** 196 **Alamy Images:** Eitan Simanor. 198 **Charles Quest-Ritson.** 200-201 **Corbis:** Tony Azzura (b). 201 **Charles Quest-Ritson:** (tr). 202 **Alamy Images:** H. Souto. 204-205 **Charles Quest-Ritson.** 208 **Alamy Images:** Robert

Harding Picture Library Ltd. **210 Alamy Images:** Cephas Picture Library / Mick Rock (tr). **Corbis:** Owen Franken (c). **211 Alamy Images:** G.P. Bowater (b). **212 Charles Quest-Ritson. 213 Charles Quest-Ritson:** (tr). **215 Charles Quest-Ritson. 216 Charles Quest-Ritson. 218 Charles Quest-Ritson. 219 Charles Quest-Ritson:** (t). **223 Charles Quest-Ritson:** (tr). **224 Alamy Images:** John Lens. **226-227 Charles Quest-Ritson. 228 Corbis:** Chris Lisle (t). **Charles Quest-Ritson:** (bl). **229 Charles Quest-Ritson. 230 Charles Quest-Ritson. 231 Charles Quest-Ritson:** (t). **232-233 Charles Quest-Ritson. 235 Bläuel Greek Organic Products:** (cb). **237 Charles Quest-Ritson:** (t). **238-239 Charles Quest-Ritson. 240-241 Charles Quest-Ritson. 245 Charles Quest-Ritson. 246 Charles Quest-Ritson:** (t). **248-249 Alamy Images:** AA World Travel Library. **250 Alamy Images:** Cephas Picture Library / Ted Stefanski. **251 Getty Images:** National Geographic / Ira Block. **252-253 Charles Quest-Ritson. 256 Cephas Picture Library:** Kevin Judd. **257 Charles Quest-Ritson. 258-259 Alamy Images:** Cephas Picture Library / Mick Rock (b). **263 Cephas Picture Library:** Kevin Judd (t). **264-265 Cephas Picture Library:** Kevin Judd (b). **266 Alamy Images:** Gary Cook (tl); Jon Arnold Images / Hanan Isachar (tr) ; Ernst Wrba (bl). **Charles Quest-Ritson:** (br). **267 Alamy Images:** David Wyatt. **270 Cephas Picture Library:** Andy Christodolo. **271 Getty Images:** Stone+ / Gustavo Di Mario. **272-273 Corbis:** Roger Wood (b). **274 Alamy Images:** Eitan Simanor. **277 Charles Quest-Ritson:** (tr).

All other images © Dorling Kindersley: Fritz Curzon.

For further information see: www.dkimages.com

AUTHOR'S ACKNOWLEDGMENTS

This book is dedicated to everyone who has helped me to write it including: Jemima Dunne, Deirdre Headon, and David Lamb, all lately of Dorling Kindersley; the many generous producers who encouraged me to taste their oils; Fabrizio Vignolini of ONAOO who taught me the vocabulary of tasting; my wife, our children and their spouses, who have enjoyed discovering the world of olive oil with me; and, not least, my mother (who says that olive oil is good for cradle cap) and my grandsons (who know that it is).

I would like to thank the following for their help in writing this book; Nicola Amati, Pamela Amato, Antonino Anastasi, Judy Anderson, David Angwin, Abdellatif Bahous, Evelynne Bakinta, Giovanni Bandino, Manfredi Barbera, Anna Beloni, Omar Benattia, Jenny Birrell, Christopher & Katharine Blair, Fritz Bläuel, Giancarlo Bonamini, Arthur Brown, Annamaria Bruni, Maria Caterina Burgarella, Juan Caballero, Pietro Calò, Charles Carey, Lucio Carli, Peter & Eleo Carson, Luciano Carta, Judith Carter, Roberto Cerraudo, Gordon Cheers, Colin Clere, Stefano Conti, Peter Cooling, Maurizio Cortese, Matty Cremona, Pierluigi Crescimanno, Stefano Cuccuini, Fritz & Joanna Curzon, Gabriele & Giuseppe d'Alì, Elio D'Ambrosio, Alessandro de Cillis, Stefano de Pieri, Filippo De Santis, Ria Deckx Boost, Antonio del Balzo, Pietro Di Caro, Alessandro Di Pasquale, Stefano Di Piero, Evángelos Dimarákis, Maisie Elliott, Domenico Fazari, Antonella Fineschi, Giuseppe Fois, Sebastiano Galioto, Paqui Garcia, Christiane Garnero Morena, Giovanni Genovese, Massimiliano Geraci, Nicky Giavroglou, Bill Grant, Maria Guarini, Carolyn Hanbury, Chris James, Raoudha Jerbi Abbes, Tish Jones, Olga Kafianis, Stylianos Kaitanides, Alessandros Korizi, Klaudia Koumadorakis, Charalambos Koutsoukos, Francesco Maria Lagani, Mandy Lebentz, Luca Leccisotti, Barbara Levy, Angela & Antonio Lioi, Christian Lo Conte, Celso Madeira, Francesco Marcello Marcianò, Marilena Massara, Andreas Mathioudakis, Evangelos Melas, Ronald & Christine Mickelsen, Helen Morgan, Massimo Neri, Trevor Nottle, Felipe Núñez de Prado, Giorgio Pannelli, Niki Papadopoulou, Fernando Paternò, Grigoris Pavlopoulos, Paolo Pejrone, Giampaolo Perra, Elisa & Francesco Petrucci, Roger Phillips, Gianni Pizzo, Nikos Plevritakis, Eleni Psarrea, Kostas Psypolias, Umberto & Paola Quattrocchi, Wojtek & Madeline Rakowicz, Christine Reid, Keith Richmond, Colin & Camilla Roberts, Angelo Romano, Giuseppe Rosso, Margarida Salavessa, Daniele Salvagno, Hanan Samara, Francesco Schettino, Marcello Scoccia, Filotas Sfikas, Irene Stamatakou, Christine Stephan, Gunnar Strømsholm, Pierluigi Taccone de Sitizano, Judith Taylor, Lluis Terès, Martí Terès i Rios, Xisco Terrassa, Antonella Titone, Cleopatra Triantafyllou, Laura & Marco Turri, Leopoldo Vaccaro, Juan Valderrama, Giuseppe Vergari, John Vertelis, Christine Vestfals, Fabrizio Vignolini, Phanis Vrettos, Mario Zadro, and Mme. Bouchra Zkhiri.